Authentication in Insecure Environments

Sebastian Pape

Authentication in Insecure Environments

Using Visual Cryptography and Non-Transferable Credentials in Practise

 Springer Vieweg

Dr. Sebastian Pape
Dortmund, Germany

Doctoral thesis at the University of Kassel, Department Electrical Engineering and Computer Science, defended on September 2nd, 2013, submitted with the title "The Challenge of Authentication in Insecure Environments" by Sebastian Pape

ISBN 978-3-658-07115-8 ISBN 978-3-658-07116-5 (eBook)
DOI 10.1007/978-3-658-07116-5

The Deutsche Nationalbibliothek lists this publication in the Deutsche Nationalbibliografie; detailed bibliographic data are available in the Internet at http://dnb.d-nb.de.

Library of Congress Control Number: 2014948456

Springer Vieweg
© Springer Fachmedien Wiesbaden 2014

Printed on acid-free paper

Springer Vieweg is a brand of Springer DE.
Springer DE is part of Springer Science+Business Media.
www.springer-vieweg.de

For my parents

Preface

For scientific research it is essential to have interested conversational partners who come up with helpful suggestions, references and especially criticism. At this point, I like to thank them for their kind support when writing this thesis.

I particularly owe thanks to my supervisor Prof. Dr. Lutz Wegner, who in the first place made this work possible, supported me at any time with thematically and scientific advice and also untiringly encouraged me regarding all other aspects.

I thank Prof. Dr. Jan Jürjens for enabling me to finish my work at his chair, for his active support and for appraising this work.

Furthermore, I appreciate very constructive and helpful discussions about the application of anonymous credentials with Prof. Dr. Andreas Pfitzmann. I am also very thankful to Dipl.-Inf. Marit Hansen for her valuable advice, which facilitated entering the topic of privacy-enhancing technologies.

I also like to thank Dr. Sebastian Gajek and M.Sc. Denise Doberitz for fruitful discussions on visual cryptography which had a large influence that this subject was examined to this extent.

I extend my thanks to all to my former colleagues at Kassel University as well as to my current colleagues at Dortmund Technical University and the Fraunhofer Institute for Software and Systems Engineering. In particular, my thanks go to Dipl.-Ing. Michael Möller for his active support and to Dipl.-Inf. Christian Wessel for numerous helpful comments and suggestions.

I am grateful to Bruce Schneier and Kim Cameron for the permission to include photographs from their blogs in this work. I also like to thank the anonymous reviewers whose comments helped to improve the papers which were published previously and which this work is based on.

I express my sincere gratitude to all the persons mentioned here. Nevertheless, without saying all possible errors and inaccuracies go completely to my account. I am grateful for further suggestions or comments on this work.

Dortmund   Sebastian Pape

Contents

List of Figures

List of Tables

1 Introduction

> Man should be master of his
> environment, not its slave. That is
> what freedom means.
>
> Robert Anthony Eden

1.1 Authentication in Insecure Environments

During the last decades there has been an enormous growth of computing, communication, and storage capacities [HL11]. The reasons for this growth are manifold. Commerce uses the internet as a basis for sales and customer relationship management, the industry computerises their processes, and communication and discussion in the society is changed by social websites, permanent accessibility via mobile devices and omnipresent internet access. In this environment users face the problem that they lose track of what is going on in their devices and which parties they can trust. Given this fact, we need to clarify what we mean by the term *insecure*. While there are lots of scenarios imaginable regarding an insecure environment, we focus on two cases in this work. In the first scenario, we assume the user's device is not trustworthy, but he nevertheless wants to be able to use it for secure authentications. In the second scenario, a user has a trustworthy device, but does not want to be tracked by the party verifying the authentication. Additionally, the user should not be able to lend his credentials to someone else. In the next paragraphs we discuss both scenarios in more detail.

Secure Authentication via Untrusted Devices   There are numerous reasons why a device may not be considered trustworthy. First of all, the user has to rely on the manufacturer of the device's operating system. Second, the user is also reliant on the manufacturer of the device since many manufacturers install custom software on the devices. To have confidence in the device, users have not only to trust the manufacturers that they will not harm them, but also that they roll out secure software, monitor their application stores, and fix known vulnerabilities. SCHNEIER denotes this scenario as "feudal internet" [Sch11, Sch13b], where the users rely on vendor-controlled computing devices and the user has to decide which vendor (literally: which lord) he trusts. In the described scenario this affects even more moving data in "the lord's" cloud environment. However, we do not want to discuss threats to users storing their data in cloud environments here, since the focus of this work is on authentication. Thus, we return to implications of feudalism on devices. SHABTEI et al. [SFK⁺10] list threats and give a list of malicious applications and Trojan horses. Further studies show that many applications for mobile devices (e.g. for the operating system Android [Goo13]) ask for too many privileges [FCH⁺11] and many users are unable to understand and cope with Android's privilege system [FHE⁺12]. Thus the user's device is at risk by security relevant bugs in the software, malicious applications which pretend a harmless behaviour and sophisticated Trojan horses such as "Backdoor.AndroidOS.Obad.a" [Sul11, Unu13]. These are altogether good reasons to at least doubt if such a device may be considered trustworthy.

Another reason not to trust devices is the possibility of bugs or intentional backdoors in the central processing unit (CPU). DUFLOT et al. [Duf08, Duf09] study security implications on x86 CPUs and show a proof of concept in an emulation. KING et al. [KTC⁺08] demonstrate how to build general purpose backdoors to support various attacks including attacks interfering with higher levels. The basic idea of hardware Trojan horses is to change one of the main circuits during manufacturing in a way that a special value or event triggers some potentially bad behaviour. Due to the enormous number of hundreds of million transistors on the CPUs [INT08, AMD09] and the Trojan horses' behaviour, hardware Trojan horses are hard to detect. In practise, there have been claims about hardware Trojan horses in the wild [SW12]. However, it cannot be proven that they were inserted intentionally and for which particular purpose. Similarly, there also have been rumours about secret accumulators in CPUs produced by AMD[1] [Hir10]. Actually, in the end it does not matter whether it is a bug or a backdoor, if it is possible to exploit it. Although there is research on detection of backdoors [WPBC08, CWP⁺09, WS10] and prevention of Trojan horses [CB09], the user still needs to believe the manufacturer's claims.

One approach to allow secure authentication on untrusted devices is visual cryptography. The main idea is that the user has a transparency acting as a key, i.e. a see-through foil with an imprinted key, which he holds in front of his display. The image composed of the transparency and the image shown on the device's display result in "something meaningful to the user". Since the adversary is not able to see the content of the transparency, he may have full control of the used device, but is not able to conclude, what the composed image is. This way a secure channel *to*

---

[1] Advanced Micro Devices, Inc.

the user is established. A secure channel *from the user* may be constructed by a protocol where the user clicks on certain parts of the composed image. However, one problem of this approach is that the transparencies may only be used once or a strictly limited number of times. Therefore, it would be desirable to have a scheme which allows to securely re-use the transparencies a large number of times.

To emphasise the importance of such an approach, we end this section with a quote of Karen Seubert, a privacy and security expert at Chase Bank [Seu13]: "*At Chase Bank, we recognise the value of online banking – it's quick, convenient, and available any time you need it. Unfortunately, though, the threats posed by malware and identity theft are very real and all too common nowadays. That's why, when you're finished with your online banking session, we recommend three simple steps to protect your personal information: log out of your account, close your web browser, and then charter a seafaring vessel to take you 30 miles out into the open ocean and throw your computer overboard.*" Other scenarios may be found in Chap. 3.

Authentication under Surveillance   First of all, it is worth to mention that the remarks above regarding a "feudal internet" hold even more if the user suspects his service provider is observing him. In general, the user chooses only a few service providers which cover all of his needs. Since service providers expand their service offers and merge existing services, they are able to collect all-embracing data on their users. Thus, the user has to trust the suppliers of services that they handle his data with care and that they do not spy on him. Besides threats from service providers, the users' privacy may also be invaded by governments and their intelligence services which collect and correlate data in a much larger range. It is essential to notice the importance of privacy. With the evidence that privacy is explicitly part of the United Nations' Universal Declaration of Human Rights[2], we take the importance of privacy as given for the rest of this work. For a more extensive discussion of privacy we refer to works of WESTACOTT [Wes10] and SOLOVE [Sol07, Sol11], who argue for the importance of privacy. In particular, SOLOVE explains the alleged tradeoff between privacy and security and describes how the law may protect privacy.

For users to trust their service providers or a specific system, laws can be enacted or technical measures against surveillance can be taken. There is no universally accepted belief whether laws or technical measures are preferable. On the one hand, SCHNEIER proposes to protect privacy by law and compares it to the way we

---

[2]"*No one shall be subjected to arbitrary interference with his privacy, family, home or correspondence, nor to attacks upon his honour and reputation. Everyone has the right to the protection of the law against such interference or attacks.*" [Uni48, Article 12]

protect ourselves from murder [Sch13a]. Clearly, we are insignificantly protected by technical measure and predominantly by laws. On the other hand, PFITZMANN et al. [PWP90a, PWP90b, PWP00] state that laws alone are not sufficient to ensure privacy verifiably to the user. It is important that the user is able to check the status of his privacy and has not to solely rely on promises of service providers and/or the government. Otherwise, there are scenarios where a service provider wants to be sure that the right to use a service is personalised and may not be transferred without the provider's consent (e.g. streaming services for music or videos). For these applications in principle the technical solution of *non-transferable anonymous credentials* exists. Non-transferability can be achieved by either making sure the user has a strong interest not to share his credentials – say by including a valuable secret – or by technical means – say biometrics. Both approaches offer a certain level of non-transferability which we discuss in Chap. 9. On the other hand, the service provider may want to reduce the provided anonymity in case of a cheating user. Thus, there may be anonymity revocation under certain conditions or legal regulations.

In summary, this work deals with two particular aspects of authentication. First of all, authentication with untrustworthy devices where the user has make the best out of a possibly hostile environment. Secondly, authentication where the user wants to stay anonymous while the service provider wants to be sure that the credentials are not transferred and only the legitimate person is using the service.

1.2 Overview

After an introduction to notation and fundamentals in Chap. 2, we present the motivation and propose scenarios for visual encryption schemes in Chap. 3. Based on previous research of visual cryptography, we give a description of visual encryption schemes by distinguishing between encoding and encryption in Chap. 4. Furthermore, we define the notion of *human decipherable encryption schemes* (HDES), which are a generalisation of visual encryption schemes, and give the notion of *sample-or-random ciphertext only* (SOR-CO) security and their relation to real-or-random chosen plaintext security. In Chap. 5, we give a security analysis of a scheme based on dice codings proposed by DÖBERITZ and enhance it by adding noise to the encryption part. We conclude in Chap. 6 with an extensive section on future work with ideas on how to use other senses than vision, use multiple key transparencies or rotate key transparencies.

The last part of this work deals with non-transferable anonymous credentials. After describing related work and suitable scenarios in Chap. 7, we discuss the usage of biometrics for access control in Chap. 8. In Chap. 9, we compare two different approaches aiming at non-transferability: biometric access control and embedded valuable secrets. Since the first approach makes use of tamper-proof devices, we take a closer look at the risks if the device's tamper-resistance is overcome. Therefore, we compare simple access control by biometrics with access control based on fuzzy extractors. We propose an approach which combines fuzzy extractors with a stored secret on the tamper-resistant device. The third part concludes with a future work section in Chap. 10. The work ends with a summary and an outlook in Chap. 11.

Part I

Preliminaries

2 Mathematical and Cryptographic Foundation

> There are two types of encryption: one that will prevent your sister from reading your diary and one that will prevent your government.
>
> Bruce Schneier

2.1 Preliminaries and Notation

This section introduces cryptographic primitives and their foundation. The presentation follows common notations and definitions. To keep these preliminaries short and readable, we omit some special cases and slightly simplify certain definitions when the omitted exceptions are of no interest here. We assume the reader is familiar with general probability theory and basic group theory, even though we give a short introduction into the latter in Sect. 2.1.2.

2.1.1 Functions and Algorithms

Deterministic and Probabilistic Algorithms

We start with the notion of deterministic and probabilistic algorithms. While *deterministic algorithms* behave predictably, and thus, always compute the same output given a particular input using the same procedure, *probabilistic algorithms* use a source of randomness. Therefore either the running time or the output of probabilistic algorithms will be affected by randomness. This behaviour can be useful to avoid "malicious input", which would result in bad running times of the algorithm (see Worst-Case and Average-Case Complexity below) or to create algorithms producing output influenced by randomness. Allowing randomness to influence the algorithm's output can be useful to create algorithms solving problems with some (hopefully small) error rate or for algorithms giving different outputs when run on the same input, which is useful in cryptographic encryption schemes, for example.

Definition 2.1. (Deterministic Functions and Algorithms) Let $f : X \to Y$ be a *deterministic function* or *algorithm* with input x from domain X and output y from codomain Y, then we denote f results with input x in output y with:

$$y = f(x) \quad \text{or} \quad y := f(x).$$

Definition 2.2. (Probabilistic Functions and Algorithms) Let $f : X \to Y$ be a *probabilistic function* or *algorithm* with input x from domain X and output y from codomain Y, then we denote f generates output y with input x with:

$$y \in_R Y_{f(x)} \quad \text{or} \quad y \leftarrow f(x).$$

Definition 2.3. (Equality of Probabilistic Functions and Algorithms) Let $f, g : X \to Y$ be probabilistic functions or algorithms with input x, x' from domain X and output y, y' from codomain Y. By the equality $f(x) = g(x')$ we require that both functions or algorithms return the same values with the same probability $\Pr$:

$$f(x) = g(x') \quad \Leftrightarrow \quad \{y | y \leftarrow f(x)\} = \{y | y \leftarrow g(x')\} \wedge \Pr[y \leftarrow f(x)] = \Pr[y \leftarrow g(x')]$$

To compare algorithms with respect to running time or memory usage, we introduce the Big O notation which describes the behaviour of a function when its argument tends to infinity. A common use case is to express an algorithm's running time as a function of its input length using the Big O notation. The Big O notation makes a statement about a function's growth rate and allows to simplify these functions by suppressing multiplicative constants and low order terms. This allows an easy comparison of functions' growth, and thus can be used to conveniently compare algorithms' running times for "large input lengths" but sacrifices predictions for concrete instances.

Definition 2.4. (Big O notation) Let $f, g : X \to \mathbb{R}$ be functions defined on the same totally ordered set X with codomain $\mathbb{R}$ and let be $c \in \mathbb{R}$ and $x_0, x \in X$. Then we define the *Big O notation* or *Landau notation*:

$$f \in \mathcal{O}(g) \stackrel{\text{def}}{=} \exists\, c > 0\ \exists\, x_0\ \forall\, x > x_0 : |f(x)| \leqslant c \cdot |g(x)|$$

Following common conventions we also mean $f \in \mathcal{O}(g)$ when writing $f = \mathcal{O}(g)$.

In other words if $f \in \mathcal{O}(g)$ then, beginning from a certain value x_0, $f(x)$ is not significantly larger[1] than $g(x)$.

---

[1] In this case, not significantly larger means maximum a constant c times larger.

Remark 2.5. (**Security Parameter**) In cryptography it is common practise to view the running time as a function of n, often called the *security parameter*. But as previously mentioned the standard convention in complexity theory is to measure the running time of an algorithm as a function of the length of its input. To be consistent with the latter notion, we provide the algorithms with the security parameter in unary as 1^n (for example a string of n 1's) when necessary.

Now that we have a comfortable way of comparing algorithms' resources, we are able to elaborate which algorithms are feasible (for large instances).

Efficient Algorithms and Negligible Probability

KERCKHOFF is mostly known for his principle saying that the security of the cryptosystem should not rely on its secrecy (see Sect. 2.2). It is less known that he formulated six principles in total, one of them saying *"The system must be practically, if not mathematically, indecipherable"* [Ker83]. That means, when considering the security of a cryptosystem, an attacker should not be able to break the cryptosystem in "reasonable time" with "reasonable success probability". Thus, before proceeding with the definition of cryptosystems, we need to give appropriate definitions of "reasonable". At first we equate "doing something in reasonable time" with the definition of *efficient computation*.

Definition 2.6. (**Efficient Computation**) We define *efficiently computable algorithm* as algorithm with access to a fair coin, solving the underlying problem in polynomial time with an error rate of at most $\frac{1}{3}$.

Note that the choice of $\frac{1}{3}$ is arbitrary, as long as it is a constant, independent of the input, and below $\frac{1}{2}$. The idea is to repeat the algorithm several times, and thus, increase the accuracy by taking a majority vote. We refer to GILL [Gil77] for an exact definition of "Bounded-Error Probabilistic Polynomial-Time"-algorithms and to AARONSON [AKG13] for an overview about its relations to other complexity classes.

Having a definition of efficient computation now, we continue by defining "reasonable success probability" as a *not negligible* success probability.

Definition 2.7. (**Negligible function**) A function $f : \mathbb{N} \to \mathbb{R}$ is *negligible* iff

$$\forall c \in \mathbb{N} \; \exists k_c \in \mathbb{N} \; \forall k \geqslant k_c \; : \; |f(k)| \leqslant \frac{1}{k^c}$$

In other words, a function that increases slower than any inverse polynomial is called *negligible*.

Note that k_c is a natural number, since in complexity-based cryptography, the input of the negligible function is usually the cryptographic key length or a corresponding security parameter. For example, an encryption scheme is defined as secure (see indistinguishability in Sect. 2.2.1), if the probability of an attacker's success is negligible in terms of cryptographic key length. Therefore, we continue with the definition of negligible success probability.

Definition 2.8. (Negligible success probability) The success probability of an algorithm is *negligible* iff the success probability, as a function of its input length, is bounded by a negligible function.

This complements our definition of efficient computation, since repeating an algorithm with negligible success probability polynomially (in the input length) many times, results in a new algorithm with also negligible success probability.

One-Way and Trapdoor Functions

Informally speaking, one-way functions have the property that they are easy to compute, but hard to invert given the function's result of a random input.

Definition 2.9. (One-Way Function) Let $f : \{0,1\}^* \rightarrow \{0,1\}^*$ be an efficient computable function. f is a *one-way function* if for every probabilistic polynomial-time algorithm $\mathcal{A}$ the success probability Pr of finding a x' for a given $y := f(x)$, so that $f(x') = y$, is negligible:

$$\forall c \in \mathbb{N} \; \exists k_c \in \mathbb{N} \; \forall k \geqslant k_c \; : \; Pr[f(\mathcal{A}(f(x))) = f(x)] < \frac{1}{k^c}$$

Note that any one-way function can be inverted if the adversary is given enough time and thus able to simply try all values $x \in \{0,1\}^*$ until a value x' is found, such that $f(x') = y = f(x)$. Using this algorithm an adversary always succeeds, but would require exponential running time. Hence, the assumption that a function is one-way is strongly related to computational complexity and computational hardness assumptions [KL08]. Consequently, the existence of one-way functions is still an open question. A proof of their existence would also imply that the complexity classes P and NP are distinct, which is one of the most important unsolved problems in theoretical computer science [Gol01]. An up-to-date survey on the current status of P versus NP has been published recently by FORTNOW [For09]. However, it is also unknown if P unequals NP – which is widely believed – is a sufficient condition for the existence of one-way functions.

Candidates for one-way functions (cf. Sect. 2.3) are:

Multiplication and factoring Let p and q be two prime numbers in binary notation with length k. Then the multiplication of p and q can be computed in time $\mathcal{O}(k^2)$, while reverting it requires to find the factors of a given integer N with length n and the best factoring algorithm known, the general number field sieve [Cop93, Pom96], runs in time $2^{\mathcal{O}(n^{1/3}(\log n)^{2/3})}$ on average [KL08, p. 298].

Modular squaring and square roots Let N be the product of two prime numbers p and q. The modular squaring of $N > k \in \mathbb{Z}$ means to compute the remainder of k^2 divided by N, which can be done in time $\mathcal{O}(k^2)$ [HyOY96]. Obviously inverting it requires computing a square root modulo N, which has been shown to be computationally equivalent to factoring N [CGG86].

Discrete exponential function and logarithm Let p be a prime number in binary notation with length n and $k \in \mathbb{Z}$ between 0 and $p-1$. The remainder of 2^k divided by p (the discrete exponential function) can be computed in time $\mathcal{O}(n^3)$, while inverting this function requires computing the discrete logarithm modulo p. Currently, the best known algorithm, the general number field sieve – which shares many of the underlying ideas with its factoring counterpart – runs also in time $2^{\mathcal{O}(n^{1/3}(\log n)^{2/3})}$ on average [AH99, KL08].

Cryptographically secure hash functions Even though earlier versions of hash functions [MvOV97, p. 33] (see also Def. 2.76) like MD5 and SHA-1 have been successfully attacked by WANG et al. [WFLY04, WY05, WYY05], recent attacks on the latest family of hash functions – SHA-2 – by SANADHYA et al. work only on a reduced version [SS08a, SS08b]. Thus, as of today, the SHA-2 family offers practical and efficient computable one-way functions.

A special form of one-way functions with additional properties are one-way permutations.

Definition 2.10. (One-Way Permutation) Let $f : \{0,1\}^* \to \{0,1\}^*$ be a one-way function. f is a *one-way permutation* if f is injective and surjective.

Since one-way permutations are bijective, it follows, that any value $f(x)$ uniquely determines its preimage $f^{-1}(x)$: $\forall x, x' \in \{0,1\}^* : f(x) = f(x') \Leftrightarrow x = x'$. Note the difference when talking about inversion referring to one-way functions and one-way permutations, respectively. While the inversion is uniquely determined for one-way permutations, it is sufficient for the inversion of one-way functions to find any appropriate preimage value.

Strongly related to one-way permutations are trapdoor permutations. One can imagine trapdoor permutation as one-way permutation, but with the aid of special information (the trapdoor), it becomes easy to invert the permutation.

Definition 2.11. **(Trapdoor Permutation)** Let $f : \{0,1\}^* \to \{0,1\}^*$ be an efficiently computable function. f is a *trapdoor permutation* if for every probabilistic polynomial-time algorithm $\mathcal{A}$ the success probability of finding x for a given $y := f(x)$ is negligible and there exists an efficient algorithm $\mathcal{J}$, which outputs x on input $f(x)$, using trapdoor td:

$$\forall c \in \mathbb{N} \; \exists k_c \in \mathbb{N} \; \forall k \geqslant k_c \; : \; Pr[\mathcal{A}(f(x)) = x] < \frac{1}{k^c}$$

and

$$\exists \, \mathcal{J} : \mathcal{J}(f(x), td) \; = \; x$$

Trapdoor functions are an important component for public-key encryption techniques (see Sect. 2.41) and the best known trapdoor function candidates are based on the RSA [RSA78] and Rabin [Rab79] families of functions, which both rely on the problem of prime factorisation.

The term of "families of functions" is quite intuitive, but there is a formal definition [KL08] and we show their application on one-way functions and one-way and trapdoor permutations. Most known candidates of one-way functions (or one-way permutations or trapdoor permutations, respectively) do not naturally fit in the concept of families of functions. Instead, there is an algorithm generating some parameters I which define some function f_I and the requirement then is that except with negligible probability f_I is a one-way function (or one-way permutation or trapdoor permutation, respectively). Because each value of I defines a different function, we refer to families of one-way functions, one-way permutations and trapdoor permutations.

Definition 2.12. **(Family of Functions)** A tuple $(Gen, Samp, f)$ of probabilistic polynomial-time algorithms is a *family of functions* if the following holds:

- Each run of the *parameter-generation algorithm* Gen outputs a parameter I with $|I| > n$ on input 1^n. Each value of I defines the domain $\mathcal{D}_I$ and the range $\mathcal{R}_I$ of a function f_I defined below.

- The *sampling algorithm* $Samp$ outputs a uniformly distributed element of $\mathcal{D}_I$ on input I (except possibly with probability negligible in $|I|$).

- The deterministic *evaluation algorithm* f outputs an element $y \in \mathcal{R}_I$ on input I and $x \in \mathcal{D}_I$. We write this as $y := f_I(x)$.

Definition 2.13. **(Family of Permutations)** A tuple $\Pi = (Gen, Samp, f)$ of probabilistic polynomial-time algorithms is a *family of permutations* if Π is a family of functions and for each value of I output by $Gen(1^n)$, it holds that $\mathcal{D}_I = \mathcal{R}_I$ and the function $f_I : \mathcal{D}_I \to \mathcal{D}_I$ is bijective.

Definition 2.14. (Families of One-Way Functions and Permutations) A family of functions or permutations is *one-way* if for all I, output by $\mathsf{Gen}(1^n)$, the deterministic evaluation function respective permutation f_I is one-way (except possibly with probability negligible in $|I|$).

Definition 2.15. (Families of Trapdoor Permutations) A tuple $(\mathsf{Gen}, \mathsf{Samp}, f, \mathfrak{I})$ of probabilistic polynomial-time algorithms is a *family of trapdoor functions* if the tuple $(\mathsf{Gen}, \mathsf{Samp}, f)$ is a family of one-way permutations and for each value of I output by $\mathsf{Gen}(1^n)$, there exists an efficient algorithm $\mathfrak{I}_I$, which outputs x on input $f_I(x)$ by using trapdoor td_I.

As already indicated above, most candidates of one-way functions and one-way or trapdoor permutations belong to families of functions and permutations. Thus, even though each value of I defines a different function f_I, all members of a specific one-way function or one-way or trapdoor permutation rely on the same computational hardness assumption.

Pseudorandom Functions

Pseudorandomness is a computational relaxation of true randomness. Computational relaxation means, a polynomial bound observer is unable to distinguish a pseudorandom distribution from the uniform distribution. On an intuitive level, pseudorandomness helps in the construction of encryption schemes, since an adversary faced with ciphertexts which seem random to her (he cannot distinguish their distribution from the uniform distribution), should not be able to learn any information from them about the underlying plaintexts. Thus, many secure encryption schemes fundamentally rely on the use of pseudorandom functions as cryptographic primitives.

It is possible to construct pseudorandom functions based on one-way functions with the intermediate step of a pseudorandom generator. Therefore this section starts with the definition of pseudorandom generators before defining pseudorandom functions.

Definition 2.16. (Pseudorandom Generator) Let $\ell(\cdot)$ be a polynomial and let G be an efficient, deterministic algorithm: $G : \{0,1\}^n \rightarrow \{0,1\}^{\ell(n)}$. G is a cryptographically secure *pseudorandom generator* (PRG), if G outputs a long pseudorandom string $s' \in \{0,1\}^{\ell(n)}$ on the input of a short truly random seed $s \in \{0,1\}^n$, for every n it holds that $\ell(n) > n$ and the pseudorandom string s' is (except with negligible probability in n) computationally indistinguishable from a truly random string. The function $\ell(\cdot)$ is denoted as *expansion factor* of G.

Note that the output of a pseudorandom generator is not even close to real random-ness, if regarded from a higher level of abstraction. This can be seen easily since the pseudorandom generator with input $s \in \{0,1\}^n$ has at most 2^n different outputs due to its deterministic nature. Since the length of its output $s' \in \{0,1\}^{\ell(n)}$ is $\ell(n)$ and $\ell(n) > n$, there is a gap of $2^{\ell(n)} - 2^n$ strings which will never occur as output of the regarded pseudorandom generator, but would be output of a uniform distribution over $\{0,1\}^{\ell(n)}$. That means an adversary with unlimited computational power could on an output s' simply brute-force all seeds and see if there is a seed $s \in \{0,1\}^n$ such that $G(s) = s'$. Since only for the fraction $\frac{2^n}{2^{\ell(n)}} = 2^{n-\ell(n)}$ of G's outputs there will exist a seed s, the adversary is able to distinguish between a pseudorandom and an uniform distribution. However, this procedure cannot be done by an efficient algorithm, which runs polynomial in n. From the above argument also follows that the seed s for a pseudorandom generator must be kept secret, chosen uniformly at random, and must be long enough that it is unfeasible for the distinguisher to brute-force all possible seeds.

Unfortunately it is not known, if pseudorandom generators exist, even if it is strongly believed. The belief is based on the fact that LEVIN et al. proved that a a cryptographically secure pseudorandom bit generator can be constructed from a one-way function [Lev87, ILL89] and one-way functions are believed to exist as stated earlier in the section.

Definition 2.17. (Pseudorandom Function) Let F be an efficient, deterministic function: $F : \{0,1\}^* \times \{0,1\}^* \to \{0,1\}^*$. F outputs a string $s' \in \{0,1\}^*$ on the input of a key $k \in \{0,1\}^*$ and a string $s \in \{0,1\}^*$. In general the key k will be chosen uniformly at random and then fixed. We denote this with $F_k : \{0,1\}^* \to \{0,1\}^*$ with $F_k(x) = F(k,x)$. F_k is called a cryptographically secure *pseudorandom function* (PRF), if F_k is (except with negligible probability in n) computationally indistinguishable from an uniformly at random chosen function of the set of functions mapping strings of F_k's domain to strings of F_k's codomain.

Since F_k is a set of functions, F_k may also be denoted as pseudorandom function family if k is not fixed. In analogy to the reasoning in the above paragraph, the distribution over pseudorandom functions has a smaller range than the distribution over all functions with the same domain and range. For a more detailed description we refer to KATZ and LINDEL [KL08, p. 86-87]. Likewise, the consequence is that the key k for a pseudorandom function must be kept secret, chosen uniformly at random, and must be long enough that it is unfeasible for the distinguisher to brute-force all possible keys.

GOLDREICH, GOLDWASSER and MICALI show how to construct pseudorandom function families from pseudorandom generators [GGM86]. In theory it is known that pseudorandom functions exist iff pseudorandom generators exist [KL08]. In practise, block ciphers like AES [DR00] are widely believed to work as pseudorandom functions.

For the sake of clarity, the difference between pseudorandom generators and pseudorandom functions is that a pseudorandom generator's output appears random if the input was chosen uniformly at random, while the output of a pseudorandom function appears random, regardless of its input, as long as the function was chosen randomly from the pseudorandom function family.

If a pseudorandom function is a length-preserving bijection it is also a pseudorandom permutation:

Definition 2.18. (Pseudorandom Permutation) Let P be an efficient, deterministic permutation: $P : \{0, 1\}^* \times \{0, 1\}^n \to \{0, 1\}^n$. P outputs a string $s' \in \{0, 1\}^n$ on the input of a key $k \in \{0, 1\}^*$ and a string $s \in \{0, 1\}^n$. In general the key k will be chosen uniformly at random and then fixed. We denote this with $P_k : \{0, 1\}^n \to \{0, 1\}^n$ with $P_k(x) = P(k, x)$. P_k is called a cryptographically secure *pseudorandom permutation (PRP)*, if P_k is (except with negligible probability in n) computationally indistinguishable from an uniformly at random chosen permutation of the set of permutations on n-bit strings.

It may be necessary for one or more parties participating in an encryption scheme to compute not only the pseudorandom permutation P_k, but also its inverse P_k^{-1}, which may introduce security issues not covered by cryptographically secure pseudorandom permutations. If P_k is indistinguishable from a random permutation, although the adversary is granted oracle access to the inverse of the permutation, we call P_k a strong pseudorandom permutation.

Definition 2.19. (Strong Pseudorandom Permutation) Let PRP_k be an pseudorandom permutation, PRP_k is called a *strong pseudorandom permutation* if PRP_k is (except with negligible probability) computationally indistinguishable from an uniformly at random chosen permutation of the set of permutations, even if the distinguisher is granted oracle access to the inverse of the permutation.

Worst-Case and Average-Case Complexity

Studies on *computational complexity theory* began in the fifties and sixties with publications by TRAKHTENBROT [Tra56, Tra67], RABIN [Rab59, Rab60], and HARTMANIS and STEARNS [HS65]. The aim of computational complexity theory is to analyse the difficulty of computational problems and to classify problems concerning the required resources (time, memory, ...) needed to solve all instances of a certain problem. Naturally, if problems are divided into classes of problems which can be solved with a certain amount of resources, the most significant instances of the problem are the worst-cases referring to a specific algorithm. An efficient algorithm would be required to solve *all instances* of a certain problem efficiently, even if there is only one extreme case resulting in a poor performance of the algorithm. That means in many cases worst-case analysis is too pessimistic, because there may exist efficient algorithms, which perform quite good on random (average) instances.

Thus, for example, in mathematical optimisation theory, the simplex algorithm, created by DANTZIG [Dan63], is an algorithm to numerically solve linear programming tasks. Although its worst-case running time is exponential [KM72, Zad80] and even so KHACHIYAN [Kha79] presented an algorithm with polynomial running time, the simplex algorithm is widely used because it performs well in practise (on average). Besides the previously mentioned extreme cases, it is important to notice that comparing algorithms asymptotically does not necessarily allow conclusions regarding relevant instances in practise. The reason is that exponential functions with "small coefficients" in the exponent may increase slower up to a certain value than polynomials of a "high degree" with "large coefficients".

In regard to complexity-based cryptography it is necessary to point out the difference between *worst-case complexity* and *average-case complexity* related to the security of a cryptosystem. In public-key encryption schemes (see Def. 2.41) the problem of finding the secret key sk from the public key pk is based on the hardness (cf. Sect. 2.3) of a certain problem. It is obvious, that computing sk from pk should be hard on average and thus the underlying problem should be hard on average. Otherwise an adversary confronted with a problem that is only hard in the worst-case may succeed with reasonable probability.

The emerging gap between average-case and worst-case analysis regarding the security of a cryptosystem may be further amplified if the algorithm's runtime is given in Big O notation. Since Big O notation describes the limiting behaviour of an algorithm on the one hand algorithms with exponential runtime may nevertheless be feasible regarding relevant instances, for example if the exponent's coefficient is very small, while on the other hand algorithms with polynomial runtime may likewise not be feasible regarding relevant instances, for example if the degree and the leading coefficient of the polynomial are very large.

2.1.2 Basic Group Theory

Divisibility and Modular Arithmetic

Definition 2.20. (Division) Let $a, b, c \in \mathbb{Z}$ be integers. We say that a *divides* b if there exists an integer c such that $ac = b$ and denote this by $a|b$. If a does not divide b we write $a \nmid b$. If a is positive and divides b, we call a a *divisor of* b. If furthermore $a \notin \{1, b\}$ holds, we call a a *factor* or *non-trivial divisor of* b.

Proposition 2.21. *(Division with Remainder) Let $a \in \mathbb{Z}$, and $1 < b \in \mathbb{Z}$ be integers. Then there exist unique integers $q \in \mathbb{Z}$, $0 \leqslant r \in \mathbb{Z} < b$ such that $a = qb + r$ and we call q the* quotient *and r the* remainder. *We denote the remainder a upon the division by b with $[a \mod b]$.*

Definition 2.22. (Greatest Common Divisor) Let $a, b \in \mathbb{Z}$ be integers. We call the largest, positive integer that divides a and b without a remainder the *greatest common divisor* and denote this by $\gcd(a, b)$.

Definition 2.23. (Composites, Primes, Semiprimes and Coprimes) Let $n, p \in \mathbb{N}$ be integers. We denote $p > 1$ as *prime* if p has no non-trivial divisors. A positive integer $n > 1$ that is not prime is called *composite*. By definition 1 is neither prime nor composite. Let $p, q \in \mathbb{N}$ be primes then we call their product $n = pq$ a *semiprime*. Let furthermore $a, b \in \mathbb{Z}$ be integers. If $\gcd(a, b) = 1$ we say that a and b are *relatively prime* or *coprime*.

Definition 2.24. (Euler's φ-function) *Euler's φ-function* is named after the Swiss mathematician Leonard Euler and $\varphi(n)$ is defined to be the number of positive integers less than or equal to n that are coprime to n.

Groups

Groups are an algebraic structure consisting of a set along with a binary function which maps any two of its elements to a third of its elements satisfying the following conditions:

Definition 2.25. (Monoid) Let $\mathbb{G}$ and $\mathbb{G}'$ be a set and $\circ : \mathbb{G} \times \mathbb{G} \to \mathbb{G}'$ a binary function on $\mathbb{G}$, which takes two arguments of $\mathbb{G}$ as input. A *monoid* is a set $\mathbb{G}$ along with a binary operation $\circ$ for which the following holds:

Associativity: $\forall g_1, g_2, g_3 \in \mathbb{G} : (g_1 \circ g_2) \circ g_3 = g_1 \circ (g_2 \circ g_3)$

Closure: $\forall g, h \in \mathbb{G} : g \circ h \in \mathbb{G}$

Existence of Identity: $\exists e \in \mathbb{G} . \forall g \in \mathbb{G} : e \circ g = g = g \circ e$
With e called the *identity*.

Definition 2.26. (Group) Let $(\mathbb{G}, \circ)$ be a monoid. We call $(\mathbb{G}, \circ)$ a *group* if the following holds:

Existence of Inverses: $\forall g \in \mathbb{G} . \exists h \in \mathbb{G} : g \circ h = e = h \circ g$
Such an h is called an *inverse of g*.

When the binary operation ∘ is self-evident, we may omit it and simply refer to $\mathbb{G}$ as group. Depending on the discussed group we will use additive or multiplicative notation. In *additive notation* the group operation is denoted by $g + h$, the identity is denoted by 0 and the inverse of g is denoted by $-g$. Analogous in *multiplicative notation* the group operation is denoted by $g \cdot h$ or simply gh, the identity is denoted by 1 and the inverse of g is denoted by g^{-1}. Note that this does not mean that the group operation corresponds with integer addition or multiplication.

Definition 2.27. (Group Exponentiation) Let $\mathbb{G}$ be a group then we define *exponentiation by* m as applying the group operation m times.
When using *additive notation* we denote this as:

$$mg = m \cdot g \overset{\text{def}}{=} \underbrace{g + \ldots + g}_{m \text{ times}}$$

When using *multiplicative notation* we denote this as:

$$g^m \overset{\text{def}}{=} \underbrace{g \ldots g}_{m \text{ times}}$$

Definition 2.28. (Abelian Group) Let $(G, \circ)$ be a group. We say $\mathbb{G}$ is an *abelian group* if ∘ is commutative:

Commutativity: $\forall g, h \in \mathbb{G} : g \circ h = h \circ g$

Definition 2.29. (Finite Group and Group Order) Let $(G, \circ)$ be a group. We say $\mathbb{G}$ is a *finite group* if $\mathbb{G}$ has a finite number of elements. We denote the number of elements in $\mathbb{G}$ with $|\mathbb{G}|$ and denote it as the *order of the group* $\mathbb{G}$.

Definition 2.30. (Subgroup) Let $(G, \circ)$ be a group. We say $\mathbb{G}'$ is a *subgroup* of $\mathbb{G}$ if $\mathbb{G}' \subseteq \mathbb{G}$ and $\mathbb{G}'$ itself is a group under the same operation associated with $\mathbb{G}$. If additionally $\mathbb{G}' \subset \mathbb{G}$ holds, we call $\mathbb{G}'$ a *strict subgroup* of $\mathbb{G}$.

Since associativity (and commutativity) are inherited from $\mathbb{G}$, one need to verify closure and the existence of identity and inverse to check that $\mathbb{G}'$ is a subgroup of $\mathbb{G}$.

Definition 2.31. (Order of Group Elements) Let $\mathbb{G}$ be a finite group of order m. For arbitrary $g \in \mathbb{G}$ we define the set

$$\langle g \rangle \overset{\text{def}}{=} \left\{ g^0, g^1, \cdots \right\}$$

Furthermore let $i \leqslant m$ be the smallest positive integer such that $g^i = 1$. Then the sequence repeats after i terms, and thus

$$\langle g \rangle = \left\{ g^0, g^1, \cdots, g^{i-1} \right\}$$

It can easily be proven that $\langle g \rangle$ is a subgroup of $\mathbb{G}$ with order i. And we name $\langle g \rangle$ the *subgroup generated by* g.

Definition 2.32. (Cyclic Group and Generator) Let $\mathbb{G}$ be a finite group of order m. If there exists an element $g \in \mathbb{G}$ with order m, then $\langle g \rangle = \mathbb{G}$ and we call $\mathbb{G}$ a *cyclic group* and denote g as a *generator* of $\mathbb{G}$.

Definition 2.33. (Congruence modulo N) Let $a, b, N \in \mathbb{Z}$ with $N > 1$. We say that a and b are *congruent modulo* N, denoted as $a = b \pmod{N}$, if $[a \bmod N] = [b \bmod N]$. We also understand an expression such as $a = b = c = \ldots = z \pmod{N}$ in such a manner that every equal sign in this sequence refers to congruence modulo N.

Definition 2.34. ($\mathbb{Z}_N$) Let $1 < N \in \mathbb{Z}$. The set of congruence classes modulo N is denoted as $\mathbb{Z}_N$ or $\mathbb{Z}/n\mathbb{Z}$ and defined by

$$\mathbb{Z}_N \stackrel{\text{def}}{=} \{[a \bmod N] | a \in \mathbb{Z}\} = \{0, 1, \ldots, N-1\}$$

It can easily be verified that $(\mathbb{Z}_N, *)$ is a monoid. If N is prime, there exists an inverse for each group element of $\mathbb{Z}_N$ under multiplication, and thus for $1 < p \in \mathbb{Z}$ and p is prime, $(\mathbb{Z}_p, *)$ is a group.

Definition 2.35. ($\mathbb{Z}_N^*$) Let $1 < N \in \mathbb{Z}$. Then we define the set of invertible elements with respect to multiplication modulo N by

$$\mathbb{Z}_N^* \stackrel{\text{def}}{=} \{a \in \{1, \ldots, N-1\} | \gcd(a, N) = 1\}$$

$\mathbb{Z}_N^*$ obviously consists of integers in the set $\{1, \ldots, N-1\}$ that are relatively prime to N. By requesting $\gcd(a, N) = 1$ elements that are not invertible are eliminated and it can be easily verified that $(\mathbb{Z}_N^*, *)$ is a group [KL08, p. 249, 255].

Bilinear Maps

A bilinear map is a function with two arguments which is linear in both of them. Therefore, bilinear maps are also called *pairings* because they associate pairs of elements from $\mathbb{G}_1$ and $\mathbb{G}_2$ with elements in $\mathbb{G}_T$. An illustrative example of a bilinear map is the multiplication of integers.

Definition 2.36. (Bilinear Map) Let $\mathbb{G}_1$, $\mathbb{G}_2$ and $\mathbb{G}_T$ be cyclic groups of the same order, then a *bilinear map* B: $\mathbb{G}_1 \times \mathbb{G}_2 \to \mathbb{G}_T$ is a function such that for all $g_1 \in \mathbb{G}_1$, $g_2 \in \mathbb{G}_2$ and $a, b \in \mathbb{Z}$,

$$B(g_1^a, g_2^b) = B(g_1, g_2)^{ab}$$

holds.

Since this definition allows degenerated (trivial) mappings, which map everything to the identity of $\mathbb{G}_T$ and nothing is said if the mapping operation can be computed efficiently we successively extend our definition to obtain only interesting bilinear maps.

Definition 2.37. (Non-degenerated Bilinear Map) Let $\mathbb{G}_1$, $\mathbb{G}_2$ and $\mathbb{G}_T$ be cyclic groups of the same order, g_1 and g_2 be generators of $\mathbb{G}_1$ and $\mathbb{G}_2$, respectively, and B: $\mathbb{G}_1 \times \mathbb{G}_2 \to \mathbb{G}_T$ be a bilinear map. B is a *non-degenerated bilinear map* if $B(g_1, g_2)$ is a generator of $\mathbb{G}_T$.

Definition 2.38. (Admissible Bilinear Map) Let $\mathbb{G}_1$, $\mathbb{G}_2$ and $\mathbb{G}_T$ be cyclic groups of the same order, and B: $\mathbb{G}_1 \times \mathbb{G}_2 \to \mathbb{G}_T$ be a bilinear map. A map e is an *admissible bilinear map* if it is non-degenerated and its mapping is efficiently computable.

Remark 2.39. For the rest of this work, if we use the term bilinear map we implicitly mean admissible bilinear maps if not stated otherwise.

ARTIN gives a more detailed introduction to bilinear maps [Art93].

2.2 Encryption Schemes

We first define private-key encryption schemes (also known as symmetric encryption schemes) based on KATZ and LINDEL [KL08] followed by the definition of public-key encryption schemes (also known as asymmetric encryption schemes). The definitions do not differ much from other definitions, e.g. given by BUCHMANN [Buc99] and MENEZES et al. [MvOV97].

Definition 2.40. (Private-Key Encryption Scheme) A *private-key encryption scheme* is a tuple of probabilistic polynomial-time algorithms (GenKey,Enc,Dec) such that:

- The *key-generation algorithm* GenKey takes as input the security parameter 1^n and outputs a key k; we write this as $k \leftarrow \text{GenKey}(1^n)$ (thus emphasising the fact that GenKey is a randomised algorithm). We will assume without loss of generality that any key k output by $\text{GenKey}(1^n)$ satisfies $|k| \geq n$.

- The *encryption algorithm* Enc takes as input a key k and a plaintext message $m \in \{0,1\}^*$ from some underlying plaintext space $\mathcal{M}$, and outputs a ciphertext c. Since Enc may be randomised we write this as $c \leftarrow Enc_k(m)$.

- The *decryption algorithm* Dec takes as input a key k and a ciphertext c, and outputs a message m or a special symbol $\perp$ denoting failure. We assume that Dec is deterministic, and so write this as $m := Dec_k(c)$.

It is required that for every n, every k output by $GenKey(1^n)$, and every $m \in \mathcal{M}$, it holds that[2]

$$Dec_k(Enc_k(m)) = m$$

The definition of public-key encryption is very similar, except that instead of working with a single key, distinct encryption and decryption keys are defined.

Definition 2.41. (Public-Key Encryption Scheme) A *public-key encryption scheme* is a tuple of probabilistic polynomial-time algorithms (GenKey,Enc,Dec) such that:

- The *key-generation algorithm* GenKey takes as input the security parameter 1^n and outputs a pair of keys (pk, sk); we refer to the first of these as the *public key* and the second as the *private key*. We write this as $(pk, sk) \leftarrow GenKey(1^n)$. We assume for convenience that pk and sk each have length at least n, and that n can be determined from pk,sk.

- The *encryption algorithm* Enc takes as input a public key pk and a plaintext message $m \in \{0,1\}^*$ from some underlying plaintext space $\mathcal{M}$ (that may depend on pk). It outputs a ciphertext c, and we write this as $c \leftarrow Enc_{pk}(m)$.

- The *decryption algorithm* Dec takes as input a private key sk and a ciphertext c, and outputs a message m or a special symbol $\perp$ denoting failure. We assume without loss of generality that Dec is deterministic, and write this as $m := Dec_{sk}(c)$.

It is required that (except with possibly negligible probability over (sk, pk) output by $GenKey(1^n)$ and any randomness used by Enc) for every n, every (sk, pk) output by $GenKey(1^n)$, and every $m \in \mathcal{M}$ it holds that

$$Dec_{sk}(Enc_{pk}(m)) = m$$

Note that this definition of public-key encryption scheme allows a negligible decryption error, either resulting from error when the keys are generated or from

---

[2]Given this, the assumption that Dec is deterministic is without loss of generality.

randomness used when a message is encrypted. This means that the result of decrypting a ciphertext could either be wrong or $\perp$ with negligible probability.

One possible source of decryption errors are prime generation algorithms producing primes with probability close to 1, thus GenKey obtains a composite instead of a prime when generating the key pair. As an example for encryption errors due to the use of randomness we refer to the AJTAI-DWORK-Cryptosystem [AD97], where encryption is done bitwise and 0s are encrypted following a specific procedure, while 1s are chosen randomly from the ciphertext space, and thus, with negligible probability may decrypt to 0.

Definition 2.42. (Symmetric and Asymmetric Encryption Schemes) Derived from the use of the secret key k respective the public/private pair of keys (pk, sk), private-key encryption schemes are also named *symmetric encryption schemes* and public-key encryption schemes are named as *asymmetric encryption schemes*.

Remark 2.43. Encryption schemes may also be considered to be symmetric, if different keys are used for decryption and encryption, which can efficiently be computed from each other.

Since it should be computationally hard in asymmetric encryption to derive the private key from the corresponding public key, it is possible for all users to publish their public key. Thus, in contrast to symmetric encryption schemes, keys do not need to be exchanged secretly and pairwise between all communication partners. If Alice wants to send Bob a message, she retrieves Bob's public key pk, encrypts the message, sends it to Bob, and Bob is able to decrypt it with his private key sk. However, Alice has to be sure, that she really receives Bob's public key (see Sect. 2.2.4), changing the challenge from secure key distribution to providing authentic public keys. The concept to ensure the authenticity of Bob's public key with electronic signatures (see Sect. 2.4.2) and one ore more trusted certification authority is referred to as key management and results in a *public key infrastructure* (*PKI*). This in general includes procedures to create, manage, store, distribute, and revoke digital certificates [MvOV97, TS08].

In practise, asymmetric encryption schemes are computationally more intensive than symmetric encryption schemes, and thus, substantially slower (typically by a factor of hundreds to thousands times). Hence, a widespread use of asymmetric encryption schemes is, to transport keys of a symmetric encryption scheme, which are later used for encrypting bulk data [MvOV97]. We omit an example of an encryption scheme in this section and refer to RSA in Sect. 2.3.1 instead.

Cryptographic Protocols

In general, protocols define the way two or more parties interact with each other by declaring a formal step-by-step procedure. If the protocol's objective is related to security and employs cryptographic primitives or functions, we also speak of *cryptographic protocols* or *security protocols*.

Definition 2.44. (Cryptographic Protocol) A *cryptographic protocol* is a distributed algorithm defined by a sequence of steps precisely specifying the actions required of two or more entities in order to achieve a specified security objective [MvOV97, p. 33].

Common objectives of cryptographic protocols are:

Key establishment A shared secret is made available to two or more parties, e.g. for subsequent use in an encryption scheme or protocol.

Authentication To one party some degree of assurance regarding the true identity of another party with which it is assumedly communicating is provided.

Authenticated key establishment protocol A party establishes a shared secret with another party whose identity has been approved.

It is important to recognise the difference between cryptographic primitives and protocols. A cryptographic protocol may fail even though the employed cryptographic primitives are secure. Reasons of failure include security guarantees of the cryptographic primitive which are only assumed or not clearly understood by the protocol's designer, violations of the cryptographic primitive's assumptions, such as an uniform distribution of a certain value or a severe amplification of a slight weakness in a cryptographic primitive.

Definition 2.45. (Protocol Failure) A *protocol failure* occurs if a cryptographic protocol does not achieve its intended security objective, whereby the attacker does not take her advantage of breaking the underlying cryptographic primitives directly.

Names of Participating Parties

Following cryptographic traditions [RSA78, Sch95], we keep at widely used names for the participants when following cryptographic protocols. In encryption schemes the sender Alice wants to send a message to Bob, the receiver, while Eve is an eavesdropper also referred to as *passive attacker* (see Sect. 2.2.2). In contrast, an *active attacker* will be called Mallory (see Sect. 2.2.4).

Kerckhoff's principle

An essential part of cryptosystems is the use of keys for encryption and decryption. Although one could argue that it is possible to construct cryptosystems without using keys, KERCKHOFF gave convicting arguments why this does not make sense. Following KERCKHOFF's *principle* [Ker83] the security of a cryptosystem should completely rely on the secrecy of the keys and not on the secrecy of the algorithm. SHANNON later rephrased this as SHANNON's *maxim*: *"the enemy knows the system being used"* [Sha49].

There are several reasons supporting KERCKHOFF's principle:

- It is much more difficult to ensure the secrecy of an algorithm than the secrecy of the key.

- It is much easier to change (only) a compromised key than to change the compromised encryption scheme.

- If a group of several people want to encrypt their pairwise communication, it is significantly easier for them to use the same program/algorithm and change only the keys than to use a different program/algorithm depending on the person communicating with.

- Secret algorithms may (intentionally) include backdoors [PT67].

- Public algorithms allow a better analysis of the cryptosystem.

The last item is subject of recurring discussion with supporters of the opposite philosophy (called *security through obscurity*), who also want to keep the encryption scheme secret. In practice, many systems using security through obscurity have been shown to be based on inadequate encryption schemes, which were broken, once they were known. There are diverse causes that the underlying encryption scheme gets known, leakage through (ex-)employees or close analysis by experts using reverse engineering [CCI90, vdBKV97], for example. Experience has shown that the process of publishing encryption schemes, respectively an open competition and evaluation, is able to produce reasonable secure schemes like RSA [RSA77, RSA78] (cf. Sect. 2.3.1), DES [nis77, Mat94], and AES (Rijndael) [DR00]. Furthermore, the MI-FARE Classic Chip [NXP07] used for payments in public transport systems in London and the Netherlands, for example, was reverse engineered [NP07, NESP08a] and broken afterwards [CNO08, KGHG08, GdKGM+08]. As an other example, we name DECT, whose encryption algorithm was partly reverse engineered and whose implementations where found to sometimes lack the use of authentication and encryption [SWT+10, MOTW09, LST+09, Men09]. These examples strongly suggest that KERCKHOFF's principle is sound. For a further discussion of the question "When does disclosure actually help security?" we refer to SWIRE [Swi04].

Before dealing with security models we introduce notions of security and attacker models in the next subsections. We then proceed with attacks, which affect implementations of or protocols using encryption schemes, before we end this section with some thoughts about practical security.

2.2.1 Notions of Security

There are different notions a user might have in mind when using a cryptosystem, apart from the classical idea of keeping the transmitted message secret. We first present the user's obvious aim that the attacker is not able to gain any useful information from ciphertexts, formalised as *indistinguishability* by GOLDWASSER and MICALI [GM84]. Afterwards we introduce another aim – called *non-malleability* due to DOLEV, DWORK and NAOR [DDN91] – with the notion that the attacker is not able to transform a given ciphertext into another ciphertext, so that the according plaintexts are 'meaningfully related'.

On the other hand, considering a possible attacker's strength, one could think of different abilities being at an attacker's disposal, e.g. *chosen-plaintext attacks* and *chosen-ciphertext attacks*. When evaluating the security of a cryptosystem, it is essential to contrast the user's aims with the attacker's abilities. BELLARE et al. came up with the idea to regard security aims and attacks as independent. In this section we follow their idea to obtain definitions of secure encryption as a pairing of a particular goal and a particular attack model [BDPR98, BDPR01]. BELLARE et al. also proved dependencies between these, for example they showed that a non-malleable cryptosystem also fulfils indistinguishability.

This section outlines the previously mentioned notions of security to give a general idea of their intention. A formal definition, taking into account also the resources and abilities of the attacker (see Sect. 2.2.2), will be given in Sect. 2.2.3.

Indistinguishability

The idea and definition of *indistinguishability* (*IND*) were introduced by GOLD-WASSER and MICALI [GM84] in the context of chosen-plaintext attacks (see Sect. 2.2.2). Since we refer to it later, we outline the presentation of BELLARE et al. [BDPR98, BDPR01] in this section.

Let Enc be an encryption algorithm, k a key, and p_0 and p_1 two plaintexts of the same length. We regard the following experiment: The adversary chooses the two plaintexts p_0 and p_1 and receives a ciphertext c which is either the encryption of p_0 or p_1. The adversary's task is to determine if $c = Enc_k(p_0)$ or $c = Enc_k(p_1)$. She succeeds if her probability to take the correct decision is more than negligibly better than flipping a coin or guessing. If the resource $\mathcal{R}$ is available to the adversary and she is not successful, the cryptosystem denoted as *indistinguishable under $\mathcal{R}$*.

Obviously this is equivalent with the requirement that the adversary does not gain any information from the ciphertext, since her probability to determine the corresponding plaintext does not increase when she learns the ciphertext [MRS87].

Non-Malleability

An encryption scheme is *non-malleable (NM)*, if the adversary is not able to change a given ciphertext in a way so that the corresponding plaintexts are 'meaningfully related'. As an example, consider an auction with secret bids and an adversary who is able to eavesdrop on the other participants' encrypted bids. If she is able to enter a bid which exceeds the other participants' bids by one – even if she does not know the value of their bid – the auction will come up to an irregular end.

Non-malleability was originally defined as *simulation based non-malleability* by Dolev et al. [DDN91, DDN95, DDN00]. Later Bellare et al. gave an at first sight different definition called *comparison based non-malleability* [BDPR98, BDPR01], but Bellare and Sahai were able to prove that both definitions specify an equivalent security model [BS99]. Bellare and Sahai also showed that non-malleability can be reduced to a certain model of indistinguishability, which has been shown to be a more practical formalisation.

Plaintext Awareness

For the sake of completeness we also introduce *plaintext awareness*, which goes back to Bellare and Rogaway in 1994 [BR94, BR95a] and was improved in 1998 by Bellare et al. [BDPR98, BDPR01]. An encryption scheme is plaintext aware, if efficient algorithms can not come up with a valid ciphertext without "knowing" the corresponding plaintext (except with negligible probability). The formal definition of plaintext awareness and most related encryption schemes fundamentally rely on the random oracle model [BR95b] which we do not want to discuss here. However, a variant of the Cramer and Shoup cryptosystem [CS98] has been shown to be plaintext aware under the "knowledge of exponent assumption" in the standard model [Den06a].

2.2.2 Passive Attacks

As already mentioned above, it is also necessary to take the attacker's resources or (assumed) strategy into account when dealing with the security of an encryption scheme or cryptographic protocol. In this subsection we concentrate on *passive attacks* where – in contrast to active attacks (see Sect. 2.2.4) – the adversary Eve is only capable of monitoring the communication channel and not able to alter the transmission on the channel in any way. Thus, the adversary's strategy can be imagined as recording data of the communication channel and analysing it afterwards threatening the confidentiality of data. Passive attacks may be further classified in respect to the adversary's capabilities [MvOV97]. The list of following common passive attacks is by no means exhaustive.

Attacks on the Encryption Scheme

Brute-Force Attack   The *brute-force attack* is also known as *exhaustive key search attack*. The attacker's strategy is to find the used key by searching through the space of all possible keys until the correct one is found. Its practical feasibility depends on the size of the key space, the rate with which keys can be tested, and the ability to determine the correct key when testing. The most obvious way to determine the key is if the attacker possesses a plaintext/ciphertext-pair. If the attacker only obtains ciphertexts, she is also capable of checking if the outcome of a decryption is, for instance, a meaningful text in English.

Ciphertext-Only Attack   A *ciphertext-only attack* (*COA*) is one where the imaginary adversary attacks the encryption scheme only by observing ciphertext. If an adversary is able to succeed with ciphertext-only attacks, the encryption scheme is considered to be completely insecure.

Known-Plaintext Attack   If an adversary does not only know ciphertext, but also knows the corresponding plaintexts for a quantity of ciphertexts, the attack is referred to as *known-plaintext attack*.

Chosen-Plaintext Attack   Attacks where the adversary is able to create the ciphertext of any chosen plaintext are denoted *chosen-plaintext attack*. If the adversary is allowed to chose the plaintexts depending on the ciphertexts created in previous encryption the attack is called *adaptive chosen-plaintext attack* (*CPA*). Note that in public encryption schemes this kind of attack cannot be prevented, since obviously the adversary is able to receive the victim's public key and encrypt arbitrary plaintexts without the participation or even the knowledge of her victim.

Chosen-Ciphertext Attack   A *chosen-ciphertext attack* is one where the adversary is able to decrypt arbitrary ciphertexts and its formal definition originates from NAOR and YUNG [NY90, NY95]. Analogous to the denomination of chosen-plaintext attacks, the *chosen-ciphertext attack* is called *adaptive (CCA)* if the adversary's choice of ciphertexts may depend on prior decryptions. One way an adversary might be able to decrypt ciphertexts is by gaining access to the victim's equipment used for decryption, even if she is unable to extract the key, for instance, by stealing a tamper-resistant cryptographic smartcard.

A special variant of this attack is known as *lunchtime attack* or *midnight attack* alluding that the adversary exploits a brief absence of her victim [BDPR98, CS98]. Here the adversary is allowed to make adaptive chosen-ciphertext queries until she receives the challenge ciphertext (*CCA1*) and thus improves her attack. A stronger form of this attack (*CCA2*) goes back to RACKOFF and SIMON [RS92] and allows the adversary to make adaptive chosen-ciphertext queries after receiving the challenge ciphertext. Obviously she would directly succeed, if she asked for a decryption of the challenge ciphertext, thus, her queries may depend on the challenge ciphertext but may not be identical to it.

Parallel Attack The definition of *parallel attacks* was developed by BELLARE and SAHAI to connect non-malleability with indistinguishability [BS99] as described in more detail in Sect. 2.47. The model of parallel attacks extends chosen-plaintext, respective chosen-ciphertext, attacks by giving the adversary the possibility to ask for the decryption of a certain quantity of ciphertexts after she has obtained the challenge ciphertext. Of course, she is not allowed to ask for the challenge ciphertext, which would render the attack model useless. Since the decryption requests may not depend on the result of each other, one can imagine the requests as being processed in parallel, therefore yielding the name parallel attack. Due to stronger underlying attacks (CPA, CCA1, CCA2), ascending digits in the abbreviated form (PA0, PA1, PA2) represent stronger attacks. It is obvious that CCA2 and PA2 represent the same attack model, since the adversary does not gain any additional resources by the extension due to the fact, that she is already allowed to ask for decryptions in CCA2.

Related-Key Attack A *related-key attack* is one where the adversary observes communication encrypted with two or more related keys which are tied in some mathematical relationship which is known by the adversary. At the beginning of the attack, the adversary does not know initial values of the keys or parts of them, but she might know which parts of them are identical. At first sight, this seems to be quite fanciful, because no cautious cryptographer would encrypt plaintexts with multiple keys who are in a certain relationship known to the attacker. But since some cryptographic protocols are developed by people without solid cryptographic background and not analysed by cryptographers, this attack is not unrealistic. One of the best-known applications for related-key attacks is the WEP protocol [IEE97] used to encrypt wireless networking. Due to a weakness in the key-generation algorithm, WEP creates related keys for different connections. We refer the reader to FLUHRER et al. [FMS01], CHAABOUNI [Cha06], and TEWS et al. [TWP07] for more details.

Ciphertext-Verification Attack   In 1999 HALEVI and KRAWCZYK introduced *ciphertext-verification attacks* for public-key cryptosystems [HK98, HK99]. In this scenario the adversary gets access to the public key of her victim and a *plaintext-checking oracle*, which answers on input of a plaintext/ciphertext-pair if the ciphertext is a valid encryption of the corresponding plaintext. Seemingly this attack is weaker than a chosen-ciphertext attack. Since in public-key cryptosystems the attacker is always able to generate valid plaintext/ciphertext-pairs, this attack is only useful if the encryption scheme is probabilistic. If it was deterministic, an adversary would be able to verify plaintext/ciphertext-pairs himself by encrypting the relevant plaintext. Later this attack was also denoted as *plaintext-checking attack* by NGUYEN and POINTCHEVAL [NP02].

Reaction Attack   HALL, GOLDBERG and SCHNEIER propose a scenario where an adversary utilises decryption errors by observing the receiver's reactions when decrypting [HGS99]. We speak of decryption errors, which may appear in probabilistic encryption schemes, if the decryption of an encryption does not result in the original plaintext. They occur, for instance, in the original version of the AJTAI-DWORK encryption scheme [AD97]. The so-called *reaction attack* does not directly attack the underlying problem of the encryption scheme, rather information is gathered from the reactions of the receiver. This is accomplished by presenting the owner of a private key a ciphertext that may contain errors, in which case a signature (see Sect. 2.4.2) or hash (see Sect. 2.4.1) checksum verification fails. By watching the reaction, for example in a protected system, such as a tamper-proof smartcard (see Sect. 8.3.1), the adversary gains information about the plaintext or the key. Other examples rely on the use of social engineering (see Sect. 2.2.4) to bring the receiver of a message to reveal information. The exact way the attack is launched depends on the adversary's imagination and the victim's naivety.

   We admit that especially the classification of reaction attacks as passive attacks is questionable. But in cases where the adversary attacks a tamper-proof smartcard, the attack mainly consists of observation and eavesdropping and thus legitimates the classification as passive attack.

Attacks on the User

Another form of passive attack is to physically observe the victim. This includes for example, catching a glimpse of the victim as he enters his keyphrase or using reflections of the monitor on spoons, teacups, walls or even the human iris [BDU08, BCD$^+$09]. Also, hardware keyloggers are cheaply available [Kee09]. Depending on how much information is revealed, we are either done, for example if these attacks reveal the full key, or we can use the gained information for further evaluation which is referred to as *side-channel attack* and covered in Sect. 2.2.2. This also includes users rendering an encryption scheme useless by choosing too simple passwords, reusing them or writing them at their monitor or on the backside of their keyboards (see also the work by FLORÊNCIO and HERLEY [FH07], and SCHNEIER [Sch06, Sch07b]).

Attacks on Implementations and Hardware

Instead of attacking the underlying cryptosystem and thus trying to break the intractability of the underlying problems, *attacks on the implementation* try to obtain information about the plaintext or the private key by observing the computations or communication of a given implementation. Hence, the adversary does not attack a weakness in the algorithms of the encryption scheme, but rather gathers information on the execution of the encryption scheme's algorithms on a real device.

Traffic Analysis   By observing network traffic, an adversary may gain important information to compute or speed up a brute-force computation of the secret key. SONG et al. exploited the fact that the SSH protocol [BSB05] transmits each keystroke in a separate packet during interactive sessions, thus leaking the inter-keystroke timing of the users' typing. This allowed them to infer information on the users' passwords from the frequency and timing of network packets using statistical models resulting in an fifty times faster attack than brute force [SWT01].

In general, *traffic analysis* is the procedure of deducing information from patterns in communication. In this context communication traffic is usually encrypted and the adversary is unable to decrypt it. However, she may collect, for instance, delay, length, timing, sender and receiver of the messages in order to deduce information. For a more detailed treatment of traffic analysis we refer to DANEZIS et al. [Dan03], DANEZIS and MURDOCH [MD05], and MATHEWSON and DINGLEDINE [MD04].

Side-Channel Attacks   In order to recover secret parameters of the computation, *side-channel attacks* make use of unintended physical leakage resulting from implementation-specific characteristics of cryptographic primitives. For example, any electrical device produces electromagnetic radiation, which an adversary might listen to. If the implementation is straightforward and no countermeasures are taken, such a leakage can be sufficient to extract enough information to successfully recover the secret key. It is important to point out that side-channel attacks apply to a specific implementation on specific hardware and do not attack the mathematical or computational security of the used cryptographic algorithms.

On the opposite side, there are *tamper-proof* or *tamper-resistant* devices, such as smartcards (cf. Sect. 8.3.1) and secure (co)processors [SW99], which are built to prevent attackers with physical access from retrieving or altering the sensitive information stored on the device. The measures to achieve tamper-resistance range from screws with special heads to special packaging and protection of semiconductors [CLLW92]. Information stored on the chip should only be accessible by the software running on the device and the predetermined interfaces, which are then able to enforce access control. It is very hard – if not impossible – to achieve tamper-resistance, since an adversary who is in possession of the device may try to tamper with it as long as she wishes. Therefore, in practise, the measures focus on the group of potential tamperers, aiming to withstand the supposed level of knowledge and available tools.

Side-channel attacks are a quite new research area and were brought to attention by KOCHER in the mid nineties [Koc96], even though this technique has been known since the forties [Sin08].

The first target of side-channel attacks are tamper-proof devices, such as smartcards, but this kind of attack affects other cryptographic devices as well. In analogy to communication attacks, the term *passive attack* is also commonly used in this context if the adversary only observes the cryptographic hardware without trying to manipulate or disturb its proper functioning. Fault-attacks, the according active counterpart of side-channel attacks, are described in Sect. 2.2.4.

In literature, side-channel attacks are also classified as invasive and non-invasive attacks. *Invasive attacks* require exposing the chip in order to get direct access to its components. *Non-invasive attacks* only analyse externally available information such as emissions and power consumption. SKOROBOGATOV and ANDERSON [SA02] additionally introduced *semi-invasive attacks*, where the chip of the smartcard is depackaged to get access to the chips surface, but the passivation layer, an extra shield to hide the internal behaviour of the chip, remains untouched. Note that the axes of active/passive and invasive/non-invasive are orthogonal. A non-invasive attack, such as a fault attack using a much faster clock frequency (see Sect. 2.2.4), may completely change the card's behaviour, while an invasive attack may simply observe the card after depackaging. For example, when the MIFARE Crypto-1 Cipher was broken, an invasive, passive attack gave a detailed description of the chips gates which provided a basis for further investigations [NESP08b].

Depending on the source of information, the following list states examples for side-channel attacks.

Timing attack The idea of *timing attacks* was first introduced by KOCHER [Koc96] and practically implemented by DHEM et al. against an RSA implementation [DKL+98]. The main idea of this attack is to deduce valuable information on the private key from the running time of a cryptographic algorithm or device. This can either be applied to a complete run of a cryptographic algorithm or tried on internal operation stages. The latter especially affects smartcards, since, in general, smartcards have no internal clock [RE08, p. 73f] and therefore clock ticks have to be generated externally. This heavily eases the attacker's effort to measure the timing of certain sub-parts of the cryptographic algorithm.

As an example, we regard MONTGOMERY's algorithm for modular multiplication [Mon85] which also efficiently performs modular exponentiation [MvOV97, p. 603]. We do not describe MONTGOMERY's algorithm in detail here, it is sufficient to know, that its running time – for a fixed modulus – is independent of the factors with the exception that the intermediary result of the multiplication may me greater than the modulus. If so, an additional subtraction has to be computed which can be easily determined by an attacker and supplies him with additional information on the factors.

Power analysis attack Similar to timing attacks, *power analysis attacks* can provide valuable information about operations and parameters to the attacker by observing the power consumption of a cryptographic device, in particular its central processing unit. KOCHER et al. was the first who introduced the ideas of *simple power analysis attacks*, where the power consumption measurements are directly interpreted, and *differential power analysis attacks*, where statistical functions are applied to the power consumption measurements [KJJ99]. Again the attack on smartcards is especially easy since their power supply is provided by the terminal [RE08, p. 67ff] and thus is easy to measure.

Electromagnetic analysis attack Fundamentally with the same idea, *electromagnetic analysis attacks* gather information by measuring the electromagnetic fields near the processor of a cryptographic device. This kind of attack was first introduced by QUISQUATER and SAMYDE [QS01] and shortly after proven to be feasible by GANDOLFI et al. [GMO01]. Electromagnetic analysis attacks apply to all kind of electronic devices, since electromagnetic fields are inevitable whenever the electric charges move. In connection with display devices, which produce human readable images and thus are highly patterned, this attack is also known as *Van Eck phreaking* after the Dutch researcher VAN ECK, who showed a proof of concept in the mid eighties regarding cathode ray tube monitors [vE85]. Keyboards are often used to enter sensitive information such as passwords and pins, so attacking them is a quite straightforward approach which was first suggested by KUHN and ANDERSON [KA98] and ten years later shown to be practically feasible [VP09].

Acoustic Cryptanalysis As a last resource of information for side-channel attacks, we mention low level acoustic emissions from cryptographic devices. Since electrical currents heat material and this material gives off heat to its environment, noise emissions (mostly above 10kHz) from an operating processing unit occur which can be used to locate a HLT instruction [Int99, p. 3-291], for example. A proof of concept of this attack has been show recently by SHAMIR and TROMER [ST11]. Earlier ASONOV et al. have shown how to recognise the key being pressed by acoustic emanation of a keyboard [AA04, ZZT05].

Naturally all described attacks can be combined with each other, but the combination of timing and power analysis is most common.

As can be inferred from the above paragraphs, the efforts needed for side-channel attacks may be quite low, while, on the other side, the development and deployment of countermeasures is not trivial. We do not discuss applicable countermeasures here. Instead we refer the reader to a survey from QUISQUATER and KOEUNE [QK02] for a deeper discussion of side-channel attacks and possible countermeasures and to "The Side Channel Cryptanalysis Lounge" from the European Network of Excellence for Cryptology [AV13].

2.2.3 Security Models

Now that we have described various notions of security and possible attacks, we are able to examine security models used to evaluate the security of an encryption scheme. We start this section with classical security models and then continue with formal security models where we limit ourselves to game-based models for asymmetric and symmetric encryption schemes.

Classical Security Models

Parts of the following classification are due to SHANNON [Sha49], who introduced perfect, provable and ad hoc security already in 1949. There were also definitions of perfect security for a polynomially constrained adversary by GOLDWASSER and MICALI [GM84], and y-security which goes back to YAO [Yao82]. Since MICALI et al. have shown them to describe an equivalent security model [MRS87], we do not want to go into more detail here. Instead, we have a look at the classification of security models, dividing them into five models, given by MENEZES et al. [MvOV97].

Unconditional Security   The strongest security model is *unconditional security* also denoted as *perfect security* by Sʜᴀɴɴᴏɴ [Sha49]. An adversary should not be able to gain any information from the ciphertext, even if she is granted unlimited resources. That means – analogous to indistinguishability – by learning the ciphertext, the adversary may not gain any information about the related plaintext. By defining an empty message it is also possible to hide the information if or that information has been transmitted. The major drawback is that the length of the key must have at least the length of the plaintext. As a consequence of this, each key may only be used once to preserve perfect security, since otherwise information may be leaked.

A well-known example for this is the *Vernam-One-Time-Pad* (*OTP*, cf. [Buc99, p. 89]) where the message is encrypted by XORing (cf. Def. 4.60) it into a randomly chosen key of the same length resulting in a ciphertext of random data. But despite the fact that *one-time pads* are the only cryptosystems providing perfect security in theory, in practice they only trade the transmission of a message for the transmission of an at least equally long key (the one time pad). The main advantage – which may be useful in specialised situations – is a shift of time [Sch02]. The one-time pad may be securely transmitted beforehand, while the message obviously has to be transmitted after was generated. As a drawback, care has to be taken to generate a truly random key and to store it securely after its transmission.

Complexity-Theoretic Security   In *complexity-theoretic security* an appropriate model of computation is defined and the adversary is modelled as having polynomial bounded computational power (time and space). Then security is proven relative to the previously defined model. In this context, it is important to notice that an algorithm solving all instances of a given problem yields automatically an upper bound on the complexity of the problem, which is determined by its worst-case analysis. On the contrary, finding a lower bound of a problem implies to make a statement about *all possible* (as yet undiscovered) algorithms which solve this problem, which may be quite hard to prove.

Since complexity-theoretic security makes use of asymptotic analysis and worst-case analysis, care has to be taken to identify the practical value of this model. As already stated in Sect. 2.1.1, results of asymptotic and worst-case analysis must be interpreted with care, since computations in contrast to the proof may or may not be feasible for real parameters. However, complexity-theoretic analysis may lead to a better understanding of security for the analysed encryption scheme.

Provable Security   An encryption scheme is regarded as *provable secure*, if it can be proven that breaking the encryption scheme is as least as hard as solving an assumed hard problem. In the majority of cases, assumed hard problems are number-theoretic, like factorisation or computing discrete logarithms. An example for provable security is RSA [RSA77, RSA78] under the assumption that the adversary's aim is to get the victim's private key. It can be shown that getting the private key is as difficult as factorising the RSA-modulus [DeL84, Mil75, Mil76]. A more detailed description of cryptographic hardness assumptions is given in Sect. 2.3.

It is important to note that the hardness of the underlying problem has not to be proven, instead the hardness assumption is regarded sufficient. As KOBLITZ mentions that the security is rather conditional than provable and could mislead outsiders [Kob07]. In a series of publications, KOBLITZ and MENEZES analyse and criticise several results of provable security and discuss the question of how to interpret reduction arguments in cryptography [KM04, KM, KM07] and provoked responses among others from GOLDREICH [Gol06] and DAMGÅRD [Dam07a].

Computational Security In *computational security* it is assumed, that the encryption scheme has been well studied. On that condition, computational security aims to measure the amount of computational effort required to break the cryptosystem with the best known algorithms. An encryption scheme is characterised as *computationally secure*, if the effort needed to break the system exceeds the hypothetical adversary's available resources by an adequate margin.

Encryption schemes in this class are often related to hard problems, but lack proof of equivalence as required for provable security. As in the above paragraph, we take RSA as an example, but this time we assume the adversary wants to construct the plaintext from its underlying ciphertext. Since RSA is a public-key encryption scheme, it is also assumed the adversary knows the public key used for encrypting the plaintext. It is an open question if the adversary has to calculate the private key in order to decrypt the ciphertext or if she has more feasible options [RK03]. Again we have to refer to Sect. 2.3 for a more detailed description of RSA.

Ad hoc Security Clearly the weakest security offers the model of *ad hoc security* which is based on a variety of plausible and convincing arguments, that the resources needed for a successful attack exceed the resources of a potential adversary. Even though this is a widespread "prove of security", it obviously is the least satisfying method, since possibly unknown attacks represent a permanent threat.

Game-Based Security Models

An excellent overview on formal security models and the problems of inferring from statements in the security model to conclusions regarding the practical use is given by DENT [Den06b]. This subsection covers game-based security models for asymmetric encryption proposed by RACKOFF and SIMON [RS92] and symmetric encryption proposed by BELLARE et al. [BDJR97].

Asymmetric Encryption Schemes   Our presentation follows BELLARE et al. [BDPR98, BDPR01] where a particular goal (indistinguishability, non-malleability) is paired with a particular attack model (chosen-plaintext and chosen-ciphertext attacks). The previously mentioned papers also show relations between the security models as shown in Fig. 2.1. Unsurprisingly, if an encryption scheme is secure in the sense of a particular security model, it is also secure in the sense of all security models where the adversary is weaker (from CCA2 to CPA). Before we address the reason why non-malleability is harder to achieve (CPA,CCA1) or equivalent to indistinguishability (CCA2) we need to deal with the indistinguishability-based security models.

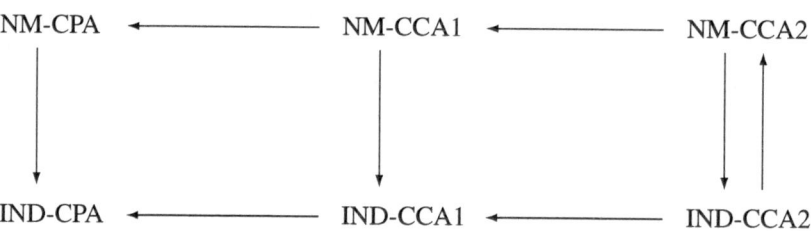

Figure 2.1: Relations between Security Models for Asymmetric Encryption $\mathcal{SM}$ after BELLARE et al. [BDPR98, BDPR01]. An arrow from $\mathcal{SM}_1$ to $\mathcal{SM}_2$ indicates that $\mathcal{SM}_1 \Rightarrow \mathcal{SM}_2$ holds.

Before we regard the formal definition of the security models, we take a look at the following experiment which is shown in Fig. 2.2. The key-generation algorithm of the encryption scheme creates a pair of keys (pk, sk). The adversary gets the public key pk and – depending on her allowed capabilities (CCA1, CCA2) – may ask a decryption oracle $\mathcal{O}_{Dec}$ in order to learn information about the secret key. She then outputs two different plaintexts m_0, m_1 of the same length. From those plaintexts one is uniformly at random selected and the encryption is given to the adversary. Her challenge is to decide which of the two plaintexts was encrypted. In the case of CCA2 she may again ask a decryption oracle $\mathcal{O}_{Dec}$ except for the decryption of the challenge ciphertext. If the adversary is significantly better than

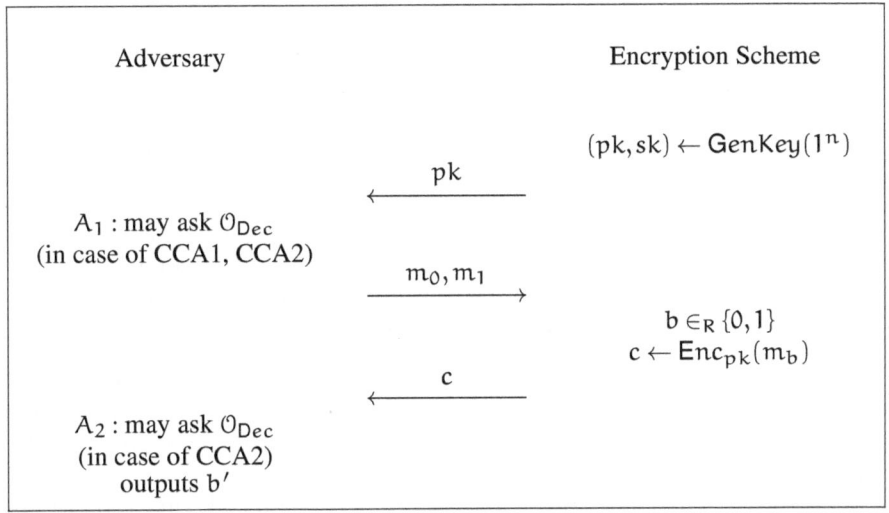

Figure 2.2: Visualisation of Game-Based IND-atk Security Models

guessing she succeeds and the encryption scheme is not secure in the sense of the regarded security model.

Now that we have an idea how this approach works, we follow the definitions of BELLARE et al. [BDPR98] and come up with a formal definition. Since the only difference between the three security models is the access to the decryption oracle we handle altogether. $\mathcal{O}_{Dec}$ denotes a decryption oracle for the previously generated secret key and ϵ denotes an oracle which returns the empty string on any input. Formally, the adversary is modelled by two algorithms and the second stage may get some status information s from the first stage.

Definition 2.46. (IND-CPA, IND-CCA1, IND-CCA2) Let $\Pi = (GenKey, Enc, Dec)$ be a public key encryption scheme as in Def. 2.41 and let $A = (A_1, A_2)$ be an adversary consisting of two sub-algorithms. For attack $atk \in \{cpa, cca1, cca2\}$ and the security parameter $n \in \mathbb{N}$ the adversary's success probability is

$$\mathbf{Adv}_{A,\Pi}^{ind-atk}(n) \overset{def}{=} \Pr[\mathbf{Exp}_{A,\Pi}^{ind-atk-1}(n) = 1] - \Pr[\mathbf{Exp}_{A,\Pi}^{ind-atk-0}(n) = 1]$$

where the experiment $\mathbf{Exp}_{A,\Pi}^{ind-atk-b}(n) = b'$ for $b \in \{0,1\}$ is given as follows:

$$
\begin{array}{rcll}
(pk, sk) & \leftarrow & \mathsf{GenKey}(1^n) & \text{key-generation} \\
(m_0, m_1, s) & \leftarrow & A_1^{O_1}(pk); & \text{first stage of A (find)} \\
b & \in_R & \{0,1\} & \text{random selection of b} \\
c & \leftarrow & \mathsf{Enc}_{pk}(m_b) & \text{encryption} \\
b' & \leftarrow & A_2^{O_2}(m_0, m_1, s, c) & \text{second stage of A (guess)}
\end{array}
$$

with:

$$
\begin{array}{llll}
O_1(\cdot) = \epsilon & \text{and} & O_2(\cdot) = \epsilon & \text{for atk} = cpa \\
O_1(\cdot) = O_{Dec}(\cdot) & \text{and} & O_2(\cdot) = \epsilon & \text{for atk} = cca1 \\
O_1(\cdot) = O_{Dec}(\cdot) & \text{and} & O_2(\cdot) = O_{Dec}(\cdot) & \text{for atk} = cca2
\end{array}
$$

The messages m_0 and m_1 from the plaintext space $\mathcal{M}$ may be freely chosen by the adversary under the condition that their length is equal: $|m_0| = |m_1|$ and that they are different. Furthermore, if $atk = cca2$ the adversary is not allowed to ask the oracle O_2 for the decryption of c.

If the success probability $\mathbf{Adv}_{A,\Pi}^{ind-atk}(n)$ of a polynomial bound adversary is negligible in n, we say the encryption scheme Π is *secure in the sense of* $\mathrm{IND-atk}$.

Regarding non-malleability Bellare and Sahai [BS99] have shown that the notions of comparison based and simulation based non-malleability are equivalent. Furthermore, they also give a formulation of non-malleability in terms of indistinguishability under a certain type of attack, which they call parallel attack. Since its definition is very similar to Def. 2.46 we give only a short definition:

Definition 2.47. (IND-PA0, IND-PA1, IND-PA2) Let $\Pi = (\mathsf{GenKey}, \mathsf{Enc}, \mathsf{Dec})$ be a public key encryption scheme as in Def. 2.41 and let $A = (A_1, A_2)$ be an adversary consisting of two sub-algorithms as in Def. 2.46. For attack $atk \in \{pa0, pa1, pa2\}$ and the security parameter $n \in \mathbb{N}$ the adversary's success probability is

$$
\mathbf{Adv}_{A,\Pi}^{ind-atk}(n) \overset{\mathrm{def}}{=} \Pr[\mathbf{Exp}_{A,\Pi}^{ind-atk-1}(n) = 1] - \Pr[\mathbf{Exp}_{A,\Pi}^{ind-atk-0}(n) = 1]
$$

where the experiment $\mathbf{Exp}_{A,\Pi}^{ind-atk-b}(n) = b'$ for $b \in \{0,1\}$ is for $atk = pa0$ ($pa1, pa2$) almost the same experiment as for $atk = cpa$ ($cca1, cca2$) in Def. 2.46. The only difference is that the second stage A_2 of the adversary's algorithm may additionally ask a decryption oracle a polynomial number of times with the restriction that the different queries are not allowed to depend on the result of each other. The decryption oracle may also not be asked for the decryption of the challenge ciphertext c.

Questioning the additional oracle can be imagined as asking the oracle only once for a decryption of a vector of ciphertexts. The oracle then returns a vector of plaintexts where each plaintext is the decryption of the corresponding ciphertext. It is obvious that in the case of PA2 the availability of the additional oracle is of no use, since the adversary already has access to a decryption oracle and hence the notions of IND-PA2 and IND-CCA2 are equivalent. Returning to the equivalence of non-malleability and indistinguishability under parallel attacks the models from NM-CPA via NM-CCA1 to NM-CCA2 are equivalent to IND-PA0 to IND-PA2.

As a last statement before we turn to security models for symmetric encryption, we point out that BAUDRON et al. [BPS00] were able to proof that an adversary has no advantage if she possesses multiple public keys in any of the security models given in this paragraph.

Symmetric Encryption Schemes   BELLARE et al. [BDJR97] give four defini-tions of security for symmetric encryption models. Each definition captures two notions depending if the adversary is given access to only an encryption oracle (CPA) or also an decryption oracle (CCA). It is worthwhile to mention that in contrast to asymmetric encryption in symmetric encryption the adversary is not able to create ciphertexts by herself and hence is provided with an encryption oracle. The first two of the four notions were introduced by BELLARE et al. while the other two are adaptions from notions given by GOLDWASSER and MICALI [GM84] for asymmetric encryption. We give slightly simplified definitions here.

We start with the description of left-or-right indistinguishability (LOR). The adversary is allowed to ask an oracle, the *left-or-right oracle*, for the encryption of plaintexts. Her query consists of a pair of plaintexts (m_0, m_1) and her task is to determine if the left-or-right oracle answers with the encryption of the left (m_0) or right (m_1) plaintext, which is arbitrary but fixed for each run of the experiment. If the adversary is not able to gain a significant advantage, the encryption scheme is considered to be secure in the sense of left-or-right indistinguishability. If chosen ciphertext attacks are considered, the adversary is given access to a decryption oracle, but may not query it at a ciphertext she received from the left-or-right oracle, since she would obviously always succeed otherwise.

Definition 2.48. (LOR-CPA, LOR-CCA) Let $\Pi = (\mathsf{GenKey}, \mathsf{Enc}, \mathsf{Dec})$ be a sym-metric encryption scheme as in Def. 2.40 and $b \in \{0, 1\}$. Let A_{cpa} be an adversary with access to the left-or-right oracle $\mathcal{O}_{\mathcal{LR}}(\cdot, \cdot, b)$ and let A_{cca} be an adversary with access to the left-or-right oracle $\mathcal{O}_{\mathcal{LR}}(\cdot, \cdot, b)$ and to a decryption oracle $\mathcal{O}_{\mathsf{Dec}}(\cdot)$.

The left-or-right oracle $\mathcal{O}_{\mathcal{LR}}(\cdot, \cdot, b)$ takes as input two messages m_0 and m_1 from the plaintext space $\mathcal{M}$ and depending on b it returns the encryption $\mathsf{Enc}(m_b)$.

For attack $atk \in \{cpa, cca\}$ and the security parameter $n \in \mathbb{N}$ the adversary's success probability is

$$\mathbf{Adv}_{A_{atk},\Pi}^{lor-atk}(n) \overset{def}{=} \Pr[\mathbf{Exp}_{A_{atk},\Pi}^{lor-atk-1}(n) = 1] - \Pr[\mathbf{Exp}_{A_{atk},\Pi}^{lor-atk-0}(n) = 1]$$

where the experiment $\mathbf{Exp}_{A_{atk},\Pi}^{lor-atk-b}(n) = b'$ for $b \in \{0,1\}$ is given as follows:

$$
\begin{array}{lll}
k & \leftarrow & \mathsf{GenKey}(1^n) \\
b & \in_R & \{0,1\} \\
b' & \leftarrow & A_{atk}^{O_1,O_2};
\end{array}
\quad
\begin{array}{l}
\text{key-generation} \\
\text{random selection of } b \\
\text{adversary tries to determine } b'
\end{array}
$$

with:

$$
\begin{array}{llll}
O_1(\cdot) = O_{\mathcal{LR}}(\cdot,\cdot,b) & \text{and} & O_2(\cdot) = \epsilon & \text{for } atk = cpa \\
O_1(\cdot) = O_{\mathcal{LR}}(\cdot,\cdot,b) & \text{and} & O_2(\cdot) = O_{\mathsf{Dec}}(\cdot) & \text{for } atk = cca
\end{array}
$$

The messages m_0 and m_1 from the plaintext space $\mathcal{M}$ may be freely chosen by the adversary as input for the left-or-right oracle $O_{\mathcal{LR}}(\cdot,\cdot,b)$ under the condition that their length is equal: $|m_0| = |m_1|$. Furthermore, if $atk = cca$ the adversary is not allowed to ask the decryption oracle $O_{\mathsf{Dec}}(\cdot)$ for the decryption of any ciphertext she received by $O_{\mathcal{LR}}(\cdot,\cdot,b)$.

If the success probability $\mathbf{Adv}_{A_{atk},\Pi}^{lor-atk}(n)$ of a polynomial bound adversary is negligible in n, we say the encryption scheme Π is *secure in the sense of* LOR − atk.

Real-or-random indistinguishability (ROR) is very similar to left-or-right indistinguishability. Essentially the experiment is unchanged, only the available oracle is now a *real-or-random oracle* which answers either the encryption of the queried message or an encryption of a randomly chosen string of the same length. Again, for each run of the experiment the oracle's behaviour is arbitrary but fixed. The adversary's task is to determine the oracle's operating mode. The encryption scheme is considered to be secure in the sense of real-or-random indistinguishability if the adversary cannot gain a significant advantage. As before if chosen ciphertext attacks are considered, the adversary may not query the decryption oracle at a ciphertext she received from the real-or-random oracle.

Definition 2.49. (ROR-CPA, ROR-CCA) Let $\Pi = (\mathsf{GenKey}, \mathsf{Enc}, \mathsf{Dec})$ be a symmetric encryption scheme as in Def. 2.40 and $b \in \{0,1\}$. Let A_{cpa} be an adversary with access to the real-or-random oracle $O_{\mathcal{RR}}(\cdot,b)$ and let A_{cca} be an adversary with access to the real-or-random oracle $O_{\mathcal{RR}}(\cdot,b)$ and to a decryption oracle $O_{\mathsf{Dec}}(\cdot)$.

The real-or-random oracle $\mathcal{O}_{\mathcal{RR}}(\cdot, b)$ takes as input a message m from the plaintext space $\mathcal{M}$ and depending on b it returns either the encryption $\mathsf{Enc}(m)$ of the message m (if $b = 0$) or an encryption $\mathsf{Enc}(r)$ of an equal-length randomly chosen string r (if $b = 1$).

For attack $atk \in \{cpa, cca\}$ and the security parameter $n \in \mathbb{N}$ the adversary's success probability is

$$\mathbf{Adv}_{A_{atk},\Pi}^{ror-atk}(n) \overset{\mathrm{def}}{=} \Pr[\mathbf{Exp}_{A_{atk},\Pi}^{ror-atk-1}(n) = 1] - \Pr[\mathbf{Exp}_{A_{atk},\Pi}^{ror-atk-0}(n) = 1]$$

where the experiment $\mathbf{Exp}_{A_{atk},\Pi}^{ror-atk-b}(n) = b'$ for $b \in \{0,1\}$ is given as follows:

$$
\begin{array}{llll}
k & \leftarrow & \mathsf{GenKey}(1^n) & \text{key-generation} \\
b & \in_R & \{0,1\} & \text{random selection of } b \\
b' & \leftarrow & A_{atk}^{\mathcal{O}_1,\mathcal{O}_2}; & \text{adversary tries to determine } b'
\end{array}
$$

with:

$$
\begin{array}{llll}
\mathcal{O}_1(\cdot) = \mathcal{O}_{\mathcal{RR}}(\cdot, b) & \text{and} & \mathcal{O}_2(\cdot) = \epsilon & \text{for } atk = cpa \\
\mathcal{O}_1(\cdot) = \mathcal{O}_{\mathcal{RR}}(\cdot, b) & \text{and} & \mathcal{O}_2(\cdot) = \mathcal{O}_{\mathsf{Dec}}(\cdot) & \text{for } atk = cca
\end{array}
$$

If $atk = cca$ the adversary is not allowed to ask the decryption oracle $\mathcal{O}_{\mathsf{Dec}}(\cdot)$ for the decryption of any ciphertext she received by $\mathcal{O}_{\mathcal{RR}}(\cdot, \cdot, b)$.

If the success probability $\mathbf{Adv}_{A_{atk},\Pi}^{ror-atk}(n)$ of a polynomial bound adversary is negligible in n, we say the encryption scheme Π is *secure in the sense of* $\mathrm{ROR} - atk$.

An adaption of indistinguishability models for asymmetric encryption (IND-CPA, IND-CCA) is find-then-guess security. The main difference to asymmetric security is that the adversary is not able to encrypt by herself and has to ask an encryption oracle instead. Therefore, we give only a short repetition of the shared notion. The adversary has to specify two plaintexts of the same length. One of them is randomly chosen and encrypted. The adversary obtains the ciphertext and has to determine which plaintext was encrypted. If she is significantly better than by guessing, she succeeds. Again, the formal definition divides the adversary's algorithm into two stages: finding and guessing.

Definition 2.50. (FTG-CPA, FTG-CCA) Let $\Pi = (\mathsf{GenKey}, \mathsf{Enc}, \mathsf{Dec})$ be a symmetric encryption scheme as in Def. 2.40 and $b \in \{0,1\}$. Let $A = (A_1, A_2)$ be an adversary consisting of two sub-algorithms with access to an encryption oracle $\mathcal{O}_{\mathsf{Enc}}(\cdot)$ (CPA) respectively with access to an encryption oracle $\mathcal{O}_{\mathsf{Enc}}(\cdot)$ and to a decryption oracle $\mathcal{O}_{\mathsf{Dec}}(\cdot)$ (CCA).

For attack $atk \in \{cpa, cca\}$ and the security parameter $n \in \mathbb{N}$ the adversary's success probability is

$$\mathbf{Adv}_{A_{atk},\Pi}^{ftg-atk}(n) \stackrel{def}{=} \Pr[\mathbf{Exp}_{A_{atk},\Pi}^{ftg-atk-1}(n) = 1] - \Pr[\mathbf{Exp}_{A_{atk},\Pi}^{ftg-atk-0}(n) = 1]$$

where the experiment $\mathbf{Exp}_{A_{atk},\Pi}^{ftg-atk-b}(n) = b'$ for $b \in \{0,1\}$ is given as follows:

k	$\leftarrow$	$\mathsf{GenKey}(1^n)$	key-generation
(m_0, m_1, s)	$\leftarrow$	$A_1^{O_1, O_2}$	first stage of A (find)
b	$\in_R$	$\{0, 1\}$	random selection of b
c	$\leftarrow$	$\mathsf{Enc}_k(m_b)$	encryption
b'	$\leftarrow$	$A_2^{O_1, O_2}(m_0, m_1, s, c)$	second stage of A (guess)

with:

$$O_1(\cdot) = O_{\mathsf{Enc}}(\cdot) \quad \text{and} \quad O_2(\cdot) = \epsilon \qquad \text{for } atk = cpa$$
$$O_1(\cdot) = O_{\mathsf{Enc}}(\cdot) \quad \text{and} \quad O_2(\cdot) = O_{\mathsf{Dec}}(\cdot) \qquad \text{for } atk = cca$$

The messages m_0 and m_1 from the plaintext space $\mathcal{M}$ may be freely chosen by the adversary as challenge plaintexts under the condition that their length is equal: $|m_0| = |m_1|$. If $atk = cca$ the adversary is not allowed to ask the decryption oracle $O_{\mathsf{Dec}}(\cdot)$ for the decryption of the challenge ciphertext c.

If the success probability $\mathbf{Adv}_{A_{atk},\Pi}^{ftg-atk}(n)$ of a polynomial bound adversary is negligible in n, we say the encryption scheme Π is *secure in the sense of* FTG − atk.

Since it is comparison-based, we do not give the definition of the missing notion of security– called semantic security– but shortly describe its idea. The notion of semantic security is that whatever can be efficiently computed about the plaintext given the ciphertext can also be computed in absence of the ciphertext. More formally, the adversary runs two stages. First, she chooses an advantageous message distribution of equal-length strings. In the second stage, according to the chosen distribution two plaintexts m_0, m_1 are selected. The adversary gets the encryption of m_1 and has to output a function f and a function value α such that $\alpha = f(m)$. The encryption scheme is secure if the adversary is not able to perform this task significantly better than the probability $\alpha = f(m_0)$ with m_0 randomly drawn from the previously mentioned message distribution.

BELLARE et al. also showed that the notions of LOR-ATK and ROR-ATK respectively FTG-ATK and SEM-ATK are equivalent. They also showed that the first provides a stronger notion of security than the latter although, intuitively it may appear vice versa. An overview of the relation between the notions is shown in Fig. 2.3.

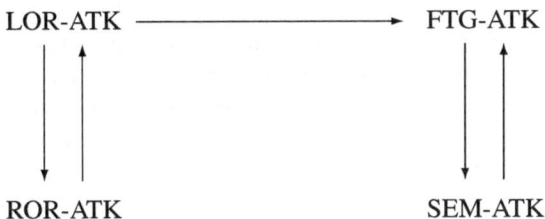

Figure 2.3: Relations between Securitymodels $\mathcal{SM}$ for Symmetric Encryption after BEL-LARE et al. [BDJR97]. An arrow from $\mathcal{SM}_1$ to $\mathcal{SM}_2$ indicates that there exists a security-preserving reduction from $\mathcal{SM}_1$ to $\mathcal{SM}_2$.

2.2.4 Active Attacks

In contrast to passive attackers, *active attackers* may also attempt to delete, add, or replay messages, or more generally, to alter the transmission on the communication channel in some way. Therefore, it is assumed that the communication between Alice and Bob is held over an unprotected network. The modelled adversary, Mallory, is then able to completely control the data sent between Alice and Bob as shown in Fig. 2.4. Compared to Eve, Mallory not only threatens data confidentiality but also data integrity and authentication.

Figure 2.4: Setup of Active Attacks on the Communication Channel

Note that some sources also consider chosen-plaintext and chosen-ciphertext attacks as an active attack, since the adversary chooses the plaintext respectively the ciphertext she wants to have encrypted respectively decrypted. However, in these cases the adversary does not change any message nor tampers any device, thus her attack mainly relies on eavesdropping. Therefore, we continue to categorise these attacks as passive attacks.

In general, active attacks are harder to carry out than passive attacks, but have a more devastating impact when they succeed. For example, an active attack on a communication channel requires that the attacker not only listens to the communication and breaks the cryptography to send a corrupted message, but he also has to block the delivery of the original message, because the receiver would become suspicious if he receives messages "twice". Moreover, the attacker has to be fast enough to avoid a network failure and thus alert her victim(s). Otherwise, there are also scenarios from which an attacker benefits, for example if encrypted documents can be found on a server or the attacker is in possession of the cryptographic device and mounts fault-attacks. Below we describe some common active attacks, but this list is by no means complete.

Attacks on the Encryption Scheme

Rewrite Attack   A basic active attack is the *rewrite attack* where the attacker can replace a message with anything she chooses. Of course the attacker will use her ability in conjunction with cryptanalysis as described in Sect. 2.2.2. Injecting new, changed or corrupted messages might help the attacker to gather enough information to successfully attack the encryption scheme.

Attacks on the User

Even though they are not attacks on the used encryption scheme itself, we shortly mention physical or social pressure on the user to compromise a cryptosystem.

The majority of cryptographic tools are designed from a theoretical perspective and assume users will not disclose their keys. But in reality, the security of computer-based security systems does not only depend on the used encryption scheme but also on the involved user and the security of the used computer. Bribery, which is with a hint of sarcasm often called *purchase-key attack*, coercion, blackmail, and deception culminating in torture may be very effective attacks against human weaknesses. The latter is also referred to as *rubber-hose attack* [Sch08b, Sog08] having organisations in mind beating their victims with a rubber-hose to avoid traces. As illustrated in a comic strip by Munroe [Mun10, #538], all these attacks share the idea of attacking human weaknesses or poor security procedures in an organisation's work flow instead of attacking the encryption scheme itself.

From a cryptographic perspective, this also applies to laws ordering disclosure of the secret or private key in cases of encrypted data. This was legislated, for example, in the United Kingdom[3] [Koo13]. The law has already been applied in practice against some animal rights activists [War07] not much after it came into force. Since this aspect focuses on legal and social aspects, we do not elaborate on this topic and refer to Koops [Koo99] for a discussion on the use of strong cryptography by criminals. He describes the conflict between the law enforcement

---

[3] see part III of the Regulation of Investigatory Powers Act 2000 (c. 23) which came into force on 1st October 2007 [Kin00]

and the legitimate needs of the information society to use strong cryptography. His arguments are based on experiences in the Netherlands.

A more subtle way is the use of *social engineering*, where the user is manipulated to give his key or his password away voluntarily. This can for example be done by pretending to be another person and the success depends on the victim's naivety, the attacker's creativity and her knowledge about work flows and company internals [MS02]. A recent example of social engineering are *phishing attacks* which ask users – most commonly via email – to enter private and/or authentication data into an imitated, fraudulent website by impersonating a trustworthy third party [JJJM07]. Among many other factors it was shown that a high personalisation of the attack creates more trust at the victim's side [Jak07]. So called *spear phishing attacks*, which use gathered information about the victim to mount a specific attack, are often highly efficient.

Attacks on Implementations and Hardware

Again, instead of attacking the underlying cryptosystem, *attacks on the implementation* try to obtain information about the plaintext or the private key by observing the computations or communication of a concrete implementation. Compared with passive side-channel attacks, active attackers additionally try to induce errors in the computation to gather auxiliary information in order to find the secret key.

Fault Induction Attacks Regarding cryptographic hardware, we also consider attacks where an adversary manipulates the proper functioning of cryptographic hardware, thus consequently called *fault induction attacks*, as active attacks. Fault induction attacks are the active counterpart of side-channel attacks (see Sect. 2.2.2). The main idea of fault induction attacks is to apply stress, for example radiation, to the cryptographic device with the objective of provoking errors in the computation. By choosing the position and time of the error, for example a single-bit error in a specific sub-part of the attacked algorithm, and comparing the correct and erroneous output, the attacker tries to gain information about internal states of the algorithm. In this manner conclusions may be drawn concerning the secret/private key.

There are two orthogonal characteristics of fault induction attacks: the type of fault and the fault induction technique. Following QUISQUATER and KOEUNE [QK02] we first describe different types of faults, which an attacker might induce and then give some examples of techniques to achieve this goal.

Permanent vs. transient While a *permanent fault* damages the cryptographic device irreversible, which affects all future computations, *transient fault attacks* only induce fault(s) in the current computation. Examples for permanent faults are cutting data bus wires or freezing memory cells to constant values. Transient faults can be achieved by altering the clock frequency or the power supply's voltage to abnormal ranges outside of the hardware's specification.

Time of occurrence Some of the attacks require to induce the fault at a specific time during the computation while others allow more flexibility.

Error location Some of the attacks require to be able to induce the fault in a specific memory cell or other location while others allow more flexibility.

Error type Different outcomes of an error must be considered. The value of a bit, a byte or even longer data type can be changed, the changed value can be flipped, flipped only in one direction (from zero to one or otherwise) or permanently set to a specific value. Also the error can be induced for sure or only with a certain probability.

Glitch-attack A special kind of error type are *glitch-attacks* where the attacker prevents the execution of a certain kind of machine code instruction. The attacker watches the processor's signals and exactly induces a disruption (glitch) in that moment, when a jump was going to be executed, preventing the processor from executing that jump. This way critical subroutines can be bypassed say for avoiding an authentication routine or again to gain information on internal states.

An illustrative example of fault attacks is an attack on RSA implementations with Chinese Remainder Theorem [BDL97, JLjQ99], which is quite easy to deploy. Inducing a single fault at any time during the computation – even without the knowledge of that fault's position – is sufficient to perform this attack. Furthermore, one faulty RSA signature – even without comparison to the correct computation – is enough to determine the secret factor q (see Ex. 2.79) and thus be able to forge any number of signatures. For more details we refer the reader to the already named work from QUISQUATER and KOEUNE [QK02, p. 9f] or the papers cited above.

In the following we state some examples of fault induction techniques which apply to smartcards, but can be adapted to other cryptographic devices, as well.

Voltage ISO standards [iso06] require smartcards to work properly in a certain range ($\pm 0, 5V$) around their voltage specification (5V). However, if the deviation of the external power supply is larger than the specified tolerance, this may lead to wrong computation results, provided the card is still able to finish its computation. Since the disturbance usually consists of short peaks, this attack is known as *spike attack*. For a recent example of a non-invasive spike attack we refer the reader to SCHMIDT and HERBST [SH08].

Clock In an analogous way, a tolerance of the clock frequency is specified by ISO standards [iso06] and applying abnormal frequencies can be used to induce errors. While slowing down the clock is usually used to try to observe internal states, an increased clock rate of much more than the specified tolerance may completely change the central processing unit's (CPU) behaviour. By finely tuning the resulting clock glitches, it is possible to make the CPU omit instructions during the execution of a program [BS03]. ANDERSON and KUHN discuss an attack originating in the pay-TV hacking community, where the normal clock frequency of 5 MHz was replaced with one of more than 20MHz. By varying the precise timing and duration of the glitch, the CPU was made to execute a number of completely different instructions resulting in a loop which wrote the contents of a limited memory range to the serial port [AK96].

Temperature Another way to induce faults in the card's computation is to have it processing in extreme heat conditions. GOVINDAVAJHALA and APPEL successfully applied this attack by heating memory chips to about 100 degrees of Celsius making them generating memory faults which they could further exploit to take over a virtual machine [GA03].

Radiation It is known that correctly focused radiation, such as x-rays or microwaves, can induce errors and corrupt the processor's computations. GOVINDAVAJHALA and APPEL [GA03] discuss some types of radiation and their chances of inducing errors.

Light By use of light it is possible to induce transient fault. SKOROBOGATOV and ANDERSON used a photoflash lamp magnified with a microscope to change individual bits and jump instructions in a way that conditional branches were taken the wrong way [SA02].

Eddy current QUISQUATER and SAMYDE showed that magnetic fields produced by alternating current in a coil is able to induce eddy currents which induce faults in memory cells. This way they were able to change the value of a pin stored inside a mobile phone's card [QS02].

Most of the attacks described above are non-invasive. This means they are easier to mount as they do not require physical opening or access to electrical contacts of the chip on the card. We refer the reader to work from AUMUELLER et al. [ABF$^+$02], ANDERSON and KUHN [AK98], KÖMMERLING and KUHN [KK99], MAHER [Mah97], and MOORE et al. [MMC$^+$02] for a more intensive treatment of tamper-resistance, countermeasures to fault induction attacks, and particular methods on how to induce errors on micro controller chips.

Attacks on Protocols

In this section we describe two of the most common attacks on protocols, man-in-the-middle and replay attacks. In general, until a protocol is proven to be secure and to provide the intended service, it is possible to induce protocol failures in various ways. Thus, there never can be a complete listing of all possible attacks. For a short description of other attacks on protocols than the abovementioned, we refer to Menezes et al. [MvOV97, p. 42].

Man-in-the-Middle Attack   As shown in Fig. 2.5, *man-in-the-middle attacks* assume an attacker intercepts messages between two victims. While the victims, Alice and Bob, believe that they are communicating directly to each other, both of them effectively talk to Mallory. This way Mallory is not only able to eavesdrop on all messages before sending them along to the meant receiver, she is also able to change or inject messages. To mount this attack, the attacker must, on the one hand, be able to intercept all messages between her victims and inject new ones, on the other hand, the attacker has to convincingly impersonate both victims. While the first is a matter of the involved network structure, the latter is mainly a lack of authentication. Thus, man-in-the-middle attacks can be prevented by including some form of endpoint authentication, certificates for instance. Note that if users are involved in the authentication process, it is essential that they understand the procedure's operation and its purpose. This process has to be supported by an appropriate user interface.

As a prominent example of failure, we mention communication with secure web servers, which typically uses the Hypertext Transfer Protocol Secure (HTTPS) [Res00]. HTTPS includes an encryption layer, either the Secure Sockets Layer (SSL) [FKK96] or its successor the Transport Layer Security (TLS) [DR08]. The encryption layer protects confidentiality and integrity of the communication and offers a certificate-based server authentication, as well. Thus, in theory SSL provides a high level of security [WS96]. In practice, however, users encounter security errors frequently, say for expired or unsigned certificates or for certificates that are issued for other domains[4]. Since most browsers handle security errors in a confusing manner, allow users to view and install certificates which the browser could not verify itself, the typical reaction is to install a certificate without evaluation. The user's behaviour is mostly due to not understanding the risk of man-in-the-middle attacks and the principles of certificate-based authentication. In fact they accustom themselves a habit of ignoring risks because of a lack of feed-

---

[4]Sometimes domain owners are not willing to pay the fee for additional SSL certificates and therefore reuse certificates, for example the certificate for "domain.com" serves also for "domain.org".

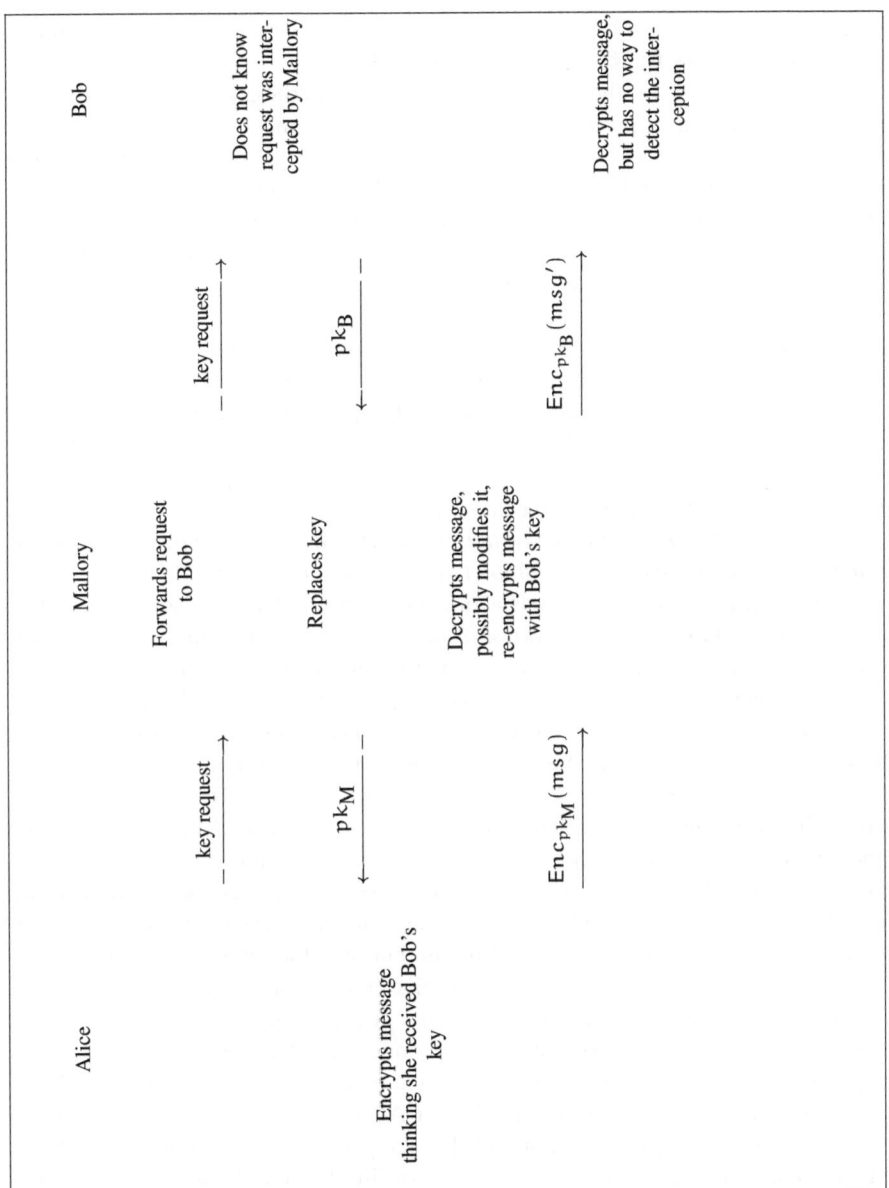

Figure 2.5: Protocol Flow of a Man-in-the-Middle Attack after Young and Aitel [YA04, p. 169]

back. For a discussion of how to harden web browsers to impede man-in-the-middle attacks see the work by Xia and Brustoloni [XB05].

Recently a flaw in the EMV[5] [EMV08a, EMV08b, EMV08c, EMV08d] protocol, the dominant protocol used for smartcard payments worldwide, has been found. The flaw allows to use a genuine card to make a payment without knowing the card's personal identification number (PIN) by performing a man-in-the-middle attack. The man in the middle tricks the terminal into believing the PIN was verified correctly by the card, while telling the issuing bank that no PIN was entered at all [MDAB10a, MDAB10b].

Replay Attacks   *Replay attacks* involve information gained from maliciously repeating or delaying a valid run of a security protocol. This can either be done by an involved party or an adversary eavesdropping on the communication and retransmitting the picked up data.

Malladi et al. generalise the definition of *replay attacks* as: *"an attack on a security protocol using relay of messages from a different context into the intended (or original and expected) context, thereby fooling the honest participant(s) into thinking they have successfully completed the protocol run."* [MAFH02, p. 77].

A very simple example is a password interception. Eve eavesdrops on Alice sending her password to Bob as proof of identity. When Alice and Bob finish their conversation, Eve contacts Bob in order to pretend being Alice and sends Alice's password, picked up from the wiretapped session, which Bob will happily accept.

Syverson [Syv94] presents a taxonomy of replay attacks on cryptographic protocols (see Tab. 2.1). At the highest level he distinguishes between external and internal runs based on the protocol run of the message's origin (in relation to the protocol run of the replay). The former is further classified into interleavings and classic replays characterising whether the attacker requires contemporaneous protocol runs. Orthogonally to the origin of the message, the destination of the message is used for further classification into reflections (message is sent back to sender), deflections (message is sent to another than the intended recipient), and straight replays (the intended principal receives the message delayed).

There are several ways to prevent replay attacks, for instance, by means of session tokens or nonces (numbers used once) sent from Bob to Alice at the beginning of the protocol or timestamps which require a synchronisation of Alice's and Bob's clock. The common idea is that Alice sends Bob a hash of a session token, a nonce or a timestamp appended to the password instead of the password alone. Thus, if Eve has picked up the according hash and wants to use it in a later session, either Bob sends Eve another session token or nonce invalidating

---

[5]EMV stands for Europay, MasterCard and Visa

Table 2.1: Taxonomy of Replay Attacks by SYVERSON [Syv94]

1. Run external attacks (replay of messages from outside the current run of the protocol)

   a) Interleavings (requiring contemporaneous protocol runs)

      i. Deflections (message is directed to other than the intended recipient)

         A. Reflections (message is sent back to sender)

         B. Deflections to a third party

      ii. Straight replays (intended principal receives message, but message is delayed)

   b) Classic replays (runs need not to be contemporaneous)

      i. Deflections (message is directed to other than the intended recipient)

         A. Reflections (message is sent back to sender)

         B. Deflections to a third party

      ii. Straight replays (intended principal receives message, but message is delayed)

2. Run internal attacks (replay of messages from inside the current run of the protocol)

   a) Deflections (message is directed to other than the intended recipient)

      i. Reflections (message is sent back to sender)

      ii. Deflections to a third party

   b) Straight replays (intended principal receives message, but message is delayed)

the hash Eve has picked up or the timestamp is already expired and the forged authentication fails. A general scheme preventing replay attacks is given by MALLADI et al. [MAFH02].

2.2.5 Practical Security

It is important to understand that developers need to cover all possible points of attack to establish a secure system while the attacker already succeeds if she is able to find only one exploit which is sufficient to break the system. This property is visualised by the well known proverb that "a chain is only as strong as its weakest link". For practical purposes it is also important to consider the strength of the attacker. While it is quite hard to establish a formal attacker model at this point, a rough classification was given by ABRAHAM et al. [ADDS91]:

Class I (clever outsiders) : They are often very intelligent but lack knowledge of the system and access to sophisticated equipment. They often try to take advantage of an existing weakness in the system, rather than try to create one.

Class II (knowledgeable insiders) : They have a substantial technical education, highly sophisticated tools and instruments for analysis, and expertise and potential understanding of the most parts of the system.

Class III (funded organisations) : Due to their great funding resources, they have teams of specialists, including Class II adversaries, with complementing skills and the most advanced analysis tools. Thus, they are capable of exhaustive and systematic analysis and of designing highly sophisticated attacks.

As already mentioned in Sect. 2.2.4 with regard to the security of a system, the encryption system is a decisive factor but the involved users and the security of the used computers need to be considered as well.

User Involvement   Recent studies show that security failures result by far more often from the users' unthoughtfulness and lack of knowledge than by them having criminal intentions [Pri07a, Pri07b, Pri09]. Therefore, it is crucial to understand "human factors". STAJANO and WILSON [SW09] examine a variety of scams and extract general principles about the recurring behavioural patterns of victims, which we describe in short:

Distraction Principle When people are distracted, attackers have it easy. Sometimes the victim might not even notice the fraud.

Social Compliance Principle Society pressures people not to question authority. An attacker impersonating as a policeman or other authority can exploit this.

Herd Principle Risks seem to be more acceptable if everyone else appears to accept them, too.

Dishonesty Principle If the attack happens while a user is himself involved in illegal or socially unacceptable actions, the victim will be reluctant to follow up the incident.

Deception Principle The victim is made to believe certain appearances, but things and people are not what they pretend to be and their identity is only forged by the attacker.

Need and Greed Principle If the attacker knows the victim's needs and desires she can easily manipulate him.

Time Principle Time pressure often makes a victim decide hastily without proper reasoning. Attackers can exploit this by pretending time pressure.

Some of the principles above can easily be identified as part of security failures in modern computer systems.

As a first observation, we notice that users are vulnerable from the *need and greed principle* and the *time principle*, since they want to accomplish a certain amount of work in a reasonable time. Despite the suggestions that users are lazy and unmotivated on security issues, Herley argues that their rejection of security advice is entirely rational from an economical perspective [Her09]. Security advices often shield users from direct consequences of attacks, but burdens them with perceived indirect costs in the form of added effort. Herley claims that often security advices are complex and growing, but their benefits are largely speculative or moot, for example regarding certificate error warnings, which appear to be false positives all the time. Thus, users decide that spending time to avoid attacks which do not appear to happen, would exceed the possible loss by two orders of magnitude and therefore reject the security advice due.

Schneier assents by saying that the user's main goal is to get their work done and that they usually get rewarded for accomplishing their work in time while ignoring security advices is often accepted: *"Well, the average computer user is going to pick dancing pigs over security any day. And we can't expect them not to."* [Sch99a].

This especially holds if security flaws in recent protocols are known and still there exists no reasonable way around if work is to get done. Schneier [Sch09c] argues that it is hard for the user to figure out which vulnerabilities are serious and which are not and even if he could, it is hard to figure out if there is anything he can do to protect himself. Furthermore, chances of becoming a victim are small, thus workarounds mostly offer a poor cost-benefit tradeoff. And last but not least, often the user himself cannot do anything, because his data is stored in corporate databases and not under his control, like webmail or data stored in the social web [NH03] or in computing clouds [Hay08].

Example 2.51. (Four-Digit Codes on Keypads)
As an example we refer to the two four-digit keypads shown in Fig. 2.6 which could, for instance, be used for access control at front doors of houses or companies.

There are ten thousand different four-digit codes, thus – depending on the needed level of security – in theory this kind of access control should be sufficient for many applications. In practice there are three issues to notice when looking at this particular keypads. First of all, an adversary probably would only have to try at most 24 codes, since both keypads suffer from erosion of keys and thus the digits of the code can easily be guessed. Moreover, people tend to chose codes they can easily remember. Thus, the first code almost certainly is "1234" while the second probably is either a date like "1986" (or maybe "1968") or a geometrically appealing choice like "1689". Notice also the marks of a pen on the second keypad's digits ("2369"). Here the code might have changed to something like "6239" which would also be quite symmetric and thus easy to remember. Last but not least, the code of the keypad is probably changed only rarely, therefore attackers will have sufficient time to test different codes.

(a) Keypad "1234"

(b) Keypad "1689"

Figure 2.6: Keypads from SCHNEIER's blog [Sch09a]

The *deception principle* is further elaborated by SCHNEIER who explains why the perception of security often diverges from reality [Sch07a, Sch08a]. SCHNEIER states that people's natural intuition about risk works quite well for risks people encounter regularly [Sch09b]. This can be exploited by exposing people to risks they do not encounter regularly, for example by means of social engineering which was shown to be effective by Mɪᴛɴɪᴄᴋ [MS02] who acted as hacker in the eighties and nineties [U.S99]. Pretending to have another identity works especially well in connection with the *social compliance principle*. When the adversary impersonates a figure of authority, the victim is likely not to question orders.

Balancing Costs and Estimated Benefits   It is also worth to take a look at costs and estimated benefits from the perspective of a company as well as from the perspective of a possible attacker.

A company may have different views on security. On the one hand, a company aims at making profits, thus any investment will be judged on profitability. The estimated gain should at least cover the expenditures of any investment. On the other hand, it is unclear how investments into information technology targeted at security directly increase a company's profit. At first glance security measures seem to decrease the company's profit due to their added costs and possibly disadvantage on the development and manufacturing of a product. At a closer view it turns out to be quite hard to assess the necessary amount of investment for security measures. The absence of successful attacks precludes the evaluation of the investment. Often, there isn't even feedback about the number of attacks prevented by a certain measure. However, successful attacks create real loss and may also have a bad influence on a company's reputation which is hard to measure in dollar and cent. As a result we claim that most companies will disburse only the absolutely necessary, even though they cannot tell what the absolutely necessary is.

Risk analysis and risk management, especially regarding business, is a large field which is far beyond the scope of this work. For a guide to risk analysis we refer to Vᴏsᴇ [Vos08] and an introduction to risk management is given by Cʀᴏᴜʜʏ et al. [CGM05]. Hᴜʙʙᴀʀᴅ [Hub09] deals with the evaluation of risk management and reveals how analysis methods can be misused and misapplied. Furthermore, plenty of work has been done discussing risk analysis and risk management regarding the characteristics of information technology [SGF02] and information security [Pel05]. For the literally interested we also recommend a short-story of Tᴡᴀɪɴ [Twa71].

Let us now regard the motivation of a possible attacker. If the attacker is a criminal, her aim is to extract money in any way from breaking the cryptographic system. Thus, it is reasonable to assume that the attacker will probably not spend more than she estimates to win. Having this in mind, it is worth to remember that – reverse from the situation for companies – an attacker may gain reputation from breaking a system, which might give him additional motivation to analyse a cryptographic system. This is particularly true for a researcher, whose aim is to investigate the according system rather than exploiting it.

2.3 Cryptographic Hardness Assumptions

As stated above, modern cryptography heavily relies on the assumption that a *particular problem* cannot efficiently be solved. We already discussed pseudorandom function families in Sect. 2.1.1 and stated that it is not known, if pseudorandom generators exist, even though it is strongly believed. The assumption, that pseudorandom functions exist, is based on

- the proof that pseudorandom permutations exist if one-way functions exist in combination with

- the belief that one-way functions exist.

This section introduces two number-theoretic problems – factoring and computing discrete logarithms – which are assumed to be hard, and thus are well-known examples of one-way function candidates.

2.3.1 The Factoring and RSA Assumption

We first want to glance at the factoring assumption and based on that continue with the closely related RSA assumption.

The Factoring Assumption

One of the oldest problems is *integer factorisation* or just *factoring*. Factoring is the task of splitting a composite number n into its non-trivial divisors $p_1, p_2, \ldots$, which, when multiplied together, return the original integer. A trivial algorithm solving this task is *trial division*, which simply checks if p divides n for all p smaller than $\lfloor \sqrt{n} \rfloor$. The running time of trial division is $O\left(\sqrt{n}(\log n)^c\right)$, since this method requires $\sqrt{n}$ divisions and each of them takes $(\log n)^c$ for some constant c. With regard to the input length, the running time of trial division is exponential. There are more efficient factoring algorithms than trial division, e.g. POLLARD's Rho factoring algorithm [Pol75], its derivations [Bre80, BP81], and the general number field sieve, which runs on average in time $2^{O\left(n^{1/3}(\log n)^{2/3}\right)}$ [Cop93, Pom96, KL08] as already stated above. Yet no *polynomial-time* algorithm that solves the factoring problem has been discovered.

Before we give a formal definition of the factoring assumption, which – roughly speaking – predicts that polynomial-time algorithm solving the factoring problem will not be found in the future, we note that not all composites of a given length are equally hard to factor. Remembering the idea of trial division, it is easy to conclude that a composite consisting of small factors is easier to factorise than a composite consisting of two primes of almost the same size. From what is known today, the hardest instances of integer factorisation seem to be semiprimes when they are both large, randomly chosen, not too close to each other but almost of the same size.

Definition 2.52. (Factoring Assumption) Let $n, p, q \in \mathbb{N}$ be integers with p, q distinct primes of large size and $n = pq$ and let $\mathbb{Z}_n^*$ be the multiplicative group mod n with size $\varphi(n) = (p-1)(q-1)$. The *factoring assumption* states that the success probability for any polynomial-time algorithm finding p, q given n is negligible.

It is worth to mention that SHOR found a polynomial-time algorithm for factoring [Sho97a, Sho99a] running on quantum computers [RP00, Fen03]. But even though there are first implementations factoring small numbers using nuclear magnetic resonance [VSB$^+$01] or a photonic chip [PMO09], it is unlikely that quantum computers become feasible within the next few years.

The RSA Assumption

In 1977 RIVEST, SHAMIR, and ADLEMAN described the first public-key cryptography algorithm suitable for signing as well as encryption [RSA78]. The algorithm was named *RSA*, obviously the initials of their surnames. Today RSA is believed to be secure given appropriate security parameters are chosen.

Assuming Alice wants to send Bob a message, the design of RSA is as follows: Given the *modulus* n, a product of two (or more) large primes, Alice encrypts the message M with Bob's public key (n, e) by computing the ciphertext

$$C = M^e \pmod{n}$$

where e, the *public exponent*, is an odd integer $e \geqslant 3$ that is relatively prime to $\varphi(n)$, the order of the multiplicative group $\mathbb{Z}_n^*$. Using his private key (n, d) Bob is able to decrypt Alice's message M by computing

$$M = C^d \pmod{n}$$

where d, the *private exponent*, is chosen such that $de = 1 \pmod{\varphi(n)}$ holds. This decryption procedure uses the fact that when $C^d = (M^e)^d = M^{ed} \pmod{n}$ and $ed = 1 + k\varphi(n)$ it follows from EULER's theorem[6] that $M^{ed} = M^{1+k\varphi(n)} \equiv m(m^{\varphi(n)})^k \equiv m \pmod{n}$.

An adversary is assumed to be able to eavesdrop C and may also know Bob's public key (n, e), but should not be able to compute the corresponding plaintext message M. The formalisation of the adversary's task is known as the RSA problem [RK03].

---

[6]EULER's theorem states that if $a, n \in \mathbb{N}$ are coprime, then $a^{\varphi(n)} = 1 \pmod{n}$ holds [Sha93, p. 21, 24].

Definition 2.53. (RSA Problem) The *RSA problem* states: Given an RSA public key (n, e) and a ciphertext $C = M^e \pmod{n}$, compute M.

Theorem 2.54. *RSA theorem The RSA problem is no harder than integer factoring.*

Theorem 2.54 holds since an adversary who is able to factor the modulus n is able to compute the private key (n, d) from the public key (n, e). However, as of today, it remains unclear if the converse is true. When n is a product of two primes, its factorisation can be computed efficiently from $\varphi(n)$, thus factoring n and computing $\varphi(n)$ are equally hard. RIVEST, SHAMIR ,and ADLEMAN [RSA78] showed that, given n, d, e with $ed = 1 \pmod{\varphi(n)}$, it is possible to compute the factorisation of n in probabilistic polynomial-time. Later, CORON and MAY [May04, CM07] presented a deterministic polynomial-time algorithm that factors n given (e, d) under the assumption that $e, d < \varphi(n)$. However, without this assumption the equivalence between finding d and factoring n is not entirely solved and remains an open problem. BONEH and VENKATESAN [BV98] have provided strong evidence that such a construction is unlikely if the exponent is very small, indicating that the RSA problem for very small exponents could be easier than factoring. So in general, given our current state of knowledge, we can not conclude that the RSA problem is as hard as factoring.

A formal notation that the RSA problem is hard to solve is given by the RSA assumption:

Definition 2.55. (RSA Assumption) The *RSA assumption* states that the RSA problem is hard to solve, provided that the modulus n is sufficiently large and randomly generated, and that the plaintext M is a random integer between 0 and $n - 1$.

Following the abovementioned arguments, the RSA assumption obviously only holds if the factoring assumption holds and, due to theorem 2.54, the RSA assumption appears to be stronger than the factoring assumption.

The strong RSA assumption states that the RSA problem is hard even though the attacker is allowed to choose the public exponent e. Since this may be easier than solving the RSA problem, the assumption that this is hard is stronger than the RSA assumption [BP97, FO97].

Definition 2.56. (Strong RSA Assumption) The *strong RSA assumption* (SRSA) states: Given an RSA modulus n (of unknown factorisation) and a ciphertext C it is hard to compute a pair consisting of *any* plaintext M and an (odd) public exponent $e \geqslant 3$ such that $C = M^e$ holds.

For a more deeper insight into the RSA problem we refer the reader to surveys by BONEH [Bon99] and KATZENBEISSER [Kat01] and to the 'Hard Problems in Cryptography Wiki' [oEiCI12b] for an overview on hard problems related to factoring.

2.3.2 The Discrete Logarithm and Diffie-Hellman Assumptions

Beside assumptions based on factoring, other well-known candidates for one-way functions rely on discrete logarithms in cyclic groups. After introducing the discrete logarithm assumption, we present a couple of continuative assumptions based on the discrete logarithm assumption, namely the computational or the much stronger decisional Diffie-Hellman assumption.

The Discrete Logarithm Assumption

If $\mathbb{G}$ is a cyclic group of order m, there exists a generator $g \in \mathbb{G}$ such that $\mathbb{G} = \{g^0, g^1, \ldots, g^{m-1}\}$. It follows that for any $h \in \mathbb{G}$ there is a unique $x \in \mathbb{Z}_m$ such that $g^x = h$.

Definition 2.57. (Discrete Logarithm) Let $\mathbb{G}$ be a cyclic group of order m and $h, g \in \mathbb{G}, x \in \mathbb{Z}_m$ with $g^x = h$. We call x the *discrete logarithm of* h *with respect to* g and denote this as $\log_g h$.

Definition 2.58. (Discrete Logarithm Problem) Let $\mathbb{G}$ be a cyclic group and g be a generator in $\mathbb{G}$. The *discrete logarithm problem* (*DL problem* or *DLP*) is to compute $\log_g h$ given a generator g and a random element $h \in \mathbb{G}$ as input.

So far, no efficient algorithms solving the discrete logarithm problem are known. The naive way to solve the discrete logarithm problem, known as *trial multiplication*, is to raise the generator g to higher powers until the result matches h. To compute a discrete logarithm with this method requires a linear running time in the size of the cyclic group $\mathbb{G}$ and is thus exponential in the number of digits of the group's size. However, there exist more elaborate versions, often based on similar algorithms for integer factorisation. Examples are the baby-step giant-step algorithm [Sha69, ST05], Pollard's rho algorithm for logarithms [Pol75, MvOV97] and the currently best known algorithm, the general number field sieve, which runs in time $2^{\mathcal{O}(n^{1/3}(\log n)^{2/3})}$ on average [AH99, KL08].

Along the lines of integer factoring, SHOR gave a polynomial-time algorithm for computing discrete logarithms on a quantum computer [Sho97a, Sho99a]. But as already mentioned, large scale quantum computers will most likely not become feasible within the next decades, thus it is widely believed that computing discrete logarithms is hard.

Definition 2.59. (The Discrete Logarithm Assumption) The assumption that there exist cyclic groups for which the discrete logarithm problem is hard is denoted as *discrete logarithm assumption* (*DL assumption*).

Note that for a particular cyclic group $\mathbb{G}$ we say that the discrete logarithm assumption holds for group $\mathbb{G}$ if we assume that the discrete logarithm problem *in this group* is hard.

The Diffie-Hellman Assumptions

Even though, the DL problem seems to be hard in appropriate groups (for example groups modulo a prime or groups defined over an elliptic curve [Wer02]) it is difficult to base cryptographic constructions on the DL problem, because there is no trapdoor information about the group making the computation of discrete logarithms efficient. Nevertheless, the DL problem can serve as a basis for a trapdoor function for various related problems around the Diffie-Hellman problem. In general there exist two variants: a computational version requiring to solve a particular problem related to the DL problem and a decisional version requiring to distinguish the solution of the underlying computational problem from a random group element. Besides the Diffie-Hellman key exchange protocol (cf. 2.64), well known applications of variants of the Diffie-Hellman problem are the ElGamal cryptosystem [EG85] and the Digital Signature Algorithm [nis09].

Definition 2.60. (Computational Diffie-Hellman Problem) Let $\mathbb{G}$ be a cyclic group of order m, $g \in \mathbb{G}$ a randomly chosen generator of $\mathbb{G}$ and $a, b \in \{0, \ldots, m-1\}$ independently chosen at random. The *computational Diffie-Hellman problem* (*CDH problem*) is to compute g^{ab} given (g, g^a, g^b).

Definition 2.61. (Computational Diffie-Hellman Assumption) The assumption that there exist cyclic groups for which the CDH problem is hard is denoted as *computational Diffie-Hellman assumption* (*CDH assumption*).

As before we say that the computational Diffie-Hellman assumption holds for a particular cyclic group $\mathbb{G}$ if we assume that the computational Diffie-Hellman problem *in this group* is hard. To ease the notation, we omit to continuously mention that the assumption means that there exist groups for which the assumption holds and that the assumption does not mean that the underlying problem is hard for all groups.

Obviously the CDH assumption is related to the discrete logarithm assumption. If computing discrete logarithms (in $\mathbb{G}$) were easy, then it would be possible to compute a or b, and thus also g^{ab} and the CDH assumption would not hold. In fact, as known today, the most efficient way to solve the CDH problem is to compute a discrete logarithm, and thus solve the DL problem. Despite some progress showing that in many groups the CDH problem is almost as hard as the DL problem or even equivalent in certain special cases, it is still an open problem whether the CDH assumption is equivalent to the DL assumption [dB90, MW96, BL96]. Besides that, except for generic groups [Nec92, Sho97b], there is no proof to date, that either the DH problem or the DL problem are hard problems.

Definition 2.62. (Decisional Diffie-Hellman Problem) Let $\mathbb{G}$ be a cyclic group of order m, $g \in \mathbb{G}$ a generator of $\mathbb{G}$ and $a, b \in \{0, \dots, m-1\}$ independently chosen at random. The *decisional Diffie-Hellman problem* (*DDH problem*) is to distinguish the value of g^{ab} from a random element $g^c \in \mathbb{G}$ given (g, g^a, g^b).

Definition 2.63. (Decisional Diffie-Hellman Assumption) The *decisional Diffie-Hellman assumption* (*DDH assumption*) states that the decisional Diffie-Hellman problem is hard, meaning that given (g, g^a, g^b) the value of g^{ab} is computationally (in the security parameter m) indistinguishable from a random element $g^c \in \mathbb{G}$.

More formally, let $\mathbb{G}$ be a cyclic group of order m, $g \in \mathbb{G}$ a generator of $\mathbb{G}$ and $a, b, c \in \mathbb{Z}_m$ independently chosen at random, then the following probability distributions are computationally (in the security parameter m) indistinguishable:

- (g^a, g^b, g^{ab}) (also denoted as *DDH triple*)

- (g^a, g^b, g^c).

The DDH assumption is closely related to the CDH assumption. Obviously, if the CDH assumption does not hold, one could compute g^{ab} and thus easily distinguish DDH triples from random triples. Thus, the DDH assumption is stronger than the CDH assumption and there exist groups where detecting DDH triples is easy, but solving the accompanying CDH problem is assumed to be hard. One case involves checking if an element is an quadratic residue[7] [Can05], which is easy. This is particularly important, because bilinear and multilinear pairings in groups over elliptic curves have been shown to be useful for cryptographic applications [BS02] in which quadratic residues play an important role.

Example 2.64. (Diffie-Hellman Key Exchange Protocol)
An application of the DH problem is the Diffie-Hellman key exchange protocol [DH76], which allows two parties to jointly establish a shared secret over an insecure communication channel. This can be useful to establish a secure communication channel by using the shared secret as symmetric key cipher. Note that the Diffie-Hellman key exchange protocol itself does not provide authentication of the communicating parties, leaving it vulnerable to man-in-the-middle attacks.

The protocol works as follows: Alice and Bob agree on a finite cyclic group $\mathbb{G}$ of size n and a generator $g \in \mathbb{G}$ which both are assumed to be public information, and thus are known to attackers. Alice picks a random number $a < n \in \mathbb{N}$ and sends

---

[7] An integer $q \in \mathbb{G}$ is called quadratic residue modulo n if $\exists x \in \mathbb{G} : x^2 = q \pmod{n}$ holds.

g^a to Bob. Vice versa, Bob picks also a random number $b < n \in \mathbb{N}$ and sends g^b to Alice. Since Alice knows a, Bob knows b and $(g^a)^b = (g^b)^a$ both participants are able to compute g^{ab} and thus share a secret group element. Since only g^a and g^b were transmitted, to compute g^{ab} Eve has to solve the CDH problem. It is worthwhile to mention that, depending on the intended use of the shared key, the property that the CDH assumption holds is necessary, but not sufficient to keep the *complete* shared key secret. Therefore, even though Eve may not be able to compute g^{ab}, recovering some bits may allow her a successful attack on the cryptosystem used later.

The protocol sequence is shown in Fig. 2.7.

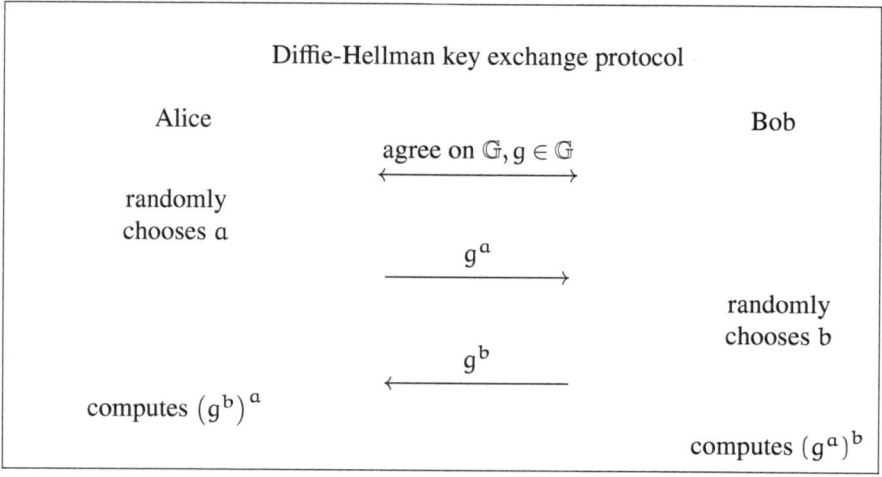

Figure 2.7: Diffie-Hellman Key Exchange Protocol

MAURER and WOLF [MW99] show that, under some assumptions for certain groups, it can be proven that breaking the Diffie-Hellman protocol is polynomial-time equivalent to computing the related discrete logarithm. Their overview paper [MW00] summarises almost 25 years of investigation of the Diffie-Hellman protocol.

Beside the famous CDH and DDH problems, there are many variants of the DH problem. The following notions are in no way meant to be complete.

Definition 2.65. (Strong Decisional Diffie-Hellman Problem) Let $\mathbb{G}$ be a cyclic group of order m, let $g \in \mathbb{G}$ be a randomly chosen generator and a, b independently and randomly chosen from $\mathbb{Z}_m^*$. Then given $g, g^a, g^b, g^{b^{-1}}, \nu \in \mathbb{G}$ the *strong decisional Diffie-Hellman problem* (*SDDH problem*) is to determine if ν is a random group element or g^{ab}.

Definition 2.66. (Strong Decisional Diffie-Hellman Assumption) The *strong decisional Diffie-Hellman assumption (SDDHI assumption)* [PS00a] states that one cannot distinguish the distributions of the SDDH problem significantly better than by guessing.

Definition 2.67. (External Diffie-Hellman Assumption) Let $\mathbb{G}_1$, $\mathbb{G}_2$ and $\mathbb{G}_T$ be cyclic groups of the same order, and B: $\mathbb{G}_1 \times \mathbb{G}_2 \to \mathbb{G}_T$ be an admissible bilinear map. The *external Diffie-Hellman assumption (XDH assumption)* states that the DDH problem is hard in $\mathbb{G}_1$. This notion is also referred to as *asymmetric XDH assumption* and the stronger version of the assumption, the *symmetric XDH assumption (SXDH assumption)* requires the DDH problem also to be intractable in $\mathbb{G}_2$.

The notion of the XDH assumption was proposed by SCOTT [Sco02] and later by BONEH et al. [BBS04], but the first formal definition was given by BALLARD et al. [BGdMM05]. GALBRAITH et al. provided evidence for the validity of the XDH assumption in two specific elliptic curve subgroups with an efficiently computable pairing [Gal01, GR04].

The DDH problem becomes easy if the groups $\mathbb{G}_1$ and $\mathbb{G}_2$ of the bilinear map B are equal, since given g, g^a, g^b, g^c it is sufficient to check whether $B(g^a, g^b) = B(g, g^c)$. Nevertheless, if $\mathbb{G}_1$ and $\mathbb{G}_2$ are distinct groups, the DDH problem may still be hard, and thus the XDH assumption may still hold for groups chosen with caution.

Definition 2.68. (y-strong Diffie-Hellman Problem) Let $\mathbb{G}_1$, $\mathbb{G}_2$ and $\mathbb{G}_T$ be cyclic groups of the same order, B: $\mathbb{G}_1 \times \mathbb{G}_2 \to \mathbb{G}_T$ be an admissible bilinear map, g_1 be a generator of $\mathbb{G}_1$ and respectively g_2 a generator of $\mathbb{G}_2$. Then, given $g_1, g_2^x, g_2^{x^2}, \ldots, g_2^{x^y} \in \mathbb{G}$, the *y-strong Diffie-Hellman problem (y-SDH problem)* is to compute a pair $\left(c, g_1^{\left(\frac{1}{x+c}\right)} \right)$.

There also exists a weaker version of the y-SDH problem which requires to compute $g_1^{\left(\frac{1}{x+c}\right)}$ for a given c [MSK02]. This version has been shown equivalent to computing $g_1^{\left(\frac{1}{x}\right)}$ [ZSNS04].

Definition 2.69. (y-strong Diffie-Hellman Assumption) The *y-strong Diffie-Hellman assumption (y-SDH assumption)* [BB04, DY05] states that the y-SDH problem can not be solved significantly better than by guessing.

The y-decisional Diffie-Hellman inversion problem [MSK02] is similar and omits the use of bilinear mappings.

Definition 2.70. (y-Diffie-Hellman Inversion Problem) Let $\mathbb{G}$ be a cyclic group of order m, let $g \in \mathbb{G}$ be a randomly chosen generator and a randomly chosen from $\mathbb{Z}_m^*$. Then the y-*Diffie-Hellman inversion problem* (y-*DHI problem*) is to compute $g^{\frac{1}{a}}$ given $g, g^a, g^{a^2}, \ldots, g^{a^y} \in \mathbb{G}$. The case $y = 1$ is also known as *(computational) Diffie-Hellman inversion problem*.

As of today, the best known algorithm to solve the y-DHI problem is to solve the underlying DH problem and it is unknown whether there are other ways to compute $g^{\frac{1}{a}}$. Therefore, the y-DHI problem is at most as hard as the DH problem and it is unknown whether they are equivalent or not.

Definition 2.71. (y-Diffie-Hellman Inversion Assumption) The assumption that the y-DHI problem is hard is denoted as y-*Diffie-Hellman assumption* (y-*DHI assumption*).

And consequently, there is also a decisional version of the inversion problem:

Definition 2.72. (y-decisional Diffie-Hellman Inversion Problem) Let $\mathbb{G}$ be a cyclic group of order m and $g \in \mathbb{G}$ a randomly chosen generator and a randomly chosen from $\mathbb{Z}_m^*$. Then the y-*decisional Diffie-Hellman inversion problem* (y-*DDHI problem*) is to determine if v equals $g^{\frac{1}{a}}$ or is a random element from $\mathbb{G}$ given $g, g^a, g^{a^2}, \ldots, g^{a^y}, v \in \mathbb{G}$.

Definition 2.73. (y-decisional Diffie-Hellman Inversion Assumption) The assumption that the y-DDHI problem cannot be solved significantly (only negligibly) better than by guessing is denoted as y-*decisional Diffie-Hellman assumption* (y-*DDHI assumption*).

Definition 2.74. (Strong Decisional Diffie-Hellman Inversion Problem) Let $\mathbb{G}$ be a cyclic group of order m, let $g \in \mathbb{G}$ be a randomly chosen generator and a randomly chosen from $\mathbb{Z}_m^*$. Let $\mathcal{O}_a(\cdot)$ be an oracle, which on input $z \in \mathbb{Z}_m^*$ outputs $g^{\frac{1}{a+z}}$. Then the *strong decisional Diffie-Hellman inversion problem* (SDDHI problem) is to nominate a pair (x, α) such that on input v, α the algorithm is able to determine whether v equals $g^{\frac{1}{a+x}}$ or whether it is a random element from $\mathbb{G}$. The nomination and the determination part of the algorithm are both allowed to query the oracle $\mathcal{O}_a(\cdot)$ except on x.

Definition 2.75. (Strong Decisional Diffie-Hellman Inversion Assumption) The assumption that the SDDHI problem cannot be solved significantly (only negligibly) better than by guessing is denoted as *strong decisional Diffie-Hellman inversion assumption*.

For a more formal treatment, reductions between related Diffie-Hellman problems and various group families we refer the reader to BONEH [Bon98]. For a study of various computational and decisional Diffie-Hellman problems and some proofs of equivalences, see BAO et al. [BDZ03] and for an overview on hard problems related to the discrete logarithm problem see also the 'Hard Problems in Cryptography Wiki' [oEiCI12a].

2.4 Hash Functions and Digital Signature Schemes

This section introduces hash functions and digital signatures. Then notions of security for digital signatures are presented and blind signatures, a special kind of digital signature, which requires a separate notion of security.

2.4.1 Hash Functions

In general, hash functions map values from a large domain (e.g. strings of arbitrary length) to a range of limited size (e.g. strings of a fixed size). The classic application area of hashes is their use in data structures such as hash tables or hash maps. The hash function is used to efficiently assign new keys to storage locations at insertion time and to permit speedy lookup thereafter. Thus it is desirable that the hash function is fast and yields as few collisions as possible. A collision occurs when a pair of distinct data items (s and s') has the same hash value ($H(s) = H(s')$). Collision-resistant hash functions used in cryptography are quite similar, except that to minimise the number of collisions is an obligatory. Note that following DIRICHLET's drawer principle, often called pigeonhole principle[8] [JJ92, p. 126], it is impossible to completely avoid collisions since the domain of a hash function in general is much larger than its codomain.

We continue with a definition of hash functions based on KATZ and LINDEL [KL08] and then define collision-resistance.

Definition 2.76. (Hash functions) A *hash function* is a pair of probabilistic polynomial-time algorithms (GenKey,Hash) such that:

- The *key-generation algorithm* GenKey takes as input the security parameter 1^n and outputs a key k. We write this as $k \leftarrow GenKey(1^n)$. We assume that 1^n is implicit in k.

---

[8]The pigeonhole principle states that, given two natural numbers $1 \leqslant p < n$, if n objects (pigeons) are put into p boxes (pigeonholes), then at least one box must contain two or more of the objects (pigeons).

- There exists a polynomial ℓ such that Hash takes as input a key k and a string $s \in \{0,1\}^*$ and outputs a string $H^k(s) \in \{0,1\}^{\ell(n)}$ (where n is the value of the security parameter implicit in s)

If $H(s)$ is defined only for inputs $s \in \{0,1\}^{\ell'(n)}$ with $\ell'(n) > \ell(n)$, then we call (GenKey,Hash) a *fixed length* hash function for inputs of length $\ell'(n)$.

We now need to define the above mentioned collision resistance as security property.

Definition 2.77. (Collision resistant hash functions) A hash function with a given key k, output by GenKey(1^n), is *collision resistant* if, for all efficient adversaries, the adversaries' probability of outputting a pair of distinct strings (s and s') with the same hash value ($H^k(s) = H^k(s')$) is negligible in n.

2.4.2 Digital Signature Schemes

In this section we first define digital signature schemes based on KATZ and LINDEL [KL08] and then take a closer look at special forms of digital signature schemes, namely blind and group signature schemes.

Digital signatures are a mathematical scheme used to preserve message integrity. Provided that the receiver of a signed message knows the public key of the signer, he is able to verify that the message originates from the claimed sender and was not altered during transportation in any way.

The notion of digital signatures was first mentioned by DIFFIE and HELLMAN in 1976 [DH76]. The first concrete scheme goes back to RIVEST, SHAMIR and ADLEMAN [RSA78], even though it was rather a proof of concept. Further work includes a one-time signature scheme by LAMPORT [Lam79], a tree-based construction by MERKLE (also known as Merkle signatures or Merkle trees [Mer87, Mer89]), and a signature scheme by RABIN based on computing square modulo composite n [Rab79].

Definition 2.78. (Digital Signature Scheme) A *digital signature scheme* is a tuple of probabilistic polynomial-time algorithms (GenKey,Sign,Vrfy) such that:

- The *key-generation algorithm* GenKey takes as input the security parameter 1^n and outputs a pair of keys (vk, sk); we refer to the first of these as the *verification key* and the second as the *signing key*. We write this as $(vk, sk) \leftarrow$ GenKey(1^n). We assume for convenience that vk and sk each have length at least n, and that n can be determined from vk,sk.

- The *signing algorithm* Sign takes as input a signing key sk and a plaintext message $m \in \{0,1\}^*$. It outputs a signature s, and we write this as $s \leftarrow$ Sign(sk, m) or $s \leftarrow$ Sign$_{sk}(m)$.

- The *verification algorithm* Vrfy takes as input a verification key vk, a message m, and a signature s and outputs true or false.

It is required that for every security parameter n, every message $m \in \{0,1\}^*$ and every pair of keys (vk, sk) output by $GenKey(1^n)$, it holds that

$$Vrfy_{vk}(m, Sign_{sk}(m)) = true$$

The last statement demands, that every signature generated for a fixed message and a fixed signing key should be valid and accepted by the verifier using the corresponding verification key. Although it is possible to lower this requirement and accept the rejection of proper computed signatures with negligible probability over (sk, vk), we do not want to take this into further account here.

EXAMPLE 2.79. (Textbook RSA Signatures)
The basic variant of RSA signatures have been shown not to fulfil the requirements of existentially unforgeable signatures, but it can be shown that the RSA signature applied to the hash of the message is secure in the random oracle model[9] [BR96]. It is sufficient here to give an idea how this variant of RSA signatures work. Its method of operation can easily be applied to the hash of messages.

- The key-generation algorithm $GenKey_{RSA}$ takes as input the security parameter 1^n and outputs a modulus N that is the product of two large random primes p and q, along with integers e and d such that $e \cdot d = 1 \pmod{\varphi(N)}$ holds. The verification key is e along with the modulus N, and the signing key consists of d.

$$((N, e), d) \leftarrow GenKey_{RSA}(1^n)$$

- The signing algorithm $Sign_{RSA}$ takes as input the signing key d and the plaintext message $m \in \{0,1\}^*$. It outputs the signature $s = m^d \pmod{N}$.

$$m^d \pmod{N} \leftarrow Sign_{RSA}(d, m))$$

- The verification algorithm $Vrfy_{RSA}$ takes as input the verification key e, a message m, and a signature s and checks if $s^e = m \pmod{N}$.

$$Vrfy_{RSA}(e, m, s) := \begin{cases} true & \text{if } s^e = m \pmod{N} \\ false & \text{if } s^e \neq m \pmod{N} \end{cases}$$

For a more detailed treatment and deeper insights into signatures, we refer to work of GOLDREICH [Gol04, ch. 6], and KATZ [Kat10].

---

[9]The random oracle model is outside the scope of this work. For a description see work by BELLARE and ROGAWAY [BR95b], or KATZ and LINDEL [KL08, p. 458-469]

Notions of Security for Digital Signature Schemes

A second obvious requirement is, that it should be hard (computationally infeasible) for an adversary to generate valid signatures without the possession of the signing key. More formally, an adversary forges a signature if she outputs a message m together with a valid signature s on m, and m was not previously signed by the regular owner of the signing key sk.

In analogy to the security models of encryption schemes, GOLDWASSER, MICALI and RIVEST give security models for digital signatures based on attack models and the notion of security [GMR88]. They distinguish between *key-only attacks* and *message attacks*, where the adversary has some knowledge of some messages' signatures. Message attacks are classified into four subclasses depending on how the messages, whose signatures the adversary sees, are chosen. The attacks are listed in order of increasing severity, i.e. the attack models represent increasing capabilities of the adversary:

Key-Only Attack The adversary knows only the signer's public key.

Message Attack Before her attempt to break the digital signature scheme, the adversary has access to some messages' signatures and again to the signer's public key. Depending on how those messages are chosen, this attack model is subclassified.

Known Message Attack The adversary is given access to signatures and messages for a set of messages not chosen by him.

Generic Chosen Message Attack The adversary is given access to signatures and messages for a set of messages chosen by the adversary, but the messages are fixed and independent of the signer's public key. Thus, the entire message list has to be generated by the adversary without knowledge of the signer's key and any signature. The name 'generic' arises from the fact, that the same attack is used against any signer, since it does not depend on the signer's key.

Directed Chosen Message Attack The adversary is given access to signatures and messages for a set of messages chosen by the adversary after seeing the signer's public key. But the entire message list has to be generated by the adversary without knowledge any signature. The name 'direct' arises from the fact, that due to the dependence on the signer's public key it is directed against a specific signer.

Adaptive Chosen Message Attack The adversary may request any signature from the signer which may depend on the signer's public key as well as on any previously obtained signatures. In other words the adversary has access to an oracle which signs any message from him with the signer's private signing key.

The notion of security is described by the meaning of breaking the signature scheme. Breakings are described in order of decreasing severity meaning that the breaks represent decreasing capabilities the adversary needs to succeed:

Total Break The adversary recovers the signer's private signing key.

Universal Forgery The adversary is able to forge signatures of any message. Thus, she has an efficient signing algorithm functionally equivalent to the signer's signing algorithm, but possibly based on a different signing key.

Selective Forgery The adversary is able to forge a signature for a particular message of her choice.

Existential Forgery The adversary forges a signature not already known by him for at least one message. The adversary has no control over the message whose signature she obtains.

Following GOLDWASSER et al. [GMR88], we say that a scheme is totally breakable, respectively universally forgeable, selectively forgeable, or existentially forgeable under key-only, known message, generic chosen message, directed chosen message or adaptive chosen message attack if it is breakable in one of the above senses with the respective resources. As specified above regarding encryption schemes, a forgery attack succeeds, if the algorithm succeeds with a non-negligible probability (in the security parameter n) and runs in polynomial time (in the security parameter n).

When combining the attack model and the break of the signature scheme, clearly, the strongest notion of security is if the digital signature scheme is secure against existential forgery under an adaptive chosen message attack. This means that an adversary should not be able to forge any signature, even though she is allowed to obtain messages on many other messages of her choice. As already mentioned, this notion is called *existentially unforgeable under an adaptive chosen message attack* and was first defined by GOLDWASSER, MICALI and RIVEST, who also gave the first signature scheme satisfying their definition [GMR88].

Definition 2.80. (Existentially Unforgeable Under a Chosen-Message Attack)
A signature scheme is *existentially unforgeable under an adaptive chosen message attack* if for all efficient adversaries with access to an oracle, which returns the signature $s_i = \text{Sign}_{pk}(m_i)$ for any message m_i of the adversary's choice, the probability of an polynomial-time adversary to output a signature $s \neq m_i, \forall i$ not previously obtained from the oracle, is negligible in n.

In practise, a hash of the message instead of the whole message is often signed. Reasons for this are

Attempts to prevent certain attacks Several approaches to prevent certain attacks by hashing the message before signing it have been proposed (e.g. on "Textbook RSA" [KL08, p. 428]). Even though most of them have not been proven to be secure, they are likely to complicate those attacks. Obviously the hash has to be collision-resistant, since otherwise finding a collision results in a forged signature.

Compatibility Even though the success of hash functions to prevent attacks is uncertain, hash functions in general provide a convenient way to reformat messages. Thus the hash function can be used to trim the message to the domain of the Sign-function.

Efficiency The hash in general will be much shorter than the message, and thus save computational power and can be signed faster.

Integrity If the message's size is too large, it must be splitted into blocks and each block has to be signed separately. Without additional effort, the receiver of the message does not know, whether the received blocks are complete and in correct order.

2.4.3 Blind Signatures

Another type of signatures are *blind signatures* introduced by CHAUM [Cha83b, Cha83a]. Basically, blind signatures are a two-party protocol between a sender Alice and a signer Bob. When Bob issues a (blind) signature on a message from Alice, he should only know that he signed a message from Alice, but he should not be able to learn which message he signed. Applications for blind signatures are cryptographic election schemes, especially if the election is run online, and digital cash schemes. In both cases, a third party is able to verify the validity of a signed message (e.g. a ballot paper or a digital coin), but allow the sender to remain anonymous.

The basic idea of blind signatures is that Alice encodes (blinds) her message, sends it to Bob, who signs it and sends the signature back to Alice, who decodes (unblinds) the signature, and thus has a valid signature of the unblinded message without Bob learning anything about the message he signed. In CHAUM's original work he gives an analogy from the physical world: blind signatures are like writing a signature on the outside of a carbon paper lined envelope, which leaves a signature on the slip of paper inside the envelope.

EXAMPLE 2.81. Example from the World of Paper Documents
To get a better idea of the concept of blind signatures and their application, we describe an example taken from the world of paper documents. CHAUM [Cha83b]

considers the problem of a secret ballot, but the electors are unable to meet. A trustee is confronted with the task to organise the ballot in such a way, that all electors' votes stay secret and each elector is able to verify that his vote is counted. The proposed solution utilises the carbon paper lined envelopes described above and works as follows:

- Each elector puts a ballot slip with his vote in a carbon lined envelope and sends the envelope along with his return address in an outside envelope to the trustee.

- The trustee opens the envelope, signs the outside of the carbon lined envelope if the sender is a valid elector and sends the carbon lined envelope back to the elector's return address in a new envelope. Due to the carbon, his signature is also on the ballot slip inside the carbon lined envelope. Of course the trustee has to use a special signature, which is only valid for the specified election.

- The elector receives the signed envelope, removes it and checks the signature on the ballot slip and mails the ballot slip in a new outer envelope without return address to the trustee.

- Once the trustee has received all ballot slips in envelopes without return address, he makes the ballot slips available publicly. Thus, anyone can count the displayed ballots and check the signatures on them. In particular, if a elector is able to identify his ballot slip due to the nature of the paper or something similar, he is able to verify his vote was counted. Assuming every signature of the trustee is identical, the trustee is unable to identify any ballot slip, because the first time he actually sees them is when he puts them on public display. Hence, the trustee cannot determine how anyone voted.

As we see in the next definition, this example visualises the functionality of digital blind signatures quite exactly, even though the carbon lined envelope is represented by mathematical functions.

Definition 2.82. (Blind Signature Protocol) A *blind signature protocol* is a two-party protocol between a sender Alice and a signer Bob, which requires a tuple of probabilistic polynomial-time algorithms (GenKey,Sign,Vrfy,Blind,Unblind) such that:

- The tuple of algorithms (GenKey,Sign,Vrfy) is a digital signature scheme for Bob.

- The functions Blind and Unblind are chosen (by the sender Alice), such that $\text{Unblind}(\text{Sign}_{sk}(\text{Blind}(m))) = \text{Sign}_{sk}(m)$ holds. Blind is called a *blinding function*, Blind(m) is called a *blinded message* and Unblind denotes the *unblinding function*.

The specification of the protocol is as follows (*see* aso Fig. 2.8):

1. **(Key generation)** The signer Bob generates a pair of keys according to the key-generation algorithm GenKey of the underlying digital signature scheme.

2. **(Message blinding)** The sender Alice secretly chooses a pair of functions Blind and Unblind, selects a message, blinds that message using Blind, and sends the blinded message to Bob.

3. **(Signature generation)** Bob computes the signature of the blinded message using the Sign algorithm of the underlying signature scheme and sends the signature of the blinded message to Alice.

4. **(Signature unblinding)** Alice unblinds the signature of the blinded message using the previously chosen Unblind function, and thus holds Bob's valid signature of the original message.

5. **(Signature verification)** The verifier Victor has Bob's verification key at his disposal, obtains a message and the corresponding signature from the sender Alice, and is able by using the Vrfy algorithm of the underlying signature scheme to reject or accept the signature.

As a consequence of the definition of the blinding functions and the signature scheme, it is required that for every security parameter n, every message $m \in \{0,1\}^*$ and every pair of keys (pk, sk) output by $GenKey(1^n)$, it holds that

$$\mathsf{Vrfy}_{pk}(m, \mathsf{Unblind}(\mathsf{Sign}_{sk}(\mathsf{Blind}(m)))) = \mathsf{true}$$

which restricts the choice of the signing algorithm and the blinding/unblinding function pair.

One may also have noticed that the protocol is denoted two-party, even though Alice communicates with Bob *and* Victor. In many cases Bob and Victor are identical, but probably there will lie some time in between the signature creation and its verification. Strictly speaking, the protocol consists of two two-party sub-protocols (signature creation and verification).

As a concrete example we show CHAUM's original contribution of a blind signature based on Textbook RSA signatures.

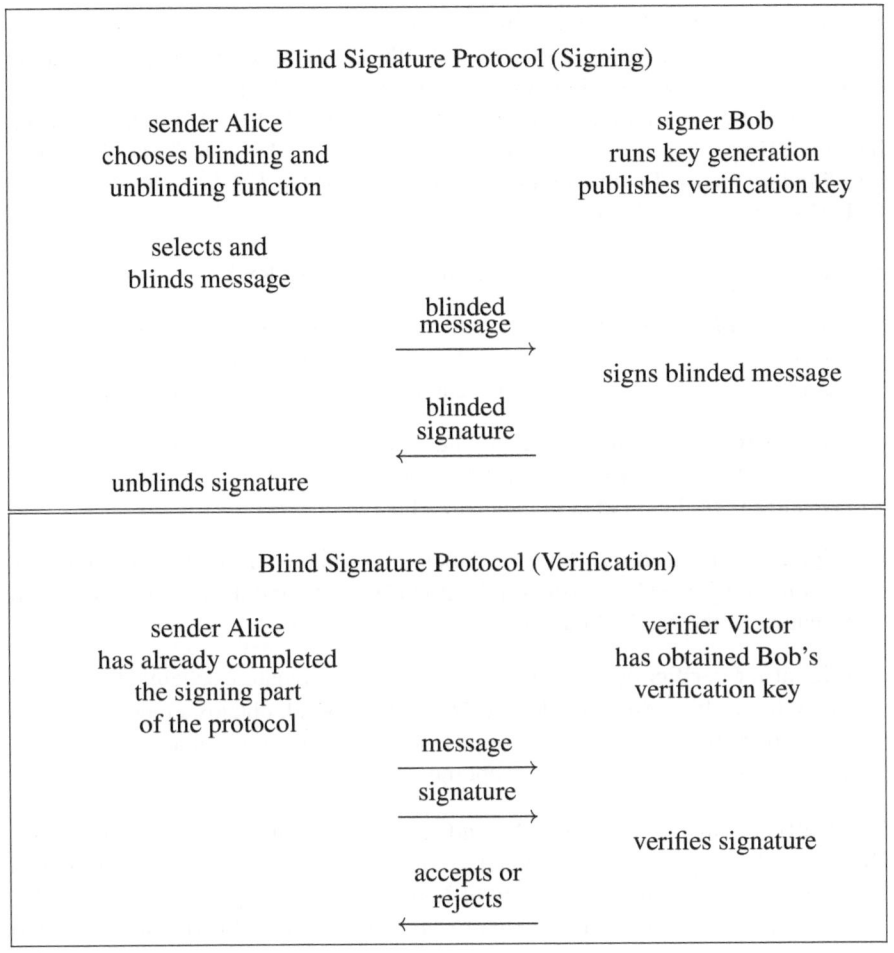

Figure 2.8: Blind Signature Scheme

EXAMPLE 2.83. (RSA Blind Signatures)

Let $(\text{GenKey}_{RSA}, \text{Sign}_{RSA}, \text{Vrfy}_{RSA})$ be the textbook RSA signature scheme from Ex. 2.79 with verification key (e, N) and signing key d.

Let $k \in \mathbb{N}$ be a random integer with $k < N$ and $\gcd(N, k) = 1$. Let the blinding function $\text{Blind}_k : \mathbb{Z}_n \to \mathbb{Z}_n$ be defined by $\text{Blind}_k(m) = k^e m \pmod{N}$. We denote k as *blinding factor*. Let the unblinding function $\text{Unblind}_k : \mathbb{Z}_n \to \mathbb{Z}_n$ be defined by $\text{Unblind}_k(s) = k^{-1} s \mod N$.

1. **(Key generation)** The signer Bob generates a pair of RSA keys.

2. **(Message blinding)** The sender Alice secretly chooses a blinding factor k, selects a message $m \in \{0, 1, \ldots, N-1\}$, blinds that message by computing $m' = \text{Blind}_k(m) = mk^e \pmod{N}$, and sends the blinded message m' to Bob.

3. **(Signature generation)** Bob computes the signature of the blinded message by computing $s' = \text{Sign}_{RSA}(d, mk^e \mod N) = km^d \mod N$ and sends the signature s' of the blinded message to Alice.

4. **(Signature unblinding)** Alice unblinds the signature of the blinded message by computing $s = \text{Unblind}_k(km^d \mod N) = m^d$, and thus holds Bob's valid signature of the original message.

5. **(Signature verification)** As in the textbook RSA signature scheme, the verifier Victor has Bob's verification key (e, N) at his disposal, obtains a message m and the corresponding signature s from the sender Alice, and is able by computing $\text{Vrfy}_{RSA}(e, m, s)$ to reject or accept the signature.

Since $\text{Blind}_k(m) = k^e m \mod N$ and $\text{Sign}_{RSA}(d, m) = m^d \mod N$ holds, $\text{Unblind}_k(\text{Sign}_{RSA}(d, \text{Blind}_k(m))) = \text{Sign}_{RSA}(d, m)$ fulfils the requirements from Def. 2.82 – due to the property of RSA-keys satisfying $k^{ed} = k^1 \pmod{N}$. The described algorithms can be used for the generation and verification of blind signatures as shown in Fig. 2.9. Furthermore, k is a random value out of all possible values with $\gcd(N, k) = 1$ and the blinding function $\text{Blind}_k(m)$ is a permutation. It follows that the result $k^e m \mod N$ of the blinding function is also random, and thus does not leak any information about the original message m.

Notions of Security for Blind Signature Schemes

Note that by unblinding a signature, the sender (Alice) computes a signature of a message which the legitimate signer (Bob) has not signed. In other words, blind signature schemes require the sender to perform an existential forgery in the sense of Def. 2.80. Thus, the security definition of digital signatures is non-applicable to

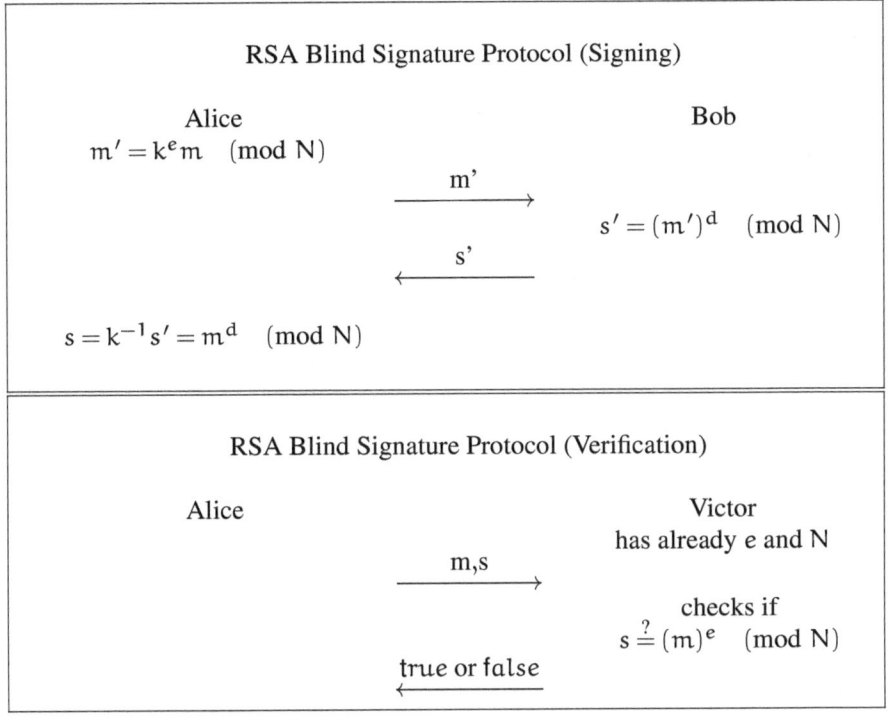

RSA Blind Signature Protocol (Signing)

Alice   Bob

$m' = k^e m \pmod N$

$\xrightarrow{\quad m' \quad}$

$s' = (m')^d \pmod N$

$\xleftarrow{\quad s' \quad}$

$s = k^{-1}s' = m^d \pmod N$

RSA Blind Signature Protocol (Verification)

Alice   Victor
                                         has already e and N

$\xrightarrow{\quad m,s \quad}$

                                         checks if
                                         $s \overset{?}{=} (m)^e \pmod N$

$\xleftarrow{\text{true or false}}$

Figure 2.9: Chaum's Blind Signature Protocol

blind signatures. POINTCHEVAL and STERN [PS00b] propose the following notion of security for blind signatures: Assuming, Alice has performed n interactions with Bob, and thus has obtained n signatures from him. Then Alice should not be able to generate a $n+1$st signature without asking Bob.

Part II

Human Decipherable Encryption Schemes

3 Introduction, Scenario, and Related Work

> To visualise is to see what is not there, what is not real – a dream . To visualise is, in fact, to make visual lies. Visual lies, however, have a way of coming true.
>
> Peter McWilliams

3.1 Background and Purpose

In today's life, the internet plays an important role. Many services shift to the internet (online banking, online shopping, media streaming and download services), business processes heavily rely on the internet (submitting claims, help desks) and it is widely used for personal communication (social networking, email). The widespread use make services an attractive aim for attackers. Thus, it is no surprise that many of this services require the user's authentication. However, often no secure channel is established to the user himself and the secure channel already ends on the user's device. If a website requires the user to log in via password, at best the site is using a connection secured with SSL. However, on the one hand, average users do not properly check SSL certificates and if certificate verification fails they ignore the warning box due to so many websites with invalid certificates. On the other hand, also the SSL certificate infrastructure has shown to be vulnerable in practice. Browsers include large lists of root certificates from 'trusted' certification authorities, but there are many issues with wrong certificates. Certification authorities issue certificates without proper checking authorisations or issue sub-certificates which allow to create arbitrary certificates [Eik13]. Researchers were able to create forged certificates [SSA+08]. Certification authorities were hacked [Art11]. For a recent survey on prominent security issues we refer to CLARK and VAN OORSHOT [CvO13].

However, even if SSL tunnels would work perfect, the channel ends on the user's computer respectively browser and leaves the user vulnerable to attacks by Trojan horses. Thus, in fact, a secure channel to the user and not his device is required.

One approach to solve this issue is to make use of trusted computing platforms [BCP+02]. Trusted computing platforms consist of a tamper-resistant core which should guarantee its integrity. Built on this core, a chain of trust is established which allows local and remote users to verify whether certain components are operating in a satisfactory way. Set up properly, this approach should prevent Trojan horses on a trusted platform. However, it is not easy to build a sufficient complex system completely from trusted components. We already pointed out some issues regarding the SSL chain of trust and do not go further into detail here. Additional concerns raised that the system is no longer under sole control of the user and may limit his freedom as already done by walled garden approaches [BVO11] seen in recent years for example on mobile devices and e-book readers [Net07]. For more elaborated thoughts on reservations against trusted computing, we refer to ANDERSON [And03] and STALLMAN [Sta07].

In online banking, many banks have come up with several approaches of authentication derived from variations of transaction authentication numbers (TAN). The user receives a list of TANs beforehand (e.g. by letter post) and has to authenticate each transaction with one of the numbers from his list. This at least ensures that an adversary cannot perform transactions by knowing the user's login and password. However, this attack is vulnerable to client side attacks such as Trojan horses or phishing. There are various attempts of banks to overcome this, such as indexed TANs (iTAN) where the user was asked for a specific TAN from his list or mobile TANs (mTAN) where a single TAN is created from transaction data and transmitted via a separate channel. In practise those variations helped against phishing, but did not succeed against Trojan horses, since the assumption that the user's mobile phone is a trusted device did not hold due to sophisticated Trojan horses which also affected the mobile devices [Sul11, Unu13]. Other approaches include special devices which are assumed to be trustworthy, but cause additional costs either at the user's or at the bank's side. Furthermore, the adversary may try to gain also control over the trusted devices by simulating to the user that the devices need to updated and connected to the computer already taken over.

Two more sophisticated approaches were proposed by SZYDLOWSKI et al. [SKK07]. The first approach, denoted as token calculation, consist of a code book instead of a TAN list and requires the user to manually compute a function depending on the intended transaction. Since the adversary does not know which function is evaluated, she is not able to transfer an eavesdropped TAN to another transaction. The second approach aims to protect against an automated adversary and proposes that the user still uses a TAN for authentication but instead of entering it with a keyboard clicks on the corresponding places on a CAPTCHA specially designed for that purpose. The idea of *Completely Automated Public Turing Test to Tell Computers and Humans Apart* (CAPTCHA) goes back to VON AHN et al. [vABHL03]. They propose to use problems hard for artificial intelligence, i.e. problems which are easy to solve for humans but cannot be solved by computers. Therefore, CAPTCHAs are inappropriate to generally protect such transactions, since they could be presented to people which solve them in return for adult entertainment (also denoted as the "Porn Turing farm" [War05]) as a kind of man-in-the-middle attack. Moreover, the usual arms race between hard CAPTCHAs and programs trying to solve them [MM03a, MM03b] applies.

Another proposal for secure authentication on untrusted computers is visual cryptography. Visual cryptography was introduced by NAOR and SHAMIR [NS94, NS96] and allows to encrypt a picture by splitting it into n shares in such a way that someone with k shares is able to reconstruct the image, while $k-1$ shares reveal no information about the original image. They proposed to print each share on a transparency, so that its re-composition can be easily done by humans by stacking their transparencies without the aid of computers (cf. Sect. 4.2.1). By using only two shares, this approach would have one physical transparency which is put in front of the display of a possibly compromised computer as shown in Fig. 3.1.

(a) transparencies side by side   **(b)** transparencies stacked

Figure 3.1: Example for Visual Cryptography with a Transparency Displayed on a Monitor and a Transparency which is Physically Put in front of the Monitor

By solving a challenge which is only solvable seeing the composed image it is ensured that a Trojan horse would only notice the points which the user clicked, but the malware cannot associate any meaning with it. However, all existing approaches are closely related to encryptions based on the XOR function (cf. Def. 4.60) which is due to humans not being able to do complex operations "on the fly". Thus, for many approaches, the key-transparency may be used only once in a secure manner. Although there are a number of schemes allowing to reuse the key-transparency, a satisfying solution for real world scenarios has not yet been found. The general idea of this work is to define human decipherable encryption schemes and regard visual cryptography as one case of human decipherable encryption schemes. To examine how key-transparencies can securely be used a couple of times, we distinguished between the coding and the encryption function. We propose a scheme where the encoding function is probabilistic and the encryption function additionally adds noise to the ciphertext making it difficult for the adversary to recover the relevant part. Samples of transparencies for visual cryptography are shown in Fig. 3.2.

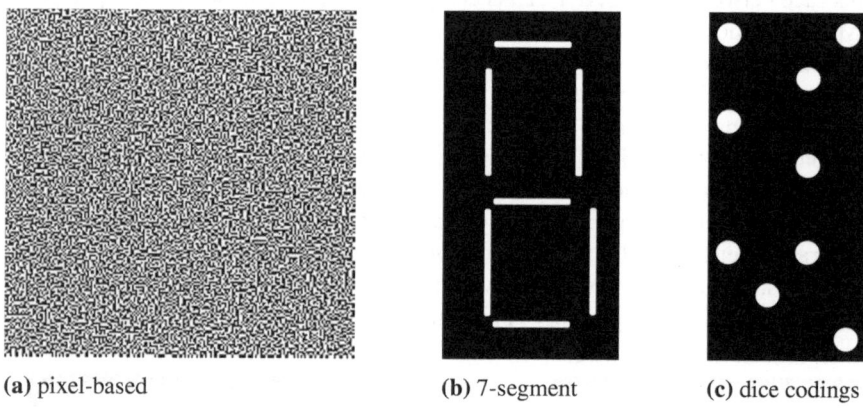

(a) pixel-based   **(b)** 7-segment   **(c)** dice codings

Figure 3.2: Transparencies for Visual Cryptography

3.2 Overview

The organisation of this part is as follows: In the remaining introduction we propose some scenarios and give a short overview of closely related work. In the next chapter we introduce the unicity distance defined by SHANNON and give notions, terms and properties of encoding and encryption schemes, distinguishing between encoding and encryption. We also define the notion of *sample-or-random ciphertext only indistinguishability* (SOR-CO) and show its relation to already existing cryptographic security models. The chapter concludes with a short introduction to visual cryptography. In Chap. 5 we introduce dice codings proposed by DOBERITZ and consider their security in different contexts before showing a successful attack and evaluating its security in the SOR-CO security model. In the second part of Chap. 5, we introduce the *human decipherable encryption scheme based on dice codings with noise* and show that it – given the proper parameters – fulfils the requirements of the ciphertext only indistinguishability security model. We conclude with a summary and detailed future work section in Chap. 6.

3.3 Scenarios

The first scenario which comes to mind, when thinking of applications for visual cryptography, is a computer infected with Trojan horses. Due to sophisticated Trojan horses – such as "Zeus mitmo" [Goo11] – the user can neither trust his computer nor his mobile device is in a clean and secure state. If he executes online banking or other sensitive tasks, he would have to ensure that his computer is not infected, which is clearly not possible. The application of visual cryptography to TANs in online banking was discussed in more detail by GREVELER [Gre07]. The user receives a list of TANs as visual cryptography *key shares* (cf. p. 83) from his bank and when performing a transaction, he has to decrypt a ciphertext containing his transaction details. After verifying the details, he confirms the transaction by clicking on special marked points inside the ciphertext.

In another scenario, the user depends on another person's hardware and again wants to execute sensitive tasks. This may either be a friend's computer, or a computer in an internet cafe. Since the user cannot ensure that the computer he is using does not log it's activities, he would be forced to trust its owner.

There is also another proposal for using visual cryptography in electronic voting by CHAUM [Cha02]. After voting, the vote is encrypted and the voting machine prints a receipt with two layers (transparencies). Stacked together, the vote is revealed and the user is able to validate it at the polling station. The user keeps one of the transparencies and the other is published after the polls are closed. With the transparency taken along, the user is able to verify that his vote was counted.

3.4 Related Work

Pixel-Based Visual Cryptography The idea and concept of visual crypto- graphy was introduced by NAOR and SHAMIR [NS94, NS96, NP97]. Their approach was pixel-based and two coloured. Since then various research proposals have appeared. They suggest to use (more) colours [VvT97, YL00, CPS04, CPS05, Shy06, CPS07], improve the contrast of pictures [BSS99, ES02, HKS00, BDSS03, HTH06, YWC08] or steganography. Steganography may be used for the detection of cheating: [HT07, SNSS08] by hiding signatures resp. watermarks in the image or by hiding the existence of a message [LYLL13] – e.g. by using letters instead of pixels. For further reading we refer to a survey by REVENKAR et al. [RAG10].

CHEN et al. [CTW08] demonstrate how to encrypt more than one image into a cipher and a key transparency. For the basic image, the scheme works like the original scheme. Additionally, it is possible to hide a number of smaller images by shifting the key transparency slide for decryption. However, the size of the composition of the smaller images may not exceed the size of the transparencies. They also give an overview of similar visual cryptography schemes which allow to reuse the transparency.

Another approach of re-using a transparency for pixel-based visual encryption goes back to FANG [Fan07, Fan09, FHL09]. His scheme allows to encrypt two images by using the key transparency twice. Given a cipher transparency c and a key transparency k, if c and k are stacked, the first image is revealed. If k is turned over before stacked on c the second image of the same size is revealed. WU and CHEN [WC98] present a related scheme where the second image is visible when one of the shares is rotated by 90 degrees. Other approaches by HSU et al. [HCL04] and WU and CHANG [WC05] use circular shift operations to shift the cipher and the key transparency. WEIR and YAN [WY09] propose two schemes. One simply uses disjoint areas of the key for decryption. The other works by using odd respectively even rows of the key transparencies to reveal two images. However, no security analysis was given.

A probabilistic model for visual encryption schemes was introduced by YANG [Yan04] and later generalised by CIMATO [CPS06]. WANG was able to avoid pixel extension, but at the cost of a probabilistic reconstruction of the original image. This means that the reconstruction is not perfect and each pixel is reconstructed correctly only with a certain probability. WANG et al. [WYL07, WYL11] extended this approach to grey-scale and colour images.

Segment-Based Visual Cryptography   BORCHERT [Bor07] extended the idea and proposes segment-based visual cryptography where instead of pixels the segments of 7-segment displays [Woo08] are the essential building blocks. Based thereupon, DOBERITZ [Dob08] presented a segment-based scheme which is also closed in the sense that all plaintexts are meaningful with the idea that the key transparency should be usable multiple times. As a consequence, several encodings are decoded to the same meaning resulting in a probabilistic encryption scheme. We extend the scheme proposed by DOBERITZ and add noise with the intention to enhance the probabilistic part to improve the re-usability of key transparencies. Moreover, we give a security model and are able to show that the scheme proposed by DOBERITZ already leaks information when the transparency is used twice. For that purpose we give a formalisation which differs between the encoding and encryption part of the scheme.

4 Human Decipherable Encryption Scheme

> Crypto is not mathematics, but crypto can be highly mathematical, crypto can use mathematics, but good crypto can be done without a great reliance on complex mathematics.
>
> William T. Shaw

4.1 Notation and Terminology

4.1.1 Messages, Codings, Ciphertexts and Keys

At first, we define four sets suitable for the domains and codomains of the encoding and encryption functions defined in the next subsections. As mentioned in Sect. 2.2, messages are encrypted with a key to ciphertexts as shown in Fig. 4.1a. Without anticipating the following subsections, we point out that messages are first encoded and then encrypted with a key distinguishing between codings and encryptions (see Fig. 4.1). Therefore the following definitions introduce messages, codings, ciphertexts and keys consisting of characters from a particular alphabet which fit into the notion one may intuitively expect.

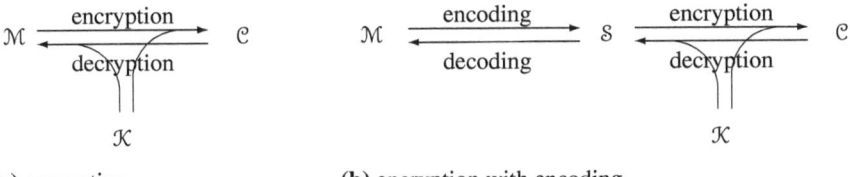

(a) encryption   (b) encryption with encoding

Figure 4.1: Relations of Encoding and Encryption Functions' (Co-)Domains

Definition 4.1. (Character, Message, Message Space) A *message* M_i with length i consists of i concatenated *characters* m_j from alphabet Ω:

$$M_i = (m_1, \ldots, m_i), \forall j \leqslant i, j \in \mathbb{N} : m_j \in \Omega$$

The *message space* of messages M_i with length i is denoted by

$$\mathcal{M}_i = \{M_i | M_i = (m_1, \ldots, m_i), \forall j \leqslant i, j \in \mathbb{N} : m_j \in \Omega\}$$

and we denote the *message space of all messages* by $\mathcal{M} = \bigcup_{\forall i} \mathcal{M}_i$.

Definition 4.2. (Symbol, Coding, Coding Space) A *code word* or *coding* S_i with length i consists of i concatenated *symbols* s_j from alphabet Σ:

$$S_i = (s_1, \ldots, s_i), \forall j \leqslant i, j \in \mathbb{N} : s_j \in \Sigma$$

The *coding space* of code words with length i is denoted by

$$\mathcal{S}_i = \{S_i | S_i = (s_1, \ldots, s_i), \forall j \leqslant i, j \in \mathbb{N} : s_j \in \Sigma\}$$

and we denote the *coding space of all codings* by $\mathcal{S} = \bigcup_{\forall i} \mathcal{S}_i$.

Definition 4.3. (Cipher Symbol, Ciphertext, Ciphertext Space) A *ciphertext* C_i with length i consists of i concatenated *ciphertext symbols* c_j from alphabet Γ.

$$C_i = (c_1, \ldots, c_i), \forall j \leqslant i, j \in \mathbb{N} : c_j \in \Gamma$$

The *ciphertext space* of ciphertexts with length i is denoted by

$$\mathcal{C}_i = \{C_i | C_i = (c_1, \ldots, c_i), \forall j \leqslant i, j \in \mathbb{N} : c_j \in \Gamma\}$$

and we denote the *ciphertext space of all ciphertexts* by $\mathcal{C} = \bigcup_{\forall i} \mathcal{C}_i$.

We are going to see in Sect. 4.2.2 that it is also useful to have an analogous fragmentation for keys.

Definition 4.4. (Key Symbol, Key, Key Space) A *key* K_i with length i consists of i concatenated *key symbols* k_j from alphabet Λ.

$$K_i = (k_1, \ldots, k_i), \forall j \leqslant i, j \in \mathbb{N} : k_j \in \Lambda$$

The *key space* of keys with length i is denoted by

$$\mathcal{K}_i = \{K_i | K_i = (k_1, \ldots, k_i), \forall j \leqslant i, j \in \mathbb{N} : k_j \in \Lambda\}$$

and we denote the *key space of all keys* by $\mathcal{K} = \bigcup_{\forall i} \mathcal{K}_i$.

Remark 4.5. Note that we may omit the index i if we have no specific length of M, S, C, or K in mind.

4.1.2 Unicity Distance

If an encryption scheme is used with a finite key and Eve intercepts n letters of encrypted communication, she may conclude a set of messages representing possible plaintexts with a certain probability. For simplicity, we assume the used encryption is deterministic and neither compressive nor expansive for the following section. Furthermore, we assume the messages sent are uniformly distributed from the message space. As the length n of the intercepted ciphertext increases, Eve may be able to narrow the field of possible plaintexts until eventually only one "solution" remains. Shannon formalised this approach [Sha49] and defined the notion of unicity distance which we develop in this subsection. For the following considerations it is assumed that Eve has unlimited time to analyse the ciphertext. Following Hellman [Hel77] we start with the definitions of plaintext redundancy.

Definition 4.6. (Language Rate and Plaintext Redundancy) Let L be a language with alphabet Ω. Then we denote the *absolute rate of language* L with $R_0 = \log_2(|\Omega|)$ and the *rate of the language* with R. The *plaintext redundancy* $D = R_0 - R$ is defined as the difference between the absolute rate and the (real) rate of the language. Both, language rate and plaintext redundancy, are measured in bits per character.

More informal, D measures how much text of a language can be omitted without losing any information, for example how much space a lossless compression would save.

Example 4.7. (Plaintext Redundancy: English language)
The English language has 26 characters, so each character may carry $\log_2 26 \approx 4.7$ bits of information. Considering meaningful English, the actual information carried per character is only about 1.5 bits per character [Hel77]. Thus, the plaintext redundancy of English is $D \approx 4.7 - 1.5 = 3.2$ bits per character. One can visualise this result by bringing to mind that the letter "q" in English words is almost always followed by the letter "u", thus "u" may be omitted without loss of information.

Let us now regard Eve's situation in more detail. Often, she has side information available, for example the language of the underlying plaintext or partial knowledge of the message, which can ease her task. Let us assume Eve intercepts a ciphertext C_n of length n and wants to determine the corresponding plaintext message M_n. In total, there are $2^{R_0 n}$ possible messages; 2^{Rn} of them are meaningful, each with the same a priori probability of 2^{-Rn} and all others are meaningless and thus are assigned a priori probabilities of 0. Let us further assume, the key used for encryption is finite. Then there will be a certain set of messages which could represent the intercepted Ciphertext. To be regarded as a possible "solution", a message has to fulfil two conditions. It has to be meaningful and there has to exist a key encrypting the regarded message to the intercepted ciphertext. Before we give some more definitions, following HELLMAN [Hel77] we take a look at the following example.

EXAMPLE 4.8. (Representation of Cipher)
Fig. 4.2 shows the message space on the left and the ciphertext space on the right. The dotted (dashed) lines show the result of the encryption with key #1 (#2) of a message at the left as an encryption on the right. Encryptions of meaningless messages are not shown, since we assume only meaningful messages are sent and thus encrypted. For the sake of clarity, the number of keys was limited to two and the number of messages respectively ciphertexts to twelve. We number the messages and ciphertexts with indices from one to twelve, starting from the top. We investigate three cases:

Message #1, Key #1 If message #1 is encrypted with key #1 the result is cipher-text #4, which – intercepted by an adversary – is obviously an encryption of message #1, since there is no other (meaningful) message into which it can be decrypted:
$$\mathsf{Enc}_{k_1}(m_1) = c_4$$

Message #1, Key #2 If message #1 is encrypted with key #2 the result is cipher-text #5, which an adversary cannot distinguish from message #2 encrypted with key #1:
$$\mathsf{Enc}_{k_2}(m_1) = c_5 = \mathsf{Enc}_{k_1}(m_2)$$

Message #4, Key #1 If message #4 is encrypted with key #1 the result is cipher-text #12. Since ciphertext #12 is also the encryption of message #4 with key #2, the adversary is able to determine which message was sent, but she does not know which key was used:
$$\mathsf{Enc}_{k_1}(m_4) = c_{12} = \mathsf{Enc}_{k_2}(m_4)$$

Note that, in the second and third case, if the adversary has no reason to assume one meaningfull message respectively key is more likely than another, the best she can do is to guess which message respectively key is correct. Naturally, there is only one correct "solution" while there can be numerous spurious message and key decipherments. More formal we define spurious message and key decipherments on the basis of HELLMAN [Hel77].

Definition 4.9. (Spurious Message and Key Decipherments) Let $(\mathsf{GenKey}, \mathsf{Enc}, \mathsf{Dec})$ be an encryption scheme, let $K \in \mathcal{K}$ be a key, let $M, M' \in \mathcal{M}$ be meaningfull plaintext messages and let $C = \mathsf{Enc}_K(M)$ be the encryption of message M with key K. We speak of a *spurious message decipherment* if there exists a key K' such that $C = \mathsf{Enc}_{K'}(M')$ and $M' \neq M$. We denote the

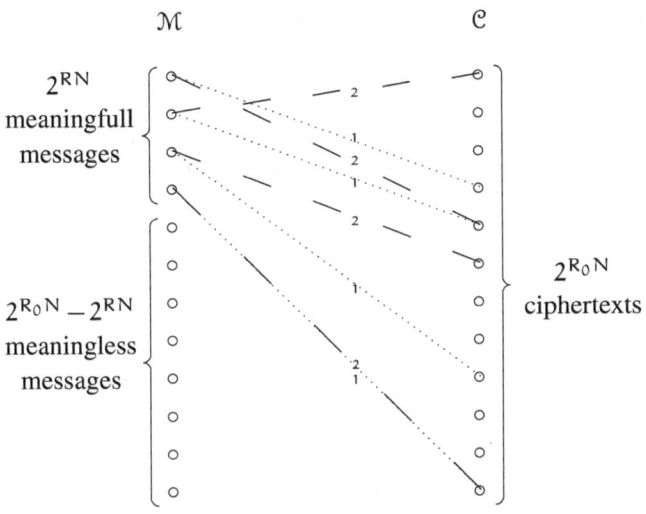

Figure 4.2: Representation of Cipher from HELLMAN [Hel77]

number of spurious messages decipherments with s_m. We speak of a *spurious key decipherment* if there exists a key $K' \neq K$ and a meaningful message M such that $Enc_K(M) = Enc_{K'}(M)$. We denote the number of spurious key decipherments with s_k.

The number of spurious message and key decipherments depends on the used encryption scheme and C. In the abovementioned example, in the second case the number of spurious key and message decipherments is both one: $s_m = 1$ and $s_k = 1$. In the third case, the number of spurious key decipherments is still one, but there is no spurious message decipherment and thus $s_m = 0$ and $s_k = 1$.

Since we assumed that the key used for encryption is finite, the number of possible and thus spurious message and key decipherments decreases, in general, as the length of the intercepted ciphertext increases. At this point, it is helpful to introduce a measure for the size of the keyspace before we are able to continue with a bound for the number of spurious key decipherments.

Definition 4.10. (Entropy of Keyspace) Let $\mathcal{K}$ be the key space, then we denote the *entropy of the key space* as $H(\mathcal{K})$. The entropy of the key space is a measure of the "size" of the key space and if all keys are a priori equally likely and independent of the message, $H(\mathcal{K})$ is the logarithm of the number of possible keys.

For a treatment of the entropy of key generators for symmetric ciphers and a statistical method to estimate it, we refer to DAWSON and GUSTAFSON [DG98]. We continue with HELLMAN's observation on the expected number of spurious key decipherments.

Theorem 4.11. *The expected number of spurious key decipherments on messages of length n is at least $2^{H(\mathcal{K})-nD} - 1$ for any uniquely encipherable, uniquely decipherable cipher.*

Proof. We refer to HELLMAN [Hel77] for the original proof. BEAUCHEMIN and BRASSARD [BB87, BB88] removed the original proof's restrictions that the distribution of keys and messages need to follow a uniform distribution.   □

Loosely speaking, this means, that a "good cryptosystem" against a computationally unbounded adversary can be built if the key rate exceeds the message redundancy. This result was obtained already be SHANNON and later LU [Lu79] extended the class of considered ciphers.

The question arises, how much ciphertext is needed that there is only one reasonable plaintext. SHANNON called the amount of needed ciphertext *unicity distance* with the intention to give a measure of the amount of ciphertext needed to break a cipher and thus measure the security of this cipher. He noticed that the unicity distance depends on the plaintext's characteristics and the used key length of the encryption algorithm [Sha49].

Definition 4.12. (Unicity Distance) Let $(\mathsf{GenKey}, \mathsf{Enc}, \mathsf{Dec})$ be an encryption scheme with key space $\mathcal{K}$ and let $M \in \mathcal{M}$ be a plaintext message of a language with plaintext redundancy D. We denote the expected amount of ciphertext (in number of letters) allowing a computationally unlimited adversary to uniquely determine the used encryption key as *unicity distance* U.

In other words, the unicity distance is the length of the message when the number of spurious key decipherments becomes zero. Taking Th. 4.11 into consideration this leads to a good approximation of the unicity distance.

Theorem 4.13. *The unicity distance U for any uniquely encipherable, uniquely decipherable cipher is approximately $\frac{H(\mathcal{K})}{D}$.*

PROOF. Following argumentations from SHANNON [Sha49] and HELLMANN [Hel77], we prove the above theorem by setting the number of spurious key decipherments in Th. 4.11 to zero and solving the inequality for n:

$$s_k \geqslant 2^{H(\mathcal{K})-nD} - 1$$
$$1 \geqslant 2^{H(\mathcal{K})-nD}$$
$$n \geqslant \frac{H(\mathcal{K})}{D}$$

∎

To get an idea for an application of the unicity distance, we take a look at an example from HELLMANN [Hel77] which also found its way to Wikipedia [Wik13f]:

EXAMPLE 4.14. (Unicity Distance: Substitution Cipher)
Let us consider a simple substitution cipher for the English language. Then there are $26! \approx 4 \cdot 10^{26}$ possible keys representing the number of ways the alphabet can be permuted. Under the assumption that all keys are equally likely, it follows that $H(\mathcal{K}) = \log_2(26!) \approx 88.4$ bits, and thus $U = \frac{H(\mathcal{K})}{D} \approx \frac{88.4}{3.2} \approx 28$ characters. Therefore, in theory 28 characters of ciphertext should be enough to elaborate a plaintext and compute the corresponding key given that the language is really English.

Obviously, the bigger the unicity distance is, the more ciphertext does an adversary need. It is easy to see that the unicity distance grows as the redundancy of the plaintext diminishes. Furthermore, the redundancy of a language does not only depend on the language itself, but also on its representation. If a message is encoded in the American Standard Code for Information Interchange (ASCII) [Ass63] or in Unicode [The11], its redundancy may be significantly higher. Otherwise, the redundancy of compressed messages may be significantly smaller. If the sender uses a perfect compression, the redundancy would be zero and thus the unicity distance would reach infinity, because there are only meaningfull messages left, making it impossible for an attacker to distinguish the correct plaintext from any incorrect plaintext. Another possibility to increase the unicity distance is to increase the entropy of the keyspace. For example, the keyspace of one time pads (cf. Sect. 2.2.3) has unbounded entropy and thus $U = \infty$, which confirms that one time pads are theoretically unbreakable.

Remark 4.15. It is important to keep in mind that the unicity distance makes a statement on how much information is enough for a *computationally unbounded adversary* to find the right key. In theory, ciphertexts with a length exceeding the unicity distance have only one meaningful decryption, but nothing is said about how much ciphertext is in practice required for an adversary with reasonably limited resources.

SHANNON also transferred the idea of equivocation, the conditional entropy of a random variable given that the value of another random variable is known, from information theory to cryptography. He used the entropy of the key or the message conditional on observed ciphertexts as a theoretical secrecy index.

Definition 4.16. (Set of Possible Keys) Let $(\text{GenKey}, \text{Enc}, \text{Dec})$ be an encryption scheme, let $M \in \mathcal{M}$ be a message with a priori probability $P(M)$, let $K \in \mathcal{K}$ be a key, and let $C \in \mathcal{C}$ be a ciphertext of the encryption scheme. We define the *set of possible keys* that can account for a ciphertext C with:

$$\mathcal{K}_C = \{K \in \mathcal{K} | P(\text{Dec}_K(C)) > 0\}$$

and its number of elements with $|\mathcal{K}_C|$. The number of possible spurious key decipherments upon seeing the ciphertext C is $\max\{(|\mathcal{K}_C| - 1), 0\}$ and denoted by $s_k(C)$. In addition, the expected number of spurious key decipherments is denoted by $\bar{s}_k = \sum_C P(C) s_k(C)$.

Definition 4.17. (Message and Key Equivocation) Let $M \in \mathcal{M}$ be a message with a priori probability $P(M)$, let $K \in \mathcal{K}$ be a key with the probability $P(K)$ being used, let $C \in \mathcal{C}$ be the ciphertext of the message M with the probability $P(C)$ being produced. The probability $P(C)$ can easily be derived from the distributions of $P(M)$ and $P(K)$. We denote the conditional probability of a key K (message M) after intercepting a ciphertext C as $P(K|C)$ respectively as $P(M|C)$. In the same manner, we denote the conditional entropy of a key respectively message upon seeing a ciphertext C by $H(K|C)$ respectively $H(M|C)$. We denote the summation of the conditional entropy over all keys and ciphertexts of length n as *key equivocation*

$$H(K|\mathcal{C}_n) = \sum_{C \in \mathcal{C}, K \in \mathcal{K}} P(C, K)\, H(K|C)$$

and the summation of the conditional entropy over all messages and ciphertexts of length n as *message equivocation*:

$$H(M|\mathcal{C}_n) = \sum_{C \in \mathcal{C}, M \in \mathcal{M}} P(C, M)\, H(M|C)$$

Key and message equivocation are measures how much information about the key respectively the message are revealed by a ciphertext.

Considering a growing length of ciphertext with a finite key size, generally key and message equivocation approach zero. In fact, this does not apply in all cases. It is possible that key and message equivocation do not approach zero and the key equivocation may even remain constant. This leads to SHANNON's definition of ideal and strong ideal systems.

Definition 4.18. (Ideal System) Let $(\mathsf{GenKey}, \mathsf{Enc}, \mathsf{Dec})$ be an encryption scheme, let $M_n \in \mathcal{M}$ be a message of length n, let $K \in \mathcal{K}$ be a key, and $\mathcal{C} \ni C = \mathsf{Enc}_K(M)$ be a ciphertext. We denote an encryption scheme as *ideal system* if the message equivocation $H(M|\mathcal{C}_n)$ and the key equivocation $H(K|\mathcal{C}_n)$ do not approach zero as the length n of the message grows to infinity. We denote an encryption scheme as *strong ideal system* if the key equivocation $H(K|\mathcal{C}_n)$ remains constant at $H(K)$ as the length of the message $n \to \infty$.

SHANNON states that, if the plaintext consists of independently and equiprobably chosen letters, then the redundancy of the plaintext is zero and therefore $H(K|\mathcal{C}_n) = H(K)$ which leads to the following theorem.

Theorem 4.19. *If all letters are equally likely and independent any closed cipher is strongly ideal [Sha49, Th. 13].*

Further research was done by JABRI, who also gave an upper bound for the probability of guessing the key if the message length is below the unicity distance [Jab96].

4.1.3 Encodings and Decodings

The following definitions of encoding and decoding functions comply with the intuition one may have of encoding and decoding. The encoding function is left-total, to ensure all messages can be encoded, and left-unique, to ensure that it is invertible. The decoding function inverts the coding function and thus has to be deterministic.

Definition 4.20. (Encoding Scheme) Let $M \in \mathcal{M}$ be a message and $S \in \mathcal{S}$ a coding. An *encoding scheme* is a tuple of algorithms $(\mathsf{Gen}, \mathsf{Encode}, \mathsf{Decode})$ such that:

- Each run of the *parameter-generation algorithm* Gen outputs a parameter I on input 1^n. Each value of I defines the domain and the range of the functions Encode_I and Decode_I defined below as well as any additional information (e.g. used font type and size, position of line breaks, arrangement of symbols), which is helpful for encoding or decoding. We furthermore require Gen to be efficient computable.

- The *encoding algorithm* $\mathrm{Encode} : \mathcal{M} \to \mathcal{S}$ takes as input a message M and outputs a coding S. Since Encode may be randomised, we write this as $S \leftarrow \mathrm{Encode}_I(M)$. Encode is an efficiently computable, probabilistic algorithm satisfying the following properties:

  - left-total: for all $M \in \mathcal{M}$ there exists a $S \in \mathcal{S}$ such that $S \leftarrow \mathrm{Encode}(M)$

  - left-unique (injective): for all $M, M' \in \mathcal{M}$ and $S \in \mathcal{S}$ it holds that if $S \leftarrow \mathrm{Encode}(M)$ and $S \leftarrow \mathrm{Encode}(M')$ then $M = M'$

- The *decoding function* $\mathrm{Decode} : \mathcal{S} \to \{\mathcal{M}, \bot\}$ takes as input a coding S and outputs a message M or a special symbol $\bot$ denoting failure. We assume without loss of generality that Decode is deterministic and write this as $\mathrm{Decode}_I(S) = M$.

It is required that for every M it holds that

$$\mathrm{Decode}(\mathrm{Encode}(M)) = M \qquad (4.1)$$

Note that we required the parameter-generation and the encoding algorithm to be efficiently computable, but not the decoding algorithm. We give the explanation for this at the end of this subsection, when we have Human Decodable Encoding Schemes (Def. 4.36) defined.

A well known example for a coding is the Morse code [Ass04], which was developed by MORSE and expanded by VAIL. It was originally designed for MORSE's electric telegraph and broadly used for wireless communication at the end of the 19th century.

EXAMPLE 4.21. (International Morse Code)
The international Morse code is used to transmit text messages, thus the used characters are letters, digits, punctuation marks, and miscellaneous signs. The corresponding code words consist of five different symbols:

1. a short mark, called 'dot' or 'dit', noted '•', one unit long

2. a longer mark, called 'dash' or 'dah', noted '—', three units long

3. an intra-character gap (used between marks within a character), one unit long

4. a short gap (between letters), three units long

5. a medium gap (between words), seven units long

It is also possible to classify intra-character gaps as technical convention and thus include them in the parameter I and use only short and longer marks, and short and medium gaps as symbols.

Tab. 4.1 shows the codings for letters. The coding goes back to GERKE, who changed nearly half of the alphabet of the original Morse coding. A fairly comprehensive description may be found in Wikipedia [Wik13c], the official document stems from the ITU Radiocommunication Assembly [Ass04].

Table 4.1: International Morse Code (letters) from the ITU Radiocommunication Assembly [Ass04]

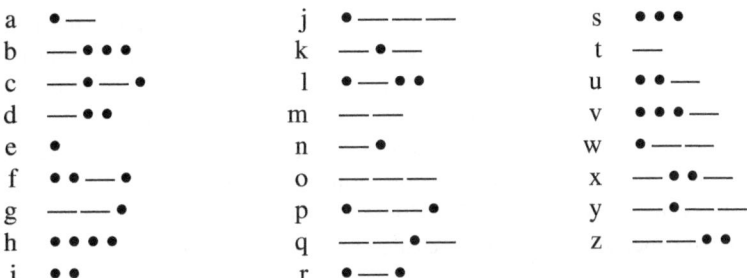

We proceed with the definition of deterministic and probabilistic encoding schemes.

Definition 4.22. (Deterministic Encoding Scheme) Let $(\mathsf{Gen}, \mathsf{Encode}, \mathsf{Decode})$ be an encoding scheme. We call an encoding scheme *deterministic* if its encoding algorithm Encode is deterministic.

Definition 4.23. (Probabilistic Encoding Scheme) Let $(\mathsf{Gen}, \mathsf{Encode}, \mathsf{Decode})$ be an encoding scheme. We call an encoding scheme *probabilistic* if its encoding algorithm Encode is probabilistic.

We continue with some definitions of useful properties for encoding schemes.

Definition 4.24. (Closed Encoding Scheme) Let $(\mathsf{Gen}, \mathsf{Encode}, \mathsf{Decode})$ be an encoding scheme. We call an encoding scheme *surjective* or *closed* if its encoding algorithm Encode is right-total (surjective): for all $S \in \mathcal{S}$ there exists a $M \in \mathcal{M}$ such that $S \leftarrow \mathsf{Encode}(M)$ and thus it holds that $\mathsf{Decode}(S) \neq \perp$.

Remark 4.25. Note that the definition of surjectivity slightly deviates from the original definition of surjectivity by BOURBAKI [Bou54, Gan59] which refers to deterministic functions only. Informally, for probabilistic functions one could imagine surjectivity that each value from the domain may cover one or more values from the codomain.

Formally, probabilistic functions may be modelled by the help of a random variable X. By giving X a certain distribution, it is possible to model the probabilistic encoding function $S \leftarrow \mathsf{Encode}(M)$ as deterministic function $\mathsf{Encode}'(M,X) = S$ and refer to surjectivity for deterministic functions. However, since the meaning of surjectivity is very much the same, we leave it at that and do not go further into details here.

The idea of closed encoding schemes is strongly related to the concept of meaningful and meaningless messages. Therefore, codings S with $\mathsf{Decode}(S) = \bot$ can be seen as meaningless and all others as meaningful. Then similar observations as in Sect. 4.1.2 apply and we will see later (cf. Sect. 4.2.2), that the notion of closed encoding schemes will become useful for encryption schemes when trying to determine if and how much information about the secret key is leaked by a ciphertext. If a coding is not closed, there exists at least one code word which cannot be the result of the corresponding encoding function.

To evaluate the amount of randomness of encoding schemes, we define the set of possible encodings for each message and its cardinality.

Definition 4.26. (Set of Possible Encodings) Let $(\mathsf{Gen}, \mathsf{Encode}, \mathsf{Decode})$ be an encoding scheme with message space $\mathcal{M}$ and let $M \in \mathcal{M}$ be a message. We denote the *set of possible encodings* for the message M with

$$\mathcal{S}_M := \{S \in \mathcal{S} | S \leftarrow \mathsf{Encode}(M)\}$$

We denote the *cardinality of* $\mathcal{S}_M$ with $|\mathcal{S}_M|$. We extend this definition also on sets. Let $\mathcal{M}' \subseteq \mathcal{M}$ then:

$$\mathcal{S}_{\mathcal{M}'} := \big\{S \in \mathcal{S} | S \leftarrow \mathsf{Encode}(M) \, . \, M \in \mathcal{M}'\big\}$$

Remark 4.27. It is possible to build an *equivalence relation* by grouping encodings in their respective sets of possible encodings:

$$S \equiv_{\mathsf{Decode}} S' \quad := \quad \mathsf{Decode}(S) = \mathsf{Decode}(S')$$

Which basically means that S and S' are both element of the same set of possible encodings $\mathcal{S}_M$.

It is easy to see that $\mathcal{S}_M$ equals $\mathcal{S}$ iff the encoding scheme is closed. Furthermore, in deterministic encoding schemes $|\mathcal{S}_M| = 1$ holds for all $M \in \mathcal{M}$, since each message cannot have different code words. In probabilistic encoding schemes there exists at least one message which has at least two different encodings. Therefore, the code words of probabilistic encoding schemes may have a quite different distribution than the messages.

This is the case when not all sets of possible encodings have the same cardinality or when the distribution among the set of all possible encodings is not uniform. This motivates the definition of distribution alike encoding schemes.

Definition 4.28. (Distribution Alike Encoding Scheme) Let $\mathcal{M}$ be the message space of the encoding scheme $(\mathsf{Gen}, \mathsf{Encode}, \mathsf{Decode})$. We call an encoding scheme *distribution alike* if

- for all messages $M_i \in \mathcal{M}$ of length i the cardinality of all sets of possible encodings $|\mathcal{S}_{M_i}|$ is equal:

$$\forall M_i, M_i' \in \mathcal{M}: \quad |\mathcal{S}_{M_i}| = |\mathcal{S}_{M_i'}|$$

- for each message $M_i \in \mathcal{M}_i$ all values of $\mathcal{S}_{M_i}$ are equally probable.

We then introduce the *cardinality of an encoding scheme* for messages of length i and denote it by $s_{\mathcal{M}_i}$.

Distribution alike schemes is ensure that if the message space follows a certain distribution, especially the uniform distribution, then the space of code words has also a very similar distribution (e.g. is also distributed uniformly). By 'very similar' we mean, that the distribution of the space of code word is, in general, the same as the message space, but we allow it to be flattened. Motivated by the definition of distribution alike encoding schemes, we prove two theorems.

Theorem 4.29. *Let* $(\mathsf{Gen}, \mathsf{Encode}, \mathsf{Decode})$ *be a distribution alike encoding scheme which maps messages* $M_i \in \mathcal{M}$ *to code words* $S_i \in \mathcal{S}$. *If a message* M_i *occurs with probability* p_i, *its encodings* $S_i \leftarrow \mathsf{Encode}(M_i)$ *occur with probability* $\frac{p_i}{s_{\mathcal{M}_i}}$.

PROOF. Since $(\mathsf{Gen}, \mathsf{Encode}, \mathsf{Decode})$ is distribution alike, there are $s_{\mathcal{M}_i}$ encodings for each message of length i, which occur for a given message with probability $\frac{1}{s_{\mathcal{M}_i}}$. Thus, the encoding of a message, which occurs with probability p_i, results in code words, which occur with probability $\frac{p_i}{s_{\mathcal{M}_i}}$. ∎

Theorem 4.30. *Deterministic encoding schemes are distribution alike with cardinality* $s_{\mathcal{M}} = 1$.

PROOF. In deterministic encoding schemes all messages have only one possible encoding. Thus, $s_{\mathcal{M}}$ equals one. ∎

Definition 4.31. (Homomorphic Encoding Scheme) Let $(\text{Gen}, \text{Encode}, \text{Decode})$ be an encoding scheme. We call an encoding scheme *homomorphic* if its encoding algorithm Encode is homomorphic: for all $M_i \in \mathcal{M} = (m_1, \ldots, m_i)$ it holds that:

$$\text{Encode}(m_1, \ldots, m_i) = \text{Encode}(m_1), \ldots, \text{Encode}(m_i) \qquad (4.2)$$

Remark 4.32. Note that the concatenation of characters is not necessarily the same, since $m_1, \ldots, m_i$ is a concatenation in the message space and $\text{Encode}(m_1), \ldots, \text{Encode}(m_i)$ is a concatenation in the coding space.

The next theorem shows that it is sufficient to require the encoding function of a homomorphic encoding scheme to be homomorphic, because the decoding function inherits this property.

Theorem 4.33. *Let* $(\text{Gen}, \text{Encode}, \text{Decode})$ *be a homomorphic encoding scheme. Then the decoding function* Decode *is also homomorphic.*

PROOF. The theorem follows from the substitution of Eq. 4.2 into Eq. 4.1 (see p. 96).

$$\begin{aligned}
\text{Decode}(s_1, \ldots, s_i) &= \text{Decode}(\text{Encode}(m_1, \ldots, m_i)) \\
&= m_1, \ldots, m_i \\
&= \text{Decode}(\text{Encode}(m_1)), \ldots, \text{Decode}(\text{Encode}(m_i)) \\
&= \text{Decode}(s_1), \ldots, \text{Decode}(s_i)
\end{aligned}$$

∎

If an encoding scheme is homomorphic, each character can be encoded independently from all other characters in the message. The already introduced Morse Code (cf. Tab. 4.1) is one example for a homomorphic encoding scheme, since each letter is encoded separately. Another example are *segmented displays*, such as the '7-Segment Display':

EXAMPLE 4.34. (7-Segment Display)
Fig. 4.3 shows the digits '0' to '9' displayed by a 7-segment display, which goes back to WOOD who invented a very similar 8-segment display [Woo08] in 1908. By varying uppercase and lowercase it is also possible to display the letters 'A' to 'F' on a 7-segment display. In general, the segments are (alphabetically) numbered clockwise as shown in Fig. 4.4.

Each digit can be displayed by switching the appropriate individual segments 'on' and 'off'. Therefore each representation of a symbol needs seven bits and thus the state of a 7-segment display can be encoded in one byte. Assumed 0 represents 'off' and 1 represents 'on', Tab. 4.2 shows the encoding function as well as the most popular bit encodings ('gfedcba' and 'abcdefg').

Figure 4.3: The Digits of the Seven-Segment Display

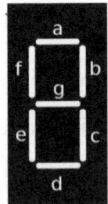

Figure 4.4: Seven-Segment Display with Segment Numbering According to Hou and
Glaser [HG05]

Table 4.2: Hexadecimal Encodings for Displaying Digits in a 7-Segment Display after
Ciarcia [Cia81], and Hou and Glaser [HG05], see also Fig. 4.4

digit	a	b	c	d	e	f	g	abcdefg	gfedcba
0	on	on	on	on	on	on	off	0x7E	0x3F
1	off	on	on	off	off	off	off	0x30	0x06
2	on	on	off	on	on	off	on	0x6D	0x5B
3	on	on	on	on	off	off	on	0x79	0x4F
4	off	on	on	off	off	on	on	0x33	0x66
5	on	off	on	on	off	on	on	0x5B	0x6D
6	on	off	on	on	on	on	on	0x5F	0x7D
7	on	on	on	off	off	off	off	0x70	0x07
8	on	on	on	on	on	on	on	0x7F	0x7F
9	on	on	on	on	off	on	on	0x7B	0x6F

Depending on the preferred alphabet and the desired quality of the produced
symbols, there are other segment displays, such as:

9-segment displays [HMC05], which have an additional segment inside each loop
of the 8, and 14- and 16-segment displays, which allow to render the latin alphabet
in more detail or to display Thai numerals [Lau91] and Persian characters [FNB89].

We realise that homomorphic encoding schemes may be easily displayed on seg-mented displays and come back to segmented displays in Sect. 4.2.2.

Furthermore, if an encoding scheme is homomorphic, it is sufficient to show that the encodings for all characters are distribution alike to conclude that the encoding scheme is distribution alike for all $M \in \Omega$ as we formalise by the next theorem.

Theorem 4.35. *A homomorphic encoding scheme is distribution alike iff:*

- *for all characters* $m \in \Omega$ *the cardinality of all sets of possible encodings* $|S_m|$ *is equal:*

$$\forall m, m' \in \Omega : \quad |S_m| = |S_{m'}|$$

- *for each character* $m \in \Omega$ *all values of* S_m *are equally probable.*

PROOF. We need to show both implications and start with the trivial one:
"General distribution alike" $\Rightarrow$ "Homomorphic, distribution alike"

- The encoding scheme is distribution alike, thus for all messages M_i of length i the cardinality of all sets of possible encodings $|S_{M_i}|$ is equal and in particular for messages M_1 of length 1, the characters $m \in \Omega$.

- The same holds for the probability with which each message occurs. By defini-tion, for each message $M_i \in \mathcal{M}_i$ all values in S_{M_i} are equally probable. Then this especially holds for messages M_1 of length 1, the characters.

The implication of the opposite direction:
"General distribution alike" $\Leftarrow$ "Homomorphic, distribution alike"

- We show the first part by mathematical induction.

  Basic Step: Under the assumption that for all characters $m \in \Omega$ the cardinality of all sets of possible encodings $|S_m|$ is equal, it is obvious that for all messages $M_1 \in \mathcal{M}$ of length 1 the cardinality of all sets of possible encodings $|S_{M_1}|$ is equal.

  Inductive step: Given a message $M_n \in \mathcal{M}$ of length n, the cardinality of all sets of possible encodings is $|S_{M_n}|$. Since Encode is homomorphic, we can derive all messages M_{n+1} of length $n+1$ by concatenation:

$$\mathsf{Encode}(M_{n+1}) = \mathsf{Encode}(M_n, M_1) = \mathsf{Encode}(M_n), \mathsf{Encode}(M_1)$$

Since the encodings of $\mathsf{Encode}(M_n)$ and $\mathsf{Encode}(M_1)$ may be chosen inde-pendently, the cardinality of all sets of possible encodings for messages of length $n+1$ is $|S_{M_{n+1}}| = |S_{M_n}| * |S_{M_1}|$. Therefore, all messages of length $n+1$ share the same cardinality of all sets of possible encodings.

- The proof that all possible encodings of messages $M_i \in \mathcal{M}_i$ occur with the same probability is right along the line of the proof above.

Thus, the equivalence of Th. 4.35 is shown. ∎

We continue with the definition of human decodable encoding schemes.

Definition 4.36. (Human Decodable Encoding Scheme) Let $(Gen, Encode, Decode)$ be an encoding scheme. We call an encoding scheme *human decodable* if the decoding algorithm Decode is feasible for most human beings.

The definition is an analogy to part (A) of the definition of CAPTCHAs (cf. Chap. 3) from AHN [vABHL03, p. 294]: "A CAPTCHA is a program that can generate and grade tests that: (A) most humans can pass, but (B) current computer programs can't pass". However, one should mention that it might be hard to decide – sometimes even on an individual basis – which algorithms are "feasible for human beings". Obviously, the used algorithm has to be chosen adequately with the target group in mind.

The definition of human decodable encoding schemes also explains why we did not require the decoding algorithm in Def. 4.20 to be efficiently computable: If we would require this property, our definition of encoding schemes would not cover CAPTCHAs, which are clearly human decodable. By choosing the definition this way, the following subsets arise:

Captcha $\subset$ Human Decodable Encoding Scheme $\subset$ Encoding Scheme

4.1.4 Human Decipherable Encryption Scheme

The next definition introduces human decipherable encryption schemes, which are a generalisation of visual encryption schemes. Visual encryption schemes allow to reconstruct concealed images without any cryptographic computation (cf. Sect. 4.2). Our definition of human decipherable encryption is not restricted to visual codings and thus covers also all other kinds of codings which do not require cryptographic computation, for example a sound based encoding could be used – similar to the already known audio CAPTCHAs [BC09, SG10, STG09]. The encryption would then be realised by overlaying a second audio track (the key) which could be reversed (decrypted) by overlaying inverse amplitudes of the same frequency. Furthermore, our definition separates encoding/decoding of a message from encrypting/decrypting it, which, as already stated, is useful when designing schemes which allow to reuse the key a certain number of times.

Definition 4.37. (Human Decipherable Encryption Scheme) Let $M \in \mathcal{M}$ be a message, let $S \in \mathcal{S}$ be a coding, let $C \in \mathcal{C}$ be a ciphertext, let $K \in \mathcal{K}$ be a key, let $n \in \mathbb{N}$ be a security parameter, and let I be some parameters. A *human decipherable encryption scheme* $\mathcal{HE}$ is a tuple of algorithms $(\mathsf{HGen}, \mathsf{HEnc}, \mathsf{HDec})$ such that:

- The *key and parameter generation algorithm* HGen takes as input a security parameter 1^n and outputs a parameter I and a key K with $I \leftarrow \mathsf{Gen}(1^n)$ and $K \leftarrow \mathsf{GenKey}(1^n)$ for Gen and GenKey defined below. We write this as

$$(I, K) \leftarrow \mathsf{HGen}(1^n) = (\mathsf{Gen}(1^n), \mathsf{GenKey}(1^n))$$

- The *human decipherable encryption algorithm* HEnc takes as input a message M and outputs a ciphertext C. $\mathsf{HEnc}_{I,K}$ is a function composition of an encryption function Enc_K and an encoding function Encode_I which are both defined below. We write this as

$$C \leftarrow \mathsf{HEnc}_{I,K}(M) = \mathsf{Enc}_K(\mathsf{Encode}_I(M))$$

- The *human decipherable decryption algorithm* HDec takes as input a ciphertext C and outputs a message M or a special symbol $\perp$ denoting failure. $\mathsf{HDec}_{I,K}$ is a function composition of a decoding function Decode_I and an decryption function Dec_K which are defined below. We write this as

$$M := \mathsf{HDec}_{I,K}(C) = \mathsf{Decode}_I(\mathsf{Dec}_K(C))$$

The algorithms $\mathsf{Gen}, \mathsf{Encode}, \mathsf{Decode}, \mathsf{GenKey}, \mathsf{Enc}, \mathsf{Dec}$ are chosen such that:

- $(\mathsf{Gen}, \mathsf{Encode}, \mathsf{Decode})$ is an encoding scheme as in Def. 4.20.

- $(\mathsf{GenKey}, \mathsf{Enc}, \mathsf{Dec})$ is a symmetric encryption scheme as in Def. 2.40 with the relaxation that we do not require the decryption algorithm Dec to run in polynomial time.

We furthermore require that the function composition $\mathsf{HDec}_{I,K}(C)$ is feasible for most human beings.

It follows from the definition of the functions that for every n, every I output by $\mathsf{Gen}(1^n)$, every K output by $\mathsf{GenKey}(1^n)$, and every $M \in \mathcal{M}$, it holds that

$$\mathsf{HDec}_{I,K}(\mathsf{HEnc}_{I,K}(M)) = \mathsf{Decode}_I(\mathsf{Dec}_K(\mathsf{Enc}_K(\mathsf{Encode}_I(M)))) = M$$

As mentioned, the definition of human decipherable encryption schemes separates encoding/decoding algorithms and encryption/decryption algorithms. The idea behind the separation is that the decryption algorithm is, in general, quite simple, mainly because it is not feasible for humans to do complex calculations with the ciphertext and the key. This also explains why – analogous to the decoding algorithm in Def. 4.20 – we do not require the decryption algorithm to run in polynomial time[1]: there may be algorithms which are feasible for humans but can not efficiently be solved by computers. However, even though we do not require it, the decryption algorithm will often run in polynomial time. Moreover, due to its simplicity it will often cause the encryption algorithm to be deterministic, too. For example, visual cryptography (cf. Sect. 4.2) makes use of the logical biconditional function (cf. Def. 4.61). As a consequence, apart from key and parameter generation, all randomisation has to be part of the encoding algorithm, while it's corresponding decoding algorithm is based on human recognition of patterns. One example would be the recognition of a sequence of letters or words on a noisy background – as shown in Fig. 4.5 in the next section.

We proceed with properties of human decipherable encryption schemes, for example whether they are probabilistic, homomorphic or distribution alike. It is easy to see that their properties are heavily based on the properties of encoding schemes. Thus the question, whether a human decipherable encryption scheme owns a particular property, will mainly rely on the underlying encoding/decoding function pair. However, since the encryption/decryption functions are not required to preserve the properties in a way so that the human decipherable encryption schemes inherits the properties from the underlying encoding scheme, we need to define them also for human decipherable encryption schemes.

We now extend Def. 4.37 to capture the definition of deterministic and probabilistic human decipherable encryption schemes.

Definition 4.38. (Deterministic Human Decipherable Encryption Scheme) Let $\mathcal{HE}$ be a human decipherable encryption scheme with the tuple of algorithms (HGen, HEnc, HDec). We denote $\mathcal{HE}$ as *deterministic* if its encryption algorithm HEnc is deterministic.

Definition 4.39. (Probabilistic Human Decipherable Encryption Scheme) Let $\mathcal{HE}$ be a human decipherable encryption scheme with the tuple of algorithms (HGen, HEnc, HDec). We denote $\mathcal{HE}$ as *probabilistic* if its encryption algorithm HEnc is probabilistic.

Similar to the abovementioned set of possible encodings, we define the set of possible encryptions of a message for a given key.

---

[1]Note that this is the only property of human decipherable encryption schemes which does not fulfil Def. 2.40.

Definition 4.40. (Set of Possible Encryptions) Let $\mathcal{HE}$ be a human decipherable encryption scheme, let $M \in \mathcal{M}$ be a message of the human decipherable encryption scheme's message space, and let $K \in \mathcal{K}$ an appropriate key. We denote the *set of possible encryptions* for the message M with key K with

$$\mathcal{C}_{K,M} := \{C \in \mathcal{C} | C \leftarrow HEnc_K(M)\}$$

and we denote the *cardinality of* $\mathcal{C}_{K,M}$ with $|\mathcal{C}_{K,M}|$.

We extend this definition also on sets of keys and messages. Let $\mathcal{K}' \subseteq \mathcal{K}$ and $\mathcal{M}' \subseteq \mathcal{M}$ then:

$$\mathcal{C}_{\mathcal{K}',M} := \left\{C \in \mathcal{C} | C \leftarrow HEnc_K(M) . K \in \mathcal{K}'\right\}$$
$$\mathcal{C}_{K,\mathcal{M}'} := \left\{C \in \mathcal{C} | C \leftarrow HEnc_K(M) . M \in \mathcal{M}'\right\}$$
$$\mathcal{C}_{\mathcal{K}',\mathcal{M}'} := \left\{C \in \mathcal{C} | C \leftarrow HEnc_K(M) . K \in \mathcal{K}', M \in \mathcal{M}'\right\}$$

Remark 4.41. It is also possible to build an *equivalence relation* by grouping encryptions in their sets of possible encryptions regarding a certain key K.

$$C \equiv_{HDec_K} C' \quad := \quad HDec_K(C) = HDec_K(C')$$

Which basically means that C and C' are both elements of the same set of possible encryptions $\mathcal{C}_{K,M}$.

Analogously to the definition of the set of possible encodings, $|\mathcal{C}_{K,M}| = 1$ holds in deterministic human decipherable encryption schemes for all $M \in \mathcal{M}, K \in \mathcal{K}$, since a message cannot have different encryptions. In probabilistic encoding schemes, there exists at least one message which has at least two different encryptions. Therefore, the encryptions of probabilistic encoding schemes may have a quite different distribution than the underlying messages. For example, if not all sets of possible encryptions have the same cardinality or if the distribution among the set of all possible encryptions is not uniform. This motivates the definition of distribution alike human decipherable encryption schemes.

Definition 4.42. (Distribution Alike) Let $\mathcal{HE}$ be a human decipherable encryption scheme with the tuple of algorithms $(HGen, HEnc, HDec)$ with message space $\mathcal{M}$ and key space $\mathcal{K}$. We denote $\mathcal{HE}$ as *distribution alike* if

- for all keys $K \in \mathcal{K}$ and for all messages $M_i \in \mathcal{M}$ of length i the cardinality of all sets of possible human decipherable encryptions $|\mathcal{C}_{K,M_i}|$ is equal:

$$\forall K \in \mathcal{K} \quad \forall M_i, M_i' \in \mathcal{M}: \qquad |\mathcal{C}_{K,M_i}| = |\mathcal{C}_{K,M_i'}|$$

- for each message $M_i \in \mathcal{M}_i$ all values of $\mathcal{C}_{K,M_i}$ are equally probable.

We then introduce the *cardinality of an human decipherable encryption scheme* for messages of length i and denote it by $c_{\mathcal{M}_i}$.

Distribution alike schemes ensure that if the message space follows a certain distribution, especially the uniform distribution, then the space of ciphertexts is also similarly distributed. The uniform distribution is particularly important since a uniformly distributed message space means that all messages are a priori equiprobable and thus the adversary has no information which messages are likely to be sent (cf. Sect. 5.3). If the ciphertext space follows another distribution, then an adversary might be able to draw some conclusion on the underlying messages. Of course, it would be desirable to achieve a uniform distribution of the ciphertext space also for other distributions of the message space. However, non-uniformly distributed message spaces offer the adversary additional information on the messages available and should be avoided. Thus we consider a uniformly distributed message space as the most interesting case.

Motivated by the definition of distribution alike encoding schemes, we prove three theorems.

Theorem 4.43. *Let* $(\mathsf{HGen}, \mathsf{HEnc}, \mathsf{HDec})$ *be a distribution alike human decipherable encryption scheme which maps messages* $M_i \in \mathcal{M}$ *to ciphertexts* $C_i \in \mathcal{C}$. *If a message* M_i *occurs with probability* p_i, *its encryptions* $C_i \leftarrow \mathsf{HEnc}(M_i)$ *occur with probability* $\frac{p_i}{c_{\mathcal{M}_i}}$.

PROOF. Since $(\mathsf{HGen}, \mathsf{HEnc}, \mathsf{HDec})$ is distribution alike, there are $c_{\mathcal{M}_i}$ encryptions for each message of length i, which occur for a given message with probability $\frac{1}{c_{\mathcal{M}_i}}$. Thus, the encryption of a message, which occurs with probability p_i, results in ciphertexts, which occur with probability $\frac{p_i}{c_{\mathcal{M}_i}}$. ∎

Theorem 4.44. *Deterministic encryption schemes are distribution alike with cardinality* $c_{\mathcal{M}} = 1$.

PROOF. In deterministic human decipherable encryption schemes all messages have only one possible encryption. Thus, $c_{\mathcal{M}}$ equals one. ∎

Definition 4.45. (Segment-based Human Decipherable Encryption Scheme)
Let $\mathcal{HE}$ be a human decipherable encryption scheme with the tuple of algorithms $(\mathsf{HGen}, \mathsf{HEnc}, \mathsf{HDec})$, message space $\mathcal{M}$, and key space $\mathcal{K}$. Let $K \in \mathcal{K}$ be a key consisting of the key symbols $k_1, \ldots, k_i$ and let $M \in \mathcal{M}$ be a message consisting of the message symbols $m_1, \ldots, m_i$. We denote $\mathcal{HE}$ as *segment-based human*

decipherable encryption scheme if its human decipherable encryption algorithm HEnc has the following property:

$$\forall K \in \mathcal{K}. \forall M \in \mathcal{M} \qquad HEnc_{k_1,\ldots,k_i}(m_1,\ldots,m_i) = HEnc_{k_1}(m_1),\ldots,HEnc_{k_i}(m_i)$$

Remark 4.46. Basically the described property is very similar to homomorphism. Each message symbol is first encoded and then encrypted with a part of the key – independently of the other message symbols. However, since each encryption $HEnc_{k_i}(m_i)$ on the right side of the equation requires knowledge about it's position to use the appropriate part of the key, strictly speaking the encryptions are not independent.

The name of the definition above is derived from the notion of segment-based visual cryptography, which was given by BORCHERT in 2007. He described a variation of visual cryptography, where – instead of pixels – segments of a 7-segment display were encrypted [Bor07] (cf. Sect. 4.2.2).

Remark 4.47. Note that the notion of segment-based encryption can easily be extended to suit multiple symbols by adjusting the spaces' alphabets or by extending the definition to match arbitrary subsets of key, message and ciphertext.

Theorem 4.48. *Let $\mathcal{HE}$ be a segment-based human decipherable encryption scheme with the tuple of algorithms* (HGen, HEnc, HDec), *message space $\mathcal{M}$, and cipher space $\mathcal{C}$. Let $K \in \mathcal{K}$ be a key consisting of the key symbols $k_1,\ldots,k_i$ and let $C \in \mathcal{C}$ be a ciphertext consisting of the ciphertext symbols $c_1,\ldots,c_i$. Then the decoding of decryptions HDec has also the following property:*

$$\forall K \in \mathcal{K}. \forall C \in \mathcal{C} \qquad HDec_{k_1,\ldots,k_i}(c_1,\ldots,c_i) = HDec_{k_1}(c_1),\ldots,HDec_{k_i}(c_i)$$

Proof. The proof is analogous to the proof of Th. 4.33.   ☐

Theorem 4.49. *A segment-based human decodable encryption scheme is distribution alike iff:*

- *for all characters $m \in \Sigma$ the cardinality of all sets of possible encryptions $|\mathcal{C}_m|$ is equal:*
$$\forall m, m' \in \Sigma: \quad |\mathcal{C}_m| = |\mathcal{C}_{m'}|$$

- *for each character $m \in \Sigma$ all values of $\mathcal{C}_m$ are equally probable.*

Proof. The proof follows the line of the proof of Th. 4.35   ☐

Another important property of human decipherable encryption schemes is whether an attacker is able to exclude some keys from the set of possibly used keys by observing ciphertext(s). Obviously, this is the case if there exists at least one ciphertext C and at least one key K for which $HDec_K(C) = \perp$ holds. Thus, by observing ciphertext C, an adversary is able to exclude the key K from the set of possibly used keys (cf. Sect. 4.1.2).

Definition 4.50. (Closed Human Decipherable Encryption Scheme) Let $\mathcal{HE}$ be a human decipherable encryption scheme with the tuple of algorithms $(HGen, HEnc, HDec)$ and the corresponding message space $\mathcal{M}$ and ciphertext space $\mathcal{C}$. We denote $\mathcal{HE}$ as *closed* if for all $K \in \mathcal{K}$ $\mathcal{C}_{K,\mathcal{M}} = \mathcal{C}$ holds:

$$\forall K \in \mathcal{K} \quad \mathcal{C}_{K,\mathcal{M}} := \{C \in \mathcal{C} | C \leftarrow HEnc_K(M) . M \in \mathcal{M}\} \quad = \quad \mathcal{C}$$

This means that each $K \in \mathcal{K}$ has to spawn the whole ciphertext space and thus an equivalent condition would be that $HDec$ never equals $\perp$ for any key $K \in \mathcal{K}$:

$$\forall K \in \mathcal{K} \, \forall C \in \mathcal{C} . HDec_K(C) \neq \perp$$

A requirement for a closed human decipherable encryption schemes is that the used encoding function is surjective. Otherwise, there would exist some codings S for which $Decode(S) = \perp$ and thus $HDec_K(Enc_K(S))$ would also result in $\perp$. This would allow an attacker to exclude all keys for a given ciphertext whose decryption Dec would result in symbols which are not in the range of the encoding function Encode (cf. Sect. 4.2.4).

Note that the notion of closed human decipherable encryption schemes is generally the same as SHANNON's notion of closed secrecy systems [Sha49, p. 664], although he only considers deterministic encryption schemes.

We continue with the notion of (strong) ideal systems for probabilistic encryption schemes.

Ideal systems for HDES

SHANNON's definition of a *(strong) ideal system* does not explicitly mention that the underlying encryption scheme has to be deterministic. To keep the definition, we have to determine its meaning for probabilistic encryption schemes.

The meaning of ideal secrecy systems stays the same, saying that an adversary should not be able to uniquely determine the used key by observing ciphertexts. The more interesting cases are strong ideal systems. As SHANNON shows, for deterministic encryption schemes *"if all letters are equally likely and independent any closed cipher is strongly ideal"* [Sha49, p. 700]. However, for probabilistic encryption schemes the property of closeness is only necessary but not sufficient to be strongly ideal. It is also necessary that an adversary is not able to gain information from the distribution of ciphertexts which in turn results from the distribution of the probabilistic encryption scheme. She is not able to do so if:

- She has no information about the distribution of the plaintexts/messages and thus is not able to link observations of the ciphertext back to the plaintext.

- The ciphertexts are uniformly distributed in the ciphertext space. If the human decipherable encryption system is distribution alike and all letters of the plaintext are equally likely and independent, the situation reflects the situation SHANNON observed. In general, if the human decipherable encryption system outputs uniformly distributed ciphertexts, an adversary has no point of attack even if the distribution of plaintexts is not uniform and she knows them. Let's regard a plaintext distribution, where one letter appears twice as often than all other letters, as an example. If the encryption system is homomorphic and there are twice as many ciphertexts for this letter than for all other letters, and adversary will not be able to identify the specific letter looking at the distribution of ciphertexts.

Among the number of disadvantages SHANNON states, the most important for human decipherable encryption systems is that the system must be closely matched to the according plaintexts which requires an extensive study of the structure of the messages by the designer. Also any change in the statistical structure of the sent messages may render the system vulnerable to analysis. Sect. 5.3.2 gives some examples how side information about the sent messages can be used to attack the system and retrieve the key.

Sample-or-Random Ciphertext Only Indistinguishability

As we will see in following sections (cf. Sect. 5.3.3 and Sect. 5.5.3), chosen-plaintext attacks (cf. Sect. 2.2.2) are often a too strong security model to rate the security of human decipherable encryption schemes. Furthermore, chosen-plaintext attacks do not reflect the capability of the adversary in all cases. Thus, the idea of *sample-or-random ciphertext only indistinguishability* (SOR − CO) is adapted from real-or-random indistinguishability, but we do not provide the adversary with an encryption oracle. Since the adversary must be capable of analysing ciphertexts, we provide a ciphertext-only oracle which returns ciphertexts with 'a certain structure' of the underlying plaintexts. The adversary is given information on the structure of the encryptions and may query a structure-or-random oracle which answers either the encryptions of a 'sample set of messages' or encryptions of an equal-sized set of randomly chosen characters of the same length than the messages. For each run of the experiment the oracle's behaviour is arbitrary but fixed. The adversary's task is to determine the oracle's operating mode.

The encryption scheme is considered to be secure in the sense of sample-or-random indistinguishability under ciphertext-only attacks if the adversary cannot gain a significant advantage. To remain the consistent, we require the adversary to be polynomial bound, even though the security parameter of the encryption scheme may be small and non-polynomial attacks may be feasible. This is especially the case if the encryption scheme is segment-based and the adversary would be able to regard all characters of the plaintext independently. Furthermore, similar to BELLARE et al. [BDJR97], we also take the number of queries to the oracle into account which allows us statements on reusing the key for a certain amount of ciphertexts and reflects a periodic change of the key. The 'certain structure of the underlying plaintexts' is modelled by the function $\mathsf{sample}_{\mathsf{struct}}$ which returns a sample set of plaintexts for each invocation.

Definition 4.51. (SOR − CO) Let $\Pi = (\mathsf{HGen}, \mathsf{HEnc}, \mathsf{HDec})$ be a human decipherable encryption scheme as in Def. 4.37 and $b \in \{0, 1\}$. Let A be an adversary with access to the *sample-or-random oracle* $\mathcal{O}_{\mathcal{SR}}(b)$. Let $\mathsf{sample}_{\mathsf{struct}}$ be a function which returns a finite set of sample plaintexts following an underlying structure struct for each invocation.

The sample-or-random oracle $\mathcal{O}_{\mathcal{SR}}(b)$ takes no input and depending on b returns either a set of encryptions $\mathsf{Enc}(m_i)$ of the messages $(m_0, \ldots, m_j) \leftarrow \mathsf{sample}_{\mathsf{struct}}$ given by $\mathsf{sample}_{\mathsf{struct}}$ (if $b = 0$) or an encryption $\mathsf{Enc}(r_i)$ of an equal-size set of uniformly at random chosen strings r_i with the same length than the corresponding messages m_i (if $b = 1$).

For the security parameter $n \in \mathbb{N}$ the adversary's success probability is

$$\mathbf{Adv}_{A,\Pi}^{sor-co}(n) \stackrel{\mathrm{def}}{=} \Pr[\mathbf{Exp}_{A,\Pi}^{sor-co-1}(n) = 1] - \Pr[\mathbf{Exp}_{A,\Pi}^{sor-co-0}(n) = 1]$$

where the experiment $\mathbf{Exp}_{A,\Pi}^{sor-co-b}(n) = b'$ for $b \in \{0, 1\}$ is given as follows:

k	$\leftarrow$	$\mathsf{GenKey}(1^n)$	key-generation
b	$\in_R$	$\{0, 1\}$	random selection of b
b'	$\leftarrow$	$A^{\mathcal{O}_{\mathcal{SR}}}(\mathsf{struct})$	adversary tries to determine b'

If the success probability $\mathbf{Adv}_{A,\Pi}^{sor-co}(n)$ of a polynomial bound adversary is negligible in n (under the restriction that A queries the sample-or-random oracle $\mathcal{O}_{\mathcal{SR}}$ at most q times), we say the encryption scheme Π is *secure in the sense of* SOR − CO *given the sample structure* struct (if the adversary is restricted to at most q queries to the sample-or-random oracle).

Remark 4.52. Since the adversary is unable to influence the sample structure struct, the value of the $SOR - CO$ security model strongly depends on an appropriate choice of struct. If struct is unreasonable close to random strings, the resulting conclusion that an encryption scheme is secure given the sample structure struct is more likely based on the adversary's inability to distinguish the distributions than on the encryption scheme's property to hide the underlying plaintexts' structure.

Relation to $ROR - CPA$ We claim that $SOR - CO$ has a different notion of security than $ROR - CPA$. We prove this by showing that, on the one hand, $ROR - CPA$ (see Def. 2.49) is at least as strong as $SOR - CO$. This is intuitively clear, since having a real-or-random oracle available allows to simulate a sample-or-random oracle. On the other hand, given an encryption scheme Π secure in the sense of $SOR - CO$ we show how to construct an encryption scheme Π, which is still secure in the sense of $SOR - CO$, but not in the sense of $ROR - CPA$.

Corollary 4.53. $[ROR - CPA \Rightarrow SOR - CO]$ *If Π is an encryption scheme, which is secure in the sense of $ROR - CPA$, then Π is secure in the sense of $SOR - CO$.*

PROOF. Let $\mathfrak{m}$ be a plaintext message from the encryption system's plaintext space $\mathcal{M}$ and $\mathsf{sample}_{\mathsf{struct}}$ be the sample function which returns a set $(\mathfrak{m}_0, \ldots, \mathfrak{m}_j)$ of sample plaintexts following an underlying structure struct for each invocation of the sample-or-random oracle $\mathcal{O}_{\mathcal{SR}}(b)$. It is easy to see that a real-or-random oracle $\mathcal{O}_{\mathcal{RR}}(\cdot, b)$ is able to simulate the sample-or-random oracle $\mathcal{O}_{\mathcal{SR}}(b)$ by asking for plaintexts that follow the underlying structure struct for each invocation. The adversary can accomplish this simply by producing a sample of messages $(\mathfrak{m}_0, \ldots, \mathfrak{m}_j) \leftarrow \mathsf{sample}_{\mathsf{struct}}$ and then asking $\mathcal{O}_{\mathcal{RR}}(\cdot, b)$ for their encryption. Thus, security in the sense of $ROR - CPA$ can be seen as security in the sense of $SOR - CO$ with an additional real-or-random oracle available.   ∎

The more challenging part is to show that if there exist encryption schemes which are secure in the sense of $SOR - CO$ that these are not automatically secure in the sense of $ROR - CPA$. The difference between both security models is intuitively plausible. For the formal proof, we need to exploit the fact that the adversaries considered by $SOR - CO$ are not able to choose the plaintexts for encryption. We show two possibilities to embed information to distinguish the states of the oracle which may easily be chosen if the adversary selects the queries to the oracle but only occur with negligible probability given the sample structure struct.

We assume there is an encryption scheme $\Pi = (\mathsf{GenKey}, \mathsf{Enc}, \mathsf{Dec})$ which is secure in the sense of $SOR - CO$. Then, based on Π, we construct an encryption scheme $\Pi' = (\mathsf{GenKey}', \mathsf{Enc}', \mathsf{Dec}')$ which is also secure in the sense of $SOR - CO$, but can easily be broken in the sense of $ROR - CPA$.

Before we formally describe the construction of Π' we shortly describe the notion of the construction. Based on the encryption algorithm Enc, we construct an encryption algorithm Enc$'$ such that it returns a special character if asked to encrypt a particular message m'. This gives the adversary an advantage when asking the random-or-real oracle. To ensure that Π' is still secure in the sense of SOR $-$ CO, we have to take care that the message m' only occurs very rarely if strings are chosen either randomly or by the sample structure struct. Otherwise an adversary may get an additional advantage to attack the encryption scheme which renders it insecure in the sense of SOR $-$ CO. We illustrate the idea by regarding two sample structures which we will use in Sect. 5.3.3. We assume, that our alphabet Γ consists of $n + 1$ characters and for simplicity assume they are represented by numbers from 0 to n.

Changing one Ciphertext   We assume $\Pi = (\mathsf{GenKey}, \mathsf{Enc}, \mathsf{Dec})$ is secure in the sense of SOR $-$ CO given a sample structure composed of one plaintext message m containing each character c_i of the alphabet Γ once:

$$\mathsf{sample}_1 \in_R \{m \mid m = m_0, m_1, \ldots, m_n \wedge \forall i, j \text{ with } 0 \leqslant i, j \leqslant n . \exists m_i = c_j\}$$

Then we regard the following algorithms for $\Pi' = (\mathsf{GenKey}', \mathsf{Enc}', \mathsf{Dec}')$

Algorithm $\mathsf{GenKey}'(1^n)$:	Algorithm $\mathsf{Enc}'_k(m)$:	Algorithm $\mathsf{Dec}'_k(c)$:
$\quad k \leftarrow \mathsf{GenKey}(1^n)$	$\quad$ if $m = 0 \ldots 0$	$\quad$ if $c = \sharp$
$\quad$ return k	$\quad\quad$ then $c := \sharp$	$\quad\quad$ then $m := 0 \ldots 0$
	$\quad$ else	$\quad$ else
	$\quad\quad\quad c \leftarrow \mathsf{Enc}_k(m)$	$\quad\quad\quad m := \mathsf{Dec}_k(c)$
	$\quad$ return c	$\quad$ return m

It is easy to see, that Π' works almost exactly like Π except when the encryption function is invoked with a string consisting of $n + 1$ zeros. Then instead of the normal encryption a special symbol is returned. While this does almost not effect the security in the sense of SOR $-$ CO, an adversary of the ROR $-$ CPA security model is able to explicitly ask the encryption oracle for that string and determine the oracle's operation mode. It remains to show the two emerging lemmas:

Lemma 4.54. $\Pi' = (\mathsf{GenKey}', \mathsf{Enc}', \mathsf{Dec}')$ *is not secure in the sense of* ROR $-$ CPA.

PROOF. This can easily be shown by exploiting the built-in weakness of Π'. We first regard the following strategy. The adversary asks the oracle for the encryption of a string consisting of $n + 1$ zeros. If the special symbol '$\sharp$' is returned she concludes that the oracle is in 'real mode' otherwise she concludes it encrypts randomly drawn strings. In the case of not seeing '$\sharp$', the adversary can be sure to be right, because when the oracle operates in 'real mode' and is given $n+1$ zeros, it returns no other encryption but the special symbol. However, if the oracle outputs the special symbol, it may nevertheless operate in random mode with a probability of $\frac{1}{(n+1)^{n+1}}$ since the alphabet consists of $n+1$ different characters and the length of the randomly drawn string is $n+1$. Thus, the resulting probabilities lead to the adversary's advantage

$$\mathbf{Adv}_{A_{cpa},\Pi'}^{ror-cpa}(n) = \Pr[\mathbf{Exp}_{A_{cpa},\Pi'}^{ror-cpa-1}(n) = 1] \quad - \Pr[\mathbf{Exp}_{A_{cpa},\Pi'}^{ror-cpa-0}(n) = 1]$$

$$= 1 - \frac{1}{(n+1)^{n+1}} \quad\quad\quad - 0$$

which is obviously not negligible. Thus, $\Pi' = (\mathsf{GenKey}', \mathsf{Enc}', \mathsf{Dec}')$ is not secure in the sense of $ROR - CPA$. ∎

But we still need to show, that this weakness preserves security in the sense of $SOR - CO$.

Lemma 4.55. $\Pi' = (\mathsf{GenKey}', \mathsf{Enc}', \mathsf{Dec}')$ *is secure in the sense of* $SOR - CO$ *given the sample structure* sample_1.

PROOF. When the oracle is in 'sample mode' the modification does not come to play, since the string consisting of $n+1$ zeros is not part of the sample. Otherwise, we already concluded that the probability that a 'random mode' oracle outputs the special symbol '♯' is $\frac{1}{(n+1)^{n+1}}$. That means when the oracle is in 'random mode', an adversary has an additional chance of getting the special symbol answered. However, since the probability is negligible and the adversary is polynomially limited, her additional advantage $Adv_\sharp$ is negligible which leads to the estimation:

$$\mathbf{Adv}_{A,\Pi'}^{sor-co}(n) = \Pr[\mathbf{Exp}_{A,\Pi'}^{sor-co-1}(n) = 1] \quad\quad - \Pr[\mathbf{Exp}_{A,\Pi'}^{sor-co-0}(n) = 1]$$

$$\leqslant \Pr[\mathbf{Exp}_{A,\Pi}^{sor-co-1}(n) = 1] + Adv_\sharp \quad - \Pr[\mathbf{Exp}_{A,\Pi}^{sor-co-0}(n) = 1]$$

$$= \mathbf{Adv}_{A,\Pi}^{sor-co}(n) + Adv_\sharp$$

Due to the assumption that Π is secure in the sense of $SOR - CO$ given the sample structure sample_1, $\mathbf{Adv}_{A,\Pi}^{sor-co}(n)$ is negligible and so is $Adv_\sharp$. Therefore, $\mathbf{Adv}_{A,\Pi'}^{sor-co}(n)$ is also negligible and Π' secure in the sense of $SOR - CO$ given the sample structure sample_1. ∎

However, it is not always possible to come back to strings of a certain length. Therefore, we show an alternative way of proving the theorem by adding stages to the encryption function of the encryption scheme.

Adding States   We assume $\Pi^* = (\mathsf{GenKey}^*, \mathsf{Enc}^*, \mathsf{Dec}^*)$ is secure in the sense of $\mathsf{SOR} - \mathsf{CO}$ given a sample structure composed of a set of all single characters c_i of the complete alphabet Γ. Thus

$$\mathsf{sample}_\Gamma \in_R \{(m_0; m_1; \ldots; m_n) \mid \forall i, j \text{ with } 0 \leqslant i, j \leqslant n . \exists m_i = j\}$$

Then we regard the following algorithms for $\Pi^* = (\mathsf{GenKey}^*, \mathsf{Enc}^*, \mathsf{Dec}^*)$:

Algorithm $\mathsf{GenKey}^*(1^n)$:	Algorithm $\mathsf{Enc}_k^*(m)$:	Algorithm $\mathsf{Dec}_k^*(c)$:
$\quad k \leftarrow \mathsf{GenKey}(1^n)$	$\quad$ if $m = 0$ then	$\quad$ if $c = \sharp$
$\quad$ return k	$\qquad$ if $s = n+1$ then	$\qquad$ then $m := 0$
	$\qquad\quad c := \sharp$	$\quad$ else
	$\qquad\quad s := 0$	$\qquad\quad m := \mathsf{Dec}_k(c)$
	$\qquad$ else	$\quad$ return m
	$\qquad\quad c \leftarrow \mathsf{Enc}_k(m)$	
	$\qquad\quad s{+}{+}$	
	$\quad$ else	
	$\qquad\quad c \leftarrow \mathsf{Enc}_k(m)$	
	$\qquad\quad s := 0$	
	$\quad$ return c	

Again, Π^* works almost exactly like Π'. This time the exception is not made for a certain string, but instead Enc^* possesses stages. If repeatedly asked for an encryption of 0, the $n+1$'s encryption will return a special symbol. This change does almost not effect the security in the sense of $\mathsf{SOR} - \mathsf{CO}$, but an adversary of the $\mathsf{ROR} - \mathsf{CPA}$ security model is able to explicitly ask the encryption oracle repeatedly for encryptions of 0 and this way determine the oracle's operation mode. It remains to show the two emerging lemmas:

Lemma 4.56. $\Pi^* = (\mathsf{GenKey}^*, \mathsf{Enc}^*, \mathsf{Dec}^*)$ *is not secure in the sense of* $\mathsf{ROR} - \mathsf{CPA}$.

PROOF. This can easily be shown by exploiting the built-in weakness of Π^*. We first regard the following strategy. The adversary asks the oracle $n+1$ times for the encryption of '0'. If the special symbol $\sharp$ is returned for the $n+1$st query she concludes that the oracle is in 'real mode' otherwise she concludes it encrypts randomly drawn strings. In the latter case, the adversary can be sure to be right, because if the oracle would operate in 'real mode' it would not return any other encryption than the special symbol for the $n+1$st query. Alternatively, if the oracle outputs the special symbol, it may nevertheless operate in random mode with a probability of $\frac{1}{(n+1)^{n+1}}$ since the alphabet consists of $n+1$ different characters and the oracle is asked $n+1$ times and resets its stage if not asked for the encryption of '0'. Thus, the resulting probabilities lead to the adversary's advantage

$$\mathbf{Adv}^{ror-cpa}_{A_{cpa},\Pi^\star}(n) = \Pr[\mathbf{Exp}^{ror-cpa-1}_{A_{cpa},\Pi^\star}(n) = 1] \quad - \Pr[\mathbf{Exp}^{ror-cpa-0}_{A_{cpa},\Pi^\star}(n) = 1]$$

$$= 1 - \frac{1}{(n+1)^{n+1}} \qquad\qquad - 0$$

which is obviously not negligible. Thus, $\Pi^\star = (\mathsf{GenKey}^\star, \mathsf{Enc}^\star, \mathsf{Dec}^\star)$ is not secure in the sense of $ROR-CPA$.   ∎

Again, we still need to show, that this weakness preserves security in the sense of $SOR-CO$.

Lemma 4.57. $\Pi^\star = (\mathsf{GenKey}^\star, \mathsf{Enc}^\star, \mathsf{Dec}^\star)$ *is secure in the sense of* $SOR-CO$ *given the sample structure* $\mathsf{sampler}$.

Since the proof is quite similar to the proof above, but would require a deeper analysis of the problem of determining the length of the longest run of heads for a coin (cf. ERDÖS [ER77]), we only give an informal proof.

Proof. We follow the work of SCHILLING [Sch90] to gain an insight into 'longest runs of head' and refer to GUIBAS and ODLYZKO [GO80] for further reading. SCHILLING regards a fair coin and analyses the expected longest head runs by using geometric random variables. This way, he arrives at the conclusion that for N trials the expected longest run of heads is approximately $EV \approx \log_2(N) - \frac{2}{3}$. Furthermore he shows that the variance is essentially constant with respect to N, the number of trials, which is remarkable. Therefore, with high probability, the longest head run for a fair coin is in a small interval around EV, the expected value[2].

Next, we regard the effect of the encryption scheme's modification. If the oracle is in 'sample mode' the modification does not come to play, since only one of the sample's set of strings is '0' and thus the encryption scheme will not get to stages higher than $s = 2$. Otherwise, if the oracle is in 'random mode' and the values are chosen randomly, a run of $n+1$ zeros would yield an output of the special symbol '♯'. That means, compared to $\Pi^\star$, an adversary has an additional chance of getting the special symbol answered when regarding $\Pi^\star$ and would then be able to determine the oracle's mode. However, since the adversary is polynomially limited and each query answers $n+1$ ciphertexts, the adversary receives at most a polynomial (in n) bounded number of ciphertexts. Without loss of generality, we assume the adversary is able to obtain $C \cdot n^c$ ciphertexts. If she would toss a coin, the expected longest

---

[2]He claims that for every n, more than 99% of the corresponding distribution accumulate on ten values [Sch90, p. 202].

run of heads would be $EV \approx \log_2(C \cdot n^c) - \frac{2}{3} = c \log_2(n) + \log_2(C) - \frac{2}{3}$. Therefore, for large values of n (compared to the constants c and C), the expected longest run of zeros is clearly smaller than $n + 1$, the number of stages of Π^*. Furthermore, the probability of randomly picking the character '0' is not $\frac{1}{2}$ like for fair coin tosses, but $\frac{1}{n+1}$ instead. This additionally reduces the probability of getting a run of zeros of length $n + 1$. For a technical proof, it remains to show that this probability is negligible (in n) for all n. We assume this probability is negligible, since (1) the distance between EV and n rises, (2) the considered estimation refers to a fair coin, and (3) the variance of EV is independent of n. Thus, the probability of randomly receiving the special symbol $\sharp$ should give the adversary no decisive advantage and thus the security of the considered encryption scheme Π^* is those of the underlying encryption scheme Π^*. □

We have shown two different methods to change encryption schemes which are secure in the sense of $SOR - CO$ to encryption schemes which are still secure in the sense of $SOR - CO$ but not in the sense of $ROR - CPA$.

Corollary 4.58. [$SOR - CO \nRightarrow ROR - CPA$] *If there exists an encryption scheme Π which is secure in the sense of $SOR - CO$, then there exists an encryption scheme Π' which is secure in the sense of $SOR - CO$ but not secure in the sense of $ROR - CPA$.*

Proof. Cor. 4.58 follows from Lem. 4.54, Lem. 4.55, Lem. 4.56, and Lem. 4.57. □

Theorem 4.59. *Security in the sense of $SOR - CO$ is a weaker notion than security in the sense of $ROR - CPA$.*

Proof. Th. 4.59 follows from Cor. 4.53 and Cor. 4.58. □

Thus, we have shown that the two security models give different notions of security and $SOR - CO$ is weaker than $ROR - CPA$.

4.1.5 XOR, EQV and Hamming Functions

The Functions XOR and EQV

In general, the encryption function in visual cryptography is quite simple. Therefore, we first introduce the two related functions: XOR and EQV on which the encryption functions are based.

Definition 4.60. (Exclusive-Or Function) We denote the *exclusive-or function (XOR)*: $\{0,1\}^n \times \{0,1\}^n \to \{0,1\}^n$ with $\oplus$ (cf. Tab. 4.3a).

Definition 4.61. (Logical Biconditional Function) We denote the *logical biconditional function (EQV)*: $\{0,1\}^n \times \{0,1\}^n \to \{0,1\}^n$ with $\leftrightarrow$ (cf. Tab. 4.3b).

Table 4.3: Truth Tables

$\oplus$	0	1
0	0	1
1	1	0

(a) XOR

$\leftrightarrow$	0	1
0	1	0
1	0	1

(b) EQV

It is easy to see, that $A \oplus B \leftrightarrow \neg(A \leftrightarrow B)$ holds. Furthermore, we extend their domain and codomain in the following way: If XOR or EQV are applied to multiple bits, they work bit by bit. Hence, XOR and EQV are homomorphic by definition.

Hamming Weight and Hamming Domain

The following notions are derived from HAMMING's work [Ham50] on error detecting and error correcting codes. If we assume the encryption function is based on XOR or EQV, the Hamming distance may be a useful measure for the distance of two ciphertexts as we will see in Sect. 5.3.1.

Definition 4.62. (Hamming Weight and Hamming Distance) Let Σ be an alphabet and let $s = b_1 \ldots b_n$ and $s' = b_1' \ldots b_n'$ with $s, s' \in \Sigma^n$ be two strings of equal length n. We denote the *Hamming weight* as the number of symbols that are different from zero:

$$\mathrm{Ham}(s) = \sum_{\substack{b_i \neq 0 \\ 1 \leqslant i \leqslant n}} 1$$

The *Hamming distance* between s and s' is the number of positions where the corresponding symbols b_i and b_i' are different:

$$\mathrm{Ham}(s, s') = \sum_{\substack{b_i \neq b_i' \\ 1 \leqslant i \leqslant n}} 1$$

With an appropriate definition of the "$-$"-operator the Hamming distance can be seen as the Hamming weight of $s - s'$ and therefore we denote it also as $\mathrm{Ham}(s - s')$.

Similar to the modulo operation, the Hamming weight and distance can be used to spawn several equivalence classes, which leads to our definition of Hamming equivalence classes and domains.

Definition 4.63. (Hamming Equivalence Class and Hamming Domain) Let $\Sigma = \{0, 1, \ldots\}^n$ and let $s = b_1 \ldots b_n$ and $s' = b'_1 \ldots b'_n$ with $s, s' \in \Sigma$ be two strings of equal length n. Then an equivalence relation on strings of length n can be built by grouping all elements with the same Hamming weight:

$$s \equiv_{\mathsf{Ham}} s' \quad := \quad \mathsf{Ham}(s) = \mathsf{Ham}(s')$$

We call the corresponding equivalence class *Hamming equivalence class* and denote it as

$$[s]_{\mathsf{Ham}} := \left\{ s' \in \Sigma^n | s \equiv_{\mathsf{Ham}} s' \right\}$$

It is also possible to build an analogous equivalence relation on all strings of length n with the same Hamming distance to a given string $\sigma = \beta_1 \ldots \beta_n$ with $\sigma \in \Sigma$ of length n:

$$s \equiv_{\mathsf{Ham}}^{\sigma} s' \quad := \quad \mathsf{Ham}(s - \sigma) = \mathsf{Ham}(s' - \sigma)$$

We call the corresponding equivalence class *Hamming domain of s on σ* and denote it as:

$$[s]_{\mathsf{Ham}}^{\sigma} := \left\{ s' \in \Sigma^n | s \equiv_{\mathsf{Ham}}^{\sigma} s' \right\}$$

It is also helpfull to have a second notation for Hamming equivalence classes, without naming a certain string by only giving the according Hamming weight. We denote this as:

$$\langle d \rangle_{\mathsf{Ham}} := \{ s \in \Sigma^n | \mathsf{Ham}(s) = d \}$$

The same applies for Hamming domains by adding σ and referring to the Hamming distance:

$$\langle d \rangle_{\mathsf{Ham}}^{\sigma} := \{ s \in \Sigma^n | \mathsf{Ham}(s - \sigma) = d \}$$

4.2 Visual Cryptography

Visual cryptography was introduced by NAOR and SHAMIR [NS94, NS96, NP97] and allows to encrypt a picture by splitting it into n shares in such a way that someone with k shares is able to reconstruct the image, while $k - 1$ shares reveal no information about the original image. They proposed to print each share on a transparency, so that its re-composition can easily be done by humans by stacking their transparencies without the aid of computers as shown in Fig. 4.5.

In this section, we describe the ideas of visual cryptography by means of binary images as an example for human decipherable encryption schemes. For a general survey we recommoned KLEIN's monograph [Kle07].

Figure 4.5: Example: Pixel-Based Visual Cryptography[3]

The layout of this section is as follows: At first, we examine fundamentals of pixel-based visual cryptography, followed by its application to the secret sharing problem and steganography. Subsequently we continue with segment-based visual cryptography which we elaborate on in the next chapter.

4.2.1 Pixel-based Visual Cryptography

We first of all deal with visual cryptography splitting the picture into two transparencies, which –stacked together– allow to reconstruct the original picture. This is a special case of secret sharing systems, NAOR and SHAMIR came up with. As the name pixel-based visual cryptography already suggests, the scheme works by encrypting the original picture pixel by pixel. For each pixel there exist n modified versions, called *shares*. Shares of a pixel consist of a certain number of subpixels. Note that the term 'subpixel' is slightly misleading since a pixel is already the smallest unit and thus cannot be further divided. What is meant, is that a certain number of the share's pixels (the subpixels) represent a pixel of the original image. The number of pixels needed to represent a pixel of the original image is called *pixel expansion* since it denotes how much bigger (than the original picture) the shares are. Fig. 4.6 shows shares with four subpixels, half black and half white[4], arranged in a 2x2-array.

The creation of transparencies works as follows: First, for each pixel of the original picture, a random share is produced, which together form the first transparency. The shares of the second transparency are chosen as a function of the original picture, such that the combination of both transparency's shares result in a pixel representing the pixel of the original image. Therefore, if the transparencies are stacked, they have to be exactly aligned. Depending on the colour of the original pixel – white or black – the stacked shares will have a certain amount of white or black subpixels as shown in the contingency table in Tab. 4.4a. In this case, the

---

[3]Transparencies and overlay can be found in more detail in App. 11.3

[4]Since the shares are stacked in order to decrypt the image, in most cases "white" actually refers to a transparent pixel, but for simplicity we use the terms of white and black pixels.

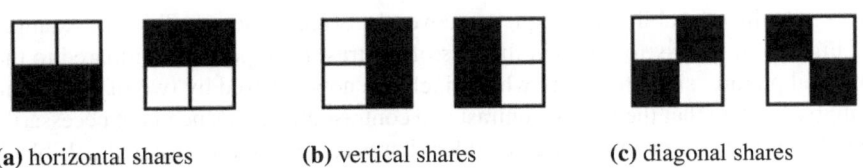

(a) horizontal shares   (b) vertical shares   (c) diagonal shares

Figure 4.6: Forms of Shares with 4 Subpixels Arranged in a 2x2 Array from NAOR and SHAMIR [NS94, p. 3]

result is either a pixel with two white and two black subpixels, which has to be interpreted as white, or a pixel with four black subpixels, which has to be interpreted as black (cf. Tab. 4.4b).

Composing the two shares can be seen as one of the functions XOR or EQV – depending on the interpretation of the result of the stacked shares. It can be easily seen, that if the part-transparent pixel is interpreted as 0, it is a matter of the XOR function, whereas if the opaque pixel is interpreted as 0 it is a matter of the EQV function.

Table 4.4: Contingency and Evaluation Table for the Overlay of Two Diagonal Pixellated Transparencies in Visual Cryptography

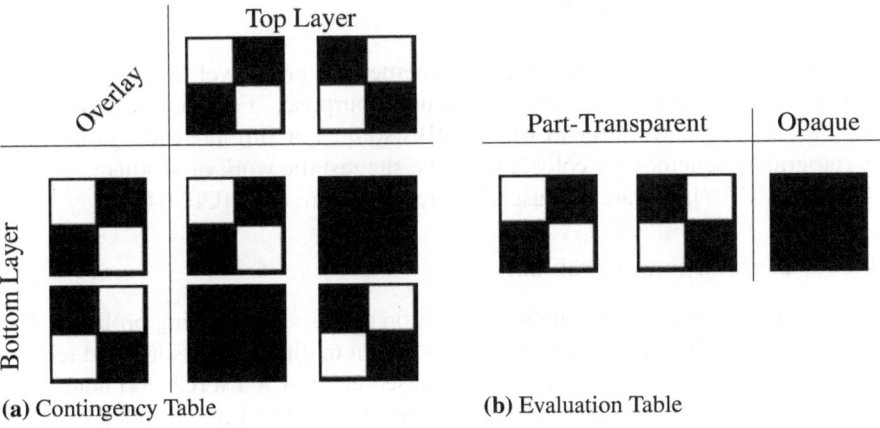

(a) Contingency Table   (b) Evaluation Table

The maximum number of black subpixels, which are allowed in order to still consider the resulting pixel as white, and the minimum number of black subpixels required to consider the resulting pixel as black, are called *contrast thresholds*. Thus, by using pixel-based virtual cryptography, a loss of contrast occurs, which does not affect the ability to uniquely recover the original picture. Take the example of Fig. 4.5, it is easy to see, that the loss of contrast is 50 percent compared to the original picture, since formerly white pixels are now covered by two of four black subpixels. Note that the loss of contrast and contrast thresholds need not necessarily be discrete. As an example, we consider shares represented by rotated half black circles as shown in Fig. 4.7. Obviously, the more white subpixels a white pixel has and the more black subpixels a black pixel has, the higher is the contrast, making it easier for the user to correctly interpret the result.

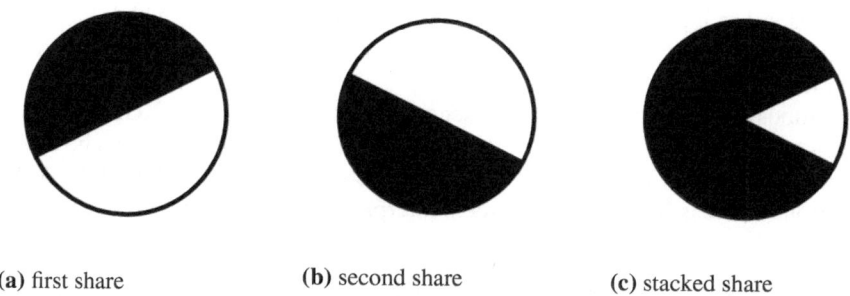

(a) first share   (b) second share   (c) stacked share

Figure 4.7: Forms of Shares Represented by Rotated Half Circles from Naor and Shamir [NS94, p. 10]

There are also visual cryptography schemes for grey level or colour images, which are not needed here for our intended purpose. For an investigation of grey level images we refer to Blundo [BSN00]. For further reading on visual cryptography schemes for color images we suggest the work of Verheul and van Tilborg [VvT97], and another useful source is Cimato et al. [CPS04].

Visual Secret Sharing Problem

We continue with the mathematical definition of the secret sharing problem. The basic idea is to share a secret into n pieces, given to different persons, and require any k pieces of them to recover the shared secret. As Chaum [Cha84] notes, this idea appeared in several places at nearly the same time with different names. In 1979 there was a technical report by Chaum [Cha79] on the use of of *partial key techniques*, Blakley [Bla79, Bla80] presented *key safeguarding techniques* at a conference, and Shamir [Sha79] submitted *threshold schemes* for publication.

Definition 4.64. (Secret Sharing Problem, Threshold Scheme) Let D be some data. The k *out of* n *secret sharing problem* is to divide the data D into n pieces $D_1, \ldots, D_n$, such that:

- D can be easily computed if k or more different pieces D_i are available.

- Given only $k-1$ or less pieces D_i, all possible values of D are equally likely, leaving D completely undetermined.

The corresponding scheme is denoted as (k, n)-*threshold scheme*.

In the visual variant of the k out of n sharing problem (cf. Sect. 4.2.1), transparencies of an image are distributed among n users, so that any k of them can see the image by stacking their transparencies, but any $k-1$ of them gain no information about it [NS94].

EXAMPLE 4.65. (4 out of 4 Visual Secret Sharing Problem)
Fig. 4.8 shows a solution of a 4 out of 4 visual secret sharing problem. It can easily be seen that any three transparencies do not leak any information about the result: Any single share contains five black subpixels, any stacked pair of shares contains seven black subpixels, and any stacked triplet contains eight black subpixels. The result of four stacked transparencies contains either eight or nine black subpixels.

In Fig. 4.8a the upper left subpixel stays white, which, of course, is not fixed and could have been any of the nine subpixels, since all permutations would also solve the visual secret sharing problem. Fig. 4.8b shows four transparencies resulting in nine black subpixels. Furthermore, it is worth to mention that the contrast is quite low. Only one out of nine subpixels determines if the result has to be interpreted as white or black.

For a more algebraic description of the 4 out of 4 visual secret sharing problem we refer to the original work [NS94, p. 4].

Steganography in Visual Cryptography

It is also possible to make use of steganography and hide a visual encrypted picture in an already existing picture. The idea can also be traced back to NAOR and SHAMIR [NS94, NS96, NP97] and is used to hide digital signatures in a share [SNSS08], for example in order to proof ownership of an image's copyright [CC02]. Consider the following example.

EXAMPLE 4.66. (Steganography in Visual Cryptography by Using 2x2-Subpixel-Arrays)
Consider Fig. 4.9. Pixels in the original picture, in which the encrypted picture is hidden, are represented by a 2x2-array with black and white subpixels. A white

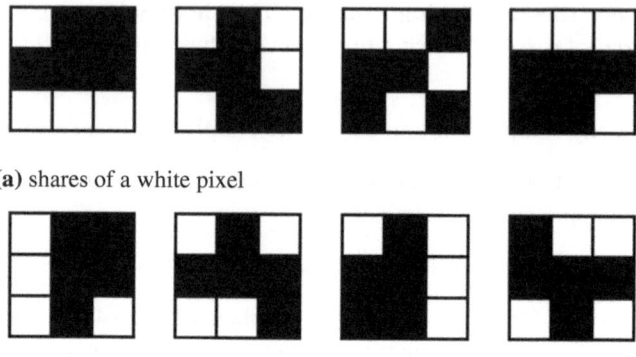

(a) shares of a white pixel

(b) shares of a black pixel

Figure 4.8: Shares of a 4 out of 4 Visual Secret Sharing Problem from Naor and
      Shamir [NS94, p. 4]

pixel in the original picture is represented by a pixel with two white (and two black)
subpixels, while a black pixel is represented by a pixel with one white (and three
black) subpixels. Pixels of the hidden image result from stacking a transparency
onto the original picture. When the shares shown in Fig. 4.9a to 4.9c, are stacked,
the resulting pixel contains three black (and one white) subpixels (cf. Fig. 4.9g) and
the result is considered to be a white pixel. Whereas a pixel containing four black
subpixels (cf. Fig. 4.9h) – as originating from stacking shares shown in Fig. 4.9d
to 4.9f – is considered to be a black pixel.

4.2.2 Segment-based Visual Cryptography

In 2007, Borchert introduced segment-based visual cryptography [Bor07]. Instead
of using pixels as smallest unit, he proposed to use segments of a segment display,
such as the 7-segment display (cf. Fig. 4.3 and 4.4), as smallest units. This way
all symbols displayable by a segment display can be encrypted. Considering the 7-
segment display, it is possible to display the digits from 0 to 9 (and the hexadecimal
digits A, b, C, d, E, F). Now the principles of visual cryptography are applied to the
segments. For every segment S, two segments S_1 and S_2 are drawn close to each
other without intersection as shown in Fig. 4.10e. The creation of transparencies
works analogous to pixel-based visual cryptography. For the first transparency, for
each segment, one of the segments S_1 and S_2 is chosen randomly. This segment
is kept white (transparent), while the other segment is turned black. One random
selection of a key k for one digit is shown in Fig. 4.10a.

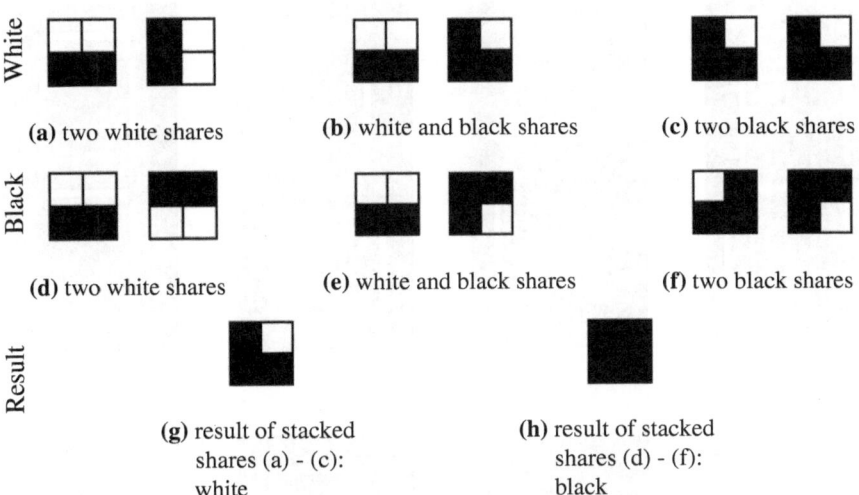

(a) two white shares   **(b)** white and black shares   **(c)** two black shares

(d) two white shares   **(e)** white and black shares   **(f)** two black shares

(g) result of stacked shares (a) - (c): white

(h) result of stacked shares (d) - (f): black

Figure 4.9: Shares Usable for Steganography in Visual Cryptography from NAOR and SHAMIR [NS94, p. 11]

The second transparency is produced according to the desired symbol to be displayed, when both transparencies are stacked. Each symbol consists of a subset of visible segments while all other segments are hidden. Consider the ciphertext c_1 in Fig. 4.10b, stacked with the key transparency k (Fig. 4.10a), the result is $p_1 = $ I (see Fig. 4.10f). Analogously, k stacked with c_2 (c_3) results in $p_2 = $ ꝛ ($p_3 = $ Ʒ), as shown in Fig. 4.10c and Fig. 4.10g (Fig. 4.10d and Fig. 4.10h). If a segment belongs to the subset of segments shown, then for this segment, the same selection of S_1 and S_2 is made as in the random share. If a segment belongs to the subset of segments hidden, then for this segment, the opposite selection of S_1 and S_2 is made as in the random share. Again, the selected segment of the second share is kept white (transparent), while the other segment is turned black.

If the transparencies are stacked, same selections of segments result in a white (transparent) segment while opposite selections of segments result in a black segment. Tab. 4.5a and 4.5b show the contingency table for horizontal and vertical segments and Tab. 4.5c and 4.5d show the evaluation table of the stacked transparencies. Considering the symbol in total, exactly the segments are shown which belong to the symbol desired to display.

Like in pixel-based visual cryptography, composing the two shares can be seen as one of the functions XOR or EQV, depending on the interpretation of the result. As

(a) k   **(b)** c_1 **(c)** c_2 **(d)** c_3

(e) all segments   **(f)** $p_1 = c_1 \leftrightarrow k$ **(g)** $p_2 = c_2 \leftrightarrow k$ **(h)** $p_3 = c_3 \leftrightarrow k$

Figure 4.10: The Principle of Visual Cryptography applied to a Seven-Segment Display according to Borchert [Bor07]

previously mentioned, the first share is random. The second share is a composition of a random value with a given value and thus also random, since the probability for each segment S choosing S_1 is $\frac{1}{2}$. Therefore, regarding only one of the two transparencies, the position of the visible segment is completely random and thus does not disclose any information on the encrypted symbol.

According to Borchert segment-based visual cryptography offers the following potential advantages as compared to pixel-based visual cryptography:
- The transparencies do not have to be aligned as exactly as in pixel-based cryptography.

Table 4.5: Contingency and Evaluation Tables for the Overlay of Two Segment-Based Transparencies in Visual Cryptography

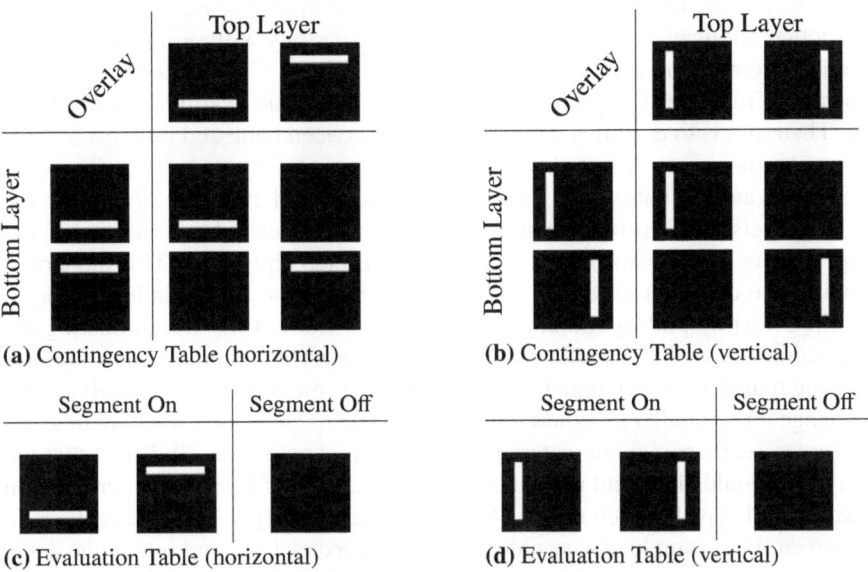

(a) Contingency Table (horizontal)   (b) Contingency Table (vertical)

(c) Evaluation Table (horizontal)   (d) Evaluation Table (vertical)

- Since no loss of contrast occurs, humans can recognise slightly malformed symbols more easily than pictures with loss of contrast.

- Less bits are needed to transmit and display the information. This may be an advantage if low bandwidth is available or the generation of random numbers is expensive, e.g. due to the use of hardware random number generators instead of pseudorandom number generators.

- It may be easier for non-experts to understand – and therefore trust – the ideas of segment-based visual cryptography.

4.2.3 Applications of Visual Cryptography

CHAUM [Cha02] described how to use visual cryptography with electronic voting machines. He showed how voters could get a receipt of their vote in order to let them be sure their vote is really counted, but makes it impossible for them to take any proof out of the polling place that could be used to show to others how they voted. In short, CHAUM proposes that after electronic voting the machine prints a two-layered receipt, that consists of two visual cryptography transparencies showing the voter's decision. The voter is asked to chose on of the transparencies as receipt while the other is destroyed at the polling place. This way he is able to check the receipt, but unable to prove how he voted to anyone outside.

Another application, is the use of visual cryptography with or instead of transaction authentication numbers (TANs) in online banking. GREVELER [Gre07] and BORCHERT [Bor07, BR08] proposed to use it to improve the security of online banking. Their aim is to establish a secure channel between bank and user, even when the user's computer is infected with malware.

The user and the bank share a key-transparency K and a secret TAN, which the customer gets from his bank. The customer sends the desired transaction t to the bank and the bank answers with a visually encrypted ciphertext. This ciphertext contains the desired transaction t and a challenge. The user is able to decrypt the ciphertext by putting the key-transparency in front of his screen making the transaction data and the challenge visible. After verifying the transaction and thus assuring that it wasn't changed[5], the user confirms the transaction by solving the challenge. The challenge could consist of the demand to click certain areas on the screen (e.g. special characters like hyphens). Another possibility is that the decryption could also yield in a randomly ordered number block (or a permutation of keys in a keypad) which enables the user to transmit digits by clicking them on the screen. For example, the user already knows a secret TAN and selects the digits t of his tan in a keypad $\pi(M)$ by revealing the positions P of his selection. More formally, the user executes the following algorithm:

Definition 4.67. (User) Let $\pi(M) = (m_1, \ldots, m_i)$ be an output by $HDec(K, C)$ and $TAN = (t_1, \ldots, t_j)$ a list of characters with $m_1, \ldots, m_i, t_1, \ldots, t_j \in \Omega$. Then $User(\pi(M), TAN) \to P$ returns $\perp$ if there exists a $t_k \in TAN$ which is $\notin \pi(M)$ or otherwise a position list $P = (p_1, \ldots, p_j)$ so that $t_1 = m_{p_1}, \ldots, t_j = m_{p_j}$ holds.

Because the adversary does neither know the content of the key-transparency put in front of the screen nor the secret TAN, she is only able to observe clicks respectively selections on the screen and does not know what they represent. In this context, it is important that the transaction and the challenge are tied together, because otherwise an attacker could unnoticedly change the transaction rendering the challenge useless. The bank server then has to verify that the challenge was solved correctly before initiating the money transfer. Fig. 4.11 shows the protocol described above.

One possibility to tie transaction data and challenge together is proposed by SZYDLOWSKI et al. [SKK07]. The user receives a code book with functions in-

---

[5]Note that the data sent from the bank is not digitally signed, which would allow the user to be sure the data wasn't changed. Instead it is assumed that only someone knowing the secret key-transparency K is able to create a ciphertext whose decryption contains the correct transaction data. While this assumption will probably hold, additional signatures may easily be added to the protocol.

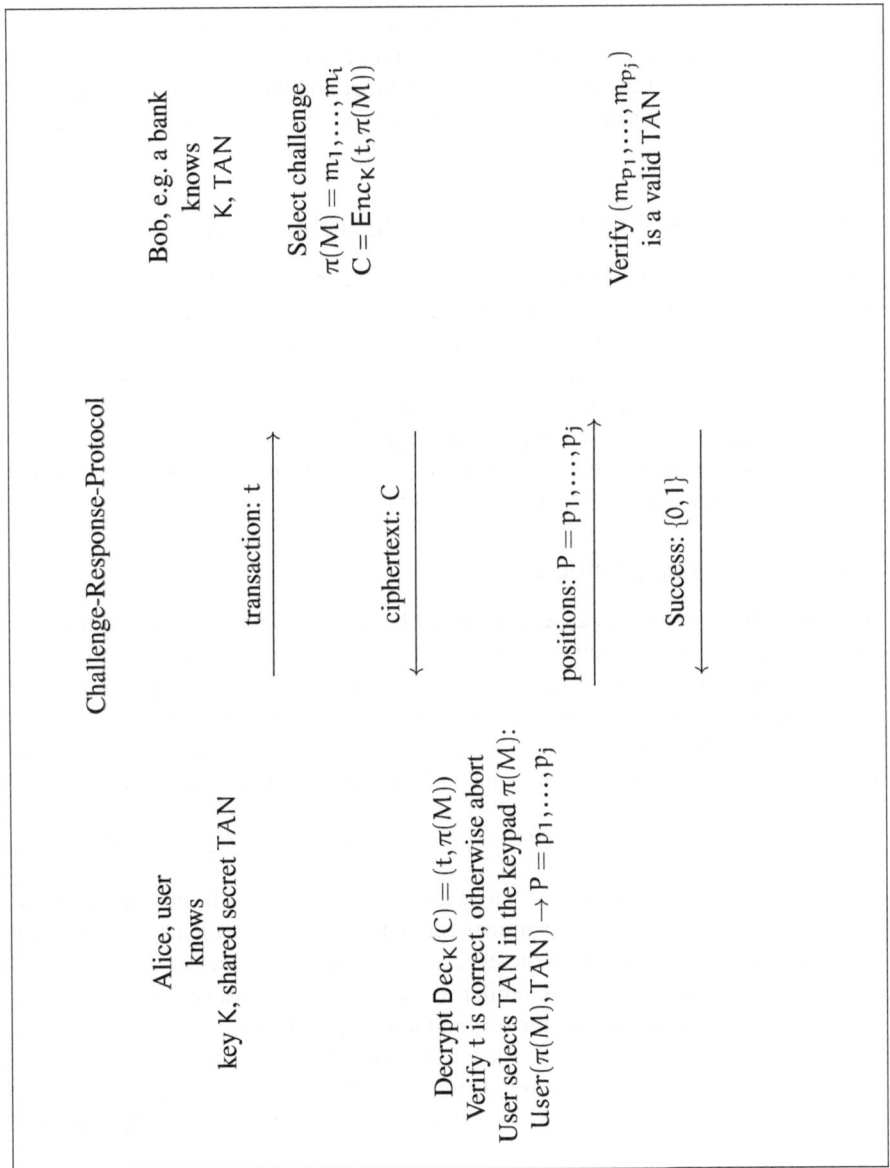

Figure 4.11: Application of Visual Cryptography: Transmission of a Transaction and Affirmation via a Mouseclick-Based Challenge-Response-Protocol

stead of a TAN list and for each authentication he is required to manually compute a function depending on the intended transaction. For example, he may be required to add certain digits of the payee's account number and the transferred amount and transmit the result of his computation by clicking on the corresponding digits of the keypad.

4.2.4 Using Key-Transparencies Multiple Times

Because pixel- and segment-based visual cryptography heavily rely on the basic principle of one time pads, they offer perfect security, provided each transparency is used only once. However, in many scenarios it would be desirable to be able to reuse the transparencies in a secure way. Although none of the presented systems was designed for reusing the transparencies, we investigate, how reuse of transparencies affects the security of the encrypted messages. In the following, the term *key-transparency* denotes the transparency we want to use multiple times, while the other transparency is called *ciphertext!transparency*.

Pixel-Based Visual Cryptography

Let us assume, two pictures are encrypted with the same key-transparency. It can be easily seen, that pixels which are white or black in both pictures, result in the same pixels on all ciphertext-transparencies when encrypted. Likewise, pixels that are different in both pictures result, when encrypted, in different (inverted) pixels. Thus, stacking two ciphertext-transparencies results in the XOR-composition of the two original pictures. Or more formally, due to XOR's associativity and commutativity[6]:

$$C_1 \oplus C_2 = (P_1 \oplus P_k) \oplus (P_2 \oplus P_k) = P_1 \oplus (P_k \oplus P_k) \oplus P_2 = P_1 \oplus P_2$$

This is especially important if a "large area" of an image is homochromatic. If this area is white, the ciphertext-transparency is identical or at least similar to the key-transparency (depending on the exact coding). In almost the same manner, if it is black, it is identical or at least similar to the inverted key-transparency, which is just as useful for an attacker as the original key-transparency.

As an example, Fig. 4.12 shows the letters 'AB' and 'XY' encrypted at the same position, as well as their XOR-composition. Of course, an adversary is not able to conclude if the result comes from the XOR-composition of 'AB' and 'XY' or 'XB'

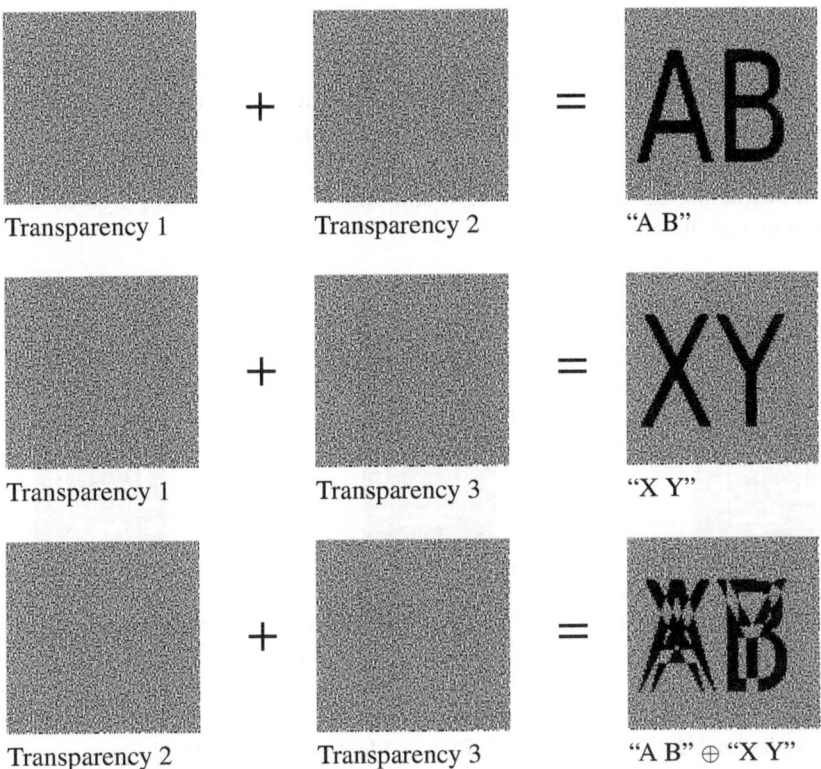

Figure 4.12: Reusing Transparencies in Pixel-Based Visual Cryptography

and 'AY' or any other combination. But depending on the context, this information is in general far more than what should be revealed.

As already mentioned in Chap. 3, a first counteraction was presented by Wu and Chen [WC98]. They designed a scheme which allowed to hide two images in two shares, where the second can be made visible by rotating one of the shares by 90 degrees. In 2007, Fang [Fan07] introduced a scheme which allows to use the transparency twice by turning it over for the second decryption. We do not want to go further into detail here and recommend Revenkar et al. [RAG10, p. 51, 54] for an entry of further reading.

---

[6]since $\neg\,(P_1 \leftrightarrow P_k) \oplus \neg\,(P_2 \leftrightarrow P_k) = (P_1 \oplus P_k) \oplus (P_2 \oplus P_k)$ this also holds if the encryption is seen as matter of the EQV-function

Segment-Based Visual Cryptography

Next, we regard the encryptions shown in Fig. 4.13, which are encrypted with the scheme proposed by Borchert [Bor07], which we already described in Sect. 4.2.2. All digits are encrypted with the same key-transparency and beginning from Fig. 4.13a show the encryption of the digits 2, 5 and 8. To ease the recognition of segments, contrary to Fig. 4.10 and Tab. 4.5, the following figures show black segments in dark grey.

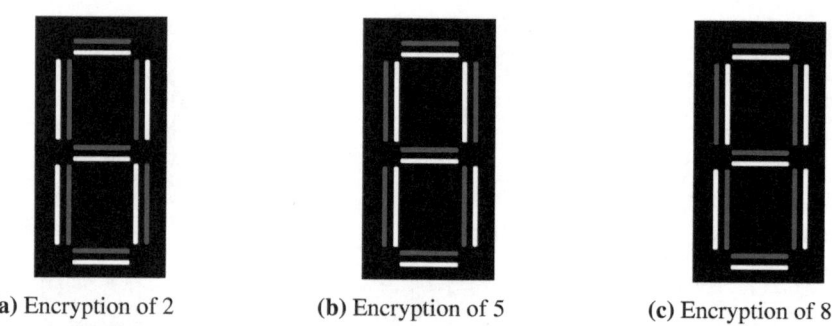

(a) Encryption of 2   (b) Encryption of 5   (c) Encryption of 8

Figure 4.13: Segment-Based Visual Cryptography: Sample Encryptions with the Same Key

Regard Fig. 4.13a first. Since there are only 10 (or 16 if we would also allow the hexadecimal digits A, b, C, d, E, F) possible digits, after eavesdropping a valid ciphertext, an adversary is able to reduce the number of possible keys from 128 (2^7, the size of the key space) to 10. The possible keys are shown in Fig. 4.14. It can be easily determined that decrypting with any other key would not result in a valid digit (cf. Fig. 4.3) which is a consequence of the fact, that the 7-segment coding is not a closed encoding scheme.

Since the key space is quite small, it is reasonable to assume, that an adversary is able to exhaustively search the whole key space and we may consider the adversary as computationally unbound. Therefore we regard the idea of the unicity distance and evaluate its suggestion of the length of the ciphertext an adversary would need to determine the key-transparency.

The number of possible keys is 2^7 and thus its entropy is $H(\mathcal{K}) = 7$ bits. The absolute rate of language for the 7-segment display is $R_0 = \log_2(2^7) = 7$ bits per character. Since there are only 10 valid digits, its (real) rate is $R = \log_2(10) \approx 3.3$ bits per character and thus its redundancy is $D \approx 3.7$ bits per character. It follows that the unicity distance is $U = \frac{H(\mathcal{K})}{D} \approx 1.9$ characters.

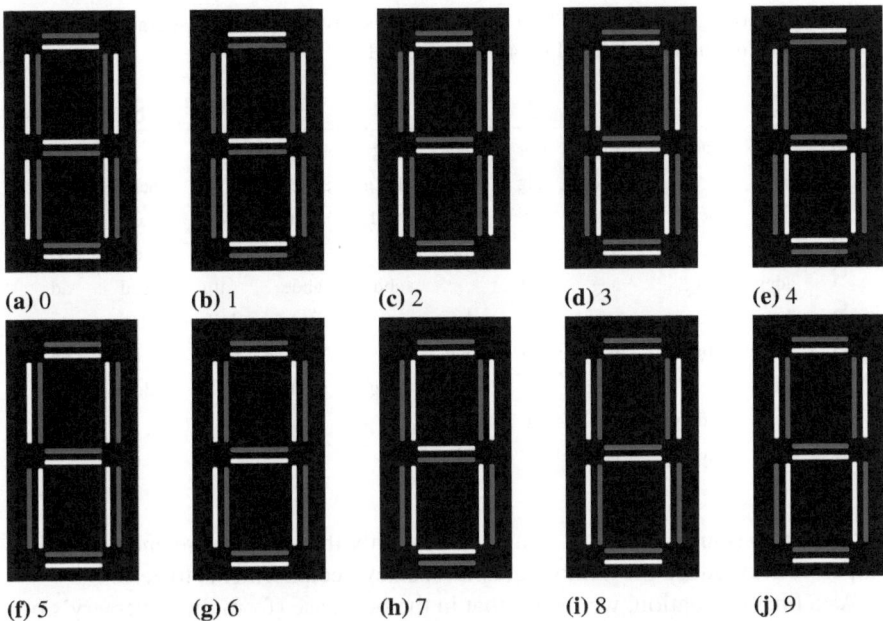

Figure 4.14: Segment-Based Visual Cryptography: Possible Keys for the Encryption Shown in Fig. 4.13a

In practice, 1.9 characters are not sufficient to determine the key, instead 3 characters are needed, as we elaborate in the following paragraph. Similar to the observations in Sect. 4.2.4, stacking two ciphertext-transparencies encrypted with the same key results in an XOR composition of the two underlying 7-segment digits. For example, the encryptions shown in Fig. 4.13a and Fig. 4.13b only differ in all vertical segments (segments b, c, e, and f, cf. Fig. 4.4). With the help of Tab. 4.6, which shows the result of an XOR operation with all legitimate 7-segment digits, it is possible to reduce the number of possible plaintexts to two (Ξ and 5). However, at this point we do not know which of the encryptions stands for Ξ since the keys shown in Fig. 4.14c and 4.14f would both yield in decryptions of Ξ and 5 and just swap the results. If we additionally consider the encryption shown in Fig. 4.13c and its differences to encryption 1 (segments c and f) and 2 (segments b and e), the puzzle can be solved.

The effects of a low plaintext redundancy, respectively closure, may be studied looking at the digits ,6,8 and 9 and the segments 'b' and 'e'. Fig. 4.15 shows that the 7-segment display includes a "closed subgroup". The named digits only

Table 4.6: Contingency Table of Two 7-Segment-Display Segments Associated with XOR using the Notation of Fig. 4.4 on page 101

⊕	0	1	2	3	4	5	6	7	8	9
0		adef	cfg	efg	adeg	beg	bg	deg	g	eg
1	adef		acdeg	adg	fg	abdfg	abdefg	a	adefg	adfg
2	cfg	acdeg		ce	aeg	bcef	bcf	cdeg	cf	cef
3	efg	adg	ce		adf	bf	bef	gd	ef	f
4	adeg	fg	aeg	adf		abd	abde	afg	aed	ad
5	beg	abdfg	bcef	bf	abd		e	bdfg	be	b
6	bg	abdefg	bcf	bef	abde	e		bdefg	b	be
7	deg	a	cdeg	gd	afg	bdfg	bdefg		defg	dfg
8	g	adefg	cf	ef	aed	be	b	defg		e
9	eg	adfg	cef	f	ad	b	be	dfg	e	

differ in two segments (b and e) and thus, if only those digits are encrypted, it is impossible to reduce the number of spurious key decipherments to zero.

As a final evaluation, we record that in the best case (from the adversary's perspective) three different ciphertext-transparencies are needed to determine the used key-transparency, while in the worst case five different ciphertext-transparencies are sufficient. The average case mainly depends on the distribution of digits used for transmission.

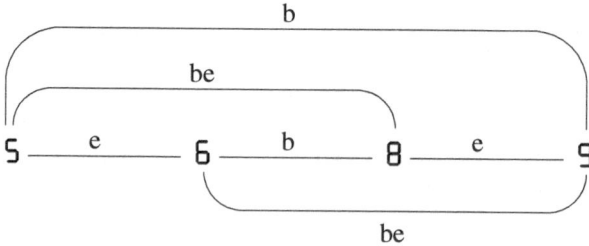

Figure 4.15: Closed Subgroup in Segment-Based Visual Cryptography: Graph of XOR Operations between the 7-Segment Display's Segments 5, 6, 8 and 9

5 Human Decipherable Encryption Schemes Based on Dice Codings

> Not only does God play dice, but
> ...he sometimes throws them where
> they cannot be seen.
>
> ―――――――――――――――
>
> Stephen Hawking

5.1 Dice Codings

This chapter introduces the original dice coding scheme invented by DOBER-ITZ [Dob08]. We show that the proposed encryption scheme based on dice codings allows adversaries to gain much more information than wanted. As a first attempt to overcome this structural weakness we propose an enhanced version which adds noise to the ciphertexts to better hide the plaintext.

5.1.1 Underlying Spaces and Parameters

Let $n \in \mathbb{N}$ be the parameter of the encoding scheme. The alphabet Ω of the *message space* $\mathcal{M}$ is the set of numbers[1] from 0 to n and thus $\Omega = \{0, \ldots, n\}$ and $\mathcal{M} = \{0, \ldots, n\}^*$. The alphabet of the *coding space* $\mathcal{S}$ can be thought to consist of symbols with n points which are either visible or not. The number of visible dots represents the corresponding character from the alphabet of the message space as shown in Fig. 5.1. The coding is not a positional (place-value) notation but an additional notation similar to unary representations of numbers [Wik13e].

――――――――――――――

[1] We treat the elements of Ω as numbers. More formally, a presentation as characters along with functions for converting from and to numbers could be chosen. However, this would significantly complicate our notation.

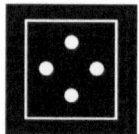
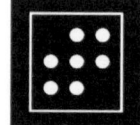
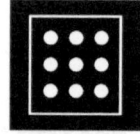

(a) An Encoding of 4   (b) An Encoding of 7   (c) An Encoding of 9

Figure 5.1: Dice Codings: Sample Encodings of 4, 7, and 9

We denote invisible dots with ● or 0 and visible dots with ○ or 1. This leads to the alphabet of the coding space $\Sigma = \{●,○\}^n = \{0,1\}^n$ with size 2^n and the coding space $S = \{\{●,○\}^n\}^* = \{\{0,1\}^n\}^*$. Since the visible dots' positions are insignificant, the number of possible symbols representing a character m follows a binomial distribution and hence is the binomial coefficient $\binom{n}{m}$. Tab. 5.1 shows the number of possible encodings for $n = 9$.

Table 5.1: Dice Codings: Numbers of possible Encodings for a 9-Dots Dice Coding

m	$|S_m|$
0	1
1	9
2	36
3	84
4	126
5	126
6	84
7	36
8	9
9	1

The alphabets Γ of *ciphertext space* C and Λ of *key space* $\mathcal{K}$ are the same and adopt the principle of visual encryption to dice codings. For each dot there exist two positions, which we denote with '○●' and '●○' respectively 'L' and 'R' to indicate where the white/transparent dot is placed. Of course, the positions could also be denoted with 0 and 1, but to prevent confusion with the coding space, we explicitly chose another notation. This leaves us with the alphabets $\Gamma = \Lambda = \{○●,●○\}^n = \{L,R\}^n$, also with size 2^n, and the ciphertext and key spaces $C = \mathcal{K} = \{\{○●,●○\}^n\}^* = \{\{L,R\}^n\}^*$. Having defined appropriate spaces, we look at dice codings applied to visual cryptography. It turns out that a notation for the inverse of messages, symbols and ciphertexts is useful (cf. Sect. 5.3.2).

Definition 5.1. (Inverses of Messages, Symbols and Ciphertexts) Let n be the parameter of the encoding scheme of an human decipherable encryption scheme based on dice codings with a message $m \in \mathcal{M}$, let $s \in \mathcal{S}$ be its encoding, and let $c \in \mathcal{C}$ be its ciphertext. We define the *inverse of a message* as $n - m$ and the *inverse of a symbol* respectively *ciphertext* if its dots are bitwise inverted. This means for symbols that '●' is changed to '○' and vice versa and for ciphertexts that '○●' is changed to '●○' and vice versa.

Based on that, we define m^* as being m or its inverse message $n - m$. Furthermore, we denote an encoding of m^* as s^* and an encryption of m^* as c^*.

5.1.2 Coding Scheme

The main idea of dice codings was already introduced in the previous subsection. We now give a more formal description of the encoding scheme which also describes the encoding and decoding algorithms. Afterwards we take a look at the properties of encoding schemes defined in Sect. 4.1.3 and determine which of them are fulfilled by dice codings.

Definition 5.2. (Dice Codings) Let n be a parameter and let message space $\mathcal{M}$ and coding space $\mathcal{S}$ be as described in Sect. 5.1.1. Then we denote $\mathrm{DICE} :=$ $(\mathrm{Gen}, \mathrm{Encode}, \mathrm{Decode})$ – with the algorithms defined below – as *dice codings*. When Encode or Decode are applied to multiple characters, they work character by character, hence the definitions below are for one character only:

- The only parameter we need for the encoding and decoding function is the number of dots on each dice. Therefore the *parameter-generation algorithm* Gen outputs on input 1^n the parameter $I = n$.

$$\mathrm{Gen}(1^n) := n \tag{5.1}$$

- The *encoding algorithm* $\mathrm{Encode} : \Omega \to \Sigma$ takes as input a number m and outputs a symbol s by randomly selecting m visible dots (1s) and $n - m$ invisible dots (0s) for the symbol s. This can also be seen as selecting an element s uniformly at random from the *Hamming equivalence class* $\langle m \rangle_{\mathrm{Ham}}$.

$$\mathrm{Encode}_n(m) := s \in_R \langle m \rangle_{\mathrm{Ham}} \tag{5.2}$$

- The *decoding function* $\mathrm{Decode} : \Sigma \to \Omega$ takes as input a symbol s and outputs the number of visible dots (1s) in s as character m. Since the number of visible dots is well-defined, a failure and thus the symbol $\perp$ never occurs. Because only the number of visible dots (1s) is counted, the decoding function is essentially the *Hamming weight* $\mathsf{Ham}(s)$ of a symbol.

$$\mathsf{Decode}_n(s) := \mathsf{Ham}(s) \tag{5.3}$$

Theorem 5.3. *Let* n *be a parameter, and let message space* $\mathcal{M}$ *and coding space* $\mathcal{S}$ *be as described in Sect. 5.1.1. Then* DICE *from Def. 5.2 fulfils the properties of an* encoding scheme *as given in Def. 4.20.*

PROOF. To prove that dice codings fulfil the definition of an *encoding scheme* as given in Def. 4.20, we have to show the following properties. Since DICE is homomorphic, it is sufficient to show that the required property is fulfilled for all characters $m \in \Omega$.

Encode **is left-total.** There exists an encoding for all characters m from the message space's alphabet $\Omega = \{0, \dots, n\}$. For example, for all characters m with $0 \leqslant m \leqslant n$ a possible encoding is $\bigcirc^m \bullet^{n-m} = 1^m 0^{n-m}$.

Encode **is left-unique.** Since there is one and only one value for the hamming weight Ham of a symbol s it holds that: For all $m, m' \in \Omega$ and $s \in \Sigma$ if $s \in_R \langle m \rangle_{\mathsf{Ham}}$ and $s \in_R \langle m' \rangle_{\mathsf{Ham}}$ then $\langle m \rangle_{\mathsf{Ham}} = \langle m' \rangle_{\mathsf{Ham}}$ and therefore $m = m'$. Hence, Encode is left-unique for all characters $m \in \Omega$.

$\mathsf{Decode}_n(\mathsf{Encode}_n(m)) = m$ **holds for all** $m \in \mathcal{M}$. Since it is easy to see that $\mathsf{Ham}(s)$ with $s \in_R \langle m \rangle_{\mathsf{Ham}}$ equals m, the property is also fulfilled.

∎

At next, we regard the properties of encoding schemes defined in Sect. 4.1.3 and determine which of them are fulfilled by dice codings.

Corollary 5.4. *Let message space* $\mathcal{M}$ *and coding space* $\mathcal{S}$ *be as described in Sect. 5.1.1. Then* DICE *from Def. 5.2 has the following* sets of possible encodings:

$$\mathcal{S}_m = \{s \in \Sigma | s \in_R \langle m \rangle_{\mathsf{Ham}}\} = \langle m \rangle_{\mathsf{Ham}}$$

Proof. Cor. 5.4 follows by the definition of the DICE encoding function. □

Corollary 5.5. *Let message space* $\mathcal{M}$ *and coding space* $\mathcal{S}$ *be as described in Sect. 5.1.1. Then* DICE *from Def. 5.2 is* probabilistic *and* homomorphic.

Proof. The properties follow by Def. 5.2. □

Corollary 5.6. *Let* n *be a parameter and let message space* $\mathcal{M}$ *and coding space* $\mathcal{S}$ *be as described in Sect. 5.1.1. Then* DICE *from Def. 5.2 is* closed *in the sense of Def. 4.24.*

PROOF. Again, we only need to regard characters since DICE is homomorphic. It is easy to see, that the encoding function is surjective: A symbol $s \in \Sigma$ contains m times the substring $\bigcirc$ and $n - m$ times the substring $\bullet$. Hence, $\text{Decode}_n(s) = m$ and therefore it holds that $\text{Decode}_n(s) \neq \perp$ and it is shown that dice codings are a closed encoding scheme. ∎

As one might already have suspected when looking at Tab. 5.1 which shows the number of possible encodings for $n = 9$, dice codings are not distribution alike.

Corollary 5.7. *Let message space* $\mathcal{M}$ *and coding space* $\mathcal{S}$ *be as described in Sect. 5.1.1. Then* DICE *from Def. 5.2 is* not distribution alike.

PROOF. Since the positions of the visible dots are insignificant, the number of possible symbols representing a character m follows a binomial distribution and hence is the binomial coefficient $\binom{n}{m}$. Thus, dice codings are not distribution alike. ∎

5.2 Basic Version

In this section we first introduce a symmetric encryption scheme which makes use of the principles of visual cryptography. This encryption scheme is then applied to dice codings resulting in the basic version of a human decipherable encryption scheme based on dice codings. We then study to which extent the proposed scheme fulfills the properties of human decipherable encryption scheme defined in Sect. 4.1.4 before we investigate its security in the next section.

5.2.1 EQV Encryption Scheme

We take a look at a symmetric encryption scheme which applies the principle of visual cryptography to dice codings. We start with the formal definition which defines the key-generation, encryption and decryption algorithms. Next we show that it is a symmetric encryption scheme in the sense of Def. 2.40. Then we are ready to show that DICE and EQV form a human decipherable description scheme according to Def. 4.37.

Definition 5.8. (EQV Encryption Scheme) Let coding space $\mathcal{S}$, ciphertext space $\mathcal{C}$ and key space $\mathcal{K}$ be as described in Sect. 5.1.1. Then we denote $\mathsf{EQV} :=$ $(\mathsf{GenKey}, \mathsf{Enc}, \mathsf{Dec})$ – with the algorithms defined below – as *EQV encryption scheme*. If Enc or Dec are applied to multiple characters, they work character by character, hence the definitions below are for one character only:

- The *key-generation algorithm* GenKey takes as input the security parameter 1^n and selects a key symbol k uniformly at random from Λ.

$$\mathsf{GenKey}(1^n) := k \in_R \{\mathsf{O\bullet}, \mathsf{\bullet O}\}^n \tag{5.4}$$

- The *encryption algorithm* $\mathsf{Enc} : \Sigma \to \Gamma$ takes as input a key symbol k and a symbol $s \in \Sigma$, and outputs a ciphertext symbol c in the following way (cf. Tab. 5.2): For each visible dot in s, the part according to the ciphertext symbol is chosen such that it equals the corresponding part of the key symbol. For each invisible dot in s, the according part of the ciphertext symbol is chosen that it is the opposite part of the key symbol.

$$\mathsf{Enc}_k(s) := s \leftrightarrow k \tag{5.5}$$

Table 5.2: Contingency Table for the Encryption with the EQV Encryption Scheme Applied to Dice Codings

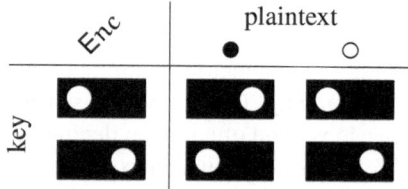

- The *decryption algorithm* $\mathsf{Dec} : \Gamma \to \Sigma$ takes as input a key symbol k and a ciphertext symbol c, and outputs a symbol s. Since encrypting and decrypting are bijective functions, a failure and thus the symbol $\bot$ never occurs. The decryption algorithm works for each dot in c and k as shown in Tab. 5.3a similar to EQV: If the corresponding parts are equal, the result is a visible dot, if they differ it is an invisible dot. Since the alphabets of the transparency's overlay and the symbol space differ, we also need a mapping function, converting the result to the symbol space's alphabet as shown in Tab. 5.3b.

$$\mathsf{Dec}_k(c) := c \leftrightarrow k$$

Table 5.3: Contingency and Evaluation Table for the Decryption with the EQV Encryption Scheme Applied to Dice Codings

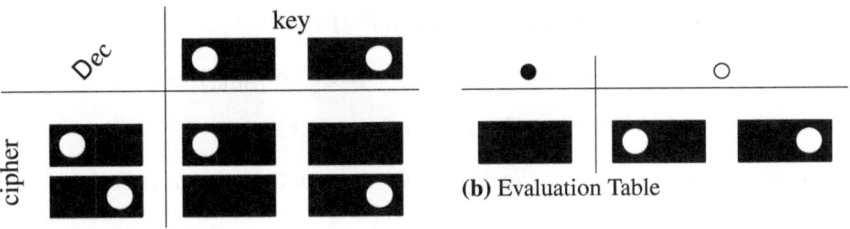

(a) Contingency Table

(b) Evaluation Table

Remark 5.9. Although, one may be curious that the encryption and decryption functions are both denoted by "↔" despite they may seem to work on different domains, we stress that the "dots" may be easily denoted as 0s and 1s as addressed in Sect. 5.1.1. Thus, one may easily convince himself that encryption and decryption implement the logical biconditional function of Def. 4.61.

It remains to show that EQV is a symmetric encryption scheme:

Theorem 5.10. *The EQV encryption scheme is a symmetric encryption scheme as defined in Def. 2.40.*

PROOF. It is easy to verify that GenKey, Enc and Dec work on the appropriate spaces and run in polynomial time. It remains to show that for every n, every k output by $GenKey(1^n)$, and every $s \in S$, it holds that $Dec_k(Enc_k(s)) = s$. This holds, since the logical biconditional function EQV is its own inverse function and thus:
$$Dec_k(Enc_k(s)) = (s \leftrightarrow k) \leftrightarrow k = s$$

∎

5.2.2 Basic Human Decipherable Encryption Scheme

The encoding scheme DICE and the symmetric encryption scheme EQV may be combined to a human decipherable encryption scheme.

Definition 5.11. Let message space $\mathcal{M}$, coding space S, ciphertext space C and key space $\mathcal{K}$ be as described in Sect. 5.1.1. We denote the tuple of combined algorithms $(HGen, HEnc, HDec)$ with $\mathcal{HE}_{DICE}$. Along the lines of the encoding scheme DICE and the encryption scheme EQV, HEnc and HDec work character by character, hence the resulting compositions below are for one character only:

- $(n,k) \leftarrow \mathsf{HGen}(1^n) = (\mathsf{Gen}(1^n), \mathsf{GenKey}(1^n))$

- $c \leftarrow \mathsf{HEnc}_{n,k}(m) = \mathsf{Enc}_k(\mathsf{Encode}_n(m)) = (s \in_R \langle m \rangle_{\mathsf{Ham}}) \leftrightarrow k$

- $m = \mathsf{HDec}_{n,k}(c) = \mathsf{Decode}_n(\mathsf{Dec}_k(c)) = \mathsf{Ham}(c \leftrightarrow k)$

We denote $\mathcal{HE}_{\mathsf{DICE}}$ as *human decipherable encryption scheme based on dice codings*.

Furthermore, we notice that $\mathcal{HE}_{\mathsf{DICE}}$ is segment-based as well as probabilistic by definition.

Corollary 5.12. *Let message space* $\mathcal{M}$, *coding space* $\mathcal{S}$, *ciphertext space* $\mathcal{C}$ *and key space* $\mathcal{K}$ *be as described in Sect. 5.1.1. Then* $\mathcal{HE}_{\mathsf{DICE}}$ *from Def. 5.11 is segment-based in the sense of Def. 4.45 and* probabilistic *in the sense of Def. 4.39.*

Proof. The proof follows by definition of $\mathcal{HE}_{\mathsf{DICE}}$.   □

Additionally, it is worth to mention that the parameter of the encoding which denotes the number of dots is also the security parameter of the encryption scheme since it determines the length of the needed key (for a single character).

Before we start to prove that $\mathcal{HE}_{\mathsf{DICE}}$ is a human decipherable encryption scheme, we have a look at a sample visualisation to get a better imagination how they look like.

EXAMPLE 5.13. (Visualisation a Dice Coding Based Scheme)
Fig. 5.2 shows two sample visualisations with the encoding, respectively security parameter, $n = 9$ where the dots are both arranged in a 3×3-matrix. Of course this is not mandatory. Since the position of the dots is not taken into account for the decryption/decoding of the message, other formats like 9×1-matrices are also imaginable. However, care has to be taken that the arrangement can easily be captured by humans. Furthermore the arrangement strongly depends on the security parameter.

To ease the recognition of elements, in Fig. 5.2b black elements are shown in dark grey.

Theorem 5.14. *Let message space* $\mathcal{M}$, *coding space* $\mathcal{S}$, *ciphertext space* $\mathcal{C}$ *and key space* $\mathcal{K}$ *be as described in Sect. 5.1.1.* $\mathcal{HE}_{\mathsf{DICE}}$ *from Def. 5.11 fulfils the properties of Def. 4.37 and therefore is a human decipherable encryption scheme.*

PROOF. The proof follows from the three simple observations (a) - (c):

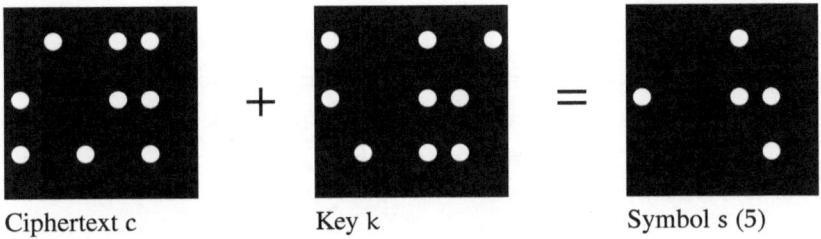

Ciphertext c   Key k   Symbol s (5)

(a) Quadratic Visualisation

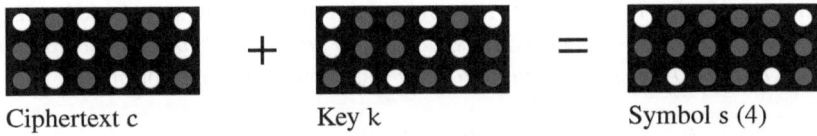

Ciphertext c   Key k   Symbol s (4)

(b) Rectangular Visualisation with Black Elements Shown in Dark Grey

Figure 5.2: Sample Visualisations of a Human Decipherable Encryption Scheme Based on Dice Codings for $n = 9$

(a) DICE is an encoding scheme as in Def. 4.20 (shown in Sect. 5.1.2).

(b) EQV is a symmetric encryption scheme as in Def. 2.40 (shown in Sect. 5.2.1), the decryption algorithm Dec is not required to run in polynomial time.

(c) The requirement that the function composition $HDec_{n,k}(c)$ is feasible for most human beings has been shown for $n = 9$ in a user study by DOBERITZ [Dob08, p. 97ff].

∎

Furthermore, it is easy to see that for every n, every k, output by $GenKey(1^n)$, and every $m \in \Omega$, it holds that:

$$HDec_{n,k}(HEnc_{n,k}(m)) = m$$

since

$$\begin{aligned}
\mathsf{HDec}_{n,k}(\mathsf{HEnc}_{n,k}(m)) &= \mathsf{Decode}_n(\mathsf{Dec}_k(\mathsf{Enc}_k(\mathsf{Encode}_n(m)))) \\
&= \mathsf{Ham}((s \in_R \langle m \rangle_{\mathsf{Ham}}) \leftrightarrow k \leftrightarrow k) \\
&= \mathsf{Ham}(s \in_R \langle m \rangle_{\mathsf{Ham}}) \qquad = \qquad m
\end{aligned}$$

Analogous to the properties of the encoding scheme DICE, we observe the properties of human decipherable encryption schemes defined in Sect. 4.1.4 and determine which of them are fulfilled by $\mathcal{HE}_{\mathsf{DICE}}$. We start with the observation of the set of possible encryptions.

Corollary 5.15. *Let* n *be the security parameter, let* m *be a message, let* k *be a key and let message space* $\mathcal{M}$, *ciphertext space* $\mathcal{C}$ *and key space* $\mathcal{K}$ *be as described in Sect. 5.1.1. Then* $\mathcal{HE}_{\mathsf{DICE}}$ *has the following* sets *of possible encryptions:*

$$\mathcal{C}_{k,m} = \{c \in \mathcal{C} | c \leftarrow \mathsf{HEnc}_k(m)\} = \langle n - m \rangle^k_{\mathsf{Ham}}$$

PROOF. Let c be a ciphertext of the message m encrypted with the key k. Then m is derived from c by determining c's distance to k. More precisely, each ciphertext c has the distance $n - m$ to the used key k. Simply because a distance of n would mean that, after decrypting, zero points are visible and if the distance from c to k shrinks by one, c and k match at another position and thus, when decrypting c with k, an additional point becomes visible which increases the message's value by one. Hence, an encryption of the message m with key k has to be in $\langle n - m \rangle^k_{\mathsf{Ham}}$ and all ciphertexts of this set decrypt with k to m. ∎

Having the set of possible encryptions in mind, it can easily be shown that the human decipherable encryption scheme based on dice codings is closed.

Corollary 5.16. *Let message space* $\mathcal{M}$, *coding space* $\mathcal{S}$, *ciphertext space* $\mathcal{C}$ *and key space* $\mathcal{K}$ *be as described in Sect. 5.1.1. Then* $\mathcal{HE}_{\mathsf{DICE}}$ *is closed in the sense of Def. 4.50.*

PROOF. We only need to regard characters since $\mathcal{HE}_{\mathsf{DICE}}$ is segment-based. We need to show that

$$\forall k \in \mathcal{K} \qquad \mathcal{C}_{k,\mathcal{M}} = \{c \in \mathcal{C} | c \leftarrow (s \in_R \langle m \rangle_{\mathsf{Ham}}) \leftrightarrow k \,.\, m \in \mathcal{M}\} \quad = \quad \mathcal{C}$$

Since dice codings are closed (cf. Cor. 5.6) and the EQV encryption scheme is – for an arbitrary but fixed k – a bijection this also holds for their composition. Note that, $\mathcal{S}$ and $\mathcal{C}$ trivially have the same number of elements since they are identical. However, this is not necessary, since for all pairs of finite sets it holds that there exists a bijection between the two sets iff they have the same number of elements [Dei10, p. 65]. Thus, $HDec_k(c) = Ham(c \leftrightarrow k)$ never equals $\perp$ and therefore $\mathcal{HE}_{DICE}$ is closed. ∎

It remains to show that $\mathcal{HE}_{DICE}$ is not distribution alike, which is obviously the case since dice codings are not and the EQV encryption scheme is deterministic and bijective and therefore preserves this property.

Corollary 5.17. *Let message space* $\mathcal{M}$*, coding space* $\mathcal{S}$*, ciphertext space* $\mathcal{C}$ *and key space* $\mathcal{K}$ *be as described in Sect. 5.1.1. Then* $\mathcal{HE}_{DICE}$ *is not distribution alike.*

Proof. Since the number of possible symbols representing a character m of DICE follows a binomial distribution and EQV is bijective, the distribution of dice codings is maintained by their composition. Hence, $\mathcal{HE}_{DICE}$ is not distribution alike. □

5.3 Security Analysis of the Basic Version

Since the decryption itself is quite simple and one time pads are only unbreakable if each key is used only once, some questions arise concerning the security of human decipherable encryption scheme based on dice codings. Are there circumstances where the key may be safely used a couple of times? If so, how often?

We assume that an adversary does not want to get discovered, and thus springs into action not before she has sufficient knowledge to perform a successful attack. An active adversary, who tampers the communication from or to the user, accepts the risk that as a result of her action the user gets suspicious and checks his computer for malicious software. Hence, in this work we cover only passive adversaries, who try to gather information for a successful attack afterwards.

It is easy to see that $\mathcal{HE}_{DICE}$ is not secure against chosen plaintext attacks. If an adversary knows any pair of ciphertext and plaintext, she is able to reduce the number of keys to the number of possible encodings for that plaintext message. Since there is only one encoding for n, an adversary may ask for an encryption of n and simply receives the key:

$$HEnc_{n,k}(n) = Enc_k(Encode_n(n)) = (s \in_R \langle n \rangle_{Ham}) \leftrightarrow k = k$$

Asking for an encryption of the message 0, which also has only one encoding, has the same consequences[2]. The only differences to known plaintext attacks consist in the fact, that the adversary may not ask for pairs of plaintext/ciphertext, otherwise

---

[2] $HEnc_{n,k}(0) = Enc_k(Encode_n(0)) = (s \in_R \langle 0 \rangle_{Ham}) \leftrightarrow k = \neg k$

she would succeed with one query. Without the plaintext/ciphertext pair, she has to reduce the number of possibly used keys for each pair she receives. We already noticed that knowing a pair of plaintext/ciphertext reduces the number of possibly used keys to the number of possible encodings for the given plaintext. If two or more pairs are known, the number of possibly used keys may be further reduced by intersecting the corresponding sets of possible keys.

However, in many applications there is no need for chosen or known plaintext security. Therefore, the next subsections deal with ciphertext-only security and slight variations. In the usual concept of ciphertext-only attacks, an adversary has only some ciphertexts and of course knowledge of the used cryptosystem. Nevertheless, an adversary often has side information about the plaintext which is less effective than one or more pairs of plaintext/ciphertext for recovering the key. She could know some restrictions or distributions regarding the plaintext. When for example, the ciphertext is the basis of a challenge-response authentication, it may be that all characters occur with the same probability or that in one challenge no symbol occurs twice.

Thus, the next subsections distinguish two cases: plain ciphertext-only attacks and ciphertext-only attacks with side information available. The side information is then further divided into side information about single dices or side information about a set of dices.

5.3.1 Ciphertext-Only Attacks Without Side Information

This subsection covers a passive adversary who has no side information available. Therefore, she obviously does not know anything about the relation of different characters. For this reason and because $\mathcal{HE}_{DICE}$ is homomorphic, the following analysis mainly deals with single characters.

If there is no side information available, an adversary may try to benefit from general attacks against one time pads. As already stated in Sect. 4.2.4, an adversary may gain information about the underlying encodings S_1 and S_2 of the plaintexts P_1 and P_2 by XORing two ciphertexts C_1 and C_2:

$$C_1 \oplus C_2 = (S_1 \leftrightarrow K) \oplus (S_2 \leftrightarrow K) = S_1 \oplus S_2$$

It is easy to see that the result above reveals the ciphertexts' *number of different dots* which is the Hamming distance between S_1 and S_2 and thus $\mathrm{Ham}(C_1 \oplus C_2) = \mathrm{Ham}(S_1 - S_2)$.

The relevance to the underlying plaintexts can be divided into the following cases, depending on the number of different dots.

0 Obviously if the number of different dots is 0, the underlying plaintexts are the same: $P_1 = P_2$.

1 If the number of different dots is 1, the difference of the plaintext messages is also 1: $P_1 = P_2 \pm 1$.

2...n-2 In contrast to the other listed cases, the number of different dots is not necessarily the difference between the plaintexts since changes may cancel each other out. Even though, an adversary may conclude whether the sum of both plaintexts is even or odd by observing if the number of different dots is even or odd: $P_1 + P_2 \overset{?}{=} 0 \mod 2$.

n-1 Analogous to "1", if the number of different dots is $n - 1$, then both plaintexts sum up to $n \pm 1$: $P_1 = n - P_2 \pm 1$.

n Analogous to "0", if the number of different dots is n, both plaintexts sum up to n. Thus P_1 would be the inverse of P_2: $P_1 = n - P_2$.

EXAMPLE 5.18. (XORing Ciphertexts of Dice Codings)
Consider $n = 9$ as an example. Tab. 5.4 shows all possible differences between ciphertexts of dice codings of the same Hamming domain. It can be easily seen that the more encodings exist for a plaintext, the more ciphertexts are possible and different numbers of dots may appear. Tab. 1 in App. 11.3 is the other way around and allows to look up all possible combinations for a given number of differing dots. Larger or smaller values of n reveal a similar picture.

Before we determine the consequences of the above for the security of the message, we take a short glance at the security of the key. It is easy to show that an adversary is not able to gain any information on the key.

Theorem 5.19. $\mathcal{HE}_{DICE}$ *is an ideal system in the sense of Def. 4.18.*

Proof. We have already shown that $\mathcal{HE}_{DICE}$ is closed. Since the adversary has no information about the sent messages, she has to consider each key equally likely and thus the message and key equivocation do not approach zero as the length of the message grows to infinity. □

Remark 5.20. It is worth mentioning, that an adversary who repeatedly eavesdrops the same ciphertext, may conclude that it is an encryption of '0' or 'n'. Although she cannot be sure that this is true, since there exists a (small) probability that another message randomly hit the same encoding.

Table 5.4: Possible Numbers of Different Dots between Ciphertexts of Dice Codings of the Same Hamming Domain with $n = 9$

$\oplus$	$\langle 0 \rangle_{Ham}$	$\langle 1 \rangle_{Ham}$	$\langle 2 \rangle_{Ham}$	$\langle 3 \rangle_{Ham}$	$\langle 4 \rangle_{Ham}$
$\langle 0 \rangle_{Ham}$	0	1	2	3	4
$\langle 1 \rangle_{Ham}$	1	0,2	1,3	2,4	3,5
$\langle 2 \rangle_{Ham}$	2	1,3	0,2,4	1,3,5	2,4,6
$\langle 3 \rangle_{Ham}$	3	2,4	1,3,5	0,2,4,6	1,3,5,7
$\langle 4 \rangle_{Ham}$	4	3,5	2,4,6	1,3,5,7	0,2,4,6,8
$\langle 5 \rangle_{Ham}$	5	4,6	3,5,7	2,4,6,8	1,3,5,7,9
$\langle 6 \rangle_{Ham}$	6	5,7	4,6,8	3,5,7,9	2,4,6,8
$\langle 7 \rangle_{Ham}$	7	6,8	5,7,9	4,6,8	3,5,7
$\langle 8 \rangle_{Ham}$	8	7,9	6,8	5,7	4,6
$\langle 9 \rangle_{Ham}$	9	8	7	6	5

$\oplus$	$\langle 5 \rangle_{Ham}$	$\langle 6 \rangle_{Ham}$	$\langle 7 \rangle_{Ham}$	$\langle 8 \rangle_{Ham}$	$\langle 9 \rangle_{Ham}$
$\langle 0 \rangle_{Ham}$	5	6	7	8	9
$\langle 1 \rangle_{Ham}$	4,6	5,7	6,8	7,9	8
$\langle 2 \rangle_{Ham}$	3,5,7	4,6,8	5,7,9	6,8	7
$\langle 3 \rangle_{Ham}$	2,4,6,8	3,5,7,9	4,6,8	5,7	6
$\langle 4 \rangle_{Ham}$	1,3,5,7,9	2,4,6,8	3,5,7	4,6	5
$\langle 5 \rangle_{Ham}$	0,2,4,6,8	1,3,5,7	2,4,6	3,5	4
$\langle 6 \rangle_{Ham}$	1,3,5,7	0,2,4,6	1,3,5	2,4	3
$\langle 7 \rangle_{Ham}$	2,4,6	1,3,5	0,2,4	1,3	2
$\langle 8 \rangle_{Ham}$	3,5	2,4	1,3	0,2	1
$\langle 9 \rangle_{Ham}$	4	3	2	1	0

Now that we examined the situation for an adversary trying to recover the secret key, we turn towards the analysis of the message's secrecy again. We already discovered that an adversary, who is able to eavesdrop two (or more) ciphertexts, may XOR them and draw some conclusions on the underlying plaintexts. Especially, she may exclude some combinations of plaintexts which do not fit the observed number of different dots. By continuously constructing sequences of valid messages which pairwise match the number of different dots, an adversary may lower the number of possible combinations of ciphertexts sent.

However, an adversary is not able to reduce the number of possible symbols for 0 below 2^n, the size of the key space. This is easy to see, since we already showed that the adversary is not able to draw conclusions on the key, 0 has only one symbol and each of the 2^n possible keys yield another ciphertext as the encryption of 0.

Thus, without side information, the adversary is not able to learn anything about the key or to reduce the number of possibly sent messages below the size of the key space. Therefore, we now examine the adversary's chances if she has side information available.

5.3.2 Ciphertext-Only Attacks With Side Information

As already stated in Sect. 4.1.2, in many cases an attacker has side information available. At first we consider side information about single characters. This means, the adversary has information about characters encrypted with the same key. In particular, we assume the adversary knows that the characters follow a certain distribution. Next, we regard an adversary who additionally knows that the plaintexts follow a certain pattern.

Security of Single Characters

As we mentioned earlier, the dice encoding scheme is not distribution alike but follows a binomial distribution instead. Let's assume the messages consist of the digits from 0 to 9, which means $n = 9$ and we recall the resulting distribution of possible encodings as shown in Tab. 5.1. Since encrypting does not change the distribution, the adversary may exploit this distribution and try to determine the ciphertext of 0 or 9 which is unique and allows to recover the secret key. Note that a restriction of the encoding characters, e.g. using only one of the possible symbols for each digit, would lead to an encoding scheme which is no longer closed. Thus, for an adversary observing ciphertexts, the distribution would no longer be helpful, but she could derive information on the used key instead (cf. Sect. 4.2.4).

Uniform Distribution In this paragraph, we assume the characters are uniformly distributed in $\Omega = \{0, \ldots, n\}$, which means the probability for an arbitrary but fixed m is $P(m) = \frac{1}{n+1}$. This distribution can be found regarding randomly generated keypads for challenge-response authentication. Since the dice encoding function changes the resulting distributions, an adversary may exploit this. Before we further discuss an adversary's strategy, we take a look at the occurring probabilities which are shown for $n = 9$ in Tab. 5.5.

For each character there are $|\mathcal{S}_m| = \binom{n}{m}$ possible Encodings. It is easy to see, that there is a huge gap between the number of encodings for 0 and $\lfloor \frac{n}{2} \rfloor$. Given an arbitrary but fixed symbol s, this leads to a conditional probability $P(s|m) = \frac{1}{|\mathcal{S}_m|}$ depending on the underlying character m which also shows large differences between the named characters. Since all characters occur with the same probability, the probabilities $P(s)$ for arbitrary but fixed symbols s reflect the originating message.

Table 5.5: Dice Codings: Probabilities of 9-Dots Dice Encodings for Uniformly Distributed Characters in Percent

m	$P(m)$	$|S_m|$	$P(s|m)$	$P(s)$
0	10.0	1	100.0	10.0
1	10.0	9	11.1	1.1
2	10.0	36	2.8	0.3
3	10.0	84	1.2	0.1
4	10.0	126	0.8	0.1
5	10.0	126	0.8	0.1
6	10.0	84	1.2	0.1
7	10.0	36	2.8	0.3
8	10.0	9	11.1	1.1
9	10.0	1	100.0	10.0

Furthermore, it is worth mentioning that the encryption is a mapping between symbols and ciphertexts and therefore not only the symbols, but also the ciphertexts reflect the corresponding probabilities.

Before we present an adversary's possible algorithm, there is one further property to notice. The inverse of a symbol s from the message m, which is obtained by 'dotwise' reversing pairs of dots, represents the inverse of the message m, namely $n - m$. This means that each message m and its inverse message $n - m$ must have the same number of possible encodings. Since all messages occur with the same probability, without additional information an adversary will not be able to distinguish between a message m and its inverse message $n - m$.

Having this in mind, we next determine an algorithm of an adversary which exploits the mentioned properties. The property that inverting a symbol s means inverting it corresponding message m is preserved by using the encryption EQV, thus the adversary does not need to differentiate between a ciphertext c and its inverse ciphertext. This means that the adversary may build classes of ciphertext by combining ciphertexts and their inverse, i.e. by inverting all ciphertexts which start with '1'. As a consequence, the probabilities for the arising classes double up[3].

To evaluate the success of an algorithm we also need to make statements about the probabilities of messages and ciphertexts. We use the following notations:

Definition 5.21. (Probabilities of Messages and Ciphertexts) Let $m \in \mathcal{M}$ be a message, $c \in \mathcal{C}$ be a ciphertext and let n be the security parameter of an human de-

---

[3]The only exception is the case when n is even and $\frac{n}{2}$ is regarded. Then, the inversion of $\frac{n}{2}$ is also $\frac{n}{2}$ and thus the corresponding sets are the same.

cipherable encryption scheme. Let N denote the number of messages or ciphertexts chosen, we introduce the following notation:

$P\left(\#c \gtreqless k|N\right)$ denotes the probability that the ciphertext c appears 'at least' / 'exactly' / 'at most' k times when doing N iterations.

$P\left(\forall c.\#c \gtreqless k|N\right)$ denotes the probability that each of the ciphertexts c appears 'at least' / 'exactly' / 'at most' k times when doing N iterations.

$P\left(\exists c.\#c \gtreqless k|N\right)$ denotes the probability that there exists a ciphertext c which appears 'at least' / 'exactly' / 'at most' k times when doing N iterations.

$P\left(\#m \gtreqless k|N\right)$ denotes the probability that the message m appears 'at least' / 'exactly' / 'at most' k times when doing N iterations.

$P\left(\forall m.\#m \gtreqless k|N\right)$ denotes the probability that each of the messages m appears 'at least' / 'exactly' / 'at most' k times when doing N iterations.

$P\left(\exists m.\#m \gtreqless k|N\right)$ denotes the probability that there exists a messages m which appears 'at least' / 'exactly' / 'at most' k times when doing N iterations.

Furthermore, if we use m^* or c^* instead of m or c, we mean that we do not distinguish between a message and its inverse and their corresponding ciphertexts.

Alg. 5.1 shows an algorithm which an adversary could use to attack the encryption scheme. At first, the algorithm inverts the ciphertexts if necessary (without loss of generality ensure that all ciphertexts start with '0') and then counts how often each 'normalised' ciphertext occurs (lines 1 to 6). If there is a ciphertext which occurred at least twice, the algorithm outputs the ciphertexts which occurred most often, otherwise it signals "failure" by returning 'noguess' (lines 7 to 12).

Depending on the security parameter n and the number of available ciphertexts N, there are four different outcomes.

1. No ciphertext occurred twice or more and the algorithm returned 'noguess'. Then, probably the number of available ciphertexts was too small and the adversary can do no better than to randomly take an available ciphertext and guess that it was '0' or respectively 'n'.

   Since we normalise ciphertexts as described above, there are $\frac{2^n}{2}$ distinct elements. Remember that we do not distinguish between a message m and it's inverse $n - m$. Thus, for $N > 2^{n-1}$ it follows from DIRICHLET's drawer principle [JJ92, p. 126] that at least one ciphertext c^* occurred twice which contradicts the specification of this class. For the rest of our analysis we require $N \leqslant 2^{n-1}$. The probability that no ciphertext occurs twice may be expressed

---

Algorithm 5.1: Probabilistic Algorithm to Attack Uniformly Distributed Messages Encrypted with $\mathcal{HE}_{\text{DICE}}$

---

input : a set of ciphertexts
output : a key or 'noguess'

1 **forall the** *ciphertexts* c **do**
    // Invert c if necessary
2   **if** c.*substring*(0)=='1' **then**
3 | c := invert(c)
4   **end**
    // Increase number of ciphertexts for c
5   NumberOf[c]++;
6 **end**

// Are there matching ciphertexts?
7 **if** $\exists$ c: NumberOf[c] > 1 **then**
    // Yes, there are.
8   **find** c with NumberOf[c] = max(NumberOf);
9   **return** c;
10 **else**
    // No, there are not.
11   **return**'noguess'
12 **end**

---

as product of conditional probabilities that no ciphertext occurs twice given the message.

$$P('noguess') = P\left(\forall c^*.\#c^* \leqslant 1|N\right)$$

$$= \sum_{\sum N_{i^*} = N}\left(\prod_{i=0}^{\lfloor \frac{n+1}{2} \rfloor} P\left(\forall c.c = HEnc\,(i^*).\#c \leqslant 1|N_{i^*}\right)\right)$$

$$= \sum_{\sum N_{i^*} = N}\left(\prod_{i=0}^{\lfloor \frac{n+1}{2} \rfloor} \frac{\prod_{j=1}^{N_i}\left(\binom{n}{i}-j+1\right)}{\binom{n}{i}}\right)$$

N_{i^*} denotes the number of times the message i or its inverse occurs. Therefore, we would need to regard all possible partitions of N into N_{i^*} and sum up their probabilities. Since this term becomes unwieldy quite fast and we are only interested in a rough estimate, we use the following observations to determine an upper bound. If a message of the class $\{0, n\}$ appears twice, its ciphertext also appears twice. Since there are $\binom{n}{i}$ different ciphertexts a message i may be encrypted to, the probability that a ciphertext occurs twice is lower the larger i is. Therefore we neglect all Terms with $0 > i > n$ and use the probability that the message 0 or n appears twice as upper bound[4]:

$$P\left(\forall c^* . \#c^* \leqslant 1 | N\right) \leqslant P\left(\forall c.c = \text{HEnc}(0) \vee c = \text{HEnc}(n).\#c \leqslant 1 | N\right)$$
$$= P\left(\#0^* = 0 | N\right) + P\left(\#0^* = 1 | N\right)$$
$$= \left(1 - \frac{2}{n+1}\right)^N + \binom{N}{1}\left(\frac{2}{n+1}\right)\left(1 - \frac{2}{n+1}\right)^{N-1}$$
$$= \left(\frac{2N+n-1}{n+1}\right)\left(\frac{n-1}{n+1}\right)^{N-1} \tag{5.6}$$

2. There is a unique ciphertext which occurred more often than all others, but it is not the encryption of '0' or 'n'. Thus, the adversary believes she has found the secret key, but she has taken a wrong one.

We already stated that the probability of hitting a ciphertext multiple times depends on its underlying message. To get a first approximate we only regard encryptions of '1' and 'n−1' as 'false occurrence'. Again we have to sum up the probabilities of all partitions of N into N_{i^*} with the condition that $N_{0^*} < N_{1^*}$. It is easy to see, that its distribution follows a multinomial distribution [LW92, p. 147]:

$$P(\text{'false'}) \geqslant \sum_{\substack{\sum N_{i^*}=N \\ N_{0^*} < N_{1^*} \\ 2 \leqslant N_{1^*}}} P\left(\exists c.c = \text{HEnc}(1^*).\#c > N_0 | N_{1^*}\right) \cdot$$
$$P\left(\#0^* = N_{0^*}, \#1^* = N_{1^*}, \#\{2,\dots,n\} = N_R | N\right)$$
$$= \sum_{\substack{\sum N_{i^*}=N \\ N_{0^*} < N_{1^*} \\ 2 \leqslant N_{1^*}}} P\left(\exists c.c = \text{HEnc}(1^*).\#c > N_0 | N_{1^*}\right) \cdot$$
$$\frac{N!}{N_{0^*}! N_{1^*}! N_R!}\left(\frac{2}{n+1}\right)^{N_{0^*}}\left(\frac{2}{n+1}\right)^{N_{1^*}}\left(\frac{n-3}{n+1}\right)^{N_R} \tag{5.7}$$

Due to the numerous classes with different numbers of elements we end up with lots of disjunctions if we want to regard all cases and exactly examine the probability. Therefor, we remember that the previous case contains some of the

---

[4]Remember that we assumed a uniform distribution of the messages.

occurrences which actually belong to this case. Since we took the outcome that an encryption of 0^* occurs at most once as upper bound for the probability that no encryption occurs more often than once, the given probability includes all outcomes that the encryption of 0^* occurs at most once and another ciphertext occurs at least twice. If the probability of the left cases – meaning $N_{0^*} \geqslant 2$ and $N_{1^*} > N_{0^*}$ is small, we may follow that $P('false') + P('noguess') \approx P(\forall c.c = \mathsf{HEnc}(0^*).\#c \leqslant 1|N)$.

Hence, we first assume there are N_{1^*} ciphertexts of 1^* and regard the probability that k_1 matching ciphertexts of 1^*occur. Again we apply DIRICHLET's drawer principle to conclude that for $N_{1^*} > (k_1 - 1)n + 1$ the probability is 1. For all other N_{1^*} and $c = \mathsf{HEnc}(1^*)$ it holds that:

$$
\begin{aligned}
P\left(\exists c.\#c = k_1|N_{1^*}\right) &\leqslant & n\binom{N_{1^*}}{k_1}\left(\frac{1}{n}\right)^k \left(\frac{n-1}{n}\right)^{N_{1^*}-k_1} \\
&=& \binom{N_{1^*}}{k_1}\left(\frac{1}{n}\right)^{N_{1^*}-1} (n-1)^{N_{1^*}-k_1} \quad (5.8)
\end{aligned}
$$

To calculate the probability of the case where $N_{0^*} \geqslant 2$ and $N_{1^*} > N_{0^*}$ we need to multiply the probability of the outcome that a specific N_{0^*} and $N_{1^*} > N_{0^*}$ occur (cf. Term 5.7) with the probability that at least $k_1 > N_{0^*}$ of the N_{1^*} 1^* match (cf. Term 5.8). For arbitrary but fixed n, N_{0^*}, k_1, N it holds that:

$$
\begin{aligned}
P\left(\#0^* = N_{0^*}; k_1|N\right) &= \sum_{N_{1^*}=k_1}^{N-N_{0^*}} \frac{N! 2^{N_{1^*}+N_{0^*}}(n-3)^{N_R}}{N_{0^*}! N_{1^*}! N_R! (n+1)^N} \\
&\cdot \binom{N_{1^*}}{k_1}\left(\frac{1}{n}\right)^{N_{1^*}-1} (n-1)^{N_{1^*}-k_1} \quad (5.9)
\end{aligned}
$$

To determine which of the above term's summands is the largest, we only regard terms depending on N_{1^*} and merge all others into X:

$$
P\left(\#0^* = N_{0^*}; k_1|N\right) = \sum_{N_{1^*}=k_1}^{N-N_{0^*}} X
$$

$$
\cdot \frac{1}{(N_{1^*}-k_1)!(N-N_{1^*}-N_{0^*})!} \quad (5.10)
$$

$$
\cdot \left(\frac{2(n-1)}{(n-3)n}\right)^{N_{1^*}} \quad (5.11)
$$

Obviously if N_{1*} increases, Term 5.10 increases until the middle of N_{1*}'s range and the decreases. Since the base in Term 5.11 is between 0 and 1, the term decreases when N_{1*} increases. Thus, the changes of both terms are contrary until N_{1*} reachs the middle of its interval. To determine the maximum of those terms we regard the change of them when N_{1*} increases:

$$\frac{(N - N_{1*} - N_{0*})}{(N_{1*} + 1 - k_1)} \cdot \left(\frac{2(n-1)}{(n-3)n} \right) \tag{5.12}$$

The term increases as long as Term 5.12 is greater than 1 and thus:

$$N_{1*} < (k_1 - 1) + 2 \frac{n(1 - k_1 + N - N_{0*}) - N + N_{0*} + k_1 - 1}{(n^2 - n - 2)} \tag{5.13}$$

Following the previous examples we assume $n = 9$. Furthermore we regard only the smallest N_{0*}, k_1 since there are n different encryptions of 1^* making high values of k_1 more unlikely to appear (cf. Tab. 2 and Tab. 3) and therefore with $N_{0*} = 2$ and $k_1 = 3$ we obtain:

$$N_{1*} < \frac{8N + 38}{35} \tag{5.14}$$

For $N < 15$ it follows that $N_{1*} = 3$, for $N \leqslant 15 < 20$ it follows that $N_{1*} = 4$, and for $N = 20$ it follows that $N_{1*} = 5$ leads to the last term which increases the summand and thus the subsequent $N_{1*} + 1$ leads to the maximum summand (cf. Tab. 5.6). This can easily be proven by multiplying the corresponding values of Tab. 4 and Tab. 2 which is essentially an evaluation of one summand of $P(\#0^* = 2; 3|N)$. It shows that even the maximum summands are quite small (remember the values are given in percent). Furthermore, from Term 5.12 it can be seen that there are not that many terms to consider, because the summands decrease fast if the maximum summand has been passed. As already said, for larger N_{0*}, k_1 this case becomes even less probable. Hence, we conclude that $P(\text{'false'}) + P(\text{'noguess'}) \approx P(\forall c.c = HEnc(0^*).\#c \leqslant 1|N)$ for sufficiently small N and therefore (cf. Term 5.6):

$$P(\text{'false'}) + P(\text{'noguess'}) \approx \left(\frac{2N + n - 1}{n + 1} \right) \left(\frac{n - 1}{n + 1} \right)^{N-1} \tag{5.15}$$

3. There are two ciphertexts which occurred more often than all others. In this case we may greatly benefit from the considerations of the previous case. Hence, we use the notation from the case above without explicitly redefining it.

Table 5.6: Evaluation of $P(\#0* = 2;3|N)$'s summands (in %) for selected N and N_{1*} with maximum summands highlighted

N	N_{1*}	Summand	Changefactor
	3	$7.7 \cdot 10^{-2}$	
	4	$1.1 \cdot 10^{-1}$	1.48
10	5	$6.8 \cdot 10^{-2}$	0.59
	6	$2.0 \cdot 10^{-3}$	0.03
	3	$7.2 \cdot 10^{-2}$	
	4	$2.1 \cdot 10^{-1}$	2.96
15	5	$2.8 \cdot 10^{-1}$	1.33
	6	$2.2 \cdot 10^{-2}$	0.08
	3	$2.9 \cdot 10^{-2}$	
	4	$1.3 \cdot 10^{-1}$	4.44
20	5	$2.7 \cdot 10^{-1}$	2.07
	6	$3.4 \cdot 10^{-1}$	1.28
	7	$3.0 \cdot 10^{-1}$	0.89

Since the probability of obtaining 'matching ciphertexts' is highest for $0*$ and $1*$ we consider only this case. We follow the line of the previous case and determine the corresponding probability on the basis of Eq. 5.7:

$$P(\#0* = k_1|N) \geq \sum_{\substack{\sum N_{i*} = N \\ N_{0*} \leq N_{1*} \\ 2 \leq N_{0*}}} P(\exists c.c = HEnc(1*).\#c = N_0|N_{1*})$$

$$\cdot \ P(\#0* = N_{0*}, \#1* = N_{1*}, \#\{2,\ldots,n\} = N_R|N)$$

$$= \sum_{\substack{\sum N_{i*} = N \\ N_{0*} \leq N_{1*} \\ 2 \leq N_{0*}}} P(\exists c.c = HEnc(1*).\#c = N_0|N_{1*})$$

$$\cdot \ \frac{N!}{N_{0*}!N_{1*}!N_R!} \cdot \frac{2^{N_{0*}+N_{1*}}(n-3)^{N_R}}{(n+1)^{N_{0*}+N_{1*}+N_R}} \quad (5.16)$$

Along the lines of the previous case we need to deal with lots of disjunctions if we want to examine the exact probability. Therefore, we begin with evaluating the probabilities for $N_{0*} = k_1 = 2$ and $N_{0*} = k_1 = 3$. We already determined the probability of k_1 matching ciphertexts of $1*$ given that there is a total of N_{1*}

ciphertexts of 1^* and came up with Term 5.8. In analogy to Eq. 5.9 and thus for arbitrary but fixed n, N_{0^*}, k_1, N we receive:

$$P(\#0^* = N_{0^*} = k_1 | N) = \sum_{N_{1^*}=k_1}^{N-N_{0^*}} \frac{N!}{N_{0^*}! N_{1^*}! N_R!}$$

$$\cdot \left(\frac{2}{n+1}\right)^{N_{1^*}+N_{0^*}} \left(\frac{n-3}{n+1}\right)^{N_R}$$

$$\cdot \binom{N_{1^*}}{k_1} \left(\frac{1}{n}\right)^{N_{1^*}-1} (n-1)^{N_{1^*}-k_1} \quad (5.17)$$

From here we follow the line of argument from Eq. 5.10 to Eq. 5.13 and continue with the values $N_{0^*} = k_1 = 2$ and $N_{0^*} = k_1 = 3$ to determine the maximum summand. This results in $N_{1^*} < \frac{8N+11}{35}$ respectively $N_{1^*} < \frac{8N+30}{35}$. Again, this can easily be proven by multiplying the corresponding values of Tab. 4 respectively Tab. 5 and Tab. 2 which also provides us with values for $P(\#0^* = 2; 2|N)$ (cf. Tab. 5.7). Since the probabilities for larger values of N_{0^*} respectively k_1 vanish fast[5] we obtain the following approximations:

$$P('tie'|N = 10) < \qquad 0.05$$
$$P('tie'|N = 15) < \qquad 0.10$$
$$P('tie'|N = 20) < \qquad 0.10$$

In summary, the probabilities of this case are slightly larger than those of the previous case. This mainly follows from on the fact that k_1 is smaller by one and therefore requires one matching ciphertext less. Otherwise, there is a fifty-fifty chance for choosing the correct key. We did not consider the very rare cases like a tie of three ciphertexts, because on the one hand, these cases have only a very low probability of occurrence and on the other hand, if they occur, it is very likely that one of these ciphertexts is an encryption of 0^* and the other two are encryptions of 1^* which provides another point of attack.

4. There is one ciphertext which occurred more often than all others, which is the encryption of '0' or 'n'.

Since we already gave upper bounds and approximations of the probabilities of all other cases we calculate the probability of this case by calculating the complementary probability:

$$P('correct') = 1 - P('false' + 'noguess') - P('tie') \quad (5.18)$$

---

[5]at least in the considered range of N (cf. Tab. 6 for an evaluation of $P(\#0^* = 3; 3|N)$)

Table 5.7: Evaluation of $P(\#0* = 2; 2|N)$'s summands (in %) for selected N and N_{1*} with maximum summands highlighted

N	N_{1*}	summand	changefactor
	2	1.0	
	3	1.9	1.85
	4	1.4	0.73
10	5	$5.1 \cdot 10^{-1}$	0.37
	6	$1.0 \cdot 10^{-1}$	0.2
	7	$1.0 \cdot 10^{-2}$	0.1
	8	$4.6 \cdot 10^{-4}$	0.04
	2	$5.3 \cdot 10^{-1}$	
	3	1.8	3.39
	4	2.6	1.46
	5	2.2	0.83
15	6	1.1	0.53
	7	$4.1 \cdot 10^{-1}$	0.36
	8	$1.0 \cdot 10^{-1}$	0.26
	9	$2.0 \cdot 10^{-2}$	0.19
	2	$1.5 \cdot 10^{-1}$	
	3	$7.2 \cdot 10^{-1}$	4.94
	4	1.6	2.18
20	5	2.0	1.29
	6	1.7	0.86
	7	1.1	0.62
	8	$5.1 \cdot 10^{-1}$	0.47
	9	$1.9 \cdot 10^{-1}$	0.37

In Tab. 5.8 the result for $N \leqslant 20$ is shown. Remember that the success probability still refers to two possible keys, since we are not able to differ between the actually used key and its inverse.

In conclusion, if characters are uniformly distributed in $\Omega = \{0, \ldots, n\}$ and encrypted with $\mathcal{HE}_{DICE}$ – depending on N – an attacker has a good chance of computing the used key which is far better than guessing. For large values of N, the law of large numbers [LW92, p. 88] takes effect and because $\mathcal{HE}_{DICE}$ is not distribution alike, an adversary will in many cases be able to read off the key (or its inverse) from the given ciphertexts.

Table 5.8: Probabilities (in %) of Success for Reducing the Number of Possible Keys to Two if Characters are Uniformly Distributed and Encrypted with $\mathcal{HE}_{DICE}$ with $n = 9$ and $N \leqslant 20$

N	P('correct')	P('false'+'noguess')	P('tie')
1	0.0	100.0	
2	4.0	96.0	
3	5.3	89.6	
4	13.1	81.9	
5	21.3	73.7	
6	29.5	65.5	
7	37.3	57.7	$\leqslant 5$
8	44.7	50.3	
9	51.4	43.6	
10	57.4	37.6	
11	57.8	32.2	
12	62.5	27.5	
13	66.6	23.4	$\leqslant 10$
14	70.2	19.8	
15	73.3	16.7	
16	75.9	14.1	
17	78.2	11.8	
18	80.1	9.9	$\leqslant 10$
19	81.7	8.3	
20	83.1	6.9	

Considerations of Other Distributions   There are many other discrete probability distributions, such as the Poisson distribution [LW92, p. 43], the binomial distribution [LW92, p. 43], the hypergeometric distribution [LW92, p. 93] or distributions according to the first-digit law going back to NEWCOMB [New81] and BENFORD [Ben38]. The first-digit law states that for many real-life sources of data, larger digits occur as the leading digit with lower and lower frequency. Whereas HILL [Hil95] has shown that this distribution rapidly converges to a uniform distribution as the position of the digit increases.

As a general idea for all distributions, the adversary may regard the expected value and the standard deviation of the considered distribution and try for which key the observed ciphertexts give the best approximation of the distribution, arithmetic mean and/or the root mean square. A drawback of this method is, that large values of N are required in order to get empirically sound results with this method. Hence,

Table 5.9: Expected Value and Standard Deviation of Distributions in General[1] and for $n = 9$

Distribution	expected Value		standard deviation	
Binomial	$n/2$	4.50	$\frac{1}{2}\sqrt{n}$	1.50
First-Digit Law[2]		3.44		6.06
Hypergeometric[3]	$\frac{ni}{i+j}$	$\frac{9i}{i+j}$	$\frac{\sqrt{nij}}{i+j}$	$\frac{3\sqrt{ij}}{i+j}$
Poisson[4]	λ	λ	λ	λ
Uniform	$n/2$	4.50	$\sqrt{\frac{(n+1)^2-1}{12}}$	2.87

[1] source: first digit law from NEWCOMB [New81], other distributions based on BARTSCH [Bar93]

[2] not considering the appearance of '0'

[3] with i being the number of ways for a "successful" selection and j being the number of ways for an "unsuccessful" selection out of a total of $i+j$ possibilities

[4] with λ being the expected number of occurrences in the given interval

we end the discussion of this method with Tab. 5.9 which shows the mentioned values for the referred distributions and turn to the discussion of a the binomial distribution of characters.

While for some of the other distributions it is possible to draw conclusions on the key given a certain amount of ciphertexts, based on similar considerations than before, this does not hold for the binomial distribution of characters as shown in Tab. 5.10. Because the distribution of characters and the distribution of the DICE encoding scheme cancel each other out, the resulting codings and therefore the ciphertexts follow a uniform distribution. Hence, the preconditions for Th. 4.19 are fulfilled, because if we only regard the codings, they are all equally likely and independently chosen. Thus – with the assumed binomial distribution of characters, the encryption system is strongly ideal. One may easily convince oneself by asserting that any (used) key results in an binomial distribution of the underlying characters. However, since this distribution is very special, it is unclear if it is of any practical use. Therefore, we do not go further into details here and continue with the security analysis for the case when the available side information ranges over several dices.

Table 5.10: Dice Codings: Probabilities of 9-Dots Dice Encodings for Binomial Distributed Characters in Percent

m	$P(m)$	$|S_m|$	$P(s|m)$	$P(s)$
0	0.2	1	100.0	0.2
1	1.8	9	11.1	0.2
2	7.0	36	2.8	0.2
3	16.4	84	1.2	0.2
4	24.6	126	0.8	0.2
5	24.6	126	0.8	0.2
6	16.4	84	1.2	0.2
7	7.0	36	2.8	0.2
8	1.8	9	11.1	0.2
9	0.2	1	100.0	0.2

Security of Multiple Characters

For this subsection, we assume that the adversary has access to ciphertexts consisting of tuples of ciphertext where underlying plaintexts are (pairwise) distinct. As an example for this scenario we refer to a challenge-response authentication with a virtual numeric keypad where the user has to enter a PIN or TAN (cf. Sect. 4.2.3 and BORCHERT [Bor07]). Although these keypads may consist of any combination of digits, e.g. if they are used for indexed TAN (iTAN) schemes [HTBB08, p. 16], where the user is asked to enter a specific i-TAN for each transaction, it is common that they consist of the digits from '0' to '9' and contain no digit twice. While for all keypads the observations from Sect. 5.3.2 – especially about uniformly distributed characters – apply, we consider here only keypads consisting of the digits from '0' to '9' which contain no duplicates. In this case we are able to give an attack algorithm with error free output. We first describe the basic concept of this algorithm with the help of two different characters before we broaden our scope to the complete keypad.

Security of Pairs of Characters   Assume we are given the ciphertexts of two characters, along with the side information, that the characters are distinct. This allows an attacker to exclude the set of possible keys which would decrypt the ciphertexts to the same character. Let n denote the encoding parameter and thus the number of dots. Then the size of the key space for encrypting two characters is 2^{2n}. The number of keys an adversary may exclude is $\sum_{i=0}^{n} \binom{n}{i}\binom{n}{i}$ which equals $\binom{2n}{n}$ by applying the Chu-Vandermonde identity [PWZ97, p. 181]. Hence, for $n = 9$, each ciphertext yields 48620 'illegal' keys out of a total of 262144 keys. Since the sets of 'illegal' keys overlap for different ciphertexts, the question arises how many ciphertexts an adversary will need to recover the secret key. First of all, we notice that with the information given, an adversary will not be able to compute the secret key. Instead of that, she can only narrow the number of possible keys to two, since inverting the key will retain the property if both characters are equal or not. Alg. 5.2 describes the basic algorithm of an adversary: A list of all possible keys is built and for each ciphertext all keys which would decrypt the two ciphertexts to the same character are gradually deleted (lines 6 to 12). Since we cannot differ between a key and its inverse for each run at most 2^{2n-1} decryptions need to be computed.

Algorithm 5.2: Deterministic Algorithm to Attack Pairs of Different Characters Encrypted with $\mathcal{HE}_{DICE}$

---

input : a set of pairs of different ciphertexts encpted with the same key
output : a key and the number of ciphertexts needed
```
// Initialise
```
1 counter:=0;
2 Possible Keys:= new set with all keys of size $2n - 1$;
```
   // Loop
```
3 **while** |Possible Keys| > 1 **do**
4 $\quad$ counter++;
5 $\quad$ get pair of different ciphertexts p_1, p_2;
6 $\quad$ **forall the** *keys in* Possible Keys **do**
```
        // derive k₁ and k₂ from key by splitting the key and
           padding the first digit of k₁ with 0
```
7 $\quad\quad$ $k_1 = 0, keys.substring(0, n/2 - 2)$;
8 $\quad\quad$ $k_2 = keys.substring(n/2 - 1, n - 2)$;
9 $\quad\quad$ **if** $HDec_{k_1}(p_1) = HDec_{k_2}(p_2)$ **then**
10 $\quad\quad\quad$ delete key from Possible Keys
11 $\quad\quad$ **end**
12 $\quad$ **end**
13 **end**
14 **return** counter, Possible Keys

Listings of an implementation (cf. List. 11.2) using a binary tree [Knu97, p. 319] (cf. List. 11.3) with Nodes (cf. List. 11.1) can be found in App. 11.3. The binary tree is built using a nested node class and each node has a pointer to its father and has 'zero' and 'one' sub-tree pointer which may be null if the key has already been dismissed.

Table 5.11: Number of Needed Ciphertexts to Recover the Secret Key from Pairs of Ciphertexts with $n-9$ and $20,000$ Runs in Total

A number of needed ciphertexts			B number of runs terminating	C aggregated number of runs
	<	40	0	0
41	-	50	640	640
51	-	60	5,024	5,664
61	-	70	6,544	12,208
71	-	80	4,656	16,864
81	-	90	2,165	19,029
91	-	100	703	19,732
101	-	110	196	19,928
111	-	120	58	19,986
	>	120	14	20,000

Tab. 5.11 shows the results from running Alg. 5.2. The experiment consisted of 20,000 runs of the program. For each run the number of randomly chosen ciphertexts is counted which was needed to eliminate all keys from the set of possible keys besides one key and its inverse. The table reads as follows. The first column A shows the number of needed ciphertexts grouped into blocks of 10. The second column B shows how many of the 20,000 runs stopped with the number of ciphertexts in the range given in column A. As can be seen, the keyspace was never reduced to two with less than 40 ciphertexts and very few of the randomly chosen key-ciphertext combinations required more than 100 ciphertexts to terminate. Column C is the summation of the values from B. The maximum number of ciphertexts needed was 153, but in general, no upper limit can be given for the reduction.

Security of Complete Keypads This subsection covers attacks on encrypted keypads consisting of the digits from '0' to 'n' without duplicates – based on the observations of the previous subsection. Such a keypad provides us with $n(n-1)$ pairs of different characters which we are able to attack. The main reason for attacking pairs and assembling the parts of the key afterwards instead of attacking the complete key to find 'illegal' keys, is that the first would need time $\mathcal{O}\left(2^{n(n+1)}\right)$ while the latter runs in time $\mathcal{O}\left(n(n-1)\cdot 2^{2n-1}\right)$.

Fortunately, we do not need to analyse all of these pairs independently. For each part of the key it is sufficient to have one result. Furthermore, we do not need to wait until the complete part of the key is recovered but may instead use partial information (excluded keys) to exclude possible keys for other pairs of ciphertexts. For each pair of ciphertexts, the key consists of two parts belonging to the corresponding ciphertext-blocks. If there is no possible key left for the second part of the key – given a certain key of the first part – we may exclude this prefix for all related combinations. Fig. 5.3 shows the representation of the keys as a binary tree. The bold nodes denote the actual path $(0100...1)$ and the second part of the key is shown in a frame.

The basic algorithm is sketched by Alg. 5.3. It inherits the part for the deletion of excluded keys from Alg. 5.2. The already addressed exchange of partial information on excluded keys to other pairs follows (lines 13 to 26). If all parts of the key are found, they need to be correctly assembled (lines 30 to 34) since – as already pointed out – the inverse of a found key is also a regular key. However, by inspecting the particular pairs, it is possible to decide whether a part of the key needs to be inverted. For example, pair $(0, 1)$ allows to append part 1 to part 0 and by continuing with the pairs $(0, 2), ..., (0, n)$ it is possible to correctly assemble the complete key and to reduce the total number of possible keys to a key and its inverse.

A first calculation shows that $(n + 1)!$ out of $(n + 1)^{n+1}$ possible messages resulting in $(n + 1)! \prod_{i=0}^{n} \binom{n}{i}$ out of $2^{n(n+1)}$ possible encodings are valid in the sense that they consist of the digits from '0' to 'n' without duplicates. For $n = 9$ this would mean that $4, 3 \cdot 10^{19} \approx 2^{66}$ out of $2^{90} \approx 1, 2 \cdot 10^{27}$ encodings are valid which gives strong evidence that a large number of possible keys may be dismissed for each intercepted ciphertext encrypted with the same key. To get an estimation on how many ciphertexts are needed to reduce the number of possible keys to two, an implementation (cf. List. 11.4) based on the already known Node (cf. List. 11.1) and an improved binary tree (cf. List. 11.5) was done.

As we can see from Tab. 5.12, in more than 85% of all tested cases, 23 ciphertexts were sufficient to reduce the number of possible keys to two. Note that this time 1,000,000 runs were executed which reduces the appearing variance compared to Tab. 5.11. Furthermore, very few outliers occured and all of them are in a narrow range of the peak. Beyond that the cpu time was in most cases around 20s on one core of an Intel Core2 Duo CPU E8400 with 3.00GHz, although a few displeasing upper outliers occured (cf. Tab. 7 in App. 11.3).

Note that if we consider only a particular character of the keypad, e.g. the first one of all keypads, it follows a uniform distribution. Therefore, one may combine the previously described idea of attacking single dices with the idea sketched above. This way the number of possible keys may be reduced faster (with fewer ciphertexts) at the price of possibly false predictions due to unfavourable occurrences of the uniform distribution.

Algorithm 5.3: Deterministic Alg. to Attack Keypads Encrypted with $\mathcal{HE}_{DICE}$

---

input : ciphertexts C_i of keypads encypted with the same key
output : a key and the number of ciphertexts needed
// Initialise
1 counter:=0;
// Full array for deleting 'impossible' keys
2 KeyPair [n][n]:= Array filled with a set of all keys of size $2n - 1$ for each combination
// Array to store the found keys
3 Found Keys [n]:= new Array
4 **while** $\exists i$ *with* $0 \leqslant i \leqslant n$ *and* Found Keys [i] *isEmpty* **do**
5   counter++;
6   **forall the** p_1, p_2 *with* $0 \leqslant p_1, p_2 \leqslant n$ *and* $p_2 \neq p_1$ **do**
7   **forall the** *keys in* KeyPair $[p_1][p_2]$ **do**   // Delete 'impossible' keys
8     $k_1 = 0, keys.\text{substring}(0, n/2 - 2)$;
9     $k_2 = keys.\text{substring}(n/2 - 1, n - 2)$;
10   **if** $HDec_{k_1}(p_1) = HDec_{k_2}(p_2)$ **then**
11   KeyPair $[p_1][p_2].\text{deleteKey}(keys)$
12   // Spread dismissed keys to other pairs
13   **if** KeyPair $[p_1][p_2]$ *with prefix* k_1 *isEmpty* **then**
14   **for** $0 \leqslant p \leqslant n$ *with* $p \neq p_1, p_2$ **do**
15   KeyPair $[p_1][p_2].\text{deletePrefix}(k_1)$;
16   **end**
17   **end**
18   **if** $|\text{KeyPair}[p_1][p_2]| = 1$ **then**   // Partial key found?
19   Found Keys $[p_1]$:=0,KeyPair$[p_1][p_2].\text{substring}(0, n/2 - 2)$;
20   Found Keys $[p_2]$:=KeyPair$[p_1][p_2].\text{substring}(n/2 - 1, n - 2)$;
    // let all subkeys start with 0
21   **if** Found Keys$[p_2].substring(0)=='1'$ **then**
22   Found Keys $[p_2] := \text{invert}(\text{Found Keys}[p_2])$
23   **for** $0 \leqslant p \leqslant n$ *with* $p \neq p_1, p_2$ **do**
24   KeyPair $[p][p_2].\text{setPrefixTo}(\text{Found Keys }[p_2])$;
25   **end**
26   **end**
27   **end**
28   **end**
29 **end**
// assemble complete key, invert Found Keys if necessary
30 **for** $1 \leqslant p \leqslant n$ **do**
31   **if** KeyPair$[0][p].substring(n/2 - 1)=='1'$ **then**
32   Found Keys$[p] := \text{invert}(\text{Found Keys}[p])$
33   **end**
34 **end**
35 **return** counter, Found Keys

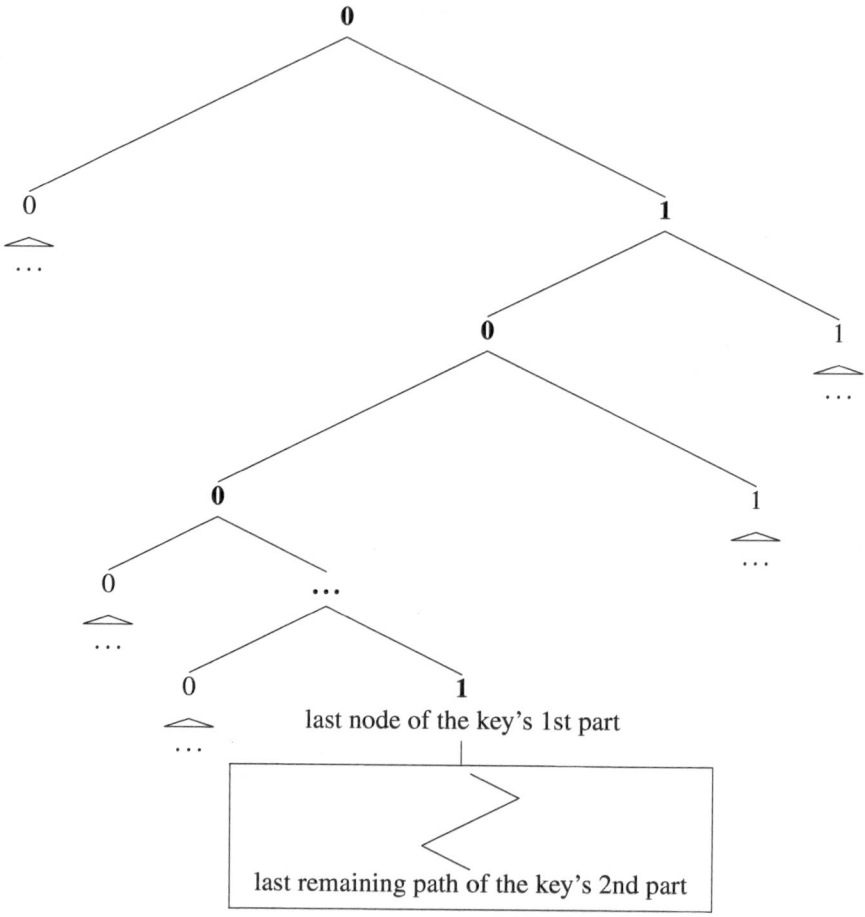

Figure 5.3: Representation of Possible Keys with a Binary Tree, the Actual Path is Denoted with Bold Nodes and the Second Part of the Key is Shown in a Frame

Remark 5.22. As a consequence of this attack, an adversary is able to mount a sophisticated replay attack on the protocol, described in Sect. 4.2.3. Assume, the adversary has installed a Trojan horse on the user's computer and already intercepted enough ciphertexts to reduce the possible keys to a key and its inverse. If the user (cf. Def. 4.67) sends his TAN to the bank by clicking on certain numbers of the keypad, the adversary blocks this transmission. When the adversary starts a new instantiation of the protocol (with an own bank transfer), she is able to transfer

Table 5.12: Number of Needed Encryptions to Recover the Secret Key from Encrypted Keypads with $n = 9$ and $1,000,000$ Runs in Total

A number of needed ciphertexts	B number of runs terminating	C aggregated number of runs
<22	0	0
22	5,467	5,467
23	854,041	859,508
24	140,338	999,846
25	152	999,998
26	2	1,000,000
>26	0	1,000,000

the user's TAN to a new keypad. For that purpose, she does not need to decrypt the digits, it is sufficient for her to correlate the symbols from the two keypads. If the bank asks for the same TAN again, i.e. when an iTAN scheme is used, it is easy for the adversary to solve the challenge with a new keypad. Following SYVERSON's classification (cf. Tab. 2.1) this is an replay attack of type "Straight replays (intended principal receives message, but message is delayed)" (1(a)ii).

5.3.3 Security Models

We conclude this section with the evaluation of selected security models. As we will see, the human decipherable encryption scheme based on dice codings is not secure in the sense of non-malleability, $LOR - CPA$, $FTG - CPA$ and $SOR - CO$ security. This strengthens our observations from the previous analysis.

Non Malleability

It is easy to see, that we do not need to consider security models to find out that $\mathcal{HE}_{DICE}$ is not non-malleable. Given the encoding parameter n and an arbitrary ciphertext c of a message m, an adversary is able to change c into an encryption c' of the message $'n - m'$. To achieve this, she simply changes all occurrences of '○●' to '●○' and vice versa. Furthermore, by flipping only one 'pair of dots', she creates a ciphertext c^* with Hamming distance of one to c. This means, she is able to create encryptions of $'m \pm 1'$, although she does not know if c^* is an encryption of $'m + 1'$ or $'m - 1'$. By a combination of both methods, an adversary is also able to create ciphertexts of $'n - m \pm 1'$.

Hence, an adversary is able to easily derive ciphertexts such that the underlying plaintexts are meaningfully related. Thus, $\mathcal{HE}_{DICE}$ is not non-malleable.

Indistinguishability

Regarding indistinguishability under chosen-plaintext attacks, the most serious problem for the human decipherable encryption scheme based on dice codings is that its encryption heavily relies on XOR. This fault cannot be compensated by randomisation of the underlying encodings since there are messages ('0','n') with only one encoding. Therefore, the adversary's strategy is to use the encryption oracle to obtain the key and with that knowledge she is able to solve the challenge. We demonstrate this on the basis of left-or-right indistinguishability and find-then-guess security.

Theorem 5.23. *The human decipherable encryption scheme based on dice codings* $\mathcal{HE}_{DICE}$ *is not secure in the sense of* LOR − CPA.

PROOF. Since $\mathcal{HE}_{DICE}$ is segment-based, we only consider single characters. The adversary does not even need to care about the used key. As sketched above, encryptions of '0' and 'n' are deterministic. Considering the experiment $\mathbf{Exp}_{A_{cpa},\Pi}^{lor-cpa-b}(n) = b'$, the adversary asks the left-or-right oracle $\mathcal{O}_{\mathcal{LR}}(\cdot,\cdot,b)$ for the encryption of the following pairs of messages: $c_0 = \mathcal{O}_{\mathcal{LR}}(0,0)$ and $c_1 = \mathcal{O}_{\mathcal{LR}}(0,n)$. If c_0 equals c_1 the oracle encrypted the left character and the adversary outputs 0. If c_0 equals the inverse of c_1 the oracle encrypted the right character and the adversary outputs 1. Thus, $\mathbf{Adv}_{A_{cpa},\Pi}^{lor-cpa}(n) = 1$ and therefore $\mathcal{HE}_{DICE}$ is not secure in the sense of LOR − CPA.   ∎

Basically, the adversary may use the same idea to prove $\mathcal{HE}_{DICE}$ is insecure in the sense of FTG − CPA, but as a proof of concept we show how she would be able to derive the used key from the encryption oracle.

Theorem 5.24. *The human decipherable encryption scheme based on dice codings* $\mathcal{HE}_{DICE}$ *is not secure in the sense of* FTG − CPA.

PROOF. Since there is only one encoding for 'n' (and '0'), an adversary may ask the encryption oracle $\mathcal{O}_{Enc}(\cdot)$ for an encryption of 'n' and simply receives the key:

$$HEnc_{n,k}(n) = Enc_k(Encode_n(n)) = (s \in_R \langle n \rangle_{Ham}) \leftrightarrow k = k$$

Obviously, with that knowledge the following challenge can easily be solved. Hence, $\mathcal{HE}_{DICE}$ is not secure in the sense of FTG − CPA.   ∎

Definition 5.25. (Sample for Set of Single Characters) We denote the sample composed of a set of all single characters c_i of the complete alphabet Γ with:

$$\mathsf{sample}_\Gamma \in_R \{(m_0; m_1; \ldots; m_n) \mid \forall i, j \text{ with } 0 \leqslant i, j \leqslant n . \exists m_i = j\}$$

Corollary 5.26. *Let S be a sample set of ciphertexts which have all been encrypted with the same key from a set of plaintexts generated by sample_Γ with the same key. Then the following properties hold:*

1. *There is at least one pair of ciphertexts in S which are inverse to each other.*

2. *Starting from the encryption of '0' or 'n' it is possible to uniquely order all other ciphertexts of S by their distance to that ciphertext.*

3. *S contains no duplicates.*

Proof. Each of the statements holds for the following reasons:

1. The plaintexts contain '0' and 'n' and since there is only one possible encryption for each of them, the corresponding ciphertexts are inverse to each other.

2. There is only one ciphertext with a certain distance between 0 and n (cf. Tab. 5.4). Otherwise it would not possible to build a sequence of underlying plaintexts ranging over the whole alphabet.

3. Duplicates may only occur if the underlying plaintexts are equal which may not occur if the sample set arises from the sample distribution sample_Γ.

□

As already discussed, in some scenarios (e.g. the online banking scenario described in Sect. 4.2.3) it is unrealistic to assume that the adversary has access to an encryption oracle. But unfortunately, even sample-or-random indistinguishability under ciphertext-only attacks shows to be a too strong security model given that the adversary obtains one sample encryption of the complete alphabet.

Theorem 5.27. *The human decipherable encryption scheme based on dice codings $\mathcal{HE}_{DICE}$ is not secure in the sense of $SOR - CO$ given that the sample sample_Γ.*

PROOF. The first question which comes to mind is: If ciphertexts are drawn randomly, which fraction of it is a valid encryption of all single characters of the complete alphabet? In total there are $2^{n(n+1)}$ possible ciphertexts. If the underlying plaintexts represent the complete alphabet, there are 2^n possibilities for '0' and for character 'i' there are $\binom{n}{i}$ possibilities since the binomial coefficient reflects the number of possibilities to get an encoding with Hamming distance i. Now that we have all different characters there are $(n+1)!$ combinations of ordering them and since we counted each case twice, because we are not able do distinguish between '0' and 'n', we end up with the following probability:

$$P('valid') = \frac{\frac{1}{2} \cdot 2^n \cdot \binom{n}{1} \cdot \ldots \cdot \binom{n}{n} \cdot (n+1)!}{2^{n(n+1)}}$$

For $n = 9$, $P('valid')$ is approximately $1.7 \cdot 10^{-3}\%$. This is small enough to determine if the underlying plaintext is composed of the complete alphabet Γ or if the ciphertext was randomly chosen.

However, the security model $SOR - CO$ requires us to randomly chose plaintexts which we then encrypt and not to randomly chose ciphertexts. Thus, the abovementioned calculation is mainly given to illustrate that the underlying structure covers only a small percentage of the corresponding ciphertext space. To distinguish the sample-distribution from a random distribution we already noticed in Cor. 5.26 when encrypting plaintexts from the sample-distribution there are certain patterns visible.

However, since the corresponding probabilities are hard to compute we do not consider all of them and concentrate on the fact that S contains no duplicates. We show how to get a non-negligible advantage and hence break the encryption scheme considering $SOR - CO$-security.

We first regard the random distribution. For simplicity we only consider the duplicates arising from the encryptions of '0' and 'n'. Therefore, we first calculate the four disjoint probabilities that at most one encryption of '0' and at most one encryption of 'n' occurs. The arising probabilities are very similar to probabilities arising from a binomial distribution:

$$P(\#0 = 0, \#n = 0 | n) = \left(\frac{n-1}{n+1}\right)^{n+1}$$

$$P(\#0 = 0, \#n = 1 | n) = \binom{n+1}{1} \frac{1}{n+1} \left(\frac{n-1}{n+1}\right)^n$$

$$P(\#0 = 1, \#n = 0 | n) = \binom{n+1}{1} \frac{1}{n+1} \left(\frac{n-1}{n+1}\right)^n$$

$$P(\#0 = 1, \#n = 1 | n) = \binom{n+1}{1} \frac{1}{n+1} \binom{n}{1} \frac{1}{n+1} \left(\frac{n-1}{n+1}\right)^{n-1}$$

Next we are able to give a lower bound on the probability that a duplicate occurs by calculating the complementary probability that at most one encryption of '0' and at most one encryption of '1' occurs:

$$P('duplicate') \geqslant 1 - P(\#0 = 0, \#n = 0|n) - P(\#0 = 0, \#n = 1|n)$$
$$- P(\#0 = 1, \#n = 0|n) - P(\#0 = 1, \#n = 1|n)$$

$$= 1 - \left(\frac{n-1}{n+1}\right)^{n+1} - 2 \cdot \left(\frac{n-1}{n+1}\right)^{n} - \frac{n}{n+1}\left(\frac{n-1}{n+1}\right)^{n-1}$$

$$= 1 - 2 \cdot \left(\frac{n-1}{n+1}\right)^{n} - \left(\frac{n-1}{n+1}\right)^{n}\left[\frac{(n-1)^2 + n(n+1)}{(n+1)(n-1)}\right]$$

$$= 1 - 2 \cdot \left(\frac{n-1}{n+1}\right)^{n} - \left(\frac{n-1}{n+1}\right)^{n}\left[2 - \frac{n-3}{n^2-1}\right] \tag{5.19}$$

$$\geqslant 1 - 4 \cdot \left(\frac{n-1}{n+1}\right)^{n} \tag{5.20}$$

$$= 1 - 4 \cdot \left(1 - \frac{2}{n+1}\right)^{n} \tag{5.21}$$

$$\geqslant 1 - \frac{4}{e^2} \quad \geqslant 0,458 \tag{5.22}$$

For rearranging terms from Eq. 5.19 to Eq. 5.20 we assumed that $n \geqslant 3$ which is justifiable since $n < 3$ generates marginal encryption schemes. The step from Eq. 5.21 to Eq. 5.22 follows because $\lim_{n \to \infty} \left(1 - \frac{2}{n+1}\right)^n = \frac{1}{e^2}$ due to the EULER limit formula [ZH04, p. 51] with e being EULER's number [OR01] and because with n rising $P('duplicate')$ is strictly monotonic decreasing since $P('duplicate')$'s derivative is slightly negative for all $n \geqslant 3$ (cf. Lemma 11.1).

That means if plaintexts are chosen randomly, there will be a good chance that 0 or n is drawn twice. Thus, the adversary may chose the following strategy: If the encryption of the challenge contains one (or more) duplicate ciphertexts she guesses that the oracle encrypted randomly chosen strings (b=1) otherwise she guesses that a sample message was encrypted (b=0). Obviously, she is correct in the first case with a probability of roughly 45% while she is never false if the oracle encrypted messages from the sample distribution.

$$\mathbf{Adv}_{A, \mathcal{HE}_{DICE}}^{sor-co}(n) = \Pr[\mathbf{Exp}_{A, \mathcal{HE}_{DICE}}^{sor-co-1}(n) = 1] - \Pr[\mathbf{Exp}_{A, \mathcal{HE}_{DICE}}^{sor-co-0}(n) = 1]$$
$$\geqslant \left(1 - \frac{4}{e^2}\right) - 0$$

Thus, the adversary is left with a non negligible advantage and hence $\mathcal{HE}_{DICE}$ is not secure in the sense of $SOR - CO$ given that a sample is composed of the complete alphabet Γ.

Note that the given advantage refers to only one query to the sample-or-random oracle. The success probability increases with each additional query. Furthermore, by taking the absence of inverse ciphertexts or 'invalid distances' between the ciphertexts into account the adversary may also improve her success probability. ∎

Certainly, the task of the adversary in the security model is slightly different than the problem an adversary faces in the online banking scenario (cf. Sect. 4.2.3). But – given that the sample is chosen appropriate – the security model is an acceptable approximation. In the addressed scenario an adversary would observe virtual keypads all encrypted with the same key. She then would try – after observing a certain number of encrypted keypads – to launch a man-in-the-middle attack and try to obtain a tan, transfer it to a new keypad and approve a money-order with it. Therefore, she has to relate fields of the attacked keypad to fields of the newly generated keypad in order to transfer the tan and legitimate the fraud. Since the fields of the keypad are arranged randomly, fortune may favour or handicap the adversary. Hence, the decision was made to give the adversary a representative sample of plaintexts which can be chosen to consider the allowed amount of fortune favouring the adversary. Especially since she has knowledge about the structure of the sample. Thus, the randomisation left in the security model completely refers to the randomisation occurring because of the encryption's randomisation.

However, it is also possible to model the security of complete keypads as previously described (cf. p. 163ff) with our security model $SOR-CO$. Therefore, we define a sample-function for keypads which contains each character of the alphabet Γ once.

Definition 5.28. (Sample for Keypads) We denote the sample composed of one plaintext message m containing each character c_i of the alphabet Γ once with:

$$sample_1 \in_R \{m \mid m = m_0, m_1, \ldots, m_n \wedge \forall i,j \text{ with } 0 \leqslant i,j \leqslant n . \exists m_i = c_j\}$$

Lemma 5.29. *Let* $m = m_0, \ldots, m_n$ *and* $m' = m'_0, \ldots, m'_n$ *be two messages from the sample structure* $sample_1$ *and let* $c = c_0, \ldots, c_n$ *respectively* $c' = c'_0, \ldots, c'_n$ *be their encryptions with* $\mathcal{HE}_{DICE}$. *Then the sum of characterwise XORing the ciphertexts is always even:*

$$\sum_{i=0}^{n} c_i \oplus c'_i = 0 \mod 2 \tag{5.23}$$

Proof. We already saw in Sect. 5.3.1 that

$$C_1 \oplus C_2 = (S_1 \leftrightarrow K) \oplus (S_2 \leftrightarrow K) = S_1 \oplus S_2$$

holds. Thus, the difference of two ciphertexts encrypted with the same key is independent of the key. Moreover, it is easy to see that the difference's parity is independent of the chosen coding. To change a symbol from value n to n' at least $|n - n'|$ dots need to be flipped. n' can then only be changed by pairwisely flipping dots. Thus, the difference's parity only depends on the underlying messages (cf. Tab. 5.4 and Tab. 1).

It remains to show that the difference's parity is even for all permutations found in sample_1. We show this by proving that changing the position of two characters does not change the difference's parity. Let the regarded characters be c_1 and c_1' respectively c_2 and c_2'. Since we are only interested in the parity,

$$|c_1 - c_1'| + |c_2 - c_2'| = c_1 + c_1' + c_2 + c_2' = |c_1 - c_2'| + |c_2 - c_1'| \quad \mathrm{mod}\ 2$$

holds.

Thus the difference's parity of two messages from the sample structure sample_1 is independent of the character's representation and the permutation of the message and thus always even. □

We already have shown for $n = 9$ that 26 ciphertexts are enough to reduce the number of possible keys to two (cf. Tab. 5.12). This is definitely sufficient to have a non negligible advantage and to conclude that $\mathcal{HE}_{\mathrm{DICE}}$ is not secure in the sense of $\mathrm{SOR} - \mathrm{CO}$ given the above sample. For only one ciphertext, the encryption scheme works like a one time pad and thus is secure. However, there is a gap between those two amounts of ciphertexts. In the proof of the following theorem we show how to close this gap with the help of Lem. 5.29.

Theorem 5.30. *The human decipherable encryption scheme based on dice codings* $\mathcal{HE}_{\mathrm{DICE}}$ *is not secure in the sense of* $\mathrm{SOR} - \mathrm{CO}$ *given the sample structure* sample_1.

PROOF. The adversary succeeds with the following strategy. She asks the oracle for two ciphertexts and determines the sum of characterwise XORing them. If the sum is even, she guesses that the oracle is in 'sample mode', if it is odd she guesses it is in 'random mode'. The corresponding probabilities are as follows:

If the oracle is in 'random mode', the sum will be in half of the cases odd and half of the cases even. Th. 5.29 shows that the sum is never odd if the underlying messages were chosen from the sample structure. Therefore, the adversary's guess is in half of the cases correct. If the oracle is in 'sample mode', the sum will always be even and thus the adversary will always be right.

Taken together, the adversary's advantage is clearly not negligible.

$$\mathbf{Adv}^{sor-co}_{A,\mathcal{HE}_{DICE}}(n) = \Pr[\mathbf{Exp}^{sor-co-1}_{A,\mathcal{HE}_{DICE}}(n) = 1] - \Pr[\mathbf{Exp}^{sor-co-0}_{A,\mathcal{HE}_{DICE}}(n) = 1]$$
$$= \frac{1}{2} - 0$$

Thus, $\mathcal{HE}_{DICE}$ is not secure in the sense of $SOR-CO$ given the sample structure $sample_1$. $\blacksquare$

We continue with a description of an enhanced version of a human decipherable encryption scheme based on dice codings which aims to enlarge the amount of information an adversary needs to recover the secret key without rendering the scheme unusable for human beings.

5.4 Dice Codings with Noise

In this section we introduce an enhanced version of the symmetric encryption scheme EQV which not only makes use of the principles of visual cryptography, but also adds some noise to the ciphertext. The idea behind adding some noise is to counter the algorithms described in the previous section. To our knowledge, this is the first visual encryption scheme which makes use of noise. Analogous to the basic version, this encryption scheme is then applied to dice codings resulting in the enhanced version of a human decipherable encryption scheme based on dice codings. We then study to which extent the proposed scheme fulfils the properties of human decipherable encryption schemes defined in Sect. 4.1.4 before we investigate its security in the next section.

Modified algorithms, variables and spaces are denoted with an additional '$\star$' to allow a better distinction between the original and the modified version. Before we are able to address the enhanced version of the EQV encryption scheme, we need to take a look at the changed ciphertext and key spaces.

5.4.1 Changes in Underlying Spaces and Parameters

Let $n \in \mathbb{N}$ be the parameter of the encoding scheme and $\nu \in \mathbb{N}$ be the security parameter of the symmetric encryption scheme. As we will see in Sect. 5.4.2, the security parameter ν defines how much noise will be used and determines the number of '$\bullet\bullet$'s in the key.

The *message space* $\mathcal{M}$ and the *coding space* $\mathcal{S}$ are as described in Sect. 5.1.1. However, as we will see later, it is helpful to have a coding space $\mathcal{S}^\star$ based on $\Sigma^\star = \{\bullet, \bigcirc\}^{n+\nu}$ with size $2^{n+\nu}$ at hand.

The alphabet Γ^* of the *ciphertext space* $\mathcal{C}^*$ not only adopts the principle of visual encryption to dice codings, it also contains some additional noise. For each position there are still two positions, which we denote with '○●' and '●○' respectively 'L' and 'R' to indicate where the white/transparent dot is placed. But the number of positions is increased by ν. This results in the alphabet $\Gamma^* = \{○●, ●○\}^{n+\nu}$ with size $2^{n+\nu}$ and the ciphertext space $\mathcal{C}^* = \{\{○●, ●○\}^{n+\nu}\}^*$.

The alphabet Λ^* of the *key space* $\mathcal{K}^*$ is changed as follows. For each dot there still exist two positions, but additionally to '○●' and '●○' respectively 'L' and 'R' – which indicate the position of a white/transparent dot – '●●' respectively 'X' indicates a position where additional noise is/was inserted. This leaves us with the alphabet $\Lambda^* = \{○●, ●○, ●●\}^{n+\nu}$ with size $3^{n+\nu}$, and the corresponding key space $\mathcal{K}^* = \{\{○●, ●○, ●●\}^{n+\nu}\}^*$.

Now that we have defined the changed spaces, we are able to take a look at the modified algorithms, to see how the additional noise is inserted in the ciphertext.

5.4.2 EQV Encryption Scheme with Noise

We start with the formal definition of the proposed symmetric encryption scheme with additional noise including its algorithms. Next, we show that it is a symmetric encryption scheme as in Def. 2.40. Then we are ready to demonstrate that DICE and EQV* also build a human decipherable description scheme as in Def. 4.37.

Definition 5.31. (EQV Encryption Scheme with Noise) Let coding space $\mathcal{S}$, ciphertext space $\mathcal{C}$ and key space $\mathcal{K}$ be as described in Sect. 5.4.1. Then we denote $\mathsf{EQV}^* := (\mathsf{GenKey}^*, \mathsf{Enc}^*, \mathsf{Dec}^*)$ – with the algorithms defined below – as *EQV encryption scheme with noise*. If Enc or Dec are applied to multiple characters, they work character by character, hence the definitions below are for one character only:

- The *key-generation algorithm* GenKey^* takes as input the parameter of the encoding scheme n and the security parameter ν as $1^n 0^\nu$ and outputs a key k^* in the following way:

  – Analogous to GenKey from Eq. 5.4, GenKey^* first uniformly at random selects a key symbol k from Λ.

  – GenKey^* then inserts ν '●●'s randomly between the pairs of dots in k (cf. Fig. 5.4). We denote this step with Ext[6].

---

[6]For the extension of the key, one may assume that the key k is linearised and the positions of the noise are randomly inserted as described. To gain a rectangular representation of the key k^*, the prime factors of $n + \nu$ need to be considered which determine the possible rectangles.

Formally, let π be a permutation of a set with length $n + v$ then $\mathsf{GenKey}^\star$ uniformly at random selects a key symbol $k^\star$ from $\Lambda^\star$ with the following properties:

$$\mathsf{GenKey}^\star(1^n 0^v) := k^\star \in_R \{k \in \Lambda^\star | \exists \pi. k = \pi(\{\bigcirc\bullet, \bullet\bigcirc\}^n \{\bullet\bullet\}^v)\} \qquad (5.24)$$

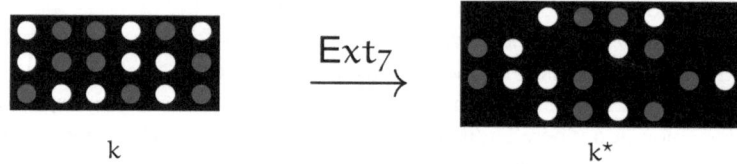

$$k \qquad\qquad k^\star$$

Figure 5.4: Sample Visualisation of the Ext Function for $n = 9$ and $v = 7$ with Black Segments Shown in Dark Grey

- The *encryption algorithm* $\mathsf{Enc}^\star : \Sigma \to \Gamma^\star$ takes as input a key symbol $k^\star \in \Gamma^\star$ and a symbol $s \in \Sigma$, and outputs a ciphertext symbol $c^\star$ in the following way:

  - For the first part of the encryption all '$\bullet\bullet$'s in $k^\star$ are disregarded and the encryption works as Enc from Eq. 5.5. We denote the intermediate result as c.

  - The second part of the encryption consists of inserting random elements of $\{\bigcirc\bullet, \bullet\bigcirc\}$ in c at exactly the positions where there are '$\bullet\bullet$'s in $k^\star$. Resulting in a ciphertext $c^\star$ where all '$\bigcirc\bullet$'s and '$\bullet\bigcirc$'s in $k^\star$ match the positions of their counterparts in $c^\star$ while all '$\bullet\bullet$'s in $k^\star$ match randomly chosen elements in $c^\star$ (cf. Fig. 5.5). We denote this part with $\mathsf{Noise}_{k^\star}$.

  We denote the encryption as:

$$\mathsf{Enc}^\star_{k^\star}(s) = \mathsf{Noise}_{k^\star}(\mathsf{Enc}_k(s)) := s \leftrightsquigarrow k^\star \qquad (5.25)$$

- The *decryption algorithm* $\mathsf{Dec}^\star : \Gamma^\star \to \Sigma$ takes as input a key symbol $k^\star$ and a ciphertext symbol $c^\star$, and outputs a symbol s. Since there are keys in the key space which are not output by $\mathsf{GenKey}^\star$ a failure and thus the symbol $\perp$ occurs if such a key is used for decryption. However, the decryption algorithm inverts the encryption algorithm straightforward:

  - The first part of the decryption consists of inverting the Noise function to recover c from $c^\star$. Since the '$\bullet\bullet$'s in $k^\star$ indicate at which positions randomly chosen elements were inserted this can be easily done. We denote this part with $\mathsf{Noise}^{-1}{}_{k^\star}$.

  - For the second part of the decryption all '$\bullet\bullet$'s in $k^\star$ are disregarded and the decryption works as Dec from Eq. 5.8.

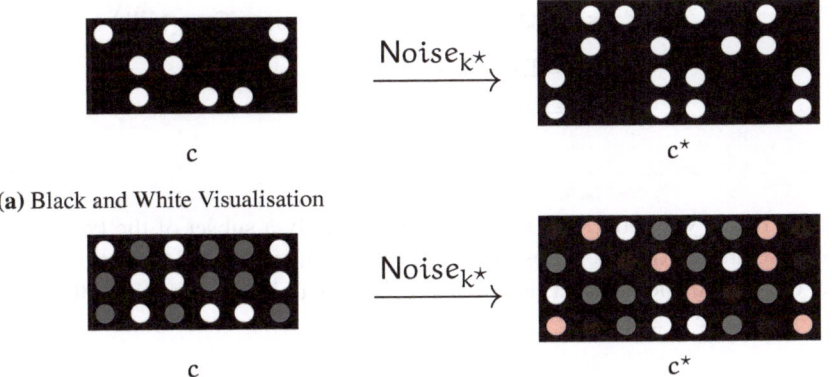

(a) Black and White Visualisation

(b) Black Segments Are Shown in Dark Grey and the Randomly Inserted Segments Are Shown in Red Respectively Dark Red

Figure 5.5: Sample Visualisations of the Noise Function with $k^\star$ from Fig. 5.4 for $n = 9$ and $\nu = 7$

We denote the decryption as:

$$Dec_{k^\star}^\star(c^\star) = Dec_k(Noise_{k^\star}^{-1}(c^\star)) := c^\star \leftrightarrow k^\star$$

Remark 5.32. The reason, why we denote the decryption with '$\leftrightarrow$' instead of '$\leftrightsquigarrow$' as in the case of the encryption will become clear after introducing the human decipherable encryption scheme. Claim 5.35 addresses this issue.

It remains to show that $EQV^\star$ is a symmetric encryption scheme:

Theorem 5.33. *The EQV encryption scheme with noise is a symmetric encryption scheme as defined in Def. 2.40.*

PROOF. It is easy to verify that $GenKey^\star$, $Enc^\star$ and $Dec^\star$ work on the appropriate spaces and run in polynomial time. It remains to show that for every n, every ν, every $k^\star$ output by $GenKey^\star(1^n)$, and every $s \in S$, it holds that $Dec_{k^\star}^\star(Enc_{k^\star}^\star(s)) = s$.

This holds, since the information about the noise inserted from the encryption $Enc^\star$ is stored in the key and thus the decryption function $Dec^\star$ is able to silently remove it:

$$Dec_{k^*}^*(Enc_{k^*}^*(s)) = Dec_k\left(Noise^{-1}{}_{k^*}[Noise_{k^*}[Enc_k(s)]]\right)$$
$$= Dec_k(Enc_k(s))$$
$$= s$$

∎

Furthermore, we notice that the used keys are only a subset of the key space. Since there are n from $n+v$ positions in k^* where the symbols '○●' and '●○' of k may be located and all other positions are filled with '●●'s, the size of the used part of key space is $2^n\binom{n+v}{n}$.

5.4.3 Human Decipherable Encryption Scheme with Noise

Now, that we became acquainted with the EQV encryption scheme with noise EQV^*, it is time to combine it with DICE to build a human decipherable encryption scheme.

Definition 5.34. Let message space $\mathfrak{M}$, coding space $\mathfrak{S}$, ciphertext space $\mathfrak{C}^*$ and key space $\mathfrak{K}^*$ be as described in Sect. 5.4.1. Then the encoding scheme DICE and the encryption scheme EQV^* build a human decipherable encryption scheme. We denote it as *dice codings based human decipherable encryption scheme with noise* and by $\mathcal{HE}_{DICE}^*$.

Before proving that $\mathcal{HE}_{DICE}^*$ is a human decipherable encryption scheme, we take a look at the tuple of combined algorithms $\mathcal{HE}_{DICE}^* = (HGen^*, HEnc^*, HDec^*)$. Along the lines of DICE and EQV^*, $HEnc^*$ and $HDec^*$ work character by character, hence the compositions below are for one character only:

- $(n, k^*) \leftarrow HGen^*(1^n0^v) = (Gen(1^n), GenKey^*(1^n0^v))$

- $c^* \leftarrow HEnc_{n,k^*}^*(m) = Enc_{k^*}^*(Encode_n(m)) = (s \in_R \langle m \rangle_{Ham}) \leftrightsquigarrow k^*$

- $m = HDec_{n,k^*}^*(c^*) = Decode_n(Dec_{k^*}^*c^*) = Ham(c^* \leftrightarrow k^*)$

Claim 5.35. *Note that the inserted noise must not necessarily be removed as shown in Fig. 5.6a. Since decoding means to compute the Hamming weight of a symbol s, it is sufficient to blacken the respective positions instead of removing them. as shown in Fig. 5.6b. The symbols of the expanded coding space no longer belong to Σ then, instead they are taken from Σ^* which has additional positions for all blackened dots.*

Bear in mind that the figures in Fig. 5.6 show only the application of the Noise^{-1} *function and that the EQV function still has to be applied for decryption. For the application of* Noise^{-1}, *one may again assume that the key* $k^\star$ *is linearised and the positions of the noise are then removed. To gain a rectangular representation of the key* k, *the prime factors of* n *need to be considered which determine the possible rectangles.*

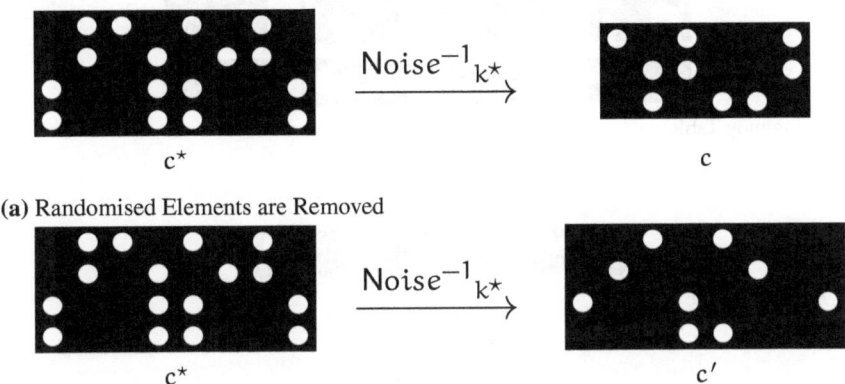

(a) Randomised Elements are Removed

(b) Randomised Elements are Blackened

Figure 5.6: Sample Visualisations of the Noise^{-1} Function with $k^\star$ from Fig. 5.4 for $n = 9$ and $v = 7$

Furthermore, the key consists of '●●'s at the positions where random elements of $\{○●, ●○\}$ *are inserted. Therefore using the basic decryption* HDec *with the key* $k^\star$ *yields blackened elements wherever noise was inserted. Tab. 5.13a shows the changed contingency table while the evaluation table Tab. 5.13b stays unchanged. This explains why we denoted the decryption* HDec* *in Def. 5.31 with* '$\leftrightarrow$'.

When noise is eliminated the previously mentioned way, it occurs unperceived by the user. The only thing a user may notice is, that there are more positions than visible dots. Ex. 5.37 shows the process of decryption for the case $s^\star = 4$.

Theorem 5.36. *The dice codings based human decipherable encryption scheme with noise,* $\mathcal{HE}^\star_{\text{DICE}}$, *fulfils the properties of Def. 4.37.*

Proof. We have to proof the following properties:

- DICE is an encoding scheme as in Def. 4.20 was shown in Sect. 5.1.2.

Table 5.13: Contingency and Evaluation Table for the Decryption with the EQV Encryption Scheme Applied with Noise to Dice Codings

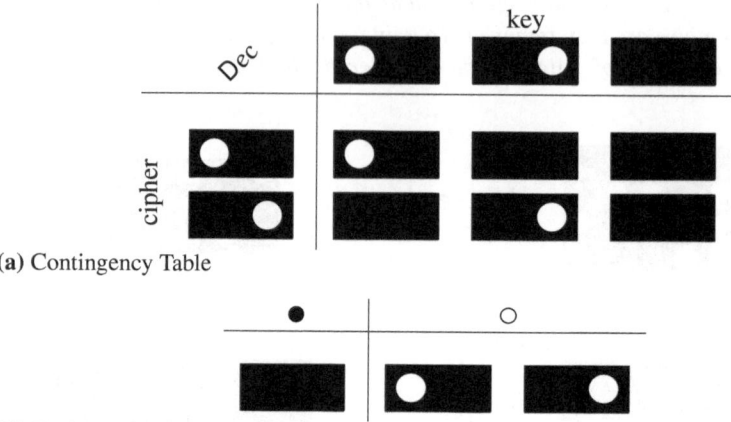

(a) Contingency Table

(b) Evaluation Table

- Since we have shown in Sect. 5.4.2 that $EQV^\star$ is a symmetric encryption scheme as in Def. 2.40, we do not need to take into account that the decryption algorithm $Dec^\star$ is not required to run in polynomial time.

- The requirement that the function composition $HDec^\star_{n,k^\star}(c^\star)$ is feasible for most human beings has not been shown in a user study. However, since $HDec_{n,k}(c)$ is feasible for $n = 9$ for most human beings, we argue that the slight deviation of the dots' positions does not render the decryption infeasible for human beings. Provided a reasonable choice for v, e.g. $v \leqslant n$, the essential principle still consists of counting dots and the results should be easily transferable.

                                                         ∎

Furthermore, it is easy to see that for every $n, v \in \mathbb{N}$, every $k^\star$ output by $GenKey^\star(1^n 0^v)$, and every $m \in \Omega$, it holds that:

$$HDec^\star_{n,k^\star}(HEnc^\star_{n,k^\star}(m)) = m$$

since

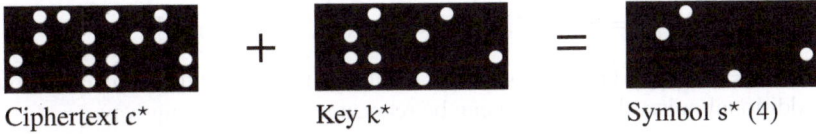

(a) Non Reduced Monochrome Visualisation

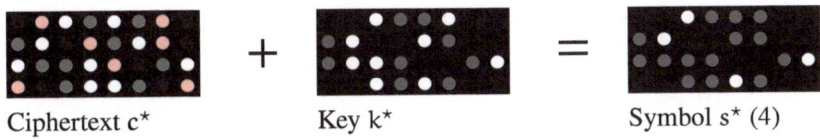

(b) Non Reduced Colored Visualisation

Figure 5.7: Sample Visualisation of a Dice Codings Based Human Decipherable Encryption Scheme With Noise for $n = 9$ and $v = 7$

$$\mathrm{HDec}^\star_{n,k^\star}(\mathrm{HEnc}^\star_{n,k^\star}(m)) = \mathrm{Decode}_n(\mathrm{Dec}^\star_{k^\star}(\mathrm{Enc}^\star_{k^\star}(\mathrm{Encode}_n(m))))$$
$$= \mathrm{Ham}((s \in_R \langle m \rangle_{\mathrm{Ham}}) \leftrightsquigarrow k^\star \leftrightarrow k^\star)$$
$$= \mathrm{Ham}(s^\star \in_R \langle m \rangle_{\mathrm{Ham}})$$
$$= m.$$

EXAMPLE 5.37. (Visualising Dice Coding Based Encryptions)
Fig. 5.7 shows the visualisation of a decryption of $\mathcal{HE}^\star_{\mathrm{DICE}}$ with the coding parameter $n = 9$ and the security parameter $v = 7$. Fig. 5.7a shows the visualisation in black and white – as is appears to a user. On the contrary, to ease the recognition of noise elements, noise is coloured red in Fig. 5.7b.

Analogous to the properties of $\mathcal{HE}_{\mathrm{DICE}}$ we regard the properties of human decipherable encryption schemes and determine which of them are fulfilled by $\mathcal{HE}^\star_{\mathrm{DICE}}$. We start with the set of possible encryptions.

Lemma 5.38. *Let m be a message, let $k^\star$ be a key and let message space $\mathcal{M}$, ciphertext space $\mathcal{C}^\star$ and key space $\mathcal{K}^\star$ be as described in Sect. 5.4.1. Further let k be the respective key of $k^\star$ with all '$\bullet\bullet$'s removed.*
Then $\mathcal{HE}^\star_{\mathrm{DICE}}$ has the following sets of possible encryptions:

$$\mathcal{C}_{k^\star,m}^\star = \{c^\star \in \mathcal{C}^\star | c^\star \leftarrow \mathsf{Noise}_{k^\star}(c) \quad . \quad c \in \mathcal{C}_{k,m}\}$$

PROOF. Since $\mathcal{HE}_{\mathsf{DICE}}^\star$ basically consists of the same algorithms as $\mathcal{HE}_{\mathsf{DICE}}$, but with additional noise, the equation can be rearranged the following way.

$$\begin{aligned}
\mathcal{C}_{k^\star,m}^\star &= \{c^\star \in \mathcal{C}^\star | c^\star \leftarrow \mathsf{HEnc}_{k^\star}^\star(m)\} \\
&= \{c^\star \in \mathcal{C}^\star | c^\star \leftarrow \mathsf{Noise}_{k^\star}(\mathsf{HEnc}_k(m))\} \\
&= \{c^\star \in \mathcal{C}^\star | c^\star \leftarrow \mathsf{Noise}_{k^\star}(c) \quad . \quad c \in \mathcal{C}_{k,m}\}
\end{aligned}$$

∎

Furthermore, we notice that $\mathcal{HE}_{\mathsf{DICE}}^\star$ is segment-based as well as probabilistic by definition.

Corollary 5.39. $\mathcal{HE}_{\mathsf{DICE}}^\star$ *from Def. 5.34 is* segment-based *and* probabilistic.

Proof. Cor. 5.39 follows by Def. 5.34.   □

It can easily be shown that the dice codings based human decipherable encryption scheme with noise is closed.

Corollary 5.40. *Let message space* $\mathcal{M}$*, coding space* $\mathcal{S}$*, ciphertext space* $\mathcal{C}^\star$ *and key space* $\mathcal{K}^\star$ *be as described in Sect. 5.4.1. Then* $\mathcal{HE}_{\mathsf{DICE}}^\star$ *is* closed *in the sense of Def. 4.50.*

Proof. Let $k^\star \in \mathcal{K}^\star$ be an arbitrary but fixed key, let $k \in \mathcal{K}$ denote the key's part without the 'randomisation part' (stripped '●●'s). We already proved that $\mathcal{HE}_{\mathsf{DICE}}$ using k is closed. Since the 'randomisation part' is independently chosen we only need to show that it covers the complete space. This is clearly the case, since each elements is randomly chosen from $\{○●, ●○\}$. Hence, $\mathcal{HE}_{\mathsf{DICE}}^\star$ is also closed.   □

It remains to show that $\mathcal{HE}_{\mathsf{DICE}}^\star$ is not distribution alike, which is obviously the case since $\mathcal{HE}_{\mathsf{DICE}}$ is not distribution alike and the additional noise does not change the corresponding distributions.

Corollary 5.41. *Let message space* $\mathcal{M}$*, coding space* $\mathcal{S}$*, ciphertext space* $\mathcal{C}^\star$ *and key space* $\mathcal{K}^\star$ *be as described in Sect. 5.4.1 and let* n *be the paramter of* DICE *and* ν *be the security parameter of* $\mathsf{EQV}^\star$*. Then* $\mathcal{HE}_{\mathsf{DICE}}^\star$ *is* not distribution alike*.

Proof. Let $k^\star$ be an arbitrary but fixed key. We first disregard the noise when encrypting and notice that the distribution of possible symbols representing a character m of DICE and the following encryption with EQV still follows a binomial distribution. Since the positions of the inserted noise are determined by the key and at each position there's a choice between two symbols, this results in $\binom{n}{m}2^\nu$ possible encryptions for the message m. Thus, the number of possible encryptions clearly depends on m. Hence $\mathcal{HE}^\star_{DICE}$ is not distribution alike. $\qquad\square$

5.5 Security Analysis of Dice Codings with Noise

This section is the counterpart to Sect. 5.3 and examines whether $\mathcal{HE}^\star_{DICE}$ allows a more secure reuse of the key for several encryptions than $\mathcal{HE}_{DICE}$. Of course, the additional noise may only be of value if the key is reused at least once. If a key is only used once, $\mathcal{HE}_{DICE}$ works as one-time pad and no noise is required. Since most of this section is based on the observations of the previously mentioned section, we keep this as short as possible.

First of all we briefly compare the key size of $\mathcal{HE}_{DICE}$ and $\mathcal{HE}^\star_{DICE}$. Let n be the encoding parameter and thus an alphabet of size $n+1$ arises and let ν be the security parameter, then $\mathcal{HE}_{DICE}$ has 2^n and $\mathcal{HE}^\star_{DICE}$ has $\binom{n+\nu}{n}2^n$ possible keys for each character which results in theory in a key length of $\log_2(2^n) = n$ respectively $\log_2\left(\binom{n+\nu}{n}2^n\right)$ bits. The latter can be estimated by the use of STIRLING's formula[7] with roughly $(n+2\nu)\log_2(n+\nu)$. Since in practise, probably a non compacted representation needs to be chosen, we consider $3^{n+\nu}$ as an upper bound of the number of possible keys which would result in a key length of $\log_2(3^{n+\nu}) \approx 1.58(n+\nu)$ bits per character. The ciphertext size is n bits per character for $\mathcal{HE}_{DICE}$ and $n+\nu$ bits per character for $\mathcal{HE}^\star_{DICE}$.

Remark 5.42. Note that in many cases it is not important to pay particular attention to the sizes of the ciphertext and key. Assume, one wants to encrypt a keypad with the numbers from 0 to 9. Then we need ten characters with nine bits which are 90 bits in total for $\mathcal{HE}_{DICE}$. Furthermore assume $\nu = n$ and wasting one bit per dot for the key, which would result in 360 bits for the key and 180 bits per ciphertext for $\mathcal{HE}^\star_{DICE}$.

Keeping this in mind, we continue start with the security analysis where we again distinguish between plain ciphertext-only attacks and ciphertext-only attacks with side information available.

---

[7]cf. FELLER[Fel08a, Sect. 2.9]: $\log(n!) \approx n\log(n) - n$

5.5.1 Ciphertext-Only Attacks Without Side Information

For this subsection we again assume a passive adversary who has no side information available. Therefore, she obviously does not know anything about the relation of different characters and because $\mathcal{HE}^{\star}_{DICE}$ is also homomorphic in relation to concatenation, the following analysis deals with single characters.

Since the adversary has no side information available, she is limited to general attacks against one time pads and may gain information about the underlying encodings S_1 and S_2 of the plaintexts P_1 and P_2 by XORing two ciphertexts C_1 and C_2. We denote the noise introduced by Noise with N_1 respectively N_2 and let Π_K be a permutation depending on K:

$$
\begin{aligned}
C_1 \oplus C_2 &= (S_1 \leftrightsquigarrow K) \oplus (S_2 \leftrightsquigarrow K) \\
&= (\Pi_K(S_1, N_1) \oplus K) \oplus (\Pi_K(S_2, N_2) \oplus K)) \\
&= \Pi_K(S_1 \oplus S_2, N_1 \oplus N_2)
\end{aligned}
$$

It follows that

$$
\mathsf{Ham}(\Pi_K(S_1 \oplus S_2, N_1 \oplus N_2)) = \mathsf{Ham}(S_1 \oplus S_2) + \mathsf{Ham}(N_1 \oplus N_2)
$$

Which is basically the same result than in Sect. 5.3.1 but with additional noise. The noise follows a binomial distribution with probability mass function $B(v, \frac{1}{2})$ since for any fixed but arbitrary N_1 the operation $\oplus N_1$ is a permutation and hence the noise has the same distribution than N_1 respectively N_2, i.e. $noise = B(v, \frac{1}{2})$. This means that an adversary needs to draw conclusions from the observation of $\mathsf{Ham}(S_1 - S_2) + B(v, \frac{1}{2})$.

To determine how much of the difference goes back to the encodings of the messages and how much originates from the noise, we need to consider the probability that the Hamming distance $ham = \mathsf{Ham}(S_1 - S_2)$ between S_1 and S_2 has a certain value ($ham = Y$), given that we observed a particular value ($obs = X$). Obviously the observed value is the sum $ham + noise$ and since ham and $noise$ are statistically independent it follows that

$$
\begin{aligned}
P(obs = X) &= \sum_{i=0}^{X} P(ham = i)P(noise = X - i) \\
&= \sum_{i=0}^{X} P(ham = i)B(v, \frac{1}{2}, X - i)
\end{aligned}
$$

and

$$P(ham = Y \cap obs = X) = P(ham = Y)P(noise = X - Y)$$

$$= P(ham = Y)B(v, \frac{1}{2}, X - Y)$$

which leads to the conditional probability

$$P(ham = Y | obs = X) = \frac{P(ham = Y \cap obs = X)}{P(obs = X)} \qquad (5.26)$$

$$= \frac{P(ham = Y)B(v, \frac{1}{2}, X - Y)}{\sum_{i=0}^{X} P(ham = i)B(v, \frac{1}{2}, X - i)}$$

Since we do not know the distribution of plaintexts, we are unable to further elaborate on this probability and postpone this to Sect. 5.5.2.

It is worth to mention that an adversary is not able to draw conclusions when the sum $P_1 + P_2$ is odd or even from observing ciphertexts as it was the case when the ciphertexts were encrypted with $\mathcal{HE}_{DICE}$. This follows from the observation that for $B(v, \frac{1}{2})$ half of the values are odd and half of the values are even, meaning that if she observed a particular value o in half of the cases the added noise causes the last bit to flip. Since we already noticed that $ham + noise = obs$, by observing the Hamming distance of two ciphertexts it is obvious that an adversary may conclude that $Ham(S_1 - S_2) \leqslant Ham(C_1 - C_2)$ and thus draw the conclusion that $|P_1 - P_2| \leqslant Ham(S_1 - S_2) \leqslant Ham(C_1 - C_2)$. In many cases this will be of limited use since the noise inserts a non marginal error which is in half of the cases $\frac{v}{2}$ or larger, but with a reasonable amount of ciphertexts and due to the birthday paradox ([KL08, p. 496]) this may leak information.

We further notice, that $\mathcal{HE}_{DICE}^{\star}$ is at least as secure as $\mathcal{HE}_{DICE}$ since an adversary is able to simulate Noise on eavesdropped ciphertexts by herself. Furthermore, by the same argumentation as for Th. 5.19, $\mathcal{HE}_{DICE}^{\star}$ is an ideal system. However, one restriction holds: An adversary who repeatedly eavesdrops a ciphertext with the same substring of length n may guess that it is an encryption of '0' or 'n' since they have the least number of possible encodings. Additionally, if the adversary observes a ciphertext c and its inversion c', she recognises that c' is the inversion of c since the inversion of noise has no influence on the decryption. However, the probability that the noise is the same for two ciphertexts (or exactly its inverse) is $\frac{1}{2^v}$, even though the birthday paradox has to be kept in mind, again.

5.5.2 Ciphertext-Only Attacks With Side Information

For this subsection, we again assume that the attacker has side information available. As in Sect. 5.3.2, we first consider side information about single characters. Then we additionally assume that the adversary knows that the plaintexts follow a certain pattern.

Security of Single Characters

Uniform Distribution   In this paragraph, we assume the characters are uniformly distributed in $\Omega = \{0,\ldots,n\}$, for which we already discussed the corresponding distribution of encodings respectively ciphertexts in Sect. 5.3.2. Since $\mathcal{HE}^\star_{\text{DICE}}$ adds additional noise, the corresponding distribution of ciphertexts would be the same with the difference that, for each character, the number of ciphertexts is given by the number of encodings multiplied by 2^n. Thus, the idea of 'identifying' an encryption of '0' or 'n' does not work as before. In this paragraph we are interested in the distribution of the Hamming distance ham between two encodings to proceed with our analysis in Sect. 5.5.1.

There are n positions (dots) for the encoding of numbers and an encoding of P_1 consists of P_1 '1's and $n-P_1$ '0's. Assume, we want regard the Hamming distance of the encoding of P_1 and P_2 (cf. Tab. 5.4). Then there are two reasons why dots may be different in the two encodings. On the one hand, if $P_1 \neq P_2$, it is obvious that there need to exist some inverted dots. On the other hand, it may be that the position of a point needs to be changed. Think of two encodings of '1' with a different position of the dot, then the Hamming distance of the two encodings of '1' is two.

This leads to the following proposition:

Proposition 5.43. *(Distribution of Hamming Distances Given Two Numbers)*
Let P_1, P_2 be two numbers uniformly at random from $\Omega = \{0,\ldots,n\}$ and S_1, S_2 their corresponding dice encodings. Let $h(n,i,j;k)$ be the hypergeometric distribution[8] with population size n, i draws, j success states and k successes. Then the distribution of the Hamming distance between S_1 and S_2 is:

$$\text{Ham}(S_1 - S_2) = P_2 - P_1 + 2k \tag{5.27}$$

where k is a hypergeometric distributed random variable with $h(n,P_1,n-P_2;k)$.

PROOF. The distribution described above is based on 'sampling without replacement' for which the hypergeometric distribution exactly represents the occurring probabilities. Each encoding of P_2 consists of P_2 '1's ('●'s) and $n-P_2$ '0's ('○'s) and the representation of S_1 consists of P_1 '1's ('●'s). To see how many of them match the

---

[8] $h(n,i,j;k) = \dfrac{\binom{i}{k}\binom{n-i}{j-k}}{\binom{n}{j}}$

positions of '1's ('●'s) in the encoding of P_2, we draw P_1 positions and regard '0's ('○'s) in P_2 as success states resulting in the distribution $h(n, P_1, n - P_2; k)$.

The Hamming distance is then the number of dots which need to be flipped (the difference between P_2 and P_1) and the number of dots given by k which count twice. k counts twice, because this means that S_1 has a '1' ('●'s) at a position where at the encoding of S_2 is a '0' ('○'s), and thus there must also be another position where it is vice versa. Otherwise there would be a deviation in the difference of $P_2 - P_1$.

Furthermore, it is easy to see that $\max(P_1 - P_2, 0) \leqslant k \leqslant \min(P_1, n - P_2)$ holds, since if there are only P_2 positions with '1's ('●'s) in the encoding of S_2 and $P_1 > P_2$ then at least $P_2 - P_1$ success must occur. On the other hand, there cannot be more successes than the number of draws or the number of successes. ■

Since we are interested in the distribution of Hamming distances for a given value, we add all values for a given Hamming distance to receive the corresponding probability mass function:

Proposition 5.44. *(Distribution of Hamming Distances) Let P_1, P_2 be two numbers uniformly at random from $\Omega = \{0, \ldots, n\}$ with their corresponding dice encodings S_1, S_2 and let $h(n, i, j; k)$ be the hypergeometric distribution. Then the distribution of Hamming distances follows*

$$P(ham = X) = \frac{1}{(n+1)^2} \sum_{\substack{0 \leqslant P_1 \leqslant n \\ 0 \leqslant P_2 \leqslant n}} h(n, P_1, n - P_2; \frac{X - P_2 + P_1}{2}) \qquad (5.28)$$

PROOF. As already described, the hypergeometric distribution reflects the particular probability that the correct number of dots match. By setting the number of required successes to $\frac{X - P_2 + P_1}{2}$ and adding the corresponding probabilities of $h(n, P_1, n - P_2; \frac{X - P_2 + P_1}{2})$ we obtain the required probability. Note that values of $\frac{X - P_2 + P_1}{2}$ which are negative or fractional have the probability 0. ■

To get an idea of the arising distribution, Tab. 5.14a shows the resulting distribution for $n = 9$ of $P(ham = X)$. Tab. 5.14b shows the distribution of $P(obs = Y)$ for $n, 9$ and $v = 9$.

We are now able to continue with our analysis and combine the result of Eq. 5.28 with Eq. 5.26:

$$P(ham = Y | obs = X) = \frac{P(ham = Y \cap obs = X)}{P(obs = X)} \qquad (5.29)$$

$$= \frac{P(ham = Y) B(v, \frac{1}{2}, X - Y)}{\sum_{i=0}^{X} P(ham = i) B(v, \frac{1}{2}, X - i)}$$

Table 5.14: Probabilities of Hamming Differences (in %) of $\mathcal{HE}^{\star}_{DICE}$ Encrypted Uniformly Distributed Characters with $n = 9$

X	P(ham = X)		Y	P(obs = Y)
0	2.3		0, 18	0.004
1	5.5		1, 17	0.05
2	9.8		2, 16	0.3
3	14.5		3, 15	1.0
4	17.9		4, 14	2.4
5	17.9		5, 13	4.9
6	14.5		6, 12	8.1
7	9.8		7, 11	11.5
8	5.5		8, 10	14.1
9	2.3		9	15.1

(a) Probabilities for $\mathcal{HE}_{DICE}$, which is the noise independent part of $\mathcal{HE}^{\star}_{DICE}$

(b) Probabilities for observing certain differences of two ciphertexts with $v = 9$

A function for GNU's basic calculator 'bc' [FSF13] to compute the probabilities for $P(ham = Y|obs = X)$ can be found in App. 11.6. But before we take a look at a concrete example of this distribution, we show that the conditional probability mass function $P(ham = Y|obs = X)$ is symmetric:

Proposition 5.45. *(Symmetry of Conditional Probability* $P(ham = Y|obs = X))$
Let $B(v, \frac{1}{2}, X)$ *be a probability mass function of a binomial distribution and* $P(ham = X)$ *be the probability mass function as defined in Eq. 5.28. Then for the resulting conditional probability the following symmetry holds:*

$$P(ham = Y|obs = X) = P(ham = (n - Y)|obs = (n + v - X)) \qquad (5.30)$$

PROOF. First we need to show that $P(ham = X) = P(ham = (n - X))$ and $B(v, \frac{1}{2}, X) = B(v, \frac{1}{2}, v - X)$:

The latter is trivial, for the first we consider the change in the summand and by swapping the roles of black and white dots (which does not change the corresponding probability) we get:

$$h(n, P_1, n - P_2; \frac{n - X - P_2 + P_1}{2}) = h(n, P_1, P_2; P_1 - \frac{n - X - P_2 + P_1}{2})$$

$$= h(n, P_1, P_2; P_1 - \frac{X - (n - P_2) + P_1}{2})$$

Since we sum over all combinations of P_1, P_2 and both run from 0 to n, it is obvious that we only changed the summand's order and therefore $P(ham = X) = P(ham = (n - X))$ holds.

Now we are able to prove the proposition:

$$P(ham = n - Y | obs = (n + v - X)) = \frac{P(ham = n - Y)B(v, \frac{1}{2}, (n + v - X) - (n - Y))}{\sum_{i=0}^{n+v-X} P(ham = i)B(v, \frac{1}{2}, (n + v - X) - i)}$$

$$= \frac{P(ham = Y)B(v, \frac{1}{2}, X - Y)}{\sum_{i=0}^{n+v-X} P(ham = i)B(v, \frac{1}{2}, (n + v - X) - i)}$$

Since the numerator is already perfectly rewritten, we need to concentrate on the denominator and start with a translation of the sum's index ($j := n - i$):

$$\sum_{i=0}^{n+v-X} P(ham = i)B(v, \frac{1}{2}, (n + v - X) - i) = \sum_{j=-v+X}^{n} P(ham = n - j)B(v, \frac{1}{2}, v - X + j)$$

By using the symmetry of $P(ham = X)$ and $B(v, \frac{1}{2}, X)$ we get

$$\sum_{j=-v+X}^{n} P(ham = j)B(v, \frac{1}{2}, X - j) \tag{5.31}$$

Now we need to adjust the range of j accordingly, which is quite easy, since for $j < 0$ we have $P(ham = j) = 0$ and for $j > X$ $B(v, \frac{1}{2}, X - j) = 0$ holds. Therefore, we obtain $\sum_{j=0}^{X} P(ham = j)B(n, \frac{1}{2}, X - j)$ and all together the definition of $P(ham = Y | obs = X)$. Hence, Pro. 5.45 is proven. ∎

The promised concrete example of the conditional probability mass function $P(ham = Y | obs = X)$ is shown in Tab. 5.15. It shows the conditional probabilities for $n = 9$ and $v = 9$ of the Hamming distance between two $\mathcal{HE}^\star_{DICE}$ encrypted uniformly at random chosen characters given that a particular value obs was observed. Values for obs > 9 may be derived by using Pro. 5.45: $P(ham = Y | obs = X) = P(ham = (9 - Y) | obs = (18 - X))$.

Since there are $\binom{n+v}{v}$ possibilities of distributing the noise in the keys, the task of the adversary is to decide which of the possibilities match the expected distribution best. If the adversary is able to solve that challenge, she may segregate noise from codings and investigate as described in Sect. 5.3.2. Whether she is successful mainly depends on the amount of eavesdropped ciphertext.

Consideration of Other Distributions The basic idea of other distributions is quite similar to the approach sketched above. The adversary may try to find the

Table 5.15: Conditional Probabilities for $n = 9$ and $v = 9$ of the Hamming Distance between Two $\mathcal{HE}^{\star}_{DICE}$ Encrypted Uniformly at Random Chosen Characters

obs \ ham	0	1	2	3	4
0	100.0				
1	79.2	20.8			
2	58.5	34.7	6.9		
3	39.3	39.9	17.8	2.9	
4	23.3	36.8	28.1	10.4	1.4
5	11.6	27.6	32.8	20.9	6.4
6	4.7	16.6	29.6	29.4	15.5
7	1.4	7.8	20.9	31.1	25.5
8	0.3	2.7	11.3	25.3	31.1
9	0.03	0.6	4.5	15.8	29.0

obs \ ham	5	6	7	8	9
0					
1					
2					
3					
4					
5	0.7				
6	3.9	0.3			
7	10.9	2.2	0.2		
8	20.7	7.2	1.2	0.1	
9	29.0	15.8	4.5	0.6	0.03

positions of the noise part by probing which partitioning matches the binomial distribution for the noise part and also the supposed distribution for the remaining part. We have already listed in Tab. 5.9 the properties, which the adversary may use. Again, this does not hold for the binomial distribution of characters as shown in Tab. 5.10 (cf. Sect. 5.3.2).

Security of Multiple Characters

In this subsection, we again assume that the adversary has access to ciphertexts consisting of tuples of ciphertext where the underlying plaintexts are (pairwise) distinct (cf. p. 161). After that we cover keypads consisting of the digits from '0' to '9' which contain no duplicates.

Security of Pairs of Characters   Given ciphertexts consisting of two characters, along with the side information that they differ allows an attacker to exclude the set of possible keys which would decrypt the ciphertexts to the same character.

Let n denote the encoding parameter and thus the number of dots without noise and let v be the security parameter which denotes the number of noise dots. Then the adversary has to do the same task described above (cf. p. 161ff). Since there are $\binom{n+v}{n}$ possible partitions of noise and encrypted encoding, the adversary has to do this task for each of them. If no possible key is left, the adversary may suspend this partitioning. But as long as there are one or more keys left, the possible key is capable of explaining all ciphertexts.

The size of the key space for encrypting two characters is $\left(2^n \binom{n+v}{n}\right)^2$. That means that the adversary has to search a $\binom{n+v}{n}^2$ times larger key space than for $\mathcal{HE}_{DICE}$. However, for a fixed position of noise, the task of the adversary is the same as for $\mathcal{HE}_{DICE}$. That means that an adversary has to compute $\binom{n+v}{n}^2$ times the task she would have to compute for $\mathcal{HE}_{DICE}$. It holds that:

$$\binom{n+v}{n}^2 \geqslant \left(\frac{n+v}{v}\right)^{2v} = \left(1+\frac{n}{v}\right)^{2v}$$

which approaches e^{2n} for large v. For $n=9$ this is roughly $6.5 \cdot 10^7$ and poses a much harder challenge to the adversary. It is worth mentioning that this is only a lower bound since for $n=9$ and $v=9$, the keyspace grows to $2.3 \cdot 10^9$. The adversary not only has to compute the task more often, she also faces the problem, that she has to solve the problem for all combinations or accept that possibly errors occur. That means her necessary effort is determined by the worst-case of the distribution of needed ciphertexts, as already shown in Tab. 5.11. Thus, as a result we conclude that the adversaries task still seems feasible but requires more ciphertexts and a non negligible amount of additional resources, while the additional resources on the user's side are manageable.

Security of Complete Keypads   Basically, the same observations as regarding the security of pairs of characters hold. If the adversary wants to try to test all possible variations of the positions of noise, she will be overwhelmed with combinations she has to prove, since there are $\binom{n+v}{n}^{n+1}$ possibilities of partitioning the key transparency into noise and non-noise parts.

5.5.3 Security Models

Non Malleability

It is easy to see, that we also do not need to consider security models to find out that $\mathcal{HE}^{\star}_{DICE}$ is not non-malleable. Given the encoding parameter n and an arbitrary ciphertext c of a message m, an adversary is able to change c into an encryption c' of the message '$n-m$'. To achieve this, she simply changes all occurrences of '$\circ\bullet$' to '$\bullet\circ$' and vice versa. Note that she does not need to be bothered by the noise since the noise is removed at the decryption and thus inverting noise does not change the result of the decryption.

Hence, an adversary is able to easily derive ciphertexts such that the underlying plaintexts are meaningfully related. Thus, $\mathcal{HE}^{\star}_{DICE}$ is not non-malleable. However, flipping a 'pair of dots' to obtain a ciphertext c^* with Hamming distance of one to c does not work as easily as in the basic version. The adversary additionally has to make sure that she is not flipping noise dots. Otherwise the result would not be changed.

Indistinguishability

Regarding indistinguishability under chosen-plaintext attacks, the most serious problem for the human decipherable encryption scheme based on dice codings with noise is that its encryption still heavily relies on XOR. This fault cannot be compensated by randomisation of the underlying encodings since there are messages ('0','n') with only one encoding. However, the additional noise slows the adversary down, since she must obtain several ciphertexts from the oracle to determine at which position in the key the noise is placed. The adversary's strategy is similar to the strategy regarding dice codings without noise. She uses the encryption oracle to obtain the key and with that knowledge she is able to solve the challenge. We demonstrate this on the basis of left-or-right indistinguishability.

Theorem 5.46. *The human decipherable encryption scheme based on dice codings with noise $\mathcal{HE}^{\star}_{DICE}$ is not secure in the sense of* $LOR-CPA$.

PROOF. Since $\mathcal{HE}^{\star}_{DICE}$ is segment-based, we only consider single characters. The encodings of '0' and 'n' are deterministic, if the adversary is able to determine the position of the noise. She then reduces the encryption scheme to $\mathcal{HE}_{DICE}$, for which Th. 5.23 states, that it is not secure in the sense of $LOR-CPA$. Thus, we only need to show how to find the noise.

Considering the experiment $\mathbf{Exp}^{lor-cpa-b}_{A_{cpa},\Pi}(n) = b'$, the adversary asks the left-or-right oracle $\mathcal{O}_{\mathcal{LR}}(\cdot,\cdot,b)$ repeatedly for the encryption of the following pairs of messages: $c = \mathcal{O}_{\mathcal{LR}}(0,0)$. Since there is only one encoding for '0', the adversary knows, wherever a dot changes its value, it is due to noise. There are ν places with noise. The we need to determine the probability that all of the noise dots at least once changed their value. If we regard k ciphertexts, the probability that *one* certain dot changed its value at least once, is:

$$P(changevalue;k) = \sum_{i=1}^{k-1} \left(\frac{1}{2}\right)^i = 1 - \left(\frac{1}{2}\right)^{k-1} \tag{5.32}$$

Thus, the probability that not all ν change their value is:

$$P(notall;k) = 1 - \left(1 - \left(\frac{1}{2}\right)^{k-1}\right)^{\nu} = 1 - \left(1 - \frac{1}{2^{k-1}}\right)^{\nu} \tag{5.33}$$

The term $1 - \frac{1}{2^{k-1}}$ approximates 1 with an exponential rate. Thus, for an arbitrary but fixed value of ν, $P(notall;k)$ tends to 1. Hence, the adversary in the LOR – CPA security model is able to determine the positions of noise with great probability. She is then able to reduce $\mathcal{HE}_{DICE}^{\star}$ to the noiseless scheme $\mathcal{HE}_{DICE}$. For $\mathcal{HE}_{DICE}$ we have already proven (cf. Th. 5.23) that it is not secure in the sense of LOR – CPA and therefore $\mathcal{HE}_{DICE}^{\star}$ is also not secure in the sense of LOR – CPA. ∎

As an example, Tab. 5.16 shows the probabilities that k ciphertexts are sufficient to determine the positions of the noise for $\nu = 9$.

Table 5.16: Probabilities of Determining the Positions of Noise in Human Decipherable Encryption Schemes Based on Dice Codings with Noise for $\nu = 9$

k	P(allnoise;k)	k	P(allnoise;k)
1	0.0	8	93.2
2	0.2	9	96.5
3	7.5	10	98.3
4	30.0	11	99.1
5	55.9	12	99.6
6	75.1	13	99.8
7	86.8	14	99.9

Basically, one may use the same idea to prove $\mathcal{HE}_{DICE}^{\star}$ is insecure in the sense of FTG – CPA and we continue without proof.

As discussed before, often it is unrealistic to assume that the adversary has access to an encryption oracle (e.g. in the online banking scenario described in Sect. 4.2.3). Hence, we close the chapter with a discussion of SOR – CO security of $\mathcal{HE}_{DICE}^{\star}$. Obviously, the security depends on the sample function $sample_{struct}$, the number of ciphertexts available to the adversary, the encoding parameter n and the security parameter ν of $\mathcal{HE}^{\star}_{\text{DICE}}$.

In general, an adversary has at least three options to break the encryption scheme and prove it insecure under sample-or-random indistinguishability for ciphertext-only attacks.

- She may learn something about the used key or at least about parts of it and check if the ciphertexts from the oracle comply with the structure of the chosen plaintexts.

- She may look for ciphertexts which do not conform to the structure of the underlying plaintexts for any key and thus conclude that the oracle is encrypting random strings.

- She may find a pattern in the distribution of ciphertexts which either suits or does not correlate to the structure of the underlying plaintexts.

The question is essentially whether the adversary is able to distinguish the distribution of samples and the distribution of random characters. The success of an attack strongly depends on the number of ciphertexts available to her and the amount of noise in the encryption scheme. The noisier the encryption scheme is (in relation to the encoding parameter), the harder the adversary's task gets. For each dice there are $\binom{n+\nu}{n}$ possibilities of arranging the 'information dots' and the 'noise dots'. Thus, raising the amount of noise, allows the adversary to have more ciphertext without being able to determine whether it is from the sample or randomly chosen. However, given a number of k ciphertexts, a sample function Samp and an encoding parameter n, it is unknown for which security parameters the human decipherable encryption scheme based on dice codings with noise is secure in the sense of $\text{SOR} - \text{CO}$ security. Although, it seems likely that there exists a lower bound N for the security parameter ν, so that for all $\nu \geqslant N$ the encryption scheme is secure.

Conjecture 5.47. *Let* $\mathcal{HE}^{\star}_{\text{DICE}}(\nu)$ *be a human decipherable encryption scheme based on dice codings with noise with the encoding parameter* n *and the security parameter* ν, *let* k *be a number of ciphertexts and let* $\text{sample}_{\text{struct}}$ *be a sample function. Then there exists a* N *so that* $\forall \nu \geqslant N$ *the encryption scheme* $\mathcal{HE}^{\star}_{\text{DICE}}(\nu)$ *is secure for* k *ciphertexts in the sense of* $\text{SOR} - \text{CO}$ *security.*

It is reasonable to assume the conjecture is true, because even for a sample which consists of a fixed message string m, the adversary has to determine where in the ciphertext the corresponding encryption of this string is located. As we already discovered when regarding $\text{LOR} - \text{CPA}$ security, the probability to determine the noise, when the dots containing the encryption of the message are fixed, depends on the number of ciphertexts k and the security parameter v. If k is fixed, there is a certain point N and for all $v \geqslant N$ the position of the noise is indeterminable.

Remark 5.48. Assume an application for $\mathcal{HE}^{\star}_{\text{DICE}}$, such as online banking. Then the parameter N answers the question how much noise one has to add to securely use the key transparency k times. After the key transparency is used that often, it is thrown away and a new one is used for the next k ciphertexts. The usability of the scheme for $v \geqslant N$ is unconsidered here. However, given a certain amount of noise v, one may derive the closely related question how often a key transparency may securely reused.

6 Conclusion and Future Work

> All work is seed sown. It grows and
> spreads, and sows itself anew.
>
> Thomas Carlyle

6.1 Summary and Conclusion

Based on previous research of visual cryptography, we gave another description of visual encryption schemes by distinguishing between encoding and encryption, which allowed us to study the properties of the used encoding and encryption schemes independently. Additionally, we defined the notion of *human decipherable encryption schemes* (HDES), a generalisation of visual encryption schemes and their relation to *Completely Automated Public Turing Tests to Tell Computers and Humans Apart* (CAPTCHAs). The observation was that existing game-based security models for indistinguishability are too strong and do not suit the requirements for human decipherable encryption schemes, we defined the notion of *sample-or-random ciphertext only* (SOR-CO) security as a consequence. We also showed that the *sample-or-random ciphertext-only* $(SOR-CO)$ security model gives a weaker notion of security than the real-or-random chosen plaintext $(ROR-CPA)$ security model.

With the idea to construct a secure HDES, where the keys may be used more than once, we showed that the basic scheme based on dice codings proposed by DOBERITZ does not fulfil the requirements of $SOR-CO$ security. We also considered its security in different contexts and presented a successful attack if the adversary has knowledge that the messages consist of pairwisely distinct characters or a keypad which does not contain a digit twice. We then showed that adding noise to the encryption part enhances the scheme. This results in the first visual encryption scheme which makes use of noise to prevent the adversary from drawing conclusions from observed ciphertexts.

In practice, HDES based on dice codings with noise can be combined with an approach proposed by SZYDLOWSKI et al. [SKK07], denoted as *token calculation*. The user receives of a code book instead of a TAN list and for each authentication he is required to manually compute a function depending on the intended transaction, e.g. a bank transfer. However, the increasing distribution of webcams may be a problem for this approach. Since mobile devices are also targeted by attackers, an infected mobile device which is incautiously positioned may be used to photograph the user when he is holding the key transparency in front of his screen.

While our proposed approach for HDES in theory is feasible, its application to 'real world scenarios' still has to be shown. This also concerns the investments to establish a system based on human decipherable encryption schemes, the running costs, which not only include administration of servers, but also training of employee and customers. It also has to be shown, whether users notice when an attacker is manipulating their communications and how the users then act.

It also seems that the well known conflict between security and usability could be a concern here, too. If the security parameter ν of HDES based on dice codings with noise is increased, the system is getting more secure. However, it may be that a large security parameter makes it harder for the user to determine the correct number of dots. Thus, to put this approach into practise, the choice of the security parameter is decisive.

6.2 Future Work

Based on the generalisation of visual encryption to human decipherable encryption schemes, many questions are open. The first part of this section deals with addressing senses other than sight. Then we discuss open questions regarding security models for human decipherable encryption schemes. The last part of this section concerns approaches on how key transparencies could be rotated, reversed or derived from a combination of transparencies – including the *human decipherable encryption scheme based on dice codings with noise*.

6.2.1 Addressing Other Senses than Sight

According to ARISTOTLE's traditional classification [AriCE] there are five senses: sight, hearing, touch, smell, and taste. Further classifications introduce additional senses such as equilibrioception[1] [Nas82], proprioception[2] [She06], thermoception[3] [Wik13d], and nociception[4] [SW07]. Furthermore, if internal senses [Dor07] are considered, which are normally stimulated from within the body, there are even

---

[1]balance
[2]body awareness
[3]heat
[4]pain

more senses to distinguish. However, any further discussion of human senses would lead to far. Although, the concept of human decodable encryption applies to all senses, we concentrate on the senses which are typically used for conscious communication between human beings: namely sight, hearing, and touch. As already described, visual cryptography uses sight, but it's concept may be easily transferred to touch, e.g. by making use of Braille [Bra94] as discussed in the next paragraph. In addition, the idea of overlaying sound may result in audible encryption which is considered in the paragraph following next.

Adopting the Principle of Visible Cryptography to Braille Braille [Bra94] is a method of encoding characters and 'touch reading' them. It was devised in 1821 by Louis BRAILLE and is a system for the blind to read and write. Braille makes use of embossed dots which are arranged in rectangular cells. Each cell consists of 2x3 dots as shown in Fig. 6.1, in general, a cell allows a blank symbol and 63 characters by embossing one or several dots in a characteristic position. Since the encoding is based on the presence or absence of dots, it is possible to build an human decodable encryption scheme on it, which works basically the same way as the described human decodable encryption scheme based on dice codings. The main difference in this case is that not only the number, but also the position of the dots is meaningful.

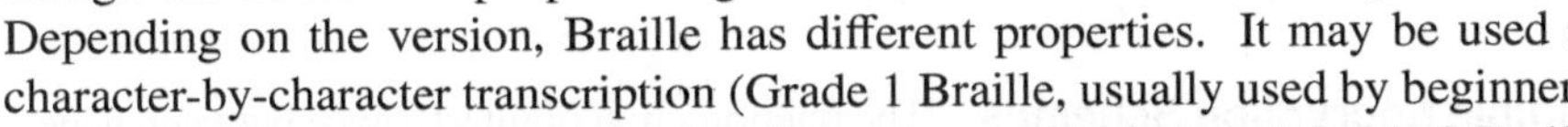

Figure 6.1: 'University of Kassel' Written in Grade 2 Braille

Braille can be seen as a deterministic human decodable encoding scheme, even though the number of people being able to read and write it, is quite small[5]. Depending on the version, Braille has different properties. It may be used as character-by-character transcription (Grade 1 Braille, usually used by beginners) and is therefore a homomorphic encoding scheme. Grade 2 and Grade 3 Braille use several contractions. They are therefore homomorphic only if the underlying alphabet structure is enlarged by a complex system of rules describing the used contractions. To reduce confusion in Braille, some combinations of selected dots are intentionally omitted because they feel the same. Therefore, the previously described versions of Braille are not closed. However, Braille patterns [The10] consisting of cells with 2x4 dots are part of Unicode (U+2800...U+28FF) and allow 256 possible patterns including the complete 2x3-dots cell range and therefore may be seen as closed encoding scheme.

---

[5]In Britain, out of roughly two million visually impaired people, only an estimated 15-20 thousand people use Braille [Wik13b].

It is certainly possible to build a touch based human decodable encryption scheme by combining one of the versions of Braille with the EQV encryption scheme (cf. Sect. 5.2.1). Further research would be needed to investigate the conditions of a secure reuse of the 'transparencies' and to build a mechanical device realising the encryption based on Braille displays (cf. Fig. 6.2). The latter requires a touchable realisation of the EQV encryption scheme. Its realisation may work either electrically by employing an intermediate switch or mechanically by bypassing pins depending on the key which represents embossed or plain dots.

Figure 6.2: Refreshable Braille Display, Photo by Ralf Roletschek via [Wik13a]

Audible Encryption Schemes   The phenomenon of interference between waves can be interpreted as EQV-function as shown in Tab. 6.1. Apart from a technical realisation it is easy to see that the underlying function is basically the same as in Tab. 5.2 and Tab. 5.3 – the EQV-function. Of course, there are other options to utilise the interference of audio waves, but first of all an appropriate coding scheme is needed. It is definitely possible to create 'beeps' and 'non beeps', which humans can count. But this would result in a very annoying human decodable encoding scheme. Otherwise, the encoding of words (or other sounds) is entirely conceivable as already done with audio CAPTCHAs [BC09, SG10, STG09]. But further research is needed to ensure that an adversary will not be able to guess the encrypted words or sounds.

A particular challenge is also the realisation of overlapping audio waves. Obviously, this can not be done at the computer used for communication. Hence, some device is needed which not only overlaps/mixes the corresponding audio ciphers and keys, but also takes care of an adequate start-stop synchronisation. Moreover, the approach should involve as less complexity as needed since otherwise the 'mixing machine' itself would be vulnerable to attacks, for example with Trojan Horses, and not transparent and trustworthy to the user.

Table 6.1: Possible Contingency Tables for Audible Encryption and Decryption with the EQV Encryption Scheme. Wave Superpositioning of a Certain Frequency Can Be Modelled by EQV

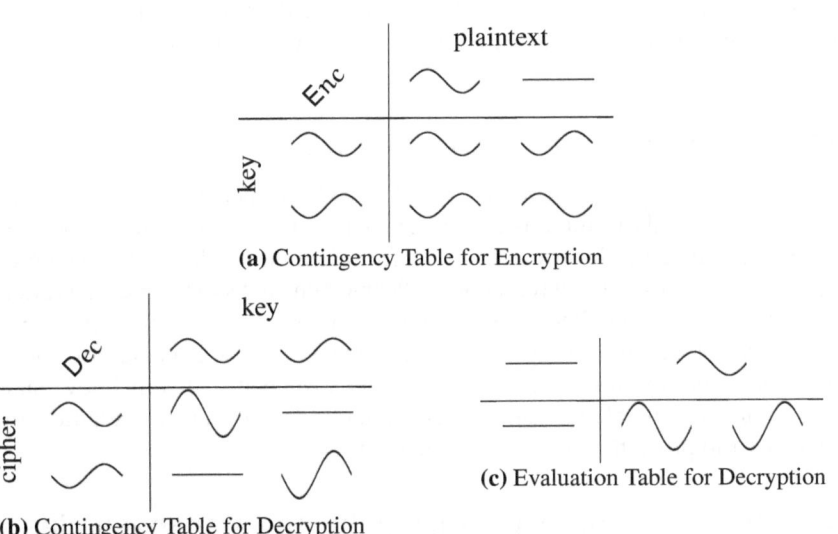

(a) Contingency Table for Encryption

(c) Evaluation Table for Decryption

(b) Contingency Table for Decryption

6.2.2 Security Assumptions and Models

Sample-or-Random Indistinguishability

It would be desirable to have a proof that encryption schemes from the class of *Human Decipherable Encryption Scheme Based on Dice Codings with Noise* with certain encoding parameters n, the security parameter v, the sample function $sample_{struct}$, and a number t representing the number of ciphertexts of the sample available to the adversary, are secure in the sense of *Sample-or-Random Ciphertext-Only Indistinguishability* (SOR − CO).

Active Adversary

We only considered a security analysis for passive adversaries. The assumption was that the adversary does not want to risk manipulating ciphertexts, since she fears that the change might result in ciphertext with a meaningless decryption, which would get the user suspicious and might lead to the detection of the adversary's Trojan horse. Thus, the adversary aims to covertly gather information up to the point when she is able to launch a successful attack.

However, it is unclear if the user can be tricked into leaking information to the adversary. For example, by using the Trojan horse for social engineering or phishing attacks and asking the user to do a 'system check', the adversary may gain additional information. It would be useful to have a model which could classify the adversary's risk of becoming detected in relation to what information a user has leaked.

Non-Malleability and Integrity of Encryptions

Since all visual encryption schemes are based on XOR, respectively EQV, it is easy for an active adversary to flip bits or change the positions of ciphertext. The user will only notice that the ciphertext was changed, when the result is not meaningful to him. It would be useful to have a non-malleable human decipherable encryption scheme. Additionally, another open question is whether there are integrity checks which are feasible for humans and would allow the receiver of a message to check whether the ciphertext was changed. It would be even better, if somebody came up with a human verifiable message authentication code, which would additionally allow the user to prove the message's authenticity.

6.2.3 Methods to Improve Reusing the Key-Transparencies

As already stated in the introduction, there is a considerable amount of work regarding the reversion of visual cryptography transparencies [CSFM05, Fan07, Fan09, FHL09, YWC08, YWLD07] which allows to use a transparency twice.

Reversing and Rotating Slides

If we consider segment-based visual cryptography with symmetrically arranged segments and symbols, rotating or a combination of rotating and reverting the transparencies becomes possible. In the case of human decipherable encryption schemes based on dice codings, there is an arrangement of rows and columns which permits rotations by 90 degrees. For example, Fig. 6.3 shows three rows and three columns for $n = 8$. By additionally using noise, it is also possible to fit other configurations into place. Note, that by rotations of 90 degrees not only the the mapping of the characters (the boxes) gets mixed, but also the mapping between the pairwisely arranged dots change from horizontal to vertical. At first,

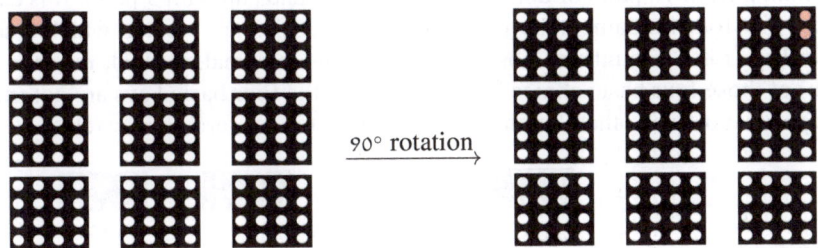

90° rotation

Figure 6.3: The Effect of Rotating Keys for a Human Decipherable Encryption Scheme Based on Dice Codings for $n = 8$

the question arises, whether the additional positions of the transparencies are of any use regarding the number of ciphertexts which can securely be encrypted with the same transparency. Furthermore the question comes up how users would get along facing the additional difficulty of positioning the transparency dependent on a certain rule. A promising approach would be if the adversary would not know the required position each time the transparency is used. Therefore, further research could investigate if the position of the slide may also be communicated by the ciphertext. For example, if the middle square is used to give instructions about the transparency's orientation. Another possibility in the online banking scenario would be to make the position of the slide dependent of the requested TAN.

Combination of Multiple Slides

The human decipherable encryption scheme based on dice codings with noise allows to split the decryption and combine two (or more) transparencies. This can be done by breaking the EQV encryption scheme with noise apart into the EQV and the Noise^{-1} function, each represented by one transparency. The EQV-transparency is enlarged to include a larger number of bits than originally included and now contains $n + v$ pairs of dots. The Noise^{-1}-transparency is needed to blind out v pairs of dots simply by containing blackened pairs of dots. By combining different EQV- and Noise^{-1}-transparencies it is possible to allow a larger number of keys with a reasonable number of transparencies, due to the 'idle dots' of the EQV-transparency. Again the question arises how users would get along facing the additional difficulty of selecting and positioning the transparencies. Furthermore, a combination of multiple slides and rotating and reverting one or both of them would allow an additional number of keys without additional slides – provided the user is able to handle this system. Tab. 6.2 shows the resulting keys for one segment if a 'full transparency' is covered with a partially blackened 'choice transparency'. Beginning from 16 pairs of dots, the resulting key ends up with 9 pairs. It is easy to see that four fundamentally different transparencies are created which result in 16 keys total through the possible orientations (original, rotated, reverted or both) of those four basic choice keys. Of course, the four basic keys are not truly independent of each other, but this may be a first step for further research.

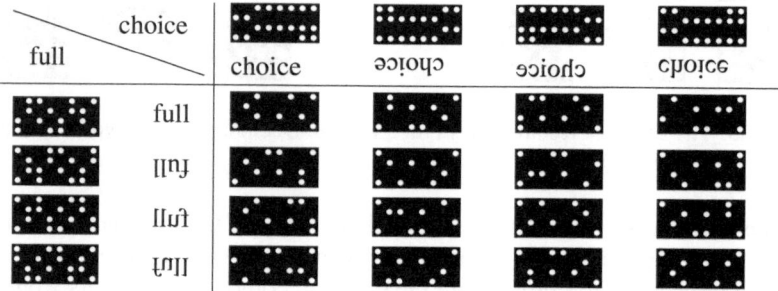

Table 6.2: Composition of Keys for a Dice Codings Based Human Decipherable Encryption Scheme with Noise for Rectangular Transparencies. The Text's Orientation Represents the Orientation of the Particular Transparency.

Closed and Segmented Displays

Another interesting question is whether there are displays similar to the 7-segment display (cf. Fig. 4.3) which only have meaningful configurations. A more graphically encoding scheme would relieve the user from the burden to count dots. However, it is unclear how to construct such a display without the need that the user has to learn new symbols.

Considering other Shapes of Key Transparencies

If the shape of the key transparency is rectangular, it is easy to see that there is only a limited number of combinations possible. It is interesting to also consider other shapes, such as squares, regular polygons and circles. This would allow more possible rotation angles. Other shapes may be useful in light of the just mentioned combination of multiple slides to derive new keys. They may also useful when the key transparency is used multiple times. Assume, key transparency and ciphertext are squares, then rotating the key transparency by 90 degrees would also switch the pairs of dots which represent one bit from horizontal ($\bigcirc\bullet$) to vertical $\left(\begin{smallmatrix}\bigcirc\\\bullet\end{smallmatrix}\right)$.

User Studies on the Variations

DOBERITZ conducted a user study which showed that the visual encryption scheme based on dice codings which she presented was commonly usable. Although it seems plausible that this also holds for human decipherable encryption based on dice codings with noise, it would be worth to study and evaluate up to which magnitude the scheme with noise remains usable. Moreover, it would also be interesting to conduct studies on the variations, where the user is require to rotate, reverse or derive key transparencies from several transparencies and evaluate the usability of the scheme and the user's capability of coping with a number of transparencies.

Part III

Non-Transferable Anonymous Credentials

7 Introduction, Scenario, and Related Work

> Once you've lost your privacy, you
> realise you've lost an extremely
> valuable thing.
>
> Billy Graham

7.1 Background and Purpose

Most cryptographic primitives for authentication schemes in the digital world are based on the knowledge of a private key or secret, for example digital signatures or zero-knowledge proofs. In many cases there is an (at least) implicit binding of the secret to a person. If you receive a signed mail, you assume it is signed by the regular owner of the private key; if you authenticate yourself with a zero-knowledge proof, you are expected not to give the secret to another person. On the other hand, one may not put too many trust into this assumption since this secrets are eventually digital data which can be copied without evidence. Two obvious situations come to one's mind: On the one hand, cryptographic secrets are not very memorisable for human beings in general, so they are usually stored somewhere, where they could be stolen. On the other hand, the user may want to share his secret with somebody while the authorising organisation does not want him to do so.

The first situation could be relieved by storing the key in a secure place (e.g. on a tamper-proof smartcard or encrypted with a human memorisable password). However, it is much harder to achieve the same in the latter situation. If you want to ensure the non-transferability of knowledge you must keep it secret from the user or make him want to keep it secret. In the following sections we especially focus on the non-transferability of anonymous credentials since they offer less contact points than e.g. digital signatures, where the user is known and could be sued for abuse. Should a user intentionally give his signing key for contracts away, the opposite party at least knows who to take to court.

Anonymous credentials introduced by Chaum [Cha85, CE87] usually consist of cryptographic tokens which allow the user to prove a statement or relationship with an organisation to another person or organisation without being identified. While some anonymous credential systems are related to the concept of untraceable or anonymous payments [Cha83b] and hence it should be possible to transfer the credentials easily to another person, there are some situations where credentials should not be transferable. We deal with anonymous credentials in more details in the next two chapters, thus this rough sketch should be sufficient at this point.

7.2 Overview

The organisation of this part is as follows: In the remaining introduction we propose some scenarios and give a short overview of closely related work. In the next chapter we introduce notions and terms of privacy and sketch the basic idea of anonymous credentials. After having a short look at smartcards, we discuss the usage of biometrics for access control and introduce the idea of fuzzy extractors. In the first part of Sect. 9.1, we introduce and compare two different approaches aiming at non-transferability: biometric access control and embedded valuable secrets. In the second part of Sect. 9.1, we take a closer look at biometric-enforced non-transferability and present a new approach. We then proceed to compare it with existing ones. We conclude with a short summary and topics for future work in Chap. 10.

7.3 Scenarios

There are at least two general cases in which non-transferable anonymous credentials are useful. The first instance tries to prevent violations of existing law by making the user prove a certain attribute, e.g. proof of age, driving licenses, a country's citizenship or special abilities such as academic degrees. These proofs have in common that they constitute a kind of access control. People who are of legal age may buy alcohol and tobacco in stores, people who own a driving license may rent cars, and so on.

In the second case, anonymous credentials act as tickets for a given service. Either the service is paid in advance, e.g. weekly or monthly tickets for travelling by train or visiting a swimming pool, or the ticket entitles its owner to a particular discount, e.g. seniors, student or handicapped ID or the German Railways BahnCard. It may not be obvious at a first glance, but the difference between the two scenarios lies in the injured party, if the system is circumvented. The first scenario's aggrieved party is the issuer who wants to enforce a certain law. In the latter scenario the user fraudulently manages to obtain a service cheaper or for free and, thus, the verifier is, or belongs to, the injured party.

IMPAGLIAZZO and MINER MORE [IM03] mention also another scenario where a health insurance company pays for a sensitive, medical test such as a human immunodeficiency virus (HIV) antibody test. On the one hand, the user would like to stay anonymous due to the sensitive nature of this test, on the other hand, the health insurance company wants the doctor to make sure, the patient is the named policyholder.

It is important to have a rough idea of the value of the credential. While this is easy, if it is used for a specific service paid in advance, the value of credentials used to prove a country's citizenship depends more on the purpose the credential is used for than on the credential itself. Assume, such a credential would be used for border control. This would make it very valuable for people smugglers and one has to expect sophisticated attacks. If the credential is used to prove this property to a social website, one may concentrate on occasional attacks.

7.4 Related Work

Basics are given by the *wallet-with-observer architecture* introduced by CHAUM and PEDERSEN [CP93]. The approach in this work is built on the wallet-with-observer architecture and so are the approaches from BLEUMER [Ble98], IMPAGLIAZZO and MINER MORE [IM03], and BHARGAV-SPANTZEL et al. [BSSB06]. BLEUMER equipped the observer with a biometric facility which only starts the protocol, if the intended biometrics are shown. IMPAGLIAZZO and MINER MORE transferred this approach to a personal digital assistant (wallet) with a tamper-resistant smartcard (observer). While BLEUMER, IMPAGLIAZZO and MINER MORE use a stored template for access control, the approach of BHARGAV-SPANTZEL et al. is based on fuzzy extractors [JW99] and used for zero-knowledge proofs [GMR89]. Since their approach does not aim to enforce non-transferability, fingerprints are read by an external device and then sent to the tamper-proof device – analogous to the match-on-card approach [Nor04]. As a consequence, the approach of BHARGAV-SPANTZEL et al. is also vulnerable by replay attacks should the adversary be able to control the wallet.

The approach presented in Sect. 9.2.1 aims to enforce non-transferability and does not rely only on fuzzy extractors but additionally stores a secret key on the tamper-proof device. Thus, it differs to the approaches of BLEUMER [Ble98], IMPAGLIAZZO and MINER MORE [IM03] by not storing a template. Compared to the approach of BHARGAV-SPANTZEL et al. it is intended for the use of anonymous credentials, aims to enforce non-transferability, relies on the system-on-card approach and additionally stores information on the tamper-proof device.

8 Privacy and Data Security

> Privacy is not something that I'm merely entitled to, it's an absolute prerequisite.

> Marlon Brando

8.1 Notions and Terms of Privacy

PFITZMANN and KÖHNTOPP give a proposal for a terminology based on early papers in this area [PK01]. Building on that, they improved the terminology [PH10] in the following years. The terms in this work are based on their work in combination with a discussion of BRANDS [Bra07] and CAMERON [Cam13] via their blogs in 2007. For this work, a vague notion of these terms is sufficient. For a more detailed discussion, we refer the reader to the literature cited above. For a taxonomy of privacy in legal terms we recommend the work of SOLOVE [Sol06].

8.1.1 Anonymity, Pseudonymity, Unlinkability and Untraceability

Anonymity means a person is able to withhold his identity regarding a certain *item of interest* (IOI), e.g. a certain action or message. The notion of anonymity is often restricted in the way that a person is not identifiable within *the anonymity set*, the set of persons which might possibly have caused the IOI. For example a sender may be anonymous only within the set of eligible senders. Naturally, the degree of anonymity depends on the size of the anonymity set.

Sometimes it is desirable to link certain IOIs to the same initiator. For this purpose, *pseudonyms* can be used as an identifier for the person, which should not allow to draw conclusions on the person's "real identity". A common real world example for pseudonyms is the use of pen names by authors.

Should an adversary not be able to link two or more IOIs, they are denoted as *unlinkable*. Unlinkability is closely related to *untraceability*, which means, that given a certain number of IOIs, the adversary is not able to trace back the identity of the person causing these IOIs. If IOIs are not unlinkable, this may allow an adversary to identify the person. For example, Peggy has the claims "I'm older than 18.", "I'm female." and "My postal code is 34121." signed by blind signatures and proves these claims consecutively, but independently of each other to a verifier Victor. If Victor is not able to link these claims, he won't be able to identify Peggy, since he does not even know, that the claims are from the same person. On the other hand, if Victor is able to link the claims and maybe some more claims collected in the future, he may be able to reduce the anonymity set sufficiently to a single person, and thus identify Peggy. Therefore, linkability of IOIs is crucial for untraceability since it may decrease the size of the anonymity set. On the other hand, if untraceability is not given, all IOIs may be attributed to the identity of the person and thus are linkable.

If Peggy is able to prove all these claims independently of each other, this is denoted as *selective disclosure*. If the statement "I'm older than 18." is needed, there is a difference between disclosing the requested statement, called *minimal disclosure* and a statement like "I'm 23 years old". The latter would disclose more information than necessary and therefore reduce the anonymity set. A scheme for selective disclosure is proposed by CANARD and LESCUYER [CL13]. By composing *sanitising signatures* [SBZ01], where a user is able to blacken parts of the original text without invalidating the signature, and anonymous credentials, the user is able to blacken all claims he does not want to show to the verifier.

8.1.2 Trust Levels Regarding Privacy

CHAUM and PEDERSEN [CP93] introduced the following trust levels regarding privacy for individuals dealing with organisations.

- If information about the individual may be revealed during the transaction with an organisation and the individual is not able to enhance his privacy by any means, the individual's privacy is denoted as *pure trust*.

- *Computational privacy* assumes that the used communication protocol has been well studied and that the individual follows the prescribed protocol. The effort needed to learn anything about the individual should then exceed the organisation's hypothetically available resources by an adequate margin.

- The individual enjoys *unconditional privacy*, if he follows the prescribed protocol and the organisation cannot learn anything extra about him, even if granted unlimited resources.

One may have noticed, that the notion of computational and unconditional security is in accordance with its counterpart of computational and unconditional security from Sect. 2.2.3. Although, CHAUM and PEDERSEN did not define it, definitions of complexity-theoretic and provable privacy in analogy to complexity-theoretic and provable security are conceivable and easily derivable.

8.2 Anonymous Credentials

The basic idea of *anonymous credentials* is that users are able to anonymously prove attributes with credentials issued by an organisation. Anonymous authentication means the verifier should not learn more information about the user than what is to be proven. The verifier should also not be able to link several authentications of the same user which would allow him to build profiles on authenticating users.

Anonymous credentials were introduced by CHAUM [Cha85, CE87] and usually consist of cryptographic tokens, such as blind [Cha83b, Cha83a] and group signatures [CvH91] in combination with proofs of knowledge (cf. Sect. 8.2.2) that allow the user (herein after also referred to as prover) to prove a statement or relationship with an organisation to another person or organisation (herein after referred to as verifier) anonymously. It is worth to mention that "knowledge" is only one authentication factor [Rel05, BJR+06] which can be transformed to "possession" by moving the secret into a tamper-proof device, such as a smartcard.

A good way to understand the properties of anonymous credentials is to compare two different payment instruments, physical money and cash cards or credit cards – leaving out the existence of anonymous credit cards [LPM94, LMP95] for the moment. Both of them fulfil the needs necessary for payments. However, while money mainly reveals the transferred amount and little other information, maybe a unique serial number on bank notes, the use of cash cards or credit cards identifies the user and thus allows the involved organisations to create highly detailed data records about the card owner. Therefore, in contrast to cash cards or credit cards, physical money in practice offers anonymity to its users, even though in theory each bank note is traceable due to its unique serial.

Similar circumstances apply during age verification, where it is common to show an identity card, say before entering a club. The procedure of age verification gets quite curious if online age verification is used, where it is common to show credit card information to a third party to prove a certain age. On the one hand, the verifier does not know, if the user shows his own credit card information. Since it is not possible to check if the user is giving his own card's information, the verifier needs to trust the user. On the other hand, the user does not know if the age verification site is trustworthy. Therefore, he probably does not want to disclose more information than needed. Giving his credit card information away makes him identifiable – even though only an age verification was required. Furthermore, the user risks fraud with his credit card information. Altogether, this procedure is quite unsatisfactory, since neither the user's privacy is preserved nor is a reliable check of his age performed.

Other examples for making use of anonymous credentials include the proof of a country's citizenship, driving license or the proof of special abilities, such as academic degrees. Note that it is unreasonable to expect anonymous credentials in border control or stop-and-search operation by the police. However, there are many national regulations also applying to websites which may make the owners of the website want to approve the user's citizenship. The scenario where a user anonymously rents a car, and his identity is only revealed should he steal or damage the car, would make it necessary that the intended driver of the car proves that he owns a valid driving license.

This issue gains in importance, if we regard the considerable increase of electronic data processing. Whereas it may be considered harmless to show an identity card to a bar's doorman for age verification, who may or may not remember the prover's identity some days later, an electronic authentication system may store timestamp and identity for a long time. This may not only worry the guest, but also lead to liability problems of the hosting organisations, as many breaches of data privacy have been shown in the past. Thus, anonymous credentials provide a way to address privacy interests without neglecting security for all involved parties when using electronic authentication.

The main idea of CHAUM's credential system is that users use different pseudonyms, which cannot be linked, when receiving credentials from an issuer or showing credentials from respective holders to a verifier. Therefore, it is occasionally referred as *pseudonym system* [LRSW00]. As stated above, pseudonyms on the one hand allow users to choose different names with each involved organisation and on the other hand they allow the involved organisations to connect users to their accounts without being able to identify them.

8.2.1 Properties of Anonymous Credentials

In this section we introduce some of the properties of anonymous credentials apart from the previously described properties untraceability, unlinkability, minimal and selective disclosure in Sect. 8.1. We roughly follow the presentation of CAMENISCH and LYSYANSKAYA [CL01].

Credentials may be denoted as *one-show*, *limited-show*, *multiple-show*, depending on their use (one-time, a limited number of times, unlimited). If limited-show and multiple-show credentials are shown to a verifier, the verifications should be unlinkable. Each pseudonym and credential should belong to a specific user [LRSW00].

For the security of the system it is crucial that no user is able to forge credentials. In particular this means that no user should be able to collaborate with other users or organisations and create a credential or obtain a credential by an organisation, which that user would not have gotten alone. A system fulfilling this requirement has *consistency of credentials*.

Anonymous credential systems are related to the concept of untraceable or anonymous payments [Cha83b, CFN88, Cha89] and hence, the credentials representing the money can be easily transferred to another person. However, there are some situations where transferring credentials is undesired and the credential should be *non-transferable*. One example would be when people have to prove their age.

Furthermore, it is sometimes desirable to identify a user, for example, if illegal actions are discovered. Revealing his identity is denoted as *global anonymity revocation*. Revealing only the user's pseudonym along with its issuing organisation is denoted as *local anonymity revocation*. Additionally revoking the anonymity of a user may only be permitted under certain conditions, e.g. if he double-spends a one-show credential.

8.2.2 Zero-Knowledge Proofs

Anonymous credentials are based on the combination of zero-knowledge proofs and signatures. The original system by CHAUM [Cha83b, CFN88, Cha89] is based on blind signatures and results in one-show credentials. Later BRANDS [Bra99] improved CHAUM's credential system by generalising it, improving its efficiency and bringing it to commercial use [Bra13]. Another credential form, unlinkable limited- or multi-show credentials by CAMENISCH et al., is based on group signatures. We give a short overview of zero-knowledge proofs in this section and outline how credential systems work by presenting the FEIGE-FIAT-SHAMIR identification scheme [FFS87, FFS88] in Ex. 8.1. This scheme also demonstrates the basic idea of zero-knowledge proofs.

Zero-knowledge proofs go back to work from GOLDWASSER, MICALI and RACK-OFF [GMR89]. For further reading, there is a survey of GOLDREICH [Gol02] and we refer to easily comprehensible presentations of QUISQUATER [QGB90] and NAOR [NNR99]. Analogous to Sect. 2.2, we stick with widely-used names for the participants when following cryptographic protocols. Regarding zero-knowledge proofs, three parties are usually needed. The *issuer* Ivan assigns some kind of certificate to Peggy. Later on, Peggy has *to prove* to the *verifier* Victor that she possesses the certificate without revealing it to him. Zero-knowledge proofs have to fulfil three properties [BFM88]:

Completeness: If the statement is true, an honest prover will be able to convince an honest verifier of the statement.

Soundness: If the statement is false, a (cheating) prover will only be able to convince an honest verifier with negligible probability.

Zero-knowledge: The proof reveals no information but the validity of the prover's statement.

EXAMPLE 8.1. Feige-Fiat-Shamir Identification Scheme
The parallel version of the FEIGE-FIAT-SHAMIR identification scheme [FFS87, FFS88, Sho99b] consists of two phases. During the initialisation phase the issuer supplies prover and verifier with the necessary data. Later, the prover may interactively demonstrate to the verifier, that he knows the data given by the issuer. No third party is needed for the proof in the second phase.

Initialisation

- Ivan chooses two large primes p, q and computes $n = pq$
- Ivan chooses $a_1, \ldots, a_k \in \mathbb{Z}_n^*$
- Ivan computes $b_i = a_i^2 \mod n$
- Ivan sends n and $a_1, \ldots, a_k$ to Peggy
- Ivan sends n and $b_1, \ldots, b_k$ to Victor
- Ivan keeps p, q secret

Protocol Run A protocol run is an interactive zero-knowledge proof as shown in Fig. 8.1. Peggy picks a random number r and sends $x := \pm r^2 \mod n$ to Victor. Having received x, Victor chooses a challenge consisting of a boolean vector $e_1, \ldots, e_k$ and sends it to Peggy. Peggy computes $y := ra_1^{e_1} \cdot \ldots \cdot a_k^{e_k} \mod n$, sends it to Victor and Victor proves if y^2 matches $\pm x b_1^{e_1} \cdot \ldots \cdot b_k^{e_k} \mod n$. The protocol is repeated until Victor is convinced that Peggy really knows the secret square roots $a_1, \ldots, a_k$ of his numbers $b_i, \ldots, b_k$.

We only give an informal reasoning of the security of the FEIGE-FIAT-SHAMIR identification scheme here and refer to the original literature for a proof. The security of the protocol is based on the factoring assumption (cf. Sect. 2.3.1). Being able to compute the modular square root, if the modulus is a composite of two primes, means being able to factor the modulus, which is the basic principle of factorisation algorithms based on quadratic sieves [Bre00, p. 8]. Therefore, it is assumed that Victor is not able to compute the modular square roots known to Peggy. If the RSA assumption holds, Victor or an eavesdropper Eve do not learn anything about Peggy's numbers a_i. If Eve knows Victor's numbers b_i and she wanted to convince Victor that she knows the modular square roots, she needs to guess Victor's challenge $e_1, \ldots, e_k$. She then could set $x := y^2 b_1^{-e^1} \ldots b_k^{-e_k}$ and when challenged simply send y to Victor. Since $y^2 = y^2 b_1^{-e^1} \ldots b_k^{-e_k} \cdot b_1^{e^1} \ldots b_k^{e_k}$ Victor would be convinced that Eve knows the modular square roots. However, if we assume, that $k = 10$ and three run's of the protocol are run, Eve's chance to correctly guess all 30 e_i is 2^{-30} which is a chance of roughly one in one billion.

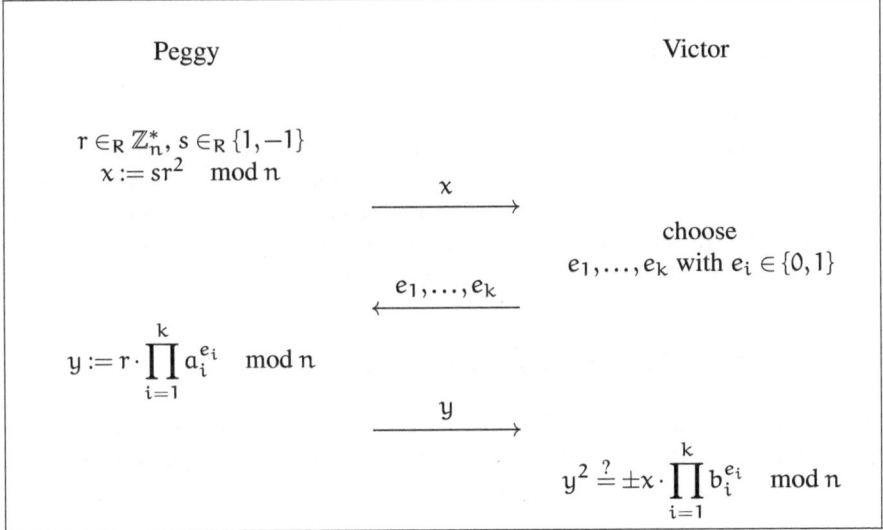

Figure 8.1: A Run of the Feige-Fiat-Shamir Identification Scheme

8.2.3 Wallet-With-Observer Architecture

In 1992 Chaum and Pedersen introduced [CP93] the *wallet-with-observer architecture*. In the wallet-with-observer-architecture there exists a user trusted device (wallet) which runs a local process (observer). The credential issuing organisation (herein after referred to as authority) trusts that the observer only performs legitimate operations. Here legitimate means in the authority's interest. The observer then works as a black box for the user and if he does not trust the manufacturer of the tamper-proof device or the issuing organisation, it is assumed that the user carefully watches the communication of the tamper-proof device with the verifier. This concept suggests that each user has a personal communication device, the *wallet*, with a tamper-resistant chip, the *observer*, which is either built-in or accessed in the form of a smartcard. This way the user is able to check and prevent the information flow from the organisation to the observer and only has to trust that the observer supports all legitimate operations. Since the observer has no direct communication channel to the verifier, the user may abort the protocol and prevent any transmission if she is not able to follow the protocol or suspects that the observer tries to send covert information to the verifier. In fact, the user is a legitimate man-in-the-middle in this case. Since the tamper-proof device uses a zero-knowledge proof, the user cannot learn anything from the responses of the card. The user may also change the challenges from the verifier to the tamper-proof device and the answers from the device to the verifier if this prevents information flow. It is only important that the user is not able to solve the verifier's challenge without the device and that the user is not able to manipulate the device.

The verifying organisation on the other hand only has to trust that the observer is still intact and prevents illegitimate operations (e.g. releasing the secret). To prevent abuse, the tamper-resistant chip may be protected by a personal identification number (PIN), resulting in a two-factor-authentication (possession of card and knowledge of the PIN) as already known from today's cash cards.

8.3 Smartcards and Biometrics

The literature on smartcards and biometrics is so extensive, one could write several books about this topics. A complete presentation is therefore not possible here and we concentrate on the combination of both areas.

8.3.1 Smartcards

The whole range of smartcards and their applications is beyond the scope of this work, and we refer the reader to the exhaustive overview by RANKL and EFFING [RE08]. In this section we focus on the interaction of smartcards with biometrics and closely related areas. In general, smartcards are considered to be tamper-proof (cf. Sect. 2.2.2).

However, adversaries able to accomplish side-channel attacks (cf. Sect. 2.2.2) or initiate fault induction attacks (cf. Sect. 2.2.4) may harm the tamper-resistance. Indications that such attacks are feasible were already given in the nineties by ANDERSON et al. [AK96, AK98]. We do not go further into details here, and refer to a survey on fault attacks in smartcard environments by GIRAUD and THIEBEAULD [GT04]. The range of applications of tamper-proof devices, and the general arms race between attackers and defenders is described by ANDERSON et al. [ABCS05, ABCS06].

Biometrics Used with Smartcards

BECHELLI et al. [BBV02] identify three general possibilities to use smartcards for biometric authentication:

Template on Card: The biometric template is stored on the smartcard, but the biometrics are acquired and compared by an external system.

Match on Card: The biometric template is stored on the smartcard, the biometrics are acquired by an external system, transmitted to the smartcard and compared there [Nor04]. An algorithm for fingerprint verification is given by PAN et al. [PGM+03] in 2003. Later, the performance of match-on-card algorithms was measured in a series of reports by the National Institute of Standards and Technology [GSW+08, GSW+09, GSW+11].

System on Card: This approach is an evolution of the match-on-card approach, where the biometric sensor is embedded in the smartcard. For example a smartcard with embedded pressure-sensitive fingerprint reader was presented by Fidelica [Fid08] and Biometric Associates [BA09].

Assume, the smartcard performs the stated operations and it is ensured (e.g. by cryptographic protocols) that only a valid smartcard is used. Then, the most secure and privacy-preserving solution is the last approach, since neither the template nor the biometrics measured are processed or transmitted outside of the smartcard. For a further discussion on caveats when using biometrics for authentication and combining them with smartcards, we refer to HACHEZ et al. [HKQ00].

8.3.2 Biometrics

Biometrics used for authentication means to measure (and compare) physiological or behavioural characteristics of a user, such as fingerprints, iris patterns, genetic codes (DNA[1]), voices or gaits. The field of biometrics is well researched[2] and too large to cover in this work. Therefore, we restrict ourselves to a short presentation of important characteristics and then start to discuss what caveats should be kept

---

[1] desoxyribonucleic acid

[2] As of today, the computer science bibliography dblp [LHA+13] returns 3581 documents when queried for "biometric".

in mind when deploying biometric systems. We continue with a brief overview of attacks on biometric templates and fuzzy extractors before we discuss which biometric attributes should be used in combination with anonymous credentials. For further reading see Wayman et al. [WJMM05].

Biometric Characteristics

There are five properties which biometrics may possess. They all refer to the relevant population for which the biometric system is intended [JaSP02, WJMM05, Way01]:

Robustness or *permanence* means that the characteristics on an individual do not change over time. Robustness is also influenced by the technical method of creating and storing the template.

Distinctiveness or *uniqueness* means that the characteristics vary over the population, so that the system is able to distinguish them.

Availability or *universality* means that the entire population should have this characteristic. Maltoni et al. [MMJP09] state that roughly 10% of the population have a poor quality of fingerprints, for instance because they are manual workers or elderly people. Additionally, it is known that gene mutations exist that cause the concerned people not to have fingerprints [NBFT+11].

Accessibility or *measurability* or *collectability* states how easy it is to measure the characteristic, preferably with an electronic sensor.

Acceptability means that people do not have objections having their biometrics captured.

Regarding the used technology, there are two other important properties. *Performance* denotes the accuracy and speed of the used technology and *circumvention* refers to how easy an adversary may imitate the biometric characteristic. Regarding the first four properties of biometric characteristics presented above, we can measure their quality by the following rates:

Robustness is measured by the *false reject rate* or *false non-match rate*, the probability that the system does not match the measured sample with the previously submitted template. Distinctiveness is measured by the *false accept rate* or *false match rate*, the probability that the system matches the measured sample with a template of another user. Availability is measured by the *failure to enroll rate*, the probability that the biometrics of a user cannot be read during the enrolment phase. The accessibility of a system may be measured by the *throughput rate*, the number of persons the system can process per time.

Another distinction is whether users have to participate explicitly. This is then denoted as *active biometrics* in contrast to *passive biometrics*, where the user might not even notice that his biometrics were measured.

Biometric Access Control

It is important to keep in mind that biometrics are substantially different from passwords or cryptographic keys [Sch99b]. First of all, most biometrics are not secret. As an example, consider fingerprints, which are unintentionally left in the environment. Fingerprints [Dil12] and iris codes [FBH+05] may also be read from distances up to 10 metres. To prove the case, CAMERON [Cam08] reports an instance, where he discovered his fingerprint on his laptop only centimetres away from the fingerprint sensor as shown in Fig. 8.2. CAMERON legitimately wonders how secure that might be.

(a) Fingerprint Reader

(b) Fingerprint Closeup

Figure 8.2: Fingerprint Charade from CAMERON [Cam08]. The Gold Blotch Was Added by CAMERON to Cover the Very Clearest Part of His Fingerprint.

There is also another difference between biometrics and passwords when used for access control. The user is relieved from the burden to choose and memorise a good password or key. Persons will naturally carry their biometrics with them at all times (unless someone figures out a way to leave their body parts at home). This is very useful in a situations like an emergency medical visit, where a patient will be unable to provide a traditional public key or password. The process of authenticating oneself to obtain a private key is very natural. One can demonstrate ownership of an identity simply by physically presenting the biometric property. However, this does not come for free, since biometrics cannot be easily revoked should they get compromised.

As in cryptographic systems, there is an arm's race between attackers and defenders. Sensors are getting better and include live detection of biometrics [GAFFOG12, GOLFOG12] for instance. But so do attack techniques. It is feasible to circumvent biometric sensors with gummy fingers easily made of cheap gelatin [MMYH02]. Even DNA profiling suffered a major attack by creating fake DNA samples [FWDG10]. For a more detailed summary on attacks on biometric systems based on fingerprints, we refer to ULUDAG et al. [UJ04].

PFITZMANN [Pfi08] points out that biometrics used for authentication also creates new security problems. Examples are forensic problems when large databases of biometric characteristics are created and valuables are protected by biometric access control, as it may give a new industry producing fake biometrics. This would not only affect the security of biometric access control, but forensic analysis as well as, e.g. regarding crimes. It is also important to consider the process rise to biometric authentication. PFITZMANN states that the user is not able to prevent third parties from passively measuring his biometrics and that at least covert passive biometrics should be outlawed to protect the user's privacy.

We conclude with two further examples, which show that biometric access control is not the Holy Grail of authentication and has to be employed carefully. In Malaysia, a car was protected by a fingerprint recognition system, and thus the thieves took the owner's finger instead of the key [Ken05]. During the last years, there has been a trend to involve biometrics in passports to prevent forgery. An investigator from the Government Accountability Office managed to get four genuine U.S. passports with his biometrics using fake names of a five year old child and a man who was more than forty years dead. With this passports he then was capable of booking and boarding a plane [Kea09]. This once more demonstrates that the process, in which the biometric access control is embedded, is also decisive.

Biometric Templates

When biometrics are used for access control, there is an enrolment phase, when templates of the biometrics are created and stored (cf. Sect. 8.3.1). When the system is on duty, access is granted or denied based on the comparison of the just measured biometrics with the stored template. The most important requirements for the templates are a small error rate when matching, *irreversibility* of the template and *revocability* of templates.

Irreversibility of the template is important for two reasons. On the one hand, if the template gets lost, the user's privacy is at risk. On the other hand, the adversary may try to extract knowledge of the original biometrics and try to create fake biometrics. Depending on the quality of the fake biometrics and the quality of the sensor, the adversary may then be able to pass the biometric access control in this way. We discuss this topic in Sect. 9.2 in the context of biometric-enforced non-transferable anonymous credentials.

Unfortunately, it shows that irreversibility is hard to achieve and creating templates from biometrics is not a one-way function. ADLER demonstrated face image reconstruction from face recognition templates [Adl03] and JAIN et al. [RSJ07, FJ09] showed how to reconstruct fingerprints based on minutiae templates. GALBALLY et al. [GRGB+12, Gal12] reconstructed iris images from iris codes.

It would be short-sighted to rely only upon a simple encryption of the templates, since also encrypted templates may be misused, for example by matching them against a global database. RATHA et al. [RCB01] introduced *cancellable biometrics*, where an intentional, repeatable distortion is added when processing the biometrics. This should ensure that the templates cannot be matched with a global template database to identify people, since every instance of enrolment may use another transformation for distortion. Moreover, if a variant of the distorted template is compromised, it is possible to revoke templates, by starting a new enrolment with another transformation. An overview of this area is given by ULUDAG, JAIN et al. [UPPJ04a, UPPJ04b, JNN08]. A review of several *template protection schemes* and existing attacks on them is given by ZHOU et al. [ZWBK09]. For a survey on this area, we refer the reader to RATHGEB and UHL [RU11].

Fuzzy Extractors

The idea of *fuzzy extractors* goes back to fuzzy vault schemes from JUELS and SUDAN [JW99]. The aim is to generate cryptographic keys from biometric data. One of the arising problems is that biometric measurements are generally noisy. Thus, fuzzy extractors have to be error-tolerant and produce the same result, provided the error is not too large. On the other hand, the output should be sufficiently random, thus one may see fuzzy extractors as "error-correcting hash-functions". Often, a helper string is used to accept biometric input similar to the original biometrics. Ideally, it is impossible to learn any information on the biometrics from the helper string. In theory this is only possible if the helper string is not related to the biometrics in any way. However, since the helper string should assist in accepting similar biometrics, it has to be related to the biometrics in some way. So the best tradeoff in practise is that at least an adversary should not learn anything useful from the helper string. Active adversaries are assumed to be able to modify also the helper string for their attacks. Fuzzy extractors, which are secure against this kind of attacks, are denoted as *robust* [DKRS06]. The output of a *uniform fuzzy extractor* follows a uniform distribution over the target set. This is desirable if the output is used for cryptographic purposes such as key generation.

Since it is sufficient for this work to have a rough understanding of fuzzy extractors, we do not go into detail here and refer for details to the literature. Examples for fuzzy extractors based on minutiae from fingerprints were given by CHANG et al. [CR07] and ARAKALA et al. [AJH07] in 2007. In 2009 YANG and YANG proposed a fuzzy extractor scheme claimed to run on smartcards [YY09]. A more formal definition of fuzzy extractors is given by DODIS et al.[DRS04, DORS08]. Some observations on multiple uses of fuzzy extractors and stronger security models are given by BOYEN [Boy04]. Finally, the existence of side-channel attacks on fuzzy extractors was shown by MERLI et al. [MSSS11].

Biometric Attributes for Access Control with Anonymous Credentials

On first glance, one might have the idea to identify a number of biometric attributes which are visible to the naked eye but not suitable for identifying the user, e.g. eye colour instead of getting the iris code. Two or three properties could be checked and if all of them match, it is assumed, that the user is legitimated. Let us assume we had ten biometric attributes, each dividing the users independent of other attributes and randomly into five subgroups of equal size. Take e.g. colour of hair (brown/black, blond, red, none, others) or iris colour (blue, brown, green, grey, hazel). In total that would split the users in roughly ten million subgroups (5^{10}). If only three attributes were checked, which were chosen by random, the anonymity set for the user would still be large enough and if those checks were unlinkable, the user could not be identified if there were enough users participating in the system. On the other hand, there would be a good chance of catching illegitimate users if they were using another person's credentials. On the average, two attributes of users will be the same. Let us assume two user with four congruent attributes would want to cheat. Since the users would not know in advance which attributes will be checked, the probability of a successful fraud would be roughly three percent[3]. Depending on the necessary level of security and the estimated penalty, this could be enough for some situations (e.g. personalised bus or train tickets).

Unfortunately, taking a closer look at biometrics reveals that it could be a problem of finding enough suitable attributes. The above mentioned hair and iris colour differ hardly outside Europe [SF04]; brown is very predominant here and, in many populations, only one iris colour is present [FDH03]. Other attributes like skin tone or seize have more fluent bounds, may vary too much (sun, ageing) or they are closer to normal distribution than to equal distribution. Thus, the only approach relying on biometrics seems to be to use a biometric attribute which is suitable to

---

[3]Unordered drawing without replacement: $h(10,3,4;3) = \binom{4}{3}\binom{10}{3}^{-1}$, where $h(\cdot)$ is the hypergeometric distribution

identify the user and to limit the information seen by the verifier. That means, that neither the verifier nor the user must have the biometric device under their control. The first would put the user's privacy at risk, while the latter would compromise the non-transferability of the tokens.

9 Analysis of Non-Transferable Anonymous Credentials

> "Who are you?"
> "No one of consequence."
> "I must know."
> "Get used to disappointment."

William Goldman
"The Princess Bride"

9.1 Approaches Aiming at Non-Transferability

As mentioned above, it is sometimes desirable to prevent users from sharing their credentials. In general, there are two well-known approaches. One approach tries to make the credential more protection deserving for the prover by embedding additional valuable secrets into the system. The aim is to make it unpleasant for the prover to share the credential by connecting it with other systems. The other approach is of more technical nature and tries to prevent the prover from sharing credentials by embedding biometric access control. Of course, it should be guaranteed that this access control does not break the user's anonymity.

In this section we shortly introduce both approaches, identify possible fields of application and compare both approaches with respect to the credentials' non-transferability.

9.1.1 Embedding Valuable Secrets

The idea of this approach is to discourage the users from sharing their credentials by equating the sharing of their credential with sharing a valuable secret. The valuable secret can be either a secret from outside the system (*PKI-assured non-transferability*) [DLN97, GPR98] or all secrets and credentials are from inside the system, e.g. credentials from other issuers (*all-or-nothing non-transferability*) [CL01]. This way the user's knowledge is made valuable beyond its primary intent and, therefore, it is assumed the user will not share it. Thus, the system's secret is personalised for each user and does not necessarily has to be kept secret from him. However, it may be tough for the issuer to verify the secret's accuracy, e.g. ensuring that the bound secret is of value for the user.

LYSYANSKAYA et al. propose a system where each user has a *master public key* [LRSW00]. They state that it is impossible to share a credential without sharing the corresponding *master private key*. To strongly encourage the users to keep their master private key secret, the authors propose to register each user's master public key at a certification authority as a legal digital signature key which can be used to sign "important legal or financial documents". In any case, depending on the certification authority and national laws – e.g. the German Digital Signature Act [Sig01] – the use of such an external master public key has to comply with regulations given by law respectively the certification authority.

In practise, this allows two possible implementations: either embedding the private key into a smartcard or delivering a personalised secret to the user. The latter is possible because the user is not technically prevented from sharing his credential. Instead, as previously mentioned, it is assumed he does not want to share the additional embedded valuable secret. It is worth mentioning that issuing a credential can be realised by an interactive protocol between issuer and user without revealing the user's credential or valuable secret to the issuer.

Nevertheless this protection will not prevent all users from sharing credentials. Either they may share their credentials incautiously, or they may really trust someone else. In addition, these valuable secrets raise the system's value – providing a larger incentive for attackers. So users have to be aware of thiefs and have to immanently trust the system's architecture. As a first conclusion, we notice that the system's effectiveness fundamentally depends on the value of the embedded secret.

9.1.2 Biometrically Enforced Non-Transferability

Another possibility to ensure the credentials are only used by the person for whom the credential was created for, implies use of the person's biometric data. Using biometrics however usually causes privacy concerns, especially since – in contrast to passwords or tokens – one cannot change biometric attributes. Therefore extraordinary care has to be taken to protect the user's data [BBB+08]. It can be easily seen that allowing the verifier to check the prover's biometric attributes conflicts with the prover's wish of anonymity. In 1998, BLEUMER [Ble98] combined anonymous credentials with biometric authentication making use of a variant of the wallet-with-observer architecture introduced by CHAUM and PEDERSEN [CP93] (cf. Sect. 8.2.3). As a new first step, the user has to show his biometrics, which are checked by the observer. Only if the user passes this verification, the proof of knowledge is started just like specified in the original scheme.

IMPAGLIAZZO and MINER MORE [IM03] transferred that design to a personal digital assistant (PDA) with a tamper-resistant smartcard. The smartcard (observer) is issued and trusted by the authority and it's tamper-resistance makes sure that the user cannot read and tamper with its content. In contrast the PDA (warden) protects the prover's interests and makes sure the smartcard does not diverge from the specified protocol. Both approaches have in common that biometric authentication is not part of the underlying credential system, but instead prerequisite for the credential protocol to start.

In practise, a system could be implemented using a smartcard with embedded fingerprint reader [BA09] or *match-on-card* systems [PGM⁺03] where an external reader delivers the biometrics directly to the card, respectively device (cf. Sect. 8.3). The advantage of system-on-card compared to match-on-card systems is that the user's biometrics are not put at risk. An example that supports this assumption is that PINs of cash cards were read out by manipulated PIN-readers [BB07]. This was only possible because PINs were entered at an external keypad and matched on the card. However, contrary to the user's PIN, one may not consider the user's fingerprints secret, because they cannot be changed and the user leaves them anywhere, e.g. at the shop's door. But even if the dealer could get the user's fingerprint at his shop's door, this would require a much larger effort than wiretapping them at an external reader. Thus, the user's privacy would be invaded if the dealer would be able to wiretap his fingerprints. We therefore assume an implementation with an embedded fingerprint reader for the comparison in Sect. 9.1.4.

9.1.3 Consideration of Other Approaches

Besides the two well-investigated approaches discussed above one may think of other schemes to prevent users from sharing their credentials. We first need to point out that the biometric access control described in the previous subsection is actually operating against the user. He is not allowed to have full control over his credentials to prevent him from passing them around. Thus, it is quite obvious that "traditional access control schemes" such as passwords are no alternative solution.

The most obvious idea for a related approach is to use a combination of the two approaches discussed above. We will take this into account when investigating the approaches' resistance to non-transferability in Sect. 9.1.4.

In the last years some scientists and technophiles had radio-frequency identification (RFID) chips implanted [Fin03, Gra06] for access control. On the one hand, if the user really trusts all parties involved in the production and implantation of the RFID chip, namely manufacturer and surgeon, this may be an option. On the other hand, the user risks an intrusion of his privacy here. Since the user cannot be sure about the chip's transmission, even if there are some means of control over the chip's transmission, the verifier may be able to communicate directly with the chip. Thus, the wallet-with-observer architecture does not apply here and the user has to trust other parties with all the consequences regarding his privacy. Furthermore, due to their limited computation power, RFID chips have to rely on lightweight cryptographic protocols which may be broken over the course of time. Moreover, the system's setup is quite complicated and from the perspective of an issuer, the connection between the user and the chip can simply be broken by another surgeon, leaving the approach quite vulnerable regarding non-transferability. Thus, we argue that implanted RFID chips are inappropriate for this scenario and do not consider them any further in this work.

9.1.4 Security Issues

Integral Parts of the Credential System's Security

Before dealing with an attacker model in the next subsection, we need to have a look at the credential system's security. Its components can be divided into three groups: the security of the basis credential system (G) and the security of the efforts trying to make those credentials non-transferable, either by biometric access control (B) or by embedding a valuable secret (S).

Moreover, the security of non-transferable anonymous credentials depends mostly on the following points:

(G1)   The security of the underlying cryptographic functions as stated above, e.g. the used zero-knowledge proof, blind or group signature schemes.

(G2)   The secrecy of the credentials created by the issuer when initialising the smartcard or combining them with an embedded valuable secret.

(B1)   The quality of the deployed device's tamper-resistance.

(B2)   The difficulty of circumventing the biometric sensors.

(S1)   The value of the embedded secret.

(S2)   The precautions taken by the users in combination with the system's potential to prevent loss, duplication or unauthorised use of credentials.

(S3)   The strength of the connection between the anonymous credential and the embedded valuable secret.

According to RATHA et al. [RCB01] there are eight places in a generic biometric system where an attack may occur as shown in Fig. 9.1. Seven of them (2 - 7) deal with attacks on the handling of the biometrics from the sensor to the matcher, for example tampering stored templates (5) or modifying a transmission of the biometrics (2). Since we assume that all those steps take place inside the tamper-proof device, an adversary would have to attack the tamper-resistance before (B1). The remaining attack (1) is circumventing the biometric sensors (B2) leading to the two points identified above.

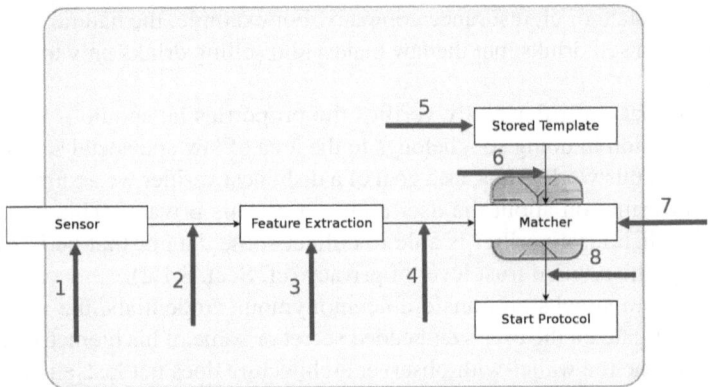

Figure 9.1: Points of Attacking a Biometric System based on RATHA et al. [RCB01]

Attacker Model

There are several parties involved in an anonymous credential system: the *issuer*, the *prover* and the *verifier* of the credential. Furthermore, the manufacturers of the software and hardware need to be trustworthy, especially when using biometric access control and, therefore, tamper-proof devices are needed. Since our main focus lies on the comparison of the strengths and weaknesses of both approaches with respect to the credentials' non-transferability, we make several assumptions leading to a narrowed field of possible attacking parties.

First of all, we assume that anonymous credentials will not be used in high-security environments – it is implausible that the access control e.g. for a nuclear power plant or in a military environment makes use of anonymous credentials since in this environments most likely the access control's security and reliability will be considered more important than the user's anonymity respectively untraceability. Furthermore, we assume that the attacking costs are proportionate to the assessed win of a breach. Therefore, we adopt a more practical view on the security of the system.

While the verifier has a natural interest to prove the credential in a scenario where he wants to sell a service, we also assume he shows at least reasonable interest to do so in compliance with the law. In the first case it is easy to see, that the verifier suffers damage if he not properly checks access to his (paid) service or collects the payment. In the latter case the assumption is based on the observation that the verifier, e.g. a police officer, either has a certain relationship to the issuer and thus cooperates. Or alternatively, the verifier is forced to prove the credential by a third party, e.g. the state or an insurance company. For example, the natural interest of a bar keeper is to sell drinks, but the law makes him selling drinks only to people of a certain age.

Ensuring that a verifier really verifies the properties he should – if he has no personal intention in doing so – belongs to the area of law and social science and is not covered in this work. Thus, as a goal of a dishonest verifier we assume, he wants to gather information about the user and to break his privacy. This could either mean that a dishonest verifier is able to collect some data or that he is somehow able to lower the assured trust level of privacy (cf. Sect. 8.1.2).

In addition to attacks on transferable anonymous credentials, the verifier may want to investigate on the user's embedded secret or some of his biometric data. But since we assume the wallet-with-observer architecture does not leak any biometrics and the embedded secret provides the verifier no additional point of attack, we conclude that the verifier is only capable of attacking the underlying credential system, even if the embedded secret may provide a stronger incentive to do so. We further assume that the issuer generates credentials or initialises the tamper-proof device without leaking any secret information to the user or verifier and, vice versa, that a protocol is used that does not reveal the user's valuable secret [LRSW00, CL01] to the issuer. In the case of biometric access control, we assume that the issuer does not copy the user's biometrics, but instead observes the enrolment phase, where the user initialises the tamper-proof device with his biometrics directly via the embedded sensor.

We note that the tamper-proof device used for biometric access control is a shared device, since it is operated by the user and either the issuer (proof of a certain attribute) or the verifier (proof of a valid ticket) wants to be sure it executes only trustworthy operations. Due to the fact that the user does not need to trust the tamper-proof device because we rely on the wallet-with-observer architecture, it is reasonable to concede the choice of the tamper-proof device to the issuer or the verifier, respectively.

This leaves us with two possible attackers: the user and a third party. If the user is seen as an attacker his aim is to trick the authentication either by creating his own credentials or by sharing a valid credential with other persons. As stated above, if the credential can be transferred or the system is broken, it can be easily seen that in most cases either a law is circumvented (proof of a certain attribute) or the verifier is affected (proof of a valid ticket). In this case, the user attacks the verifier respectively issuer. Realistically, if attacks are substantial for the system and do not occur only sporadically, we have to assume attackers of class I (clever outsiders, cf. Sect. 2.2.5). However, since attackers of this class make use of already known weaknesses in the system, it cannot be ruled out that attackers of higher classes publish their observations. On the other hand, it is not realistic, to assume that a class III adversary (funded organisations) invests time and effort to "destroy" another company's system. Thus, it is plausible to assume attackers somewhere in the range from class I to class II (knowledgeable insiders).

On the other hand, a third party may try to steal the user's credentials to use them fraudulently. Since the verifier or operating company will probably sue the user for all actions conducted in his name, this constitutes an attack on the user by a third party. Before we further investigate these third party attack scenarios, we shortly look at scenarios with colluding parties.

Collusion of Involved Parties Since there are three involved parties, there are three combinations of parties which may collude.

Apparently, the issuer and the verifier have to cooperate or may be the same organisation. This is also consistent from the perspective of the prover, since the verifier may only identify him if the issuer has placed some information in the credentials. Taken together, this is the scenario described above.

A collusion of the verifier and prover is also not particularly thrilling, since in this scenario the verifier may just skip all checks and grant the prover access to whatever service he wants to. Thus, there is no need for further investigation here.

The last remaining combination of issuer and prover does only make sense if the prover is some kind of governmental overseer. However, due to the issuer's ability to certificate the prover whatever certificate he wants and the verifier only checks that the prover has a valid certificate, this scenario is also quite uninteresting. In case of an embedded secret, the issuer abstains from requesting a valuable secret. In case of biometric access control, the question is mainly whether the issuer is able to produce some kind of blank biometrics, which would accept any biometric characteristics. This would be useful for a secret service who could demand such a smartcard and hand it out short-term to an arbitrary agents. However, due to the issuer's ability to create arbitrarily certificates, there's no big advantage to creating one or more personalised certificates.

As a sum up of the different combinations of parties, we conclude that no particular interesting scenario is resulting from the collusion of two (or more) parties.

Stealing the User's Credentials – Attacks by Third Parties

Regarding third party's attacks the first important point to notice is that they will have no more power than the involved parties. If a third party wants to gather information about the user, the verifier can be considered more powerful since he already interacts with the user. If we study attacks on the credential system or the credential's non-transferability the user is more powerful since he already has a valid credential.

This issue of a third party trying to steal the user's credentials is related to non-transferability, since in theory a non-transferable credential cannot be stolen and used by someone else. But depending on the chosen mechanisms, non-transferability is heavily based on a certain behaviour of the user. If non-transferability relies on an embedded secret of the user, most attacks on the user, which aim to make the user deviate from the required behaviour, are promising. Examples are social engineering or rubber-hose attacks (cf. Sect. 2.2.4). Depending on the purpose of the credential, even *purchase-key attacks* may come into account.

Otherwise, if biometric access control is needed, the system supports the user protecting his credentials. In addition to stealing the credentials, such as a smartcard, an attacker would be required to break the access control system, e.g. forge the user's biometrics or break the device's tamper resistance. For a comparison of the impact of possible breaches of the smartcard's tamper-resistance, we refer to Sect. 9.2.2.

Thus, regarding biometric access control, an attacker faces the same problem as the user trying to share his credential with someone else. Apart from the question of how the attacker is able to steal the user's device – which is mainly a criminalistic question – the attacker is no better than the user since the user at least has the biometric characteristics used for access control. Similar observations hold regarding backdoors and Trojan horses. Assume, a third party is capable of inserting a Trojan horse into the system, then it would be easier to steal the credentials if the approach is relying on an embedded secret. In that case it would be sufficient to inject a Trojan horse into the user's device (the wallet in the wallet-with-observer architecture) to steal the user's credential and secret. Regarding biometric access control, the credential is hidden in the tamper-proof device (the observer in the wallet-with-observer architecture). Therefore, the adversary would have to manipulate the tamper-proof device. Moreover, since the tamper-proof device is not allowed to communicate with the outside world, the adversary would additionally need to tamper the user's trusted device to get the credential.

Another possibility for the attacker would be to break the entire credential scheme. Depending on the kind of breach, it may be possible that the adversary forges credentials of a user – although it probably would be very difficult to forge the credentials of a specific user. A well-known example of a broken system is the breach of the Dutch transit card system, known as "OV-chipkaart" [Fel08b, Tan08]. Despite the fact, that the OV-chipkaart is neither non-transferable nor based on anonymous credentials, a comparable breach regarding a non-transferable anonymous credential scheme is easily imaginable. The OV-chipkaart is based on the MIFARE chip family [Sem13], which has been successfully attacked [KGHG08, NESP08b, GvRVS09]. This kind of breach leads to a completely broken system independently how non-transferability should be achieved and is thus out of the scope of this work.

Apart from completely broken systems, as already mentioned, third parties trying to steal someone's credentials still have to circumvent non-transferability, which is what we want to discuss next.

Attacks on Non-Transferability

General Attacks Before going into detail about the attacks on the specific approaches, we discuss a general attack on the wallet-with-observer architecture which can also be applied if the non-transferability of the credential is provided by an embedded secret. The verifier cannot be sure if the user is in radio contact with a legitimate user (and smartcard) who is willing to accomplish the authentication for him (see Fig. 9.2). A simple, but hard to implement countermeasure would be to isolate the user during authentication to prevent him from communicating with others. Another approach, *distance-bounding protocols*, measures round-trip-times to prevent or limit relay attacks and was proposed by BETH and DESMEDT [BD90] and the first concrete protocol was introduced by BRANDS and CHAUM [BC94].

DRIMER and MURDOCH describe an implementation of this defence for smartcards which requires only modest alterations to current hardware and software [DM07]. The setup described here is slightly different from DRIMER and MURDOCH's, since the smartcard in the wallet-with-observer architecture is not allowed to communicate directly with the verifier to protect the user's privacy. Nevertheless – if appropriate timing constraints are chosen – relay attacks may be prevented. Since this attack affects both approaches we do not further elaborate on relay attacks and their countermeasures in the further reasoning.

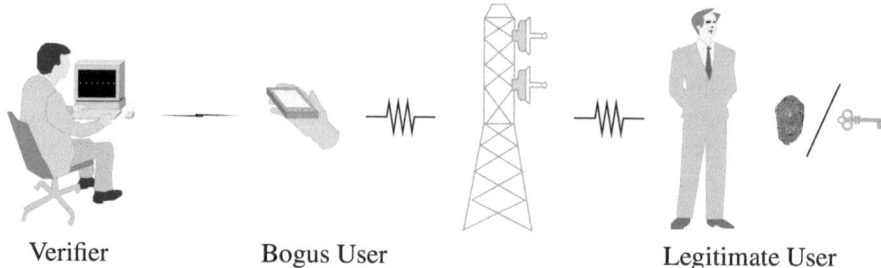

Verifier   Bogus User   Legitimate User

Figure 9.2: If They Are Able to Communicate, a Bogus and a Legitimate User Could Share a Credential.

Attacks on the Specific Approaches   In the previous section we narrowed down the field to one attacker: the user who wants to share or forge credentials. This section compares biometric access control and embedded valuable secrets. When taking a closer look at the integral parts of the credential system's security (see Sect. 9.1.4), it is obvious that both approaches do not differ much as far as the security of the basis credential system (G) is concerned. As we are interested in comparing the provided security, we may disregard (G1,2) and reduce our evaluation to the approach specific security (B1,2) versus (S1-3).

Biometric Access Control   When evaluating attacks on the approach using biometric access control there are two points of attack: the tamper-proof device and the biometric sensor. Since the biometric sensor is embedded in the device and, probably has only a moderate security level, it is reasonable to consider (B2) the weakest point. Many reports on circumvention of biometric systems include the use of photos with iris codes [GRGB+12, Gal12], facial age verification [She08, Ric08] or forged fingerprints [BT09, sta04] and suggest that unattended biometric access control, e.g. online or automated age verification, is susceptible to fraud, while it may be harder – but not unfeasible – to circumvent attended verification, e.g. at a bar or a shop.

On the other hand the tamper-resistance of devices (B1) is an arms race between manufacturers and attackers. Depending on the used device, side-channel attacks (cf. Sect. 2.2.2) and fault induction attacks (cf. Sect. 2.2.4) may be feasible.

This suggests that biometric access control restricts the group of people who are able to share a credential to those who are experts in circumventing biometric sensors or tamper-proof devices or at least profit from the experts' work by following a set of instructions.

Embedded Valuable Secrets Regarding the security of embedded secrets, it is reasonable that precautions taken by the users (S2) strongly depend on the value of the embedded secret (S1). Only if the embedded secret has some value to the user, he cares to protect it. On the other hand, if the system is set up carefully, the user cannot detach the embedded secret from the credentials. We therefore claim that the value of the secret is most important for this approach. But finding a reasonably valuable secret is quite a problem. On the one hand, the proposed master secret key proposed by LSYANKSKAYA et al. [LRSW00] seems capable of preventing most users from sharing. On the other hand, using such a powerful key seems disproportional and dangerous to protect low value credentials. Moreover, as already mentioned, there may be some regulations or laws on how to handle such a master key in a proper way, which may restrict its use for non-transferable anonymous credentials. However, if such a powerful credential already exists for other purposes, it may be used to protect many other credentials of smaller value.

We also note that these valuables might not prevent all users from sharing; be it they share their credentials incautiously, be it they really trust someone else, e.g. a close family member. Having this in mind, we refer only to users, who intentionally share credentials, e.g. parents sending their children to buy them alcohol or tobacco from a store or a family sharing a transit card.

A minor drawback of this approach is the possibility of a revocation of the master key, which would make the embedded secret useless. Since it is assumed that the embedded key is very powerful, and thus valuable, it is inevitable to permit users to revoke it. This allows the user to immediately end the validity of a previously shared credential for the cost of needing a reinitialisation of his credentials (the master key and all keys depended on it). Obviously, a simple countermeasure is to make the user pay for each reinitialisation, as it is common for cash cards or SIM cards. The price of the reinitialisation and the possible savings determine whether this is a profitable deal for the user.

Another advantage of anonymous credentials with embedded values is that they do not necessarily need an extra device. Concerning age verification at an online shop, for example, it would be enough to have additional software on the already available computer or mobile device. However, in this case the credential is most likely in a very dangerous environment and can easily be stolen, if the used device is compromised. A way to prevent this would be to delegate this task to a smartcard. This would require the user's device to have a card reader, but compared to the approach based on biometric access control, a biometric sensor is not required.

Which of those approaches is the most suitable is open, as the decision is a tradeoff between the quality respectively value of the embedded valuable secret, the required strength of non-transferability, and the economic costs.

Combination of Embedded Valuable Secrets and Biometric Access Control Comparing both approaches, it was shown that the question which approach is most suitable, depends on the user's ability to circumvent the biometric sensor or tamper the used device versus the value of the embedded secret the user is willing to risk (and which can be verified by the issuer). A combination of both approaches seems to be promising regarding the non-transferability, since a possible attacker has to circumvent the biometric sensors or break the tamper-proof device and, furthermore, the owner of the credentials must be willing to share his secret. Otherwise not only the benefits accumulate but also the restrictions. Users must have usable biometrics and a valuable secret which they are willing to embed into the system. The combination of the approaches is the most expensive, since each user needs a tamper-proof device with embedded biometric reader and the system has to be linked to an already existing "legal digital signature certification authority" which probably will not be free of charge.

Evaluation of Security

As the previous section shows, neither biometric access control nor embedded valuable secrets strictly ensures the non-transferability of anonymous credentials. While biometric access control is the more expensive and probably more error-prone solution, it might be hard to find valuable secrets to really prevent the sharing of credentials, especially since the user should be able to revoke a previously shared key at any time. Tab. 9.1 gives an overview on the elaborated attributes of both approaches.

The main disadvantage of biometric access control is that it seems feasible to bypass unattended biometric access controls and that the biometrics' missing universality[1] might restrict its usage. Otherwise biometric access control limits the possibility of unintentionally sharing the credentials for free and if the biometric measurements are attended, it is a reasonable application. Furthermore, by the use of tamper-proof devices, cloning of credentials becomes quite hard and the issuer can thus be reasonably sure the credentials are not read out.

Embedded valuables in contrast raise the system's value and thus the incentive of stealing them (with the underlying credentials) or breaking the system's architecture is increased. For low value credentials it may be possible to put a certain amount of the user's money at risk, if he shares his credential, but naturally this will not prevent all users from sharing. If there already exists a valuable credential, credentials of lower value can be bound to it, but even then the user might decide to share it, e.g. with close family members. The user is left alone with measures against

---

[1]This especially concerns fingerprints.

Table 9.1: Attributes of Different Approaches to Ensure Non-Transferability: Biometric Access Control, Embedded Valuable Secret, a Combination of both Approaches, and Embedded Valuable Secret with a Tamper-Proof Device.

attribute	biometrics	embedded secret
circumvention depends on	(un)attended access control	secret
circumvention by	experts	close family members
tamper-proof device	with biometric reader needed	not needed
universality depends on	biometrics	secret
credential cloning	hard	easy
unintended sharing	unlikely	may occur
system's value	unchanged	raised

attribute	biometrics & embedded secret	embedded secret & tamper-proof device
circumvention depends on	(un)attended AC & secret	secret
circumvention by	trusted experts	close family members
tamper-proof device	with biometric reader needed	needed
universality depends on	biometrics & secret	secret
credential cloning	hard	medium
unintended sharing	unlikely	unlikely
system's value	raised	raised

unintentionally sharing of the credential. All he can do is trying to preserve the integrity of his devices or using a tamper-proof device to protect his credentials.

Also, the combination of both approaches is not the answer to all drawbacks. While it may prevent more users from sharing, it suffers from the restrictions of both approaches and from the effort needed to put it in place. Nevertheless, it is important to keep in mind that all approaches are not able to assure non-transferability, if the user cannot be isolated but is able to communicate with the outside world during authentication. Therefore, all implementations need to take defences against relay attacks into account, e.g. based on distance-bounding protocols (remember Fig. 9.2).

We conclude that both approaches might be sufficient to prevent sharing in some applications. If the users already possess personal digital assistants, embedded valuable secrets are a quite cheap solution, even though they raise the system's value. If access control is attended, biometric sensors are reasonably secure and limit without additional effort the possibility of unintentionally sharing the credentials.

9.1.5 Limiting the Consequences of Security Breaches

Assumed a user successfully breaks the system's security there are some counter-measures limiting the consequences. If the non-transferability of the credentials is broken, there are two general restrictions which may be achieved. On the one hand, while the credential may be transferred, it is still possible to allow only one user at a time to use the credential, e.g. if there is a unique item needed for authorisation. On the other hand, depending on how the credential is used, the number of available uses in a certain time slot may be restricted.

Limiting the Number of Available Tokens

The easiest approach to limit the consequences of certain security breaches is to limit the number of possible uses respectively available tokens. If some kind of clock or trigger is available, it is also possible to limit the number of available tokens for a certain period of time. However, depending on the intended scenario, it may be difficult to give a good estimation of an upper bound on how many tokens a legitimate user may need, but chose this number low enough to restrict illegal use.

Regarding biometric access control, we already noticed that this approach relies on a tamper-proof device. If the tamper-resistance of the used device is still intact (B1), but the user is able to circumvent the biometric sensors (B2), it is easy to implement the abovementioned restriction of tokens by a simple counter. If the tamper-proof device has a clock or the used protocol involves some kind of timestamps or ticks, it is also possible to implement a counter for a given period of time. This approach is hard to implement if the non-transferability relies on an embedded secret. If a tamper-proof device is used with embedded secrets, it is because the user wants to protect his credentials. Thus, in contrast to biometric access control, the user may have full control of the device.

n-times Anonymous Authentication

To limit the number of available tokens, a more sophisticated approach is to use cryptography. DAMGÅRD et al. propose a scheme to allow only one anonymous authentication at a time [DDP06]. The security of the proposed protocol is based on the DDH assumption (cf. Def. 2.63) in the random oracle model (cf. [BR95b]). CAMENISCH et al. improved this approach by creating a credential system that lets a user anonymously authenticate at most n times per given time period [CHK$^+$06a, CHK$^+$06b]. The basic idea is that each user has a dispenser which automatically refreshes and creates n tokens per period. Each token can only be used once and should a token be used twice, the verifier is able to revoke the user's anonymity. CAMENISCH et al. also offer *glitch protection* for basically honest users who only occasionally reuse their tokens, for instance, if the user's operating system crashes. In this case, the user may not know which tokens have already been used and thus mistakenly uses a token twice, even though unused tokens would have been available to him. The security of this scheme is based on the SRSA assumption (cf. Def. 2.56) and the y-DDHI Assumption (cf. Def. 2.73) in the standard model (cf. Canetti et al. [CGH98]), where the adversary is limited only by time and computational power.

Obviously, the scheme itself does not provide non-transferability of credentials in any way, but – in combination with the precautions stated earlier in this section – it limits the extent of abuse if the number of available tokens per time period is chosen appropriately. Since the approach does not depend on a tamper-proof device, this holds for biometric access control, independently if the tamper-resistance of the device (B1) or the biometric sensors (B2) is circumvented, as well as for embedded valuable secrets. If the user spends too many tokens in a period of time, his anonymity may be revoked. Additionally, if two or more users want to use the same credentials at a time, they have to coordinate their tokens somehow to prevent double spending tokens, which would reveal the owner's identity.

Restrictions to One User at a Time

There are various attacks on the implementation of cryptographic functions on tamper-proof devices, such as side-channel (cf. Sect. 2.2.2) or fault induction attacks (cf. Sect. 2.2.4) to glean secret information from the device. One of the ideas to counter this attacks is the use of physical properties of random variations in an integrated circuit or other objects. For example, Pappu et al. [Pap01, PRTG02] took advantage of the uniqueness of light scattering particles injected in transparent material. When a laser beam meets the material, the scattering of the reflections produces a pattern depending on the angle of the laser beam and the arrangement of the scattering particles. The basic idea is that the random variations are unique and hard to copy and a challenge/response pair is given by the parameters for a certain measurement and its result, which depends on the randomness of the examined object. This system is referred to as *physically unclonable function* (PUF).

The idea of physically unclonable functions goes back to the eighties and work of Bauder [Bau83], Simmons [Sim84, Sim91] and Leighton and Micali [LM93]. A survey on the history of PUFs is given by Busch et al. [BSKS10]. There are different approaches, which are based on different applications in the real world and realise PUFs. A description and evaluation of the properties of PUFs based on application-specific integrated circuits related to security is given by Katzenbeisser et al. [KKR+12a, KKR+12b]. The two most important properties are *robustness* and *unclonability* respectively *unpredictability*. Robustness means that measurements with the same parameters produce only a slightly different response and are not highly depending on typically varying operating conditions, e.g. the ambient temperature. The unclonability of a PUF ensures that the PUF cannot be copied. This is closely related with unpredictability, which means, that an adversary given a certain set of challenge/response pairs, is not able to predict the response of a challenge which is not in the given set – except if she measures the response from the PUF. A formalisation of the properties of PUFs is given by ARMKNECHT et al. [AMS+11].

KATZENBEISSER and SCHALLER provide a table with applications and corresponding security requirements [KS12], which especially includes the storage of crypto-graphic keys and primitives. If an anonymous authentication protocol is build upon cryptographic primitives provided by an PUF or the used keys are stored by a PUF, the physical device is needed to pass the authentication challenge. Thus, even if non-transferability is broken, only the person holding the device is able to use it and as long as the PUF is unclonable, only the device can be passed around. It is not possible to extract keys or information to give away and use them for illegitimate authentication.

9.2 Biometric-Enforced Non-Transferability without Templates

In this section we look further into non-transferable anonymous credentials based on biometric access control. Analogous to the approach by IMPAGLIAZZO et al. [IM03] we prefer a setup based on the wallet-with-observer architecture, where each user has a PDA and a smartcard handed out by the credential issuing authority. Following BIERMANN et al. [BBB+08], it is obvious that the biometric device has to be connected straight to the smartcard. Moreover, since match-on-card systems cannot be assumed to be secure against replay-attacks, we consider a system-on-card setup. The only devices which fulfil our needs today are fingerprint readers, at least if price and size do matter. Pictures of samples of those cards were presented in 2008 by a number of companies (e.g. [BA09, Fid08]). However, it was neither possible to get a specimen, nor was it possible to get a rough specification. At that time, the websites vanished or the products were unlisted from the site. Nevertheless, given the technical requirements, it is plausible that these cards can be manufactured.

Based on the previous section, there are two obvious approaches to transform an anonymous credential system into a non-transferable one. The easiest approach is to simply enforce a biometric access control before the protocol of the anonymous credentials starts [IM03] as shown in Fig. 9.3a. However, this approach is based on the idea of storing a template for comparison on the tamper-proof device. The other approach is to use fuzzy extractors to generate the keys each time the protocol is started as shown in Fig. 9.3b. This was demonstrated for fingerprints by BHARGAV-SPANTZEL et al. [BSSB06]. As a third approach, we propose to combine fuzzy extractors with a secret key (see Fig. 9.3c), which is introduced in the next section.

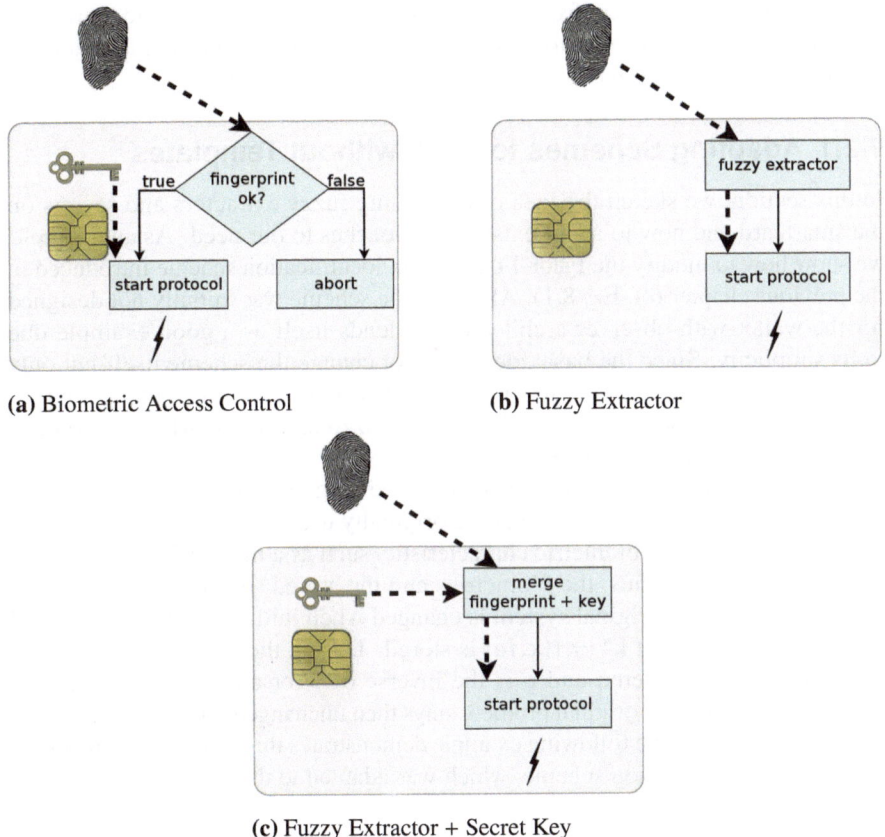

(a) Biometric Access Control

(b) Fuzzy Extractor

(c) Fuzzy Extractor + Secret Key

Figure 9.3: Different Approaches how to Combine Biometrics with Credentials: Biometric Access Control, Fuzzy Extractors and a Combination of Fuzzy Extractors with Secret Keys

Note that relying on fingerprints is only a compromise. Firstly, some people do not have suitable fingerprints. Secondly, forging fingerprints has been done with acceptable effort and there are several attacks on biometric systems based on fingerprints [UJ04]. However, fingerprint readers are the only devices which could be embedded into smartcards as of today. Following the parameters and comparison of [Jai04] the most desirable attributes for us would be to have low circumvention and high universality, uniqueness and permanence. This would lead to the use of DNA-recognition which cannot be done on a smartcard, yet. Since none of the approaches relies on special attributes of fingerprints, it is easy to switch the biometric system from fingerprints to DNA-scanning, should there exist an "on-the-fly DNA-recognition" (or any other suitable biometric identification method) some day, which could be embedded into smartcards.

9.2.1 Adapting Schemes to Work without Templates

In this section, we sketch the idea of combining fuzzy extractors and secrets on the smartcard and how to adapt existing approaches to our need. As an example, we show how to modify the FEIGE-FIAT-SHAMIR identification scheme introduced in the previous chapter (cf. Ex. 8.1). Although the scheme was initially not designed for the wallet-with-observer architecture, it lends itself as a good example due to its simplicity. Since the basic idea does not change the scheme itself but only adds a pre-computation of the scheme's keys, it works as well with more complex schemes, such as the one proposed by IMPAGLIAZZO and MINER MORE [IM03]. A security evaluation follows in Sect. 9.2.2.

Next, we demonstrate how to change an existing system for the wallet-with-observer architecture in the way that the originally used key k is composed of the fuzzy extractor fe of a biometric characteristic, such as a fingerprint, and a secret key stored on card. Thus, the biometrics and the stored secret k^* are needed to recover the key. The original system is changed when initialised, because instead of the key k, the secret $k^* := f(k, fe)$ is stored. During the protocol run, the key $k := g(k^*, fe)$ is recovered and g is the inverse of f for arbitrary, but fixed, fe: $g(f(k, fe), fe) = k$. The original protocol stays then unchanged after the original key has been recovered. The following example demonstrates this by means of the FEIGE-FIAT-SHAMIR identification scheme, which was adapted to the wallet-with-observer architecture.

EXAMPLE 9.1. Modified Feige-Fiat-Shamir Identification Protocol
The FEIGE-FIAT-SHAMIR identification scheme [FFS87, FFS88, Sho99b] is modified at the beginning of both phases:

Initialisation

- Ivan chooses two large primes p, q and computes $n = pq$
- Ivan chooses $a_1, \ldots, a_k \in \mathbb{Z}_n^*$
- Ivan computes $b_i := a_i^2 \pmod{n}$

- Ivan sends n and $a_1, \ldots, a_k$ are stored on Peggy's smartcard
- Ivan sets the smartcard in 'initialisation mode'
- Ivan sends n and $b_1, \ldots, b_k$ to Victor
- Optional: Ivan sends n and $b_1, \ldots, b_k$ to Peggy
- Ivan keeps p, q secret
- Peggy initialises the smartcard by giving samples of her fingerprint to the card
- The smartcard uses fuzzy extractors fe to derive k values f_i, overwrites a_i with $a_i^* := a_i - f_i \pmod{n}$ and switches to 'employment mode'

Protocol Run At the beginning Peggy gives her biometrics to the smartcard, the original values of a_i are recovered from the stored values a_i^* and the values of the fuzzy extractor f_i as shown in Fig. 9.4. The following protocol run is essentially the same as in the original FEIGE-FIAT-SHAMIR identification scheme. The only difference is that the scheme is adapted to the wallet-with-observer architecture and the operations Peggy did in the original protocol are executed inside the smartcard. Additionally, Peggy may change the values sent to Victor, to ensure the smartcard is not able to send information to Victor by intentionally choosing values for x. She does this by choosing a random number q and multiplying x with $\pm q^2$. If Peggy later multiplies the result of the smartcard's zero-knowledge proof with q, she does not change the result of the verifier's check, but can be sure, the value sent to Victor is sufficiently randomised. The intermediate manipulation of Peggy is of no help for Victor, since he could easily do the same manipulation by himself.

If Peggy knows $b_1, \ldots, b_k$, she may follow the protocol and abort it, if the smartcard did not compute the correct solution of the zero-knowledge proof. However, if Peggy trusts the issuer of the smartcard, she may omit to follow the protocol and mask the card's values.

One way to leak information via a covert channel is that the card stops working after n rounds of the protocol. If Victor also counts the number of protocol runs this may be used to send the number n to him. Peggy cannot prevent this, but is able to alter the number by running the protocol with the card without the participation of Victor. Since using the scheme as anonymous credential system would result in a very basic credential system, it would be necessary that all cards share the same parameters. Thus, Victor would not be able to distinguish two users and he thus is not able to count only the authentications of a specific user which prevents a covert channel.

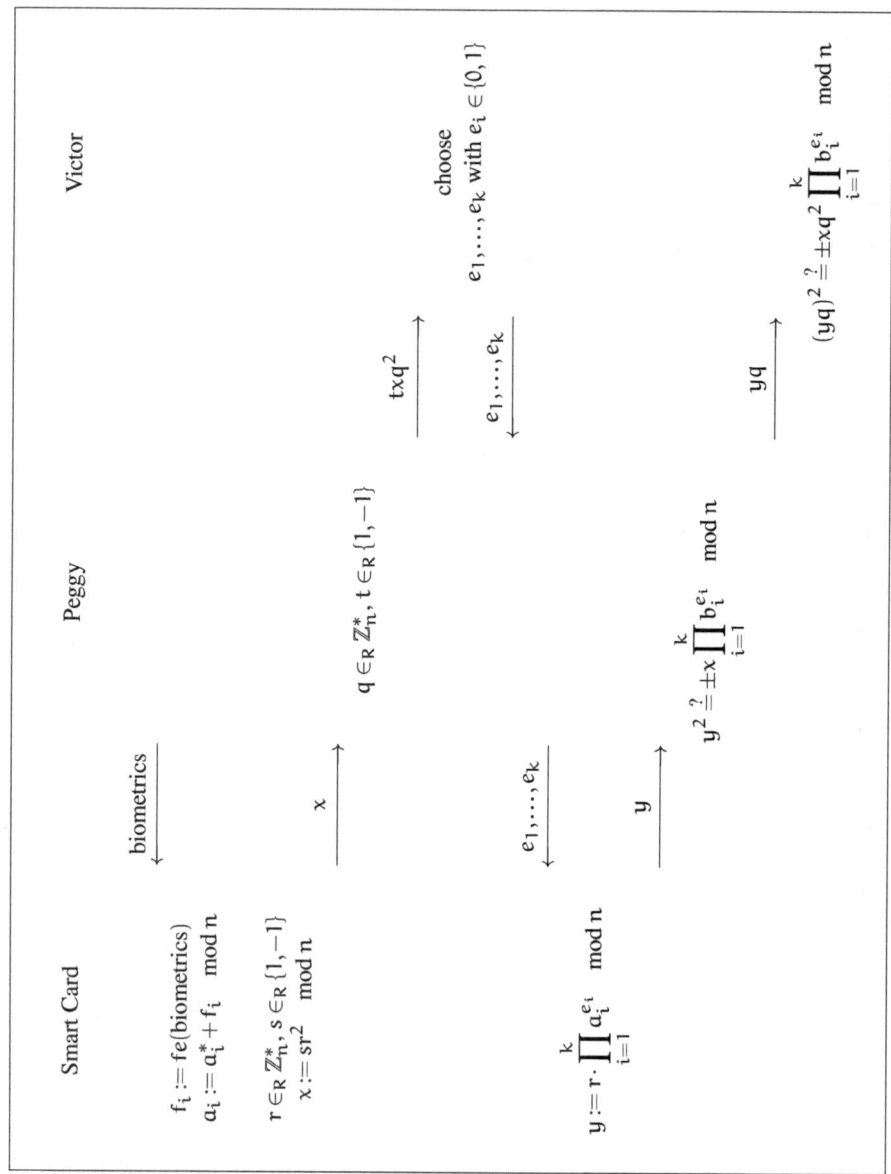

Figure 9.4: A run of the Modified FEIGE-FIAT-SHAMIR Identification Scheme

If the approach above would be used to setup an anonymous credential system, all users would have to use the same credentials and issuers and verifiers would trust, that none is able to extract the secret from the card. However, the example's purpose was to serve as illustration, the general idea of composing the credential scheme's key from the values stored at a fuzzy extractor and a secret stored on the card works also with more sophisticated approaches, which offer features such as anonymity revocation and restriction to a number of tokens per time slot. The only requirement is that it is possible to combine the secret with the result of a fuzzy extractor, e.g. by modulo addition or exclusive or.

9.2.2 Comparison of Approaches' Security

In general, for all three approaches the findings from Sect. 9.1.4 hold. If the user wants to cheat, the simplest way is to trick the biometric sensor (B2), independent of the approach which is used in the smartcard. To prevent the user from cheating via radio transmission, all approaches would additionally need to make use of distance bounding protocols as mentioned before.

Since the three approaches differ inside the card, the focus in this comparison is on the impact of possible breaches of the smartcard's tamper-resistance. It goes without saying, that the feasibility of the attacks strongly depends on the strength of the smartcard's tamper-resistance. Assuming a possible breach of the tamper-resistance also covers the scenario when the card is lost and an adversary wants to make use of the user's credentials. In this case, the remarks from Sect. 8.3.2 apply accordingly: Since the user touches the smartcard, he may leave his fingerprints on it, which may be uncovered, forged and employed to use the smartcard.

For a more systematic analysis, we adapt the security model from WANG et al. [WgMWC12] which is intended for password authentication with smartcards. Especially, we consider different capabilities of an attacker and especially the case when the attacker has either the user's biometrics or the tamper-proof device, but not both.

Biometric Access Control

If we assume the adversary knows the relevant biometrics but has no access to the tamper-proof device, it is easy to see that this is a non-critical case. Since all information to use the anonymous credential system is stored on the card, the adversary has no access to it.

Assuming, the adversary is in possession of the card, there are several possibilities of attack regarding the biometric access control (numbers refer to Fig. 9.1):

- The adversary may change the biometric data the matcher sees on the way from the sensor (2-4).

- The adversary may try to learn the stored template, e.g. by side-channel attacks (5).

- The adversary may change the stored template or influence its readout (5,6).

- The adversary may influence the matcher's process of decision making (7).

- The adversary may overwrite the matcher's decision not to start the protocol since the biometrics do not match (8).

Weighting those attacks, influencing the matcher or overwriting its decision are most likely to be feasible, since this would only require to flip a certain bit or change an instruction in the matcher's program. Note that learning the stored template also is an intrusion of the user's privacy since it may be possible to reconstruct the user's biometrics from the template as discussed before.

Beside attacks on the biometric access control, the adversary could also try to read the anonymous credential stored on the card and try to use it on its own. If she is able to bypass the biometric access control, she may try to mount side-channel or fault-injection attacks to learn the credential. The user himself, of course may try this directly.

Fuzzy Extractors

If the adversary has the user's biometrics at her disposal, the setup of the system is crucial. If the applied fuzzy extractor is essentially the same for all users, it boils down to keeping the fuzzy extractor's algorithm secret which contradicts KERCKHOFF's law. By knowing the applied fuzzy extractor and the user's biometrics, an adversary would be able to determine the underlying key of the credential system. On the other hand, if for each user another extractor is used, the approach's characteristics are quite similar to the approach presented next. Note that, these statements only hold if the system is properly set up. We work out the details in the following paragraph.

If the adversary is in possession of the card there's little she can do – besides the above mentioned attempt to find the user's biometrics on the card.

Combination of Fuzzy Extractors and Secret Key

If the adversary knows the user's biometrics, she may be able to derive the result of the fuzzy extractor, but due to the reconstruction of the key (remember $k :=$

$g(k^*, fe)$) with the key stored on the card, it is not feasible for her to learn the credential's key. The same holds vice versa.

Again, these statements only hold if the system is properly set up. It is important that the reconstruction g ranges as much as possible over the codomain if one of the parameters k^* respectively fe is fixed. We give two examples referring to the modified FEIGE-FIAT-SHAMIR identification scheme from Ex. 9.1. Remember that the adversary knows that for all $a_1, \ldots, a_k$ the restriction $\gcd(a_i, n) = 1$ holds.

Unsuffient Ranges Let us assume, that the range of the fuzzy extractors is only very small compared to the modulus n. If the adversary is able to extract the stored key from the card, she may eliminate most of the combinations for a_i, since $|a_i - a_i^*| \leqslant f_i|$. The same holds vice versa, if the stored value on the card is very small compared to the modulo n.

Reusing Values If the system stores only one secret a^* on the tamper-proof device and the adversary knows the result of the fuzzy extractor, then the adversary is able to eliminate many combinations of a_i. Due to the reconstruction of the values by $a_i := a^* + f_i \pmod{n}$, she is able to compute the differences between the numbers a_i. Instead of roughly n^k possible variations there are only n variations left for the secret of the zero-knowledge proof.

A more general advantage is that the biometric information is strongly embedded into the anonymous credential system and not only a prerequisite. A consequence of this is that the verifier may notice the fail of a biometric authentication when the following zero-knowledge proof is then performed with the wrong parameters. This is no intrusion to the user's privacy, because if the user follows the protocol, he is able to abort it at any time, and thus those failures will not leak information about him to the verifier.

Comparison

We give a short overview of the previous subsections in Tab. 9.2. The left row denotes the approach, second and third row list the relevant risks for each approach, given the adversary is in possession of the user's biometrics or tamper-proof device.

An obvious advantage of the use of fuzzy extractors is that there is no template stored. Additionally, an adversary has to somehow forge either the biometrics or the result of the fuzzy extractors to run the protocol on card. An advantage of biometric access control versus plain fuzzy extractors is that the system is not compromised should only the biometrics be known to the adversary. The combination of fuzzy extractors with a secret key stored on the smartcard combines the advantages of the other approaches.

Table 9.2: Relevant Risks for the Different Approaches Aiming to Enforce Non-Transferability by Biometrics. Not Included in the Table are Risks Concerning All Approaches.

approach	adversary knows user's biometrics	adversary has tamper-proof device
biometric access control	none	Adversary may bypass biometric access control and use credential. Adversary may learn credentials stored on card. Adversary may read biometric template and gain biometrics.
fuzzy extractor	If fuzzy extractor is known, the adversary may be able to derive the secret key and use the credential.	none
fuzzy extractor combined with secret key	none	none

10 Conclusion and Future Work

> I never think of the future. It comes soon enough.
>
> ———————————————————
>
> Albert Einstein

10.1 Summary and Conclusion

We compared two general approaches aiming to ensure non-transferability for anonymous credentials: biometric enforced non-transferability and non-transferability based on embedded valuable secrets. Not surprisingly, the weakest points are the biometric sensors and finding meaningful (valuable) secrets for the user. Both approaches are not able to ensure perfect non-transferability, but may be sufficient depending on the values to protect.

Following we investigated different realisations of biometric enforced non-transferability in more detail. We were able to propose a new derivation of how to embed biometrics in the context of the wallet-with-observer architecture used with smartcards. By binding them closer to the smartcard and the credentials, the proposed approach reduces the drawbacks. However, it remains unclear if such a system may work in practise. First of all, it is undetermined if the necessary hardware exists and if it is ready for use in productive systems. Although there were claims that those cards exist and product websites and pictures were created, none of the companies answered questions for price, availability and technical specifications. Thus it remains dubious if those cards really exist(ed) or if the claims were put in place to collect venture capital. As of today, it seems not implausible that it is possible to manufacture those cards. To judge if they could work in practise, it is essential to test the qualities of their biometric sensors, their tamper-resistance and their performance.

The performance limits the protocols used for fuzzy extractors and anonymous credentials. Since there are approaches for fuzzy extractors on smartcards [CKL03] and anonymous credentials on smartcards [MV12, BL12] this is not a problem in general. The question is how these algorithms perform on a smartcard with integrated biometric sensor.

The quality of the biometric sensors influences the effort an adversary has to undertakes to successfully circumvent them. Additionally, the quality of the sensors also limits the length of the cryptographic key computed by fuzzy extractors. It is not easy to get a reliable statement about the possible key length, but in 2003 CLANCY et al. [CKL03] proposed a system for fingerprints with 69 bits key length on smartcards, for the cost of a 30 percent false rejection rate. We refer to HAO et al. [HAD06] for an overview of achieved bit lengths with other biometrics.

Given the performance of today's smartcards which are able to utilise RSA keys up to 8192 bit length and support elliptic curve cryptography (ECC) with 192 bit key length (cf. NXP[1] card specifications [NXP13]), 69 bit seems rather short. This is also the case regarding efficient implementations of anonymous credentials on smartcards which make use of 1024 bit RSA modulo operations [MV12]. The limited key length also concerns solely fuzzy extractors, therefore the advantages of additionally using a secret stored on the tamper-proof device still holds and the proposed approach is an improvement. Since the quality of the used sensors and the performance of fuzzy extractors will increase in the future, the critical question is if they will increase faster than computational power and thus close or broaden the identified gap.

Regarding tamper-proof devices, low-cost attacks [AK96, AK98] and equipment for them exist, but also chip manufacturing becomes cheaper. Thus, it is open whether the defending or attacking party will have the edge over the other. Moreover, if the cycles of attacks and countermeasures become shorter, security turns into a logistics problem, since exchanging all devices once handed out to the customers may not be financially feasible.

Remembering that anonymous credentials will probably not be used in high-security environments, in practise approaches using fuzzy extractors may nevertheless be a reasonable choice.

10.2 Future Work

Practicable System It would be very interesting to get hands on smartcards with embedded fingerprint reader. With real world technical specifications for the fingerprint reader and the card's performance it can be determined which algorithms for fuzzy extractors and anonymous credentials come into consideration. As long as no cards are available, a proof of concept remains speculative. Relevant features of such a system are false accept and reject rates, length of the biometric key derived from the fuzzy extractor, security assumption, algorithm and key length of the used anonymous credential system and the time the system needs for a

---

[1]NXP Semiconductors N.V.

proof of knowledge. A closely related question is to which degree the application programming interfaces (API) provided by the smartcards, such as Java Card Biometric API [JCW02], BioAPI [Bio06] or the specification for the Java Card 3 Platform [Ora11], could be facilitated. In general, building schemes on methods provided by such interfaces is more efficient than using a greenfield approach and building everything on the smartcard's basic blocks. Additionally, devices based on the Universal Serial Bus (USB) may be considered. There exist storage devices with embedded fingerprint reader [Eik12] and tamper-proof storage devices (e.g. [Iro13]). A combination of both properties could also be practicable.

Other Biometrics   As described above, it is desirable to extract more bits from biometrics by fuzzy extractors and also keep the false rejection rate at a moderate level. This could either be done by raising the existing sensor's and fuzzy extractor's performance or by switching to other biometrics. However, only biometrics are suitable, where the sensor can be embedded into a tamper-proof device, preferable a smartcard. The question is which sensors are small and reliable enough for the desired approach.

Revoking Anonymity if Biometrics are False   Another open question is, whether there is a way to have anonymity revocation based on failed biometric authentication without giving the card the possibility to establish a covert channel. This is useful for unattended biometric access control, since the attendee or guard could immediately take action when the user seems to be dishonest. As a first sketch, the card could facilitate a special fuzzy extractor which maps biometrics to two different keys depending on whether the biometrics match the enrolled biometrics or not. By making use of verifiable encryption [CS03], which allows the user to verify certain properties of a ciphertext, the user may ensure that either one or the other key is used without being able to determine which one it is. Each protocol run with false biometrics may leak certain information to the verifier. If this happens a number of times, the verifier may then be able to revoke the user's anonymity. However, it is unclear, how the smartcard should be prevented from intentionally choosing the 'wrong biometrics' result to allow the verifier the identification of the user even when the user is witnessing the protocol.

Part IV

Outlook and Appendix

11 Summary, Conclusion and Outlook

> My interest is in the future because I
> am going to spend the rest of my life
> there.
>
> ———————————————
>
> Charles F. Kettering

11.1 Summary

After a short introduction on notation and fundamentals, we presented some motivation and proposed scenarios for visual encryption schemes. Based on previous research of visual cryptography, we gave alternative description of visual encryption schemes by distinguishing between encoding and encryption. This allowed us to study the properties of the used encoding and encryption scheme independently. Furthermore, we defined the notion of *human decipherable encryption schemes* (HDES), which are a generalisation of visual encryption schemes.

Due to the observation, that existing game-based security models for indistinguishability are too strong and do not suit the requirements for HDES, we defined the notion of *sample-or-random ciphertext only* (SOR-CO) security. We were able to show that the notion of SOR-CO security is a weaker notion than real-or-random chosen plaintext security. The aim was to construct a secure HDES, where the keys may be used more than once. On the way to this purpose, we showed that a scheme based on dice codings proposed by DOBERITZ does not fulfil the requirements of SOR-CO security. The scheme based on dice codings also aims to use the encryption key a couple of times. We considered its security in different contexts and presented a successful attack if the adversary has knowledge that the messages consist of pairwisely distinct characters or a keypad which does not contain a digit twice. By adding noise to the encryption part, we enhanced the scheme and showed that – given the proper parameters – it fulfils the requirements of the SOR-CO security model. To our knowledge, this is the first visual encryption scheme which uses noise to make attacks difficult. We concluded with an extensive section on future work with ideas on how to use other senses than vision, use multiple key transparencies or rotate key transparencies.

The last part deals with non-transferable anonymous credentials. We discussed the usage of biometrics for access control and compare two different approaches aiming at non-transferability: biometric access control and embedded valuable secrets. The former requires the user to show his biometrics to a trusted, tamper-proof device which then starts the protocol. The latter binds the credentials to a secret, which is valuable to the user and which he thus hopefully does not want to share. Naturally, the applicability depends on the quality of the biometric sensors and the value of the embedded secret. Since the first approach makes use of tamper-proof devices, we took a closer look at the risks if the device's tamper-resistance is overcome. Therefore, we compared simple access control by biometrics with access control based on fuzzy extractors and proposed a third approach. Our approach combines fuzzy extractors with a stored secret on the tamper-resistant device and thus reduces the drawbacks of the former approaches.

11.2 Conclusion

Recent news, which stated that vendors store users' passwords in plaintext on their servers [Rie13, WM13], suggest that users should be careful which devices (or vendors, respectively) they trust. Even if the vendors act in good faith, the users are at risk and better do not trust their devices for crucial applications. Using approaches like HDES may help to protect sensitive areas. However, there is still plenty of work to do to enhance the usability of these approaches. User should be able to reuse their key (transparencies) a good many times and be released from counting dots (cf. Chap. 5) or the need to manually do computations (cf. Sect. 4.2.3).

However, the further development of technology and especially consumer electronics may not only favour the user. The increasing distribution of webcams and cameras in mobile devices may become a problem for approaches based on visual cryptography. Since mobile devices are also targeted by attackers, an infected mobile device which is incautiously positioned may be used to photograph the user when he is holding the key transparency in front of his screen. This even more holds, when regarding approaches for anonymous authentication. Assume a perfectly working (non-transferable) anonymous credential system, but for security reasons the operator installed surveillance cameras with a face-recognition system – which may be connected to social media websites. Or similar, the user is filmed by other users with a mobile device and the images are posted onto the Net. This would completely annul the anonymous credential system in place. Thus, we conclude that it is important to not only regard the authentication system itself, but also its environment. While there are situations where it is possible to oppose technical approaches like HDES to an hostile or insecure environment, there are also environments where it is hard to find a solution without changing the environment. Especially, the use of anonymous credentials does only work if the vendor is convinced to respect its users' privacy. However, many of today's successful companies rely on profiling the user to enhance their profits, e.g. for personalised marketing, offering related products or generally optimising their products to maximise profit. Thus, they will not be willing to abandon their data collection without compensation.

This leads to the consequence that, beside the technical questions, there are many economical, social and psychological tasks to solve. Since security and privacy fundamentally depend on the user, his behaviour and his awareness of security and privacy, it is important to make the majority of users aware of the importance of security and privacy issues. This way would also affect vendors and make them offer more secure and privacy-friendly products and services due to an increasing demand. However, this outlines the connection to practical security, for which we already figured out in Sect. 2.2.5 that it is hard to achieve and strongly depends on the usability of the considered approaches.

11.3 Outlook

This section is a summary of the most significant topics for future work previously described in Chap. 6 and Chap. 10.

Visual Cryptography

The most interesting topics concerning HDES are to address other senses than sight, investigate security models for active attackers and determine approaches which improve how key transparencies could be reused.

Addressing Other Senses than Sight The concept of visual cryptography may be easily transferred to other senses, such as touch. For example, one could make use of Braille [Bra94]. Braille is a system for the blind to read and write by touching embossed dots. The dots are arranged in rectangular cells and each cell consists of 2x3 dots. Since the encoding is based on the presence or absence of pins, it is possible to build an HDES on it, which works basically the same way as the described human decipherable encryption scheme based on dice codings. The main difference in this case is that not only the number, but also the position of the dots is meaningful.

Despite only a small number of people, who is able to read and write Braille, it would be challenging to build a touch based HDES by combining one of the versions of Braille with the EQV encryption scheme (cf. Sect. 5.2.1). However, further research would be needed to investigate the conditions of a secure reuse of the 'transparencies' and to build a mechanical device realising the encryption based on Braille displays.

Security Assumptions and Models   It would be desirable to have a proof that encryption schemes from the class of *Human Decipherable Encryption Scheme Based on Dice Codings with Noise* with certain encoding parameters n, the security parameter v, the sample function sample_{struct}, and a number t representing the number of ciphertexts of the sample available to the adversary, are secure in the sense of *Sample-or-Random Ciphertext-Only Indistinguishability* $(SOR-CO)$.

Furthermore, in this work only passive adversaries were considered. The assumption was that the adversary fears detection, and thus covertly gathers information up to the point when she is able to launch a successful attack. However, it is unclear if the user can be tricked into leaking information to the adversary. A model which also covers active attacks would be useful to have. It could also classify the adversary's risk of becoming detected in relation to what information she is able to gather.

Methods to Improve Reusing the Key-Transparencies   Consider segment-based visual cryptography with symmetrically arranged segments and symbols, then it is possible to revert and rotate transparencies. It is also possible to combine two (or more) transparencies to obtain the key. It is worthwhile to investigate the security of the resulting schemes. Additionally, in the case of HDES based on dice codings with noise, the impact of noise on the security of the scheme is interesting to examine.

Regarding the usability, it would be worth to study and evaluate up to which magnitude the HDES based on dice codings with noise remains usable. Furthermore, the question comes up how users would get along facing the additional difficulty of rotating, reversing or deriving key transparencies from several transparencies.

Anonymous Credentials

It would be very interesting to try the considered approach out with existing hardware and test real world technical specifications for the fingerprint reader and the card's performance. Relevant features of such a system are false accept and reject rates, length of the biometric key derived from the fuzzy extractor, security assumption, algorithm and key length of the used anonymous credential system and the time the system needs for a proof of knowledge. A closely related question is to which degree the application programming interfaces provided by the smartcards could be facilitated.

Example of Pixel-based Visual Cryptography in Detail

All that is not perfect down to the
smallest detail is doomed to perish.

Gustav Mahler

Figure 1: Example: Pixel-based Visual Cryptography, Original Picture

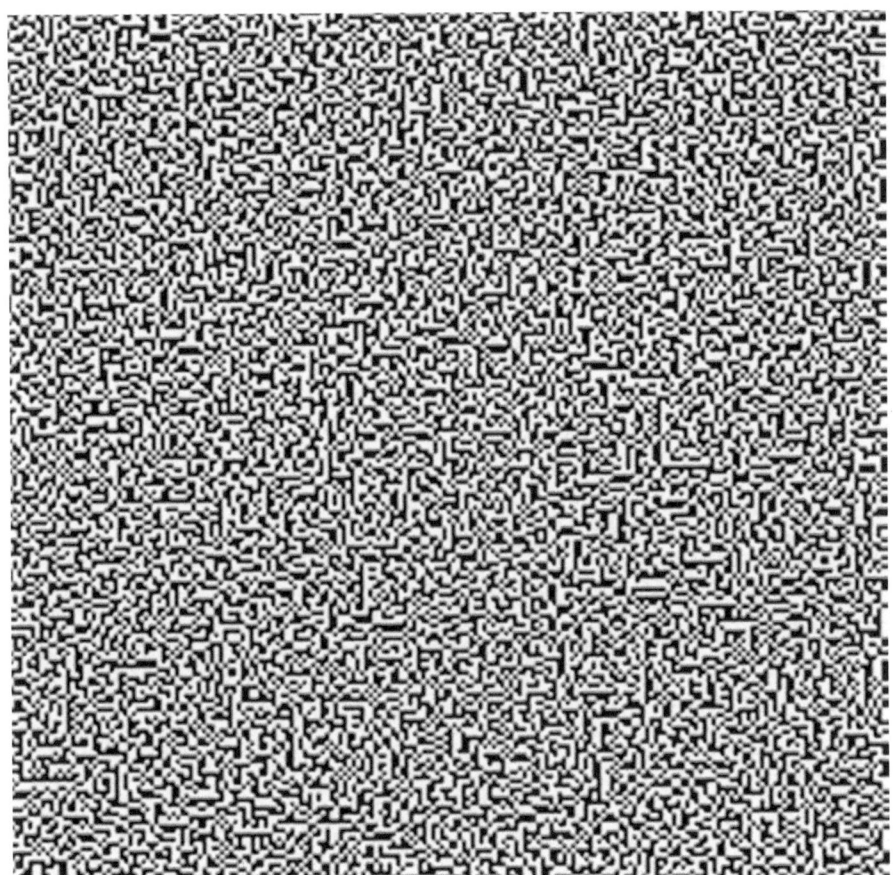

Figure 2: Example: Pixel-based Visual Cryptography, Transparency 1

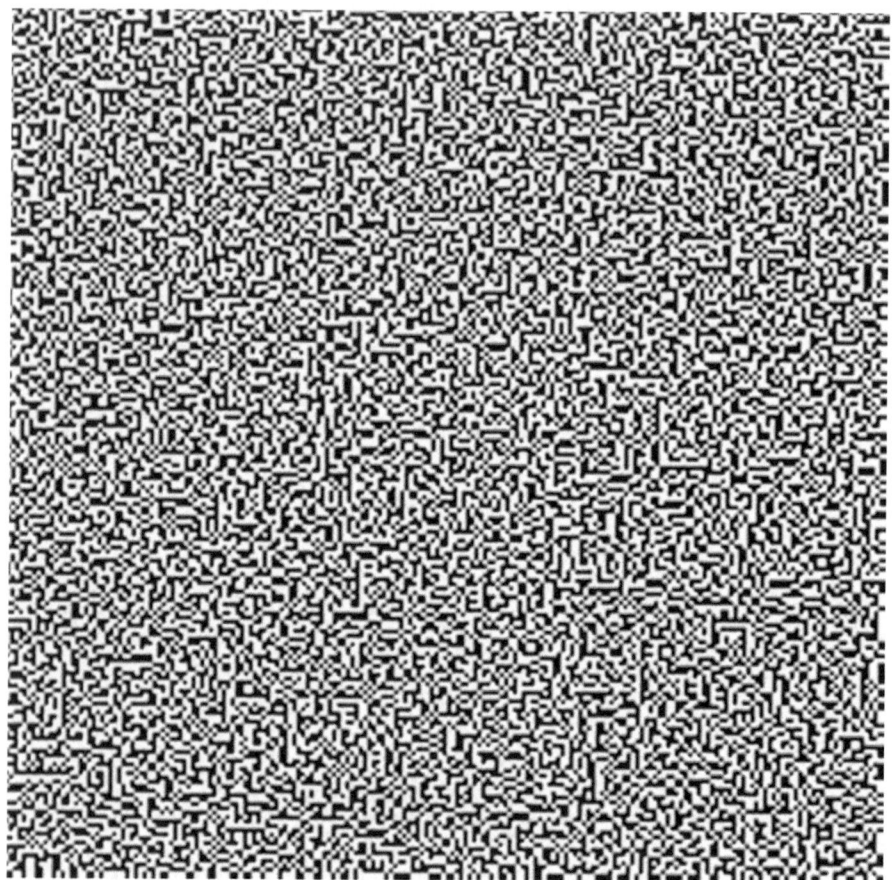

Figure 3: Example: Pixel-based Visual Cryptography, Transparency 2

Figure 4: Example: Pixel-based Visual Cryptography, Overlay

Auxiliary Tables and Proofs

> Consistency is found in that work whose whole and detail are suitable to the occasion. It arises from circumstance, custom, and nature.
>
> Marcus Vitruvius Pollio

Lemmas

Lemma 11.1. *The derivative of* $f(n) = \left(1 - \frac{2}{n+1}\right)^n$ *is positive for all* $n > 1$.

PROOF. By applying the chain rule for $\frac{df}{dn} f(n) = \frac{du^v}{du} \frac{du}{dn} + \frac{du^v}{dv} \frac{dv}{dn}$
with $u = 1 - \frac{2}{n+1}$, $v = n$, $\frac{du^v}{du} = vu^{v-1}$, and $\frac{du^v}{dv} = \log(u)u^v$ it follows:

$$\frac{df}{dn} f(n) = n\left(1 - \frac{2}{n+1}\right)^{n-1} \frac{df}{dn}\left(1 - \frac{2}{n+1}\right)$$

$$+ \left(1 - \frac{2}{n+1}\right)^n \log\left(1 - \frac{2}{n+1}\right) \frac{df}{dn}(n)$$

$$= \left(1 - \frac{2}{n+1}\right)^{n-1} \left(n\left(\frac{2}{(n+1)^2}\right) + \left(1 - \frac{2}{n+1}\right) \log\left(1 - \frac{2}{n+1}\right)\right)$$

$$= \left(1 - \frac{2}{n+1}\right)^n \left(\frac{2n}{n^2-1} + \log\left(\frac{n-1}{n+1}\right)\right)$$

Since for all $n > 1$ it holds that $\left(1 - \frac{2}{n+1}\right)^n > 0$ it remains to show that $T(n) = \left(\frac{2n}{n^2-1} + \log\left(\frac{n-1}{n+1}\right)\right) > 0$. We start with an evaluation for $n = 2$ and get $T(2) = \frac{4}{3} - \log(3) > 0$. Next, we regard the derivative of $T(n)$:

$$\frac{dT}{dn} T(n) = \frac{dT}{dn}\left(\frac{2n}{n^2-1}\right) + \frac{dT}{dn}\left(\log\left(\frac{n-1}{n+1}\right)\right)$$

$$= \frac{(n^2-1)2 - 2n(2n)}{(n^2-1)^2} + \frac{(n+1)\frac{dT}{dn}\left(\frac{n-1}{n+1}\right)}{n-1}$$

$$= \frac{-2n^2 - 2}{(n^2-1)^2} + \frac{(n+1)\left((n+1)1 - (n-1)1\right)}{(n-1)(n+1)^2}$$

$$= \frac{-2n^2 - 2}{(n^2-1)^2} + \frac{2(n^2-1)}{(n^2-1)^2}$$

$$= \frac{-4}{(n^2-1)^2}$$

This means that T(n) is stricly monotonically decreasing. Next, we consider the second derivative:

$$
\begin{aligned}
\frac{d^2 T}{dn^2} T(n) &= \frac{dT}{dn} \frac{-4}{(n^2 - 1)^2} \\
&= \frac{4 \frac{dT}{dn} (n^4 - 2n^2 + 1)}{(n^2 - 1)^4} \\
&= \frac{16n^3 - 16n}{(n^2 - 1)^4} \\
&= \frac{16n}{(n^2 - 1)^3}
\end{aligned}
$$

Since the second derivative is non-negative, $T(n)$ is strictly convex. Furthermore, since the the limit of both summands as n approaches infinity is zero, the limit of $T(n)$ as n approaches infinity is also zero:

$$
\lim_{n \to \infty} \left(\frac{2n}{n^2 - 1} + \log\left(\frac{n-1}{n+1} \right) \right) = 0
$$

This means that $T(n)$ decreases slower and slower, but is always positive until n approaches infinity. Hence, the derivative of $\left(1 - \frac{2}{n+1}\right)^n$ is also positive and therefore we showed that $\frac{df}{dn} \left(1 - \frac{2}{n+1}\right)^n > 0$ for all $n > 1$. ∎

Tables

Table 1: Possible Pairs of Dice Codings with $n = 9$ for a Given Number of Different Dots

difference	possible pairs
0	(0,0); (1,1); (2,2); (3,3); (4,4); (5,5); (6,6); (7,7); (8,8); (9,9)
1	(0,1); (1,0); (1,2); (2,1); (2,3); (3,2); (3,4); (4,3); (4,5); (5,4); (5,6); (6,5); (6,7); (7,6); (7,8); (8,7); (8,9); (9,8)
2	(0,2); (1,1); (1,3); (2,0); (2,2); (2,4); (3,1); (3,3); (3,5); (4,2); (4,4); (4,6); (5,3); (5,5); (5,7); (6,4); (6,6); (6,8); (7,5); (7,7); (7,9); (8,6); (8,8); (9,7)
3	(0,3); (1,2); (1,4); (2,1); (2,3); (2,5); (3,0); (3,2); (3,4); (3,6); (4,1); (4,3); (4,5); (4,7); (5,2); (5,4); (5,6); (5,8); (6,3); (6,5); (6,7); (6,9); (7,4); (7,6); (7,8); (8,5); (8,7); (9,6)
4	(0,4); (1,3); (1,5); (2,2); (2,4); (2,6); (3,1); (3,3); (3,5); (3,7); (4,0); (4,2); (4,4); (4,6); (4,8); (5,1); (5,3); (5,5); (5,7); (5,9); (6,2); (6,4); (6,6); (6,8); (7,3); (7,5); (7,7); (8,4); (8,6); (9,5)
5	(0,5); (1,4); (1,6); (2,3); (2,5); (2,7); (3,2); (3,4); (3,6); (3,8); (4,1); (4,3); (4,5); (4,7); (4,9); (5,0); (5,2); (5,4); (5,6); (5,8); (6,1); (6,3); (6,5); (6,7); (7,2); (7,4); (7,6); (8,3); (8,5); (9,4)
6	(0,6); (1,5); (1,7); (2,4); (2,6); (2,8); (3,3); (3,5); (3,7); (3,9); (4,2); (4,4); (4,6); (4,8); (5,1); (5,3); (5,5); (5,7); (6,0); (6,2); (6,4); (6,6); (7,1); (7,3); (7,5); (8,2); (8,4); (9,3)
7	(0,7); (1,6); (1,8); (2,5); (2,7); (2,9); (3,4); (3,6); (3,8); (4,3); (4,5); (4,7); (5,2); (5,4); (5,6); (6,1); (6,3); (6,5); (7,0); (7,2); (7,4); (8,1); (8,3); (9,2)
8	(0,8); (1,7); (1,9); (2,6); (2,8); (3,5); (3,7); (4,4); (4,6); (5,3); (5,5); (6,2); (6,4); (7,1); (7,3); (8,0); (8,2); (9,1)
9	(0,9); (1,8); (2,7); (3,6); (4,5); (5,4); (6,3); (7,2); (8,1); (9,0)

Table 2: Upper Bounds of Probabilities (in %) that k Matching Ciphertexts Occur Given N_{1*} Ciphertexts of 1^* and $n = 9$ (cf. Term 5.8)

$$P\left(\exists c.\#c = k | N_{1*}\right) = \begin{cases} 0, & \text{if } N_{1*} < k \\ 1, & \text{if } N_{1*} > (k-1)n \\ 1 - \frac{n!}{(n-N_{1*})!} \frac{1}{n^{N_{1*}}}, & \text{if } k \leqslant N_{1*} \leqslant (k-1)n, k = 2 \\ \approx \binom{N_{1*}}{k}\left(\frac{1}{n}\right)^{N_{1*}-1}(n-1)^{N_{1*}-k}, & \text{if } k \leqslant N_{1*} \leqslant (k-1)n, k > 2 \end{cases}$$

N_{1*} \ k	2	3	4	5	6
2	11.1	0	0.0	0.0	0.0
3	30.9	1.2	0.0	0.0	0.0
4	53.9	4.4	0.1	0.0	0.0
5	74.4	9.8	0.6	$1.5 \cdot 10^{-2}$	0.0
6	88.6	17.3	1.6	$8.1 \cdot 10^{-2}$	$1.7 \cdot 10^{-3}$
7	96.2	27.0	3.4	0.3	$1.1 \cdot 10^{-2}$
8	99.2	38.4	6.0	0.6	$3.7 \cdot 10^{-2}$
9	99.9	51.2	9.6	1.2	0.1
10	100.0	65.0	14.2	2.1	0.2

N_{1*} \ k	7	8	9	10
2	0.0	0.0	0.0	0.0
3	0.0	0.0	0.0	0.0
4	0.0	0.0	0.0	0.0
5	0.0	0.0	0.0	0.0
6	0.0	0.0	0.0	0.0
7	$1.9 \cdot 10^{-4}$	0.0	0.0	0.0
8	$1.3 \cdot 10^{-3}$	$2.1 \cdot 10^{-5}$	0.0	0.0
9	$5.4 \cdot 10^{-3}$	$1.6 \cdot 10^{-4}$	$2.3 \cdot 10^{-6}$	0.0
10	$1.6 \cdot 10^{-2}$	$7.4 \cdot 10^{-4}$	$2.1 \cdot 10^{-5}$	$2.6 \cdot 10^{-7}$

Table 3: Probabilities (in %) that N_{i^*} Ciphertexts of i^* out of N Ciphertexts Occur with $n = 9$ if i Follows a Uniform Distribution

$$P(\#i = N_{i^*}|N) = \binom{N}{N_{i^*}} \left(\frac{2}{n+1}\right)^{N_{i^*}} \left(1 - \frac{2}{n+1}\right)^{N-N_{i^*}}$$

N \ N_{i^*}	0	1	2	3	4	5
1	80.0	20.0	0.0	0.0	0.0	0.0
2	64.0	32.0	4.0	0.0	0.0	0.0
3	51.2	38.4	9.6	0.8	0.0	0.0
4	41.0	41.0	15.3	2.6	0.2	0.0
5	32.8	41.0	20.5	5.1	0.6	$3.2 \cdot 10^{-2}$
6	26.2	39.3	24.5	8.2	1.5	0.2
7	21.0	36.7	27.5	11.5	2.9	0.4
8	16.8	33.6	29.4	14.7	4.6	0.9
9	13.4	30.2	30.2	17.6	6.6	1.6
10	10.7	26.8	30.2	20.1	8.8	2.6
11	8.6	23.6	29.5	22.2	11.1	3.9
12	6.9	20.6	28.4	23.6	13.3	5.3
13	5.5	17.9	26.8	24.6	15.4	6.9
14	4.3	15.4	25.0	25.0	17.2	8.6
15	3.5	13.2	23.1	25.0	18.8	10.3
16	2.8	11.2	21.1	24.6	20.0	12.0
17	2.3	9.6	19.1	23.9	20.9	13.6
18	1.8	8.1	17.2	23.0	21.5	15.1
19	1.4	6.8	15.4	21.8	21.8	16.4
20	1.2	5.8	13.7	20.5	21.8	17.5

N \ N_{i^*}	6	7	8	9	10
1 to 5	0.0	0.0	0.0	0.0	0.0
6	$6.4 \cdot 10^{-3}$	0.0	0.0	0.0	0.0
7	$3.5 \cdot 10^{-2}$	$1.2 \cdot 10^{-3}$	0.0	0.0	0.0
8	0.1	$8.2 \cdot 10^{-3}$	$2.6 \cdot 10^{-4}$	0.0	0.0
9	0.3	$2.9 \cdot 10^{-2}$	$1.8 \cdot 10^{-3}$	$5.1 \cdot 10^{-5}$	0.0
10	0.6	$7.8 \cdot 10^{-2}$	$7.3 \cdot 10^{-3}$	$4.1 \cdot 10^{-4}$	$1.0 \cdot 10^{-5}$
11	1.0	0.2	$2.1 \cdot 10^{-2}$	$1.8 \cdot 10^{-3}$	$9.0 \cdot 10^{-5}$
12	1.6	0.3	$5.2 \cdot 10^{-2}$	$5.8 \cdot 10^{-3}$	$4.3 \cdot 10^{-4}$
13	2.3	0.6	0.1	$1.5 \cdot 10^{-2}$	$1.5 \cdot 10^{-3}$
14	3.2	0.9	0.2	$3.3 \cdot 10^{-2}$	$4.2 \cdot 10^{-3}$
15	4.3	1.4	0.3	$6.7 \cdot 10^{-2}$	$1.0 \cdot 10^{-2}$
16	5.5	2.0	0.6	0.1	$2.1 \cdot 10^{-2}$
17	6.8	2.7	0.8	0.2	$4.2 \cdot 10^{-2}$
18	8.2	3.5	1.2	0.3	$7.5 \cdot 10^{-2}$
19	9.5	4.4	1.7	0.5	0.1
20	10.9	5.5	2.2	0.7	0.2

Table 4: Probabilities (in %) that N_{1*} Ciphertexts of 1^* out of N Ciphertexts Occur with $N_{0*} = 2$ and $n = 9$ if i Follows a Uniform Distribution (cf. Term 5.7)

$$P(\#0^* = N_{0*}; \#1^* = N_{1*}|N) = \frac{N!}{N_{0*}!\,N_{1*}!\,(N - N_{0*} - N_{1*})!}$$
$$\cdot \left(\frac{2}{n+1}\right)^{N_{0*}} \left(\frac{2}{n+1}\right)^{N_{1*}} \left(\frac{n-3}{n+1}\right)^{N-N_{0*}-N_{1*}}$$

N \ N_{1*}	2	3	4	5	6
4	1.0	0.0	0.0	0.0	0.0
5	2.9	0.3	0.0	0.0	0.0
6	5.2	1.2	0.1	0.0	0.0
7	7.3	2.4	0.4	$2.7 \cdot 10^{-2}$	0.0
8	8.8	3.9	1.0	0.1	$7.2 \cdot 10^{-3}$
9	9.4	5.2	1.7	0.3	$3.9 \cdot 10^{-2}$
10	9.4	6.3	2.6	0.7	0.1
11	8.9	6.9	3.4	1.1	0.3
12	8.0	7.1	4.1	1.7	0.5
13	7.0	6.9	4.6	2.2	0.7
14	5.9	6.5	4.8	2.6	1.0
15	4.8	5.8	4.8	2.9	1.3
16	3.8	5.1	4.6	3.1	1.5
17	3.0	4.3	4.3	3.2	1.8
18	2.3	3.6	3.9	3.1	1.9
19	1.8	2.9	3.4	2.9	2.0
20	1.3	2.3	2.9	2.7	2.0

N \ N_{1*}	7	8	9	10
4 to 8	0.0	0.0	0.0	0.0
9	$1.8 \cdot 10^{-3}$	0.0	0.0	0.0
10	$1.1 \cdot 10^{-2}$	$4.6 \cdot 10^{-4}$	0.0	0.0
11	$3.6 \cdot 10^{-2}$	$3.0 \cdot 10^{-3}$	$1.1 \cdot 10^{-4}$	0.0
12	0.1	$1.1 \cdot 10^{-2}$	$8.1 \cdot 10^{-4}$	$2.7 \cdot 10^{-5}$
13	0.2	$2.9 \cdot 10^{-2}$	$3.2 \cdot 10^{-3}$	$2.1 \cdot 10^{-4}$
14	0.3	0.1	$8.9 \cdot 10^{-3}$	$8.9 \cdot 10^{-4}$
15	0.4	0.1	$2.0 \cdot 10^{-2}$	$2.7 \cdot 10^{-3}$
16	0.6	0.2	$3.8 \cdot 10^{-2}$	$6.4 \cdot 10^{-3}$
17	0.8	0.3	$6.5 \cdot 10^{-2}$	$1.3 \cdot 10^{-2}$
18	0.9	0.3	0.1	$2.3 \cdot 10^{-2}$
19	1.0	0.4	0.1	$3.8 \cdot 10^{-2}$
20	1.1	0.5	0.2	$5.7 \cdot 10^{-2}$

Table 5: Probabilities (in %) that N_{1*} Ciphertexts of 1^* out of N Ciphertexts Occur with $N_{0*} = 3$ and $n = 9$ if i Follows a Uniform Distribution (cf. Term 5.7)

$$P(\#0^* = N_{0*}; \#1^* = N_{1*}|N) = \frac{N!}{N_{0*}!N_{1*}!(N - N_{0*} - N_{1*})!}$$
$$\cdot \left(\frac{2}{n+1}\right)^{N_{0*}} \left(\frac{2}{n+1}\right)^{N_{1*}} \left(\frac{n-3}{n+1}\right)^{N-N_{0*}-N_{1*}}$$

N \ N_{1*}	3	4	5	6
6	0.1	0.0	0.0	0.0
7	0.5	$4.5 \cdot 10^{-2}$	0.0	0.0
8	1.3	0.2	$1.4 \cdot 10^{-2}$	0.0
9	2.3	0.6	$7.7 \cdot 10^{-2}$	$4.3 \cdot 10^{-3}$
10	3.5	1.2	0.2	$2.6 \cdot 10^{-2}$
11	4.6	1.9	0.5	$8.5 \cdot 10^{-2}$
12	5.5	2.8	0.9	0.2
13	6.1	3.6	1.4	0.4
14	6.5	4.3	2.0	0.7
15	6.5	4.8	2.5	1.0
16	6.2	5.1	3.0	1.3
17	5.7	5.3	3.5	1.8
18	5.2	5.2	3.7	2.1
19	4.5	4.9	3.9	2.4
20	3.9	4.5	3.9	2.6

N \ N_{1*}	7	8	9	10
6	0.0	0.0	0.0	0.0
7	0.0	0.0	0.0	0.0
8	0.0	0.0	0.0	0.0
9	0.0	0.0	0.0	0.0
10	$1.2 \cdot 10^{-3}$	0.0	0.0	0.0
11	$8.1 \cdot 10^{-3}$	$3.4 \cdot 10^{-4}$	0.0	0.0
12	$2.9 \cdot 10^{-2}$	$2.4 \cdot 10^{-3}$	$9.0 \cdot 10^{-5}$	0.0
13	$7.6 \cdot 10^{-2}$	$9.5 \cdot 10^{-3}$	$7.0 \cdot 10^{-4}$	$2.3 \cdot 10^{-5}$
14	0.2	$2.7 \cdot 10^{-2}$	$3.0 \cdot 10^{-3}$	$2.0 \cdot 10^{-4}$
15	0.3	$6.0 \cdot 10^{-2}$	$8.9 \cdot 10^{-3}$	$8.9 \cdot 10^{-4}$
16	0.5	0.1	$2.1 \cdot 10^{-2}$	$2.8 \cdot 10^{-3}$
17	0.7	0.2	$4.3 \cdot 10^{-2}$	$7.2 \cdot 10^{-3}$
18	0.9	0.3	$7.8 \cdot 10^{-2}$	$1.6 \cdot 10^{-2}$
19	1.1	0.4	0.1	$3.0 \cdot 10^{-2}$
20	1.4	0.6	0.2	$5.0 \cdot 10^{-2}$

Table 6: Evaluation of $P(\#0* = 3; 3|N)$'s summands (in %) for selected N and N_{1*} with maximum summands highlighted

N	N_{1*}	summand	changefactor
	3	$4.3 \cdot 10^{-2}$	
	4	$5.1 \cdot 10^{-2}$	1.18
10	5	$2.3 \cdot 10^{-2}$	0.44
	6	$4.5 \cdot 10^{-3}$	0.20
	7	$3.3 \cdot 10^{-4}$	0.07
	3	$8.0 \cdot 10^{-2}$	
	4	$2.1 \cdot 10^{-1}$	2.67
	5	$2.5 \cdot 10^{-1}$	1.19
15	6	$1.7 \cdot 10^{-1}$	0.69
	7	$7.7 \cdot 10^{-2}$	0.44
	8	$2.3 \cdot 10^{-2}$	0.30
	9	$4.5 \cdot 10^{-3}$	0.20
	3	$4.8 \cdot 10^{-2}$	
	4	$2.0 \cdot 10^{-1}$	4.15
	5	$3.8 \cdot 10^{-1}$	1.93
20	6	$4.5 \cdot 10^{-1}$	1.19
	7	$3.7 \cdot 10^{-1}$	0.82
	8	$2.2 \cdot 10^{-1}$	0.59
	9	$9.8 \cdot 10^{-2}$	0.44

Table 7: Needed CPU Time on one Core of a Intel(R) Core(TM)2 Duo CPU E8400 with
3.00GHz to Recover the Secret Key from Encrypted Keypads wth $n = 9$ and
$1,000,000$ Runs

used CPU time (in seconds)	number of runs terminating	aggregated number of runs
$\leqslant 15$	0	0
16	2	2
17	41,409	41,411
18	242,822	284,233
19	551,011	835,244
20	91,039	926,283
21	40,145	966,428
22	21,423	987,851
23	4,800	992,651
24	2,015	994,666
25	1,895	996,561
26	1,256	997,817
27	671	998,488
28	332	998,820
29	271	999,091
30	186	999,277
31	146	999,423
32	111	999,534
33	94	999,628
34	78	999,706
35	57	999,763
36	52	999,815
37	44	999,859
38	30	999,889
39	25	999,914
$40-49$	58	999,972
$50-59$	18	999,990
$60-69$	8	999,998
$70-79$	2	1,000,000
$\geqslant 80$	0	1,000,000

Source Code Listings

Life would be so much easier if we
could just look at the source code.

Dave Olson

Common Class

Listing 11.1: Node.java

```
 1  public class Node {
 2      Node zero = null;
 3      Node one = null;
 4      Node father = null;
 5
 6      boolean isLeaf = false;
 7      boolean isBorderNode = false;
 8
 9      public Node() {
10
11      }
12
13      public Node(Node father) {
14          this.father=father;
15      }
16
17      public Node(Node zero, Node one) {
18          this.zero=zero;
19          this.one=one;
20          if (this.zero != null) {zero.father=this;}
21          if (this.one != null)  {one.father=this;}
22      }
23
24      public boolean isLeafNode() {
25          return isLeaf;
26      }
27
28      public boolean isBorderNode() {
29          return isBorderNode;
30      }
31
32      public boolean isRootNode() {
33          return (this.father==null);
34      }
35
36      public int getLeftLeafs() {
37          int leafsLeft=0;
38          if (isLeaf) return 1;
39          if (zero!=null) leafsLeft=leafsLeft + zero.
                getLeftLeafs();
40          if (one!=null) leafsLeft=leafsLeft + one.getLeftLeafs
                ();
41          return leafsLeft;
42      }
43  } // end Node
```

Attacking Pairs of Characters

Listing 11.2: VisualCodingsOTP.java

```
1   import java.security.SecureRandom;
2
3   public class VisualCodingsOTP {
4
5       public static void main(String[] args) {
6           final int keylength=18;
7
8           VisualCodingsPossibleKeys keytree=new
                   VisualCodingsPossibleKeys(keylength);
9           boolean[] key = getBoolArray(keylength);
10          boolean[] field = getValidField(key);
11
12          int keynumber= (int) Math.pow(2,2*keylength −1);
13          int loopnumber=0;
14
15          System.out.print("Chosen key: "); printBoolArray(key);
16          while(keynumber>1) {
17              keytree.deleteIllegalKeys(field);
18              field = getValidField(key);
19              keynumber=keytree.getNumberOfPossibleKeys(key.
                       length);
20              loopnumber++;
21          }
22          System.out.println("Fields used: "+ ++loopnumber);
23      }
24
25      public static void printBoolArray(boolean[] boolArray) {
26          for(int i=0;i<boolArray.length;i++) {
27              if (i==boolArray.length/2) {System.out.print(" ")
                       ;};
28              if (boolArray[i]) {System.out.print("1");}
29              else {System.out.print("0");}
30          }
31          System.out.println();
32      }
33
34      private static boolean[] getBoolArray(int length) {
35          SecureRandom randomgenerator = new SecureRandom();
36          boolean[] boolArray = new boolean[length];
37          for(int i=0;i<length;i++) {
38              boolArray[i]=randomgenerator.nextBoolean();
39          }
40          return boolArray;
41      }
42
```

```
43    private static boolean[] getValidField(boolean[] key) {
44        boolean[] field;
45        do {
46            field = getBoolArray(key.length);
47        } while (! isFieldValid(key,field));
48        return field;
49    }
50
51    private static boolean isFieldValid(boolean[] key, boolean
      [] field) {
52        int sum1=0;
53        int sum2=0;
54        for(int i=0;i<key.length/2;i++) {
55            if (key[i]^field[i]) {
56                sum1++;
57            };
58            if (key[i+key.length/2]^field[i+key.length/2]) {
59                sum2++;
60            };
61        }
62        return !(sum1==sum2);
63    }
64
65 } // end VisualCodingsOTP
```

Listing 11.3: VisualCodingsPossibleKeys.java

```
 1  public class VisualCodingsPossibleKeys {
 2
 3      private Node root = new Node();
 4
 5      public VisualCodingsPossibleKeys(int level) {
 6          if (level >0) { // since we cannot differ between keys
                            //   and their inverse, we only need half of the tree
 7              root.one=null;
 8              root.zero=new Node();
 9              initializeKeyHelper(root.zero, level −1);
10          }
11      }
12
13      public void deleteKey(boolean[] key) {
14          boolean[] boolArray = key;
15          if (boolArray[0]) {
16              for(int i=0;i<boolArray.length;i++) {
17                  boolArray[i] = !boolArray[i];
18              }
19          }
20          deleteKeyHelper(root.zero, boolArray,1);
21      }
22
23      public int getNumberOfPossibleKeys(int maxlvl) {
24          return getNumberOfPossibleKeysHelper(root,1,maxlvl);
25      }
26
27      public void deleteIllegalKeys(boolean[] field) {
28          boolean[] key = new boolean[field.length];
29          boolean[] orig = new boolean[field.length];
30          // set both boxes to "0":
31          for(int j=0;j<field.length;j++) {
32              key[j]=false;
33              orig[j]=field[j];
34          }
35          // we only need to test half of the possible keys,
36          // since we cannot differ between a key an its inverse
37          delKeyCombinations(key,orig,1);
38      }
39
40      private void initializeKeyHelper(Node root, int level) {
41          if (level==0) {root.isLeaf = true;}
42          else { root.one=new Node();
43                 root.zero=new Node();
44                 initializeKeyHelper(root.one, level −1);
45                 initializeKeyHelper(root.zero, level −1);
46          }
47      }
```

```
48    private boolean deleteKeyHelper(Node root, boolean[] key,
          int position) {
49        Node nextnode;
50
51        if (root==null) {return false;}
52
53        if (key[position]){nextnode=root.one;}
54        else {nextnode=root.zero;}
55
56        if (position==key.length −1) {
57            if (key[position]) {root.one=null;}
58            else {root.zero=null;}
59            return true;
60        }
61        if (deleteKeyHelper(nextnode, key, position +1)) {
62            // no children left, tell daddy to delete
63            if ((root.one == null) && (root.zero == null)) {
64                return true;
65            }
66            // delete childless son
67            if ((root.one != null) && (root.one.one == null)
                  && (root.one.zero == null)) {
68                root.one = null;
69                return true;
70            }
71            // delete childless son
72            if ((root.zero != null) && (root.zero.one == null)
                  && (root.zero.zero == null)) {
73                root.zero = null;
74                return true;
75            }
76        }
77        return false;
78    }
79
80    private int getNumberOfPossibleKeysHelper(Node root, int
          lvl, int maxlvl) {
81        int count=0;
82        if (root.zero != null) {
83            count+=getNumberOfPossibleKeysHelper(root.zero,
                  lvl +1, maxlvl);
84        }
85        else if (lvl == maxlvl) {count++;}
86        if (root.one != null) {
87            count+=getNumberOfPossibleKeysHelper(root.one, lvl
                  +1, maxlvl);
88        }
89        else if (lvl == maxlvl) {count++;}
90        return count;
91    }
```

```
92      private void delKeyCombinations(boolean[] test, boolean[]
            orig, int position) {
93          if (position==test.length−1) {
94              if (!isKeyValid(orig,test)) {deleteKey(test);}
95          }
96          else {
97              delKeyCombinations(test, orig, position + 1);
98          }
99
100         test[position]=!test[position];
101
102         if (position==test.length−1) {
103             if (!isKeyValid(orig,test)) {deleteKey(test);}
104         }
105         else {
106             delKeyCombinations(test, orig, position + 1);
107         }
108     }
109
110     private boolean isKeyValid(boolean[] key, boolean[] field)
            {
111         int sum1=0;
112         int sum2=0;
113         for(int i=0;i<key.length/2;i++) {
114             if (key[i]^field[i]) {
115                 sum1++;
116             };
117             if (key[i+key.length/2]^field[i+key.length/2]) {
118                 sum2++;
119             };
120         }
121         return !(sum1==sum2);
122     }
123
124  } // end VisualCodingsPossibleKeys
```

Attacking of a Complete Keypad

Listing 11.4: VisualCodingsOTP2.java

```java
import java.security.SecureRandom;

public class VisualCodingsOTP2 {

    public static void main(String[] args) {
        final int dices=10;
        final int pips=9;

        boolean[][] keypad = initBoolArray(dices,pips);

        VisualCodingsPossibleKeys2 keytree = new
            VisualCodingsPossibleKeys2(dices,pips);

        int loopnumber=0;

        while(true) {
            loopnumber++;

            boolean[][] cipher = getValidCipher(keypad);

            keytree.deleteIllegalKeys(cipher);

            // key recovered?
            if (keytree.recoveredKey()) {
                System.out.println("Key_recovered_with_"+
                    loopnumber+"_ciphers.");
                break;
            }
        } // while
    }

    public static void printBoolArray(boolean[][] boolArray) {
        for(int i=0;i<boolArray.length;i++) {
            for(int j=0;j<boolArray[i].length;j++) {
                if (boolArray[i][j]) {
                    System.out.print("*");
                } else {
                    System.out.print(".");
                }
            }
            System.out.println();
        }
        System.out.println();
    }

```

```
44    private static boolean [][] initBoolArray(int dices, int
          pips) {
45    SecureRandom randomgenerator = new SecureRandom();
46    boolean [][] boolArray = new boolean[dices][pips];
47    for(int d=0;d<dices;d++) {
48        for(int p=0;p<pips;p++) {
49            boolArray[d][p]=randomgenerator.nextBoolean();
50        }
51    }
52    return boolArray;
53    }
54
55    private static boolean [][] getValidCipher(boolean [][] key)
          {
56    int pips=key[0].length;
57    int dices=key.length;
58    boolean [][] template = getRandomizedTemplate(dices,
          pips);
59    boolean [][] cipher = new boolean[dices][pips];
60
61    for(int d=0;d<dices;d++) {
62        for(int p=0;p<pips;p++) {
63            cipher[d][p]=key[d][p] ^ template[d][p];
64        }
65    }
66    return cipher;
67    }
68
69    private static boolean [][] getTemplate(int dices, int pips
          ) {
70    boolean [][] template = new boolean[dices][pips];
71
72    for(int d=0;d<dices;d++) {
73        for(int p=0;p<d && p<pips;p++) {
74            template[d][p]=true;
75        }
76        for(int k=d;k<pips;k++) {
77            template[d][k]=false;
78        }
79    }
80    return template;
81    }
82
83    private static boolean [][] getRandomizedTemplate(int dices
          , int pips) {
84    SecureRandom r=new SecureRandom();
85    boolean [][] template = getTemplate(dices,pips);
86
87
88
```

```java
89          // shuffle pips in their dices
90          for(int d=1;d<dices -1;d++) {
91              for (int p=0;p<pips;p++) {
92                  int j=p+r.nextInt(pips-p);
93                  if (p!=j)
94                  {
95                      boolean h=template[d][p];
96                      template[d][p]=template[d][j];
97                      template[d][j]=h;
98                  }
99              }
100         }
101
102         // shuffle dices
103         for(int d=0;d<dices;d++) {
104             int j=d+r.nextInt(dices-d);
105             if (d!=j)
106             {
107                 for (int p=0;p<pips;p++) {
108                     boolean h=template[d][p];
109                     template[d][p]=template[j][p];
110                     template[j][p]=h;
111                 }
112             }
113         }
114         /*
115          * Both "shuffles" traverse the array forward,
116          * repeatedly swapping a randomly selected element
117          * (from the current position to the last element)
118          * into the current position.
119          */
120         return template;
121     }
122
123     private static boolean[][] decrypt(boolean[][] key,
            boolean[][] cipher) {
124         int pips=key[0].length;
125         int dices=key.length;
126         boolean[][] plain = new boolean[dices][pips];
127
128         for(int d=0;d<dices;d++) {
129             for(int p=0;p<pips;p++) {
130                 plain[d][p]=key[d][p] ^ cipher[d][p];
131             }
132         }
133         return plain;
134     }
135
136 } // end VisualCodingsOTP2
```

Listing 11.5: VisualCodingsPossibleKeys2.java

```
 1  public class VisualCodingsPossibleKeys2 {
 2
 3      private Node[][] diceKeyPair;
 4
 5      private int dices;
 6      private int pips;
 7
 8      private int[][] keysleft;
 9
10      private boolean[][] key;
11      private boolean[] keyFound;
12
13      public VisualCodingsPossibleKeys2(int dices, int pips) {
14          this.dices=dices;
15          this.pips=pips;
16          diceKeyPair = new Node[dices][dices];
17          keysleft = new int[dices][dices];
18          key= new boolean[dices][pips];
19          keyFound=new boolean[dices];
20          if (pips>0) {
21              for(int d=0;d<dices;d++) {
22                  keyFound[d]=false;
23                  for(int e=0;e<dices;e++) {
24                      if (d==e) {continue;}
25                      // since we cannot differ between keys and
                         //     their inverse, we only need half of
                         //     the tree
26                      diceKeyPair[d][e] = new Node(new Node(),
                             null);
27                      keysleft[d][e]= (int) Math.pow(2,2*pips-1)
                             ;
28                      initializeKeyHelper(diceKeyPair[d][e].zero
                             ,0);
29                  }
30              }
31          }
32      }
33
34      public void deleteIllegalKeys(boolean[][] cipher) {
35          for(int d=0;d<dices;d++) {
36              for(int e=0;e<dices;e++) {
37                  if (d==e) {continue;}
38                  deleteIllegalKeysForPair(cipher, diceKeyPair[d
                         ][e], d, e, 0, 0);
39              }
40          }
41          cleanup();
42      }
```

```java
43        public boolean recoveredKey() {
44            boolean recovered=false;
45            boolean anchorSet=false;
46            boolean newDiceRecovered;
47            for(int d=0;d<dices;d++) {
48                if (keyFound[d]==true) {anchorSet=true;}
49            }
50
51            // anchor
52            for(int d=0;d<dices & !anchorSet;d++) {
53                for(int e=0;e<dices;e++) {
54                    if (d==e) {continue;}
55                    if (keysleft[d][e]==1) {
56                        setNodeValueFromTo(d,e);
57                        anchorSet=true;
58                    }
59                }
60            }
61
62            do {
63                newDiceRecovered=false;
64                for(int d=0;d<dices;d++) {
65                    for(int e=0;e<dices;e++) {
66                        if (d==e) {continue;}
67                        if ((keysleft[d][e]>1) || (keyFound[d] &
                                keyFound[e])) {
68                            continue;
69                            // nothing to do
70                        }
71                        if (keyFound[d] | keyFound[e]) {
72                            setNodeValueFromTo(d,e);
73                            newDiceRecovered=true;
74                        }
75                    }
76                }
77            } while (newDiceRecovered);
78
79            for(int d=0;d<dices;d++) {
80                if (!keyFound[d]) {
81                    break;
82                    // no key found
83                }
84                if (d==dices-1) {recovered=true;}
85            }
86            return recovered;
87        }
88
89
90
91
```

```
92      public void printStatus () {
93          for(int d=0;d<dices ;d++) {
94              for(int e=0;e<dices ;e++) {
95                  if (d==e) {continue ;}
96                  if (keysleft [d][e]>1) {
97                      System . out . println ("DiceKeyPair:_"+d+" ,"+e
                             +";_Keys_left :_"+keysleft [d][e]);
98                  }
99                  else {
100                     System . out . print ("DiceKeyPair:_"+d+" ,"+e+"
                             ;_Key:_");
101                     printPair (diceKeyPair [d][e]);
102                 }
103             }
104         }
105     }
106
107     public void printStatus2 () {
108         for(int d=0;d<dices ;d++) {
109             if (keyFound [d]) {
110                 System . out . print ("Key_for_dice_"+d+" :_");
111                 for(int p=0;p<pips ;p++) {
112                     if (key[d][p]) {System . out . print ("*");}
113                     else {System . out . print (".");}
114                 }
115                 System . out . println ();
116             }
117             else {
118                 System . out . println ("Key_for_dice _"+d+"_not_
                             recovered ,_yet.");
119             }
120         }
121     }
122
123     public void printPair (Node node) {
124         if (node. isLeaf ) {
125             System . out . println ();
126             return ;
127         }
128         if (node. zero !=null & node. one !=null) System . out .
                             print ("X");
129         if (node. zero !=null) {
130             if (node. isBorderNode) {System . out . print ("_");}
131             System . out . print ("."); printPair (node. zero );
132         }
133         if (node. one !=null) {
134             if (node. isBorderNode) {System . out . print ("_");}
135             System . out . print ("*"); printPair (node. one );
136         }
137     }
```

```java
138    public void printPossibleKeys (Node node) {
139        if (node.zero != null) {
140            System.out.print("0");
141            printPossibleKeysHelper(node.zero,1);
142        }
143    }
144
145    private void initializeKeyHelper(Node root, int level) {
146        if (level==pips-1) {
147            root.isBorderNode = true;
148        }
149        if (level==2*pips-1) {
150            root.isLeaf = true;
151            return;
152        }
153        root.one=new Node(root);
154        root.zero=new Node(root);
155        initializeKeyHelper(root.one, level+1);
156        initializeKeyHelper(root.zero, level+1);
157    }
158
159    private void deleteIllegalKeysForPair(boolean [][] cipher,
           Node keyPairNode, int d, int e, int pip, int sum) {
160        if (keyPairNode.isBorderNode) {
161            // finished 1st dice
162            //delete all illegal keys for the second dice
163            deleteIllegalKeysForDice(cipher, keyPairNode, d, e
                   , 0, sum, 0);
164
165            // no children left, delete Majornode
166            if (keyPairNode.zero == null & keyPairNode.one ==
                   null) {
167                deleteMajorNode(keyPairNode,d,e);
168            }
169
170            return;
171        }
172
173        //decipher depending on keyguess
174        int tmpsum[]=new int[2];
175        tmpsum[0]=sum;
176        tmpsum[1]=sum;
177        if      (cipher[d][pip]) {
178            tmpsum[0]++;
179        } else {
180            tmpsum[1]++;
181        }
182
183
184
```

```
185        // going  deeper  into  the  tree  (recursively)
186        if  (keyPairNode.zero  !=  null)  {
187            deleteIllegalKeysForPair(cipher,keyPairNode.zero,d
                   ,e,pip+1,tmpsum[0]);
188        }
189        if  (keyPairNode.one  !=  null)  {
190            deleteIllegalKeysForPair(cipher,keyPairNode.one,d,
                   e,pip+1,tmpsum[1]);
191        }
192
193    }
194
195    private  void  deleteIllegalKeysForDice(boolean[][]  cipher,
           Node  keyPairNode,  int  d,  int  e,  int  pip,  int  sum1,  int
           sum2)  {
196        if  (sum2>sum1)  {
197            return;
198            // number  of  pips  different
199        }
200
201        if  (keyPairNode.isLeaf)  {
202            // we  are  counting,  starting  with  0
203            if  (sum2==sum1)  {
204                deleteMinorNode(keyPairNode,d,e);
205            }
206            return;
207        }
208
209        int  tmpsum[]=new  int[2];
210        tmpsum[0]=sum2;
211        tmpsum[1]=sum2;
212        if      (cipher[e][pip])  {
213            tmpsum[0]++;
214        } else  {
215            tmpsum[1]++;
216        }
217
218        if  (keyPairNode.zero  !=  null)  {
219            deleteIllegalKeysForDice(cipher,keyPairNode.zero,d
                   ,e,pip+1,sum1,tmpsum[0]);
220        }
221
222        if  (keyPairNode.one  !=  null)  {
223            deleteIllegalKeysForDice(cipher,keyPairNode.one,d,
                   e,pip+1,sum1,tmpsum[1]);
224        }
225
226    }
227
228
```

```java
229    private void deleteMajorNode(Node keyPairNode, int d, int
           e) {
230        Node father=keyPairNode.father;
231        boolean[] analogRoute;
232        if (keyPairNode.isBorderNode) {
233            // inject information of impossible key into
                  other pairs
234            // side effect, writes to boolean[] analogRoute !
235            analogRoute=setAnalogNodeRoute(keyPairNode);

237            for(int f=0;f<dices;f++) {
238                if (f==d) {continue;}
239                deleteAnalogNode(d,f, analogRoute);
240            }//for
241            // delete all 2nd dices who are the same or the
                  inverse like the first dice
242            // if they are part of the right dicePairs.
243            for(int f=0;f<dices;f++) {
244                if (f==d) {continue;}
245                deleteAnalogMinorNode(diceKeyPair[f][d],f,d,
                      analogRoute);
246            }//for
247        }// if (node.isBorderNode)
248        if (father.zero == keyPairNode) {
249            father.zero = null;
250            if (father.one == null) {deleteMajorNode(father,d,
                  e);}
251        }
252        if (father.one == keyPairNode) {
253            father.one = null;
254            if (father.zero == null) {deleteMajorNode(father,d
                  ,e);}
255        }
256    }

258    private void deleteAnalogNode(int d, int e, boolean[]
           analogRoute) {
259        Node node=diceKeyPair[d][e];
260        for(int i=0;i<pips;i++) {
261            if (node == null) {
262                return;
263                //node already deleted
264            }
265            if (analogRoute[i]) {node=node.one;}
266            else {node=node.zero;}
267        }
268        //Assumption: no empty BorderNodes are left!
269        if (node.isBorderNode) {deleteMajorNodeWithChilds(node
               , d, e);}
270    }
```

```
271    private void deleteMajorNodeWithChilds(Node keyPairNode,
           int d, int e) {
272    Node father=keyPairNode.father;
273
274        // correct counter, if node isLeaf
275        if (keyPairNode.isLeaf) {keysleft[d][e]--;}
276        // if childs traverse
277        if (keyPairNode.zero != null) {
278            deleteMajorNodeWithChilds(keyPairNode.zero, d, e);
279        }
280        if (keyPairNode.one != null) {
281            deleteMajorNodeWithChilds(keyPairNode.one, d, e);
282        }
283        if (keyPairNode.isBorderNode) {
284            keyPairNode.isBorderNode=false;
285            deleteMajorNode(keyPairNode, d, e);
286        } else {
287            // delete node
288            if (father.zero == keyPairNode) {
289                father.zero = null;
290            }
291            if (father.one == keyPairNode) {
292                father.one = null;
293            }
294        }
295    }
296
297    private void deleteMinorNode(Node node, int d, int e) {
298        if (node.isBorderNode()) {
299            // inject information to other keypairs
300            deleteMajorNode(node,d, e);
301            return;
302        }
303        // delete Node; if no neighbour is left, delete father
304        if (node.father.zero == node) {
305            node.father.zero = null;
306            if (node.father.one == null) {
307                deleteMinorNode(node.father,d,e);
308            }
309            node.father = null;
310            if (node.isLeafNode()) {keysleft[d][e]--;}
311        } else
312        if (node.father.one==node) {
313            node.father.one = null;
314            if (node.father.zero == null) {deleteMinorNode(
                   node.father,d,e);}
315            node.father = null;
316            if (node.isLeafNode()) {keysleft[d][e]--;}
317        }
318    }
```

```
319     private void deleteAnalogMinorNode(Node node, int d, int e
        , boolean[] analogRoute) {
320     Node walknode;
321     if (node.isBorderNode) {
322
323         // delete minor Node
324         walknode=node;
325         for(int i=0;i<pips;i++) {
326             if (walknode == null) {
327                 break;
328                 //node already deleted
329             }
330             if (analogRoute[i]) {
331                 walknode=walknode.one;
332             }
333             else {walknode=walknode.zero;}
334         }
335         if (walknode !=null) {
336             deleteMinorNode(walknode,d,e);
337         }
338
339         // delete inverse minor Node
340         walknode=node;
341         for(int i=0;i<pips;i++) {
342             if (walknode == null) {
343                 continue;
344                 //node already deleted
345             }
346             if (!analogRoute[i]) {
347                 walknode=walknode.one;
348             }
349             else {walknode=walknode.zero;}
350         }
351         if (walknode !=null) {
352             deleteMinorNode(walknode,d,e);
353         }
354     } else {
355         //noBorderNode
356         // traversing until BorderNode is arrived
357         if (node.zero != null) {
358             deleteAnalogMinorNode(node.zero, d, e,
                    analogRoute);
359         }
360         if (node.one != null) {
361             deleteAnalogMinorNode(node.one, d, e,
                    analogRoute);
362         }
363     }
364 }
365
```

```
366    private void cleanup() {
367        for(int d=0;d<dices;d++) {
368            for(int e=0;e<dices;e++) {
369                if (d==e) {continue;}
370                if ((keysleft[d][e]==1) &&
371                    (keysleft[e][d]>=1)
372                    ) {
373                    for(int f=0;f<dices;f++) {
374                        boolean[] cleanRoute;
375                        cleanRoute=setAnalogMinorNodeRoute(
                                diceKeyPair[d][e]);
376                        if (e==f) {continue;}
377                        if (keysleft[e][f]!=1) {
378                            cleanupXYtoYstar(
379                                diceKeyPair[e][f],e,f,0,false,
380                                cleanRoute);
381                        }
382                    }
383                }
384            }
385        }
386    }
387
388    private void cleanupXYtoYstar(Node node, int d, int e, int
            counter, boolean delete, boolean[] cleanRoute) {
389
390        if (node.isBorderNode) {
391            if (delete) {
392                deleteNodeWithChilds(node,d,e);
393            }
394            return;
395        }
396
397        if (node.zero != null) {
398            cleanupXYtoYstar(node.zero,d,e, counter+1, delete
                | cleanRoute[0] ^ cleanRoute[counter],
                cleanRoute);
399        }
400
401        if (node.one != null) {
402            cleanupXYtoYstar(node.one,d,e, counter+1, delete |
                ! ( cleanRoute[0] ^ cleanRoute[counter]),
                cleanRoute );
403        }
404
405    }
406
407
408
409
```

```
410    private void deleteNodeWithChilds(Node keyPairNode, int d,
                int e) {
411        Node father=keyPairNode.father;
412
413        // correct counter, if node isLeaf
414        if (keyPairNode.isLeaf) {
415            keysleft[d][e]--;
416        }
417
418        // if childs traverse
419        if (keyPairNode.zero != null) {
420            deleteNodeWithChilds(keyPairNode.zero, d, e);
421        }
422        if (keyPairNode.one != null) {
423            deleteNodeWithChilds(keyPairNode.one, d, e);
424        }
425        if (keyPairNode.isBorderNode) {
426            deleteMajorNode(keyPairNode, d, e);
427        } else {
428            // delete node
429            if (father.zero == keyPairNode) {
430                father.zero = null;
431            }
432            if (father.one == keyPairNode) {
433                father.one = null;
434            }
435            keyPairNode.father = null;
436        }
437    }
438
439    private boolean[] setAnalogNodeRoute(Node node, int
                position, boolean[] analogRoute) {
440        if (position >=0)
441        {
442            Node father=node.father;
443
444            setAnalogNodeRoute(father,
445                               position -1,
446                               analogRoute);
447
448            if (father.zero == node) {
449                analogRoute[position]=false;
450            }
451            if (father.one == node) {
452                analogRoute[position]=true;
453            }
454        }
455        return analogRoute;
456    }
457
```

```
458    private boolean[] setAnalogNodeRoute(Node node) {
459        // takes a BorderNode and returns the path from Root to
                 BorderNode
460        boolean[] analogRoute;
461        analogRoute=new boolean[pips];
462        return setAnalogNodeRoute(node, pips -1, analogRoute);
463    }
464
465
466    private boolean[] setAnalogMinorNodeRoute(Node node) {
467        boolean[] cleanRoute;
468        cleanRoute= new boolean[pips];
469        // side effect, writes to boolean[] cleanRoute !
470        Node walknode=node;
471        int position =0;
472        while (! walknode.isBorderNode) {
473            if (walknode.zero !=null) {
474                walknode=walknode.zero;
475                continue;
476            }
477            if (walknode.one !=null) {
478                walknode=walknode.one;
479                continue;
480            }
481            System.out.println("setAnalogMinorNodeRoute:
                     Should never happen! (isBorderNode)");
482            System.exit(2);
483        }
484
485        while (! walknode.isLeaf) {
486            if (walknode.zero !=null) {
487                walknode=walknode.zero;
488                cleanRoute[position++]=false;
489                continue;
490            }
491            if (walknode.one !=null) {
492                walknode=walknode.one;
493                cleanRoute[position++]=true;
494                continue;
495            }
496            System.out.println("setAnalogMinorNodeRoute:
                     Should never happen! (isLeaf)");
497            System.exit(2);
498        }
499        return cleanRoute;
500    }
501
502
503
504
```

```
505   private void setNodeValueFromTo(int d, int e) {
506       boolean inverse=false;
507       // side effect — writes to key[][] and keyfound[];
508       // assumes there is only one entry left in diceKeyPair
509       Node tmpnode=diceKeyPair[d][e];
510       int pip=0;
511       // take a look which dice is already recovered
512       // and use inverse for second dice if necessary
513       if (keyFound[d]) {
514           if (key[d][0]) {
515               inverse=true;
516           }
517       }
518       // diceKeypair always starts with false
519       // if key[d][0] is true inverse for 2nd keypair is
             needed
520       if (keyFound[e]) {
521           Node n=tmpnode;
522           while (! n.isBorderNode) {
523               if (n.zero != null) {
524                   n=n.zero;
525               } else {
526                   n=n.one;
527               }
528           }
529           // first bit of second dice
530           if ( n.zero!=null ) {
531               if (key[e][0]) {
532                   inverse=true;
533               }
534           }
535           if ( n.one!=null ) {
536               if (!key[e][0]) {inverse=true;}
537           }
538       } // if (keyFound[e])
539       while (! tmpnode.isBorderNode) {
540           if (tmpnode.zero != null) {
541               key[d][pip]=false^inverse;
542               tmpnode=tmpnode.zero;
543               pip++;
544               continue;
545           }
546           if (tmpnode.one != null) {
547               key[d][pip]=true^inverse;
548               tmpnode=tmpnode.one;
549               pip++;
550               continue;
551           }
552       } // while
553       pip=0;
```

```
554          while (! tmpnode.isLeaf) {
555              if (tmpnode.zero != null) {
556                  key[e][pip]=false^inverse;
557                  tmpnode=tmpnode.zero;
558                  pip++;
559                  continue;
560              }
561              if (tmpnode.one != null) {
562                  key[e][pip]=true^inverse;
563                  tmpnode=tmpnode.one;
564                  pip++;
565                  continue;
566              }
567              printStatus();
568              System.out.println("setNodeValueFromTo_(Leaf):_"+d
                      +"_"+_"+e+"_"+pip);
569              System.exit(1);
570          } // while
571          keyFound[d]=true;
572          keyFound[e]=true;
573      }
574
575      private void printPossibleKeysHelper(Node root, int level)
                  {
576          if (root.zero != null) {
577              System.out.print("0");
578              printPossibleKeysHelper(root.zero,level+1);
579          }
580          if (root.one != null) {
581              if (root.zero !=null) for(int i=1;
582              i<=level;
583              i++) {
584                  if (i==pips) System.out.print(".");
585                  else System.out.print("_");
586              }
587              System.out.print("1");
588              printPossibleKeysHelper(root.one,level+1);
589          }
590          if (root.isLeaf) {
591              System.out.println();
592          }
593      }
594  } // end VisualCodingsPossibleKeys2
```

Probabilities of Hamming Differences

Listing 11.6: Functions to Compute the Probabilities of Hamming Differences of Dice Encoded Uniformly Distributed Characters

```
 1  /* helper functions */
 2
 3  define abs(n){
 4          if(n<0)return(−n)
 5          return(n)
 6  }
 7
 8  define max(a,b){
 9          if(a<b)return(b)
10          return(a)
11  }
12
13  define min(a,b){
14          if(a>b)return(b)
15          return(a)
16  }
17
18
19  define binomial(n,k){
20      auto c,i
21      if (k>n)    return(0)
22      if (k>n−k) k=n−k
23      c=1
24      for(i=0;i<k;i++) {
25              c=c*(n − i)
26              c=c/(i + 1)
27      }
28      return(c)
29  }
30
31  define mod(a,b){
32      auto c,s
33      s=scale
34      scale=0
35      /* required for % to work properly due to bc's computation */
36      c=a%b
37      scale=s
38      if(a>=0)    return(c)
39      if(c==0)    return(0)
40      return(c+b)
41  }
42
43
44
```

```
45   define factorial(n){
46       auto i,s
47       s=1
48       for(i=1;i<=n;i++)     s=s*i
49       return(s)
50   }
51
52   define prob_binomial(n,p,k){
53       auto prod,i
54       if((k<0)||(n<0)||(p<0)||(p>1)||(k>n))return(0)
55       prod=binomial(n,k)
56       for(i=1;i<=k;i++) {
57             prod=prod*p
58       }
59       for(i=1;i<=n-k;i++) {
60             prod=prod*(1-p)
61       }
62       return(prod)
63   }
64
65   /* draw "n" from "t" marbles without replacement */
66   /* "m" marbles are considered 'success' */
67   /* function computes probability of "k" successes */
68   define hypergeometric(t,n,m,k){
69       if((t<0)||(n<0)||(m<0)||(k<0))return(0)
70       if((n>t)||(m>t)||(k>m)||(k>n))return(0)
71
72       return(binomial(m,k)*binomial(t-m,n-k)/binomial(t,n))
73   }
74
75   /*   main function */
76   define prob_ham_dice(n,y) {
77       auto i,j,k,sum,index
78       scale=20
79       sum=0
80       for(k=0;k<=n;k++) { p[k]=0 }
81       for(i=0;i<=n;i++) {
82           for(j=0;j<=n;j++) {
83               for(k=max(0,i-j);k<=min(i,n-j);k++) {
84                   p[j-i+2*k]=p[j-i+2*k]+hypergeometric(n,i,n-j,k);
85               }
86           }
87       }
88
89       for(k=0;k<=n;k++) {
90           p[k]=p[k]/((n+1)*(n+1))
91           sum=sum+p[k]
92       }
93       return(p[y])
94   }
```

```
 95   define prob_ham_cond_obs(n,ham,obs) {
 96       auto denom,numer,i
 97       denom=0
 98       for(i=0;(i<=obs)&&(i<=n);i++) {
 99       if (obs-i>n) continue
100       denom=denom+prob_ham_dice(n,i)*prob_binomial(n,1/2,obs-i)
101       }
102       numer=prob_ham_dice(9,ham)*prob_binomial(n,1/2,obs-ham)
103       return(numer/denom)
104   }
```

Bibliography

[AA04]   Dmitri Asonov and Rakesh Agrawal. Keyboard acoustic emanations. In *IEEE Symposium on Security and Privacy*, pages 3–11. IEEE Computer Society, 2004.

[ABCS05]   Ross Anderson, Mike Bond, Jolyon Clulow, and Sergei Skorobogatov. Cryptographic processors - a survey. Technical Report 641, University of Cambridge – Computer Laboratory, August 2005.

[ABCS06]   Ross Anderson, Mike Bond, Jolyon Clulow, and Sergei Skorobogatov. Cryptographic processors - a survey. *Proceedings of the IEEE*, 94(2):357–369, Feb. 2006.

[ABF$^+$02]   Christian Aumüller, Peter Bier, Wieland Fischer, Peter Hofreiter, and Jean-Pierre Seifert. Fault attacks on RSA with CRT: Concrete results and practical countermeasures. In Kaliski Jr. et al. [KcKKP03], pages 261–276.

[AD97]   Miklós Ajtai and Cynthia Dwork. A public-key cryptosystem with worst-case/average-case equivalence. In *STOC '97: Proceedings of the twenty-ninth annual ACM symposium on Theory of computing*, pages 284–293, New York, NY, USA, 1997. ACM.

[ADDS91]   Dennis G. Abraham, George M. Dolan, Glen P. Double, and James V. Stevens. Transaction security system. *IBM Systems Journal – Special issue on cryptology*, 30(2):206–229, March 1991.

[Adl03]   Andy Adler. Sample images can be independently restored from face recognition templates. In *Electrical and Computer Engineering, 2003. IEEE CCECE 2003. Canadian Conference on*, volume 2, pages 1163–1166 vol.2, 2003.

[AH99]   Leonard M. Adleman and Ming-Deh A. Huang. Function field sieve method for discrete logarithms over finite fields. *Information and Computation*, 151(1-2):5–16, 1999.

[AJH07]   Arathi Arakala, Jason Jeffers, and K. J. Horadam. Fuzzy extractors for minutiae-based fingerprint authentication. In Lee and Li [LL07], pages 760–769.

[AK96]   Ross Anderson and Markus Kuhn. Tamper resistance — a cautionary note. In *Proceedings of the Second Usenix Workshop on Electronic Commerce*, pages 1–11, 1996.

[AK98]   Ross Anderson and Markus Kuhn. Low cost attacks on tamper resistant devices. In Bruce Christianson, Bruno Crispo, Mark Lomas, and Michael Roe, editors, *Security Protocols*, volume 1361 of *Lecture Notes in Computer Science*, pages 125–136. Springer Berlin Heidelberg, 1998.

[AKG13]   Scott Aaronson, Greg Kuperberg, and Christopher Granade. The complexity zoo. https://complexityzoo.uwaterloo.ca/Complexity_Zoo, 2013. last access 2013/05/13.

[AMD09]   AMD.   AMD Athlon X2 model number and feature comparisons. http://www.amd.com/us/products/desktop/processors/athlon-x2/Pages/AMD-athlon-x2-processor-model-numbers-feature-comparison.aspx, 2009. last access 2013/06/19.

[AMS⁺11]   Frederik Armknecht, Roel Maes, Ahmad-Reza Sadeghi, François-Xavier Standaert, and Christian Wachsmann. A formalization of the security features of physical functions. In *IEEE Symposium on Security and Privacy*, pages 397–412. IEEE Computer Society, 2011.

[And03]   Ross Anderson. Cryptography and competition policy: issues with 'trusted computing'. In *Proceedings of the twenty-second annual symposium on Principles of distributed computing*, PODC '03, pages 3–10, New York, NY, USA, 2003. ACM.

[AriCE]   Aristotle. *On Sense and the Sensible*. 350 B.C.E. translated by J. I. Beare.

[Art93]   Michael Artin. *Algebra*. Birkhäuser advanced texts. Birkhäuser Verlag, Basel, translated by Annette A'Campo, original published 1991 in English edition, 1993.

[Art11]   Charles Arthur. DigiNotar SSL certificate hack amounts to cyberwar, says expert. the guardian, http://www.guardian.co.uk/technology/2011/sep/05/diginotar-certificate-hack-cyberwar, September 2011. last access 2013/06/14.

[Ass63]   American Standards Association. American standard code for information interchange. ASA X3.4-1963, June 17 1963.

[Ass04]   ITU Radiocommunication Assembly. Recommendation ITU-R M.1677: International Morse code, 2004.

[AV13]   Virtual Applications and Implementations Research Lab (VAMPIRE). The side channel cryptanalysis lounge – What is already known? http://www.crypto.ruhr-uni-bochum.de/en_sclounge.html, 2013.

[BA09]   Inc. Biometric Associates. The BAI authenticator smart card datasheet. Technical report, rev. 05-2009 from http://www.biometricassociates.com/, 2009.

[Bar93]   Hans-Jochen Bartsch. *Taschenbuch mathematischer Formeln*. Fachbuchverlag Leipzig-Köln, 15. neubearbeitete edition, 1993. ISBN 3-343-00844-3.

[Bau83]   D.W Bauder. An anti-counterfeiting concept for currency systems. Technical Report PTK-11990, Sandia National Labs. Albuquerque, NM, 1983.

[BB87]   Pierre Beauchemin and Gilles Brassard. A generalization of hellman's extension of shannon's approach to cryptography (abstract). In Pomerance [Pom88], page 461.

[BB88]   Pierre Beauchemin and Gilles Brassard. A generalization of hellman's extension to shannon's approach to cryptography. *J. Cryptology*, 1(2):129–131, 1988.

[BB04]   Dan Boneh and Xavier Boyen. Short signatures without random oracles. In Christian Cachin and Jan Camenisch, editors, *EUROCRYPT*, volume 3027 of *Lecture Notes in Computer Science*, pages 56–73. Springer, 2004.

[BB07]   Mike Barwise and Daniel Bachfeld. Attack of the card cloners. IT security news and services at heise Security UK, 2007.

[BBB⁺08]   Heinz Biermann, Manfred Bromba, Christoph Busch, Gerrit Hornung, Martin Meints, and Gisela Quiring-Kock. White Paper zum Datenschutz in der Biometrie. Technical report, TeleTrusT Deutschland e.V., Verein zur Förderung der Vertrauenswürdigkeit von Informations- und Kommunikationstechnik, 2008. Edition March 2008.

[BBS04]   Dan Boneh, Xavier Boyen, and Hovav Shacham. Short group signatures. In Franklin [Fra04], pages 41–55.

[BBV02]   Luca Bechelli, Stefano Bistarelli, and Anna Vaccarelli. Biometrics authentication with smartcard. Technical Report IIT TR -8/2002, Istituto di Informatica e Telematica (IIT), Istituto di Informatica e Telematica (IIT), 2002.

[BC94]   Stefan Brands and David Chaum. Distance-bounding protocols. In *EUROCRYPT '93: Workshop on the theory and application of cryptographic techniques on Advances in cryptology*, pages 344–359, Secaucus, NJ, USA, 1994. Springer-Verlag New York, Inc.

[BC09]   Jeffrey P. Bigham and Anna Cavender. Evaluating existing audio captchas and an interface optimized for non-visual use. In Dan R. Olsen Jr., Richard B. Arthur, Ken Hinckley, Meredith Ringel Morris, Scott E. Hudson, and Saul Greenberg, editors, *CHI*, pages 1829–1838. ACM, 2009.

[BCD⁺09]   Michael Backes, Tongbo Chen, Markus Dürmuth, Hendrik P. A. Lensch, and Martin Welk. Tempest in a teapot: Compromising reflections revisited. In *IEEE Symposium on Security and Privacy*, pages 315–327. IEEE Computer Society, 2009.

[BCP⁺02]   Boris Balacheff, Liqun Chen, Siani Pearson, David Plaquin, and Graeme Proudler. *Trusted Computing Platforms: TCPA Technology in Context*. Prentice Hall, 2002.

[BD90]   Thomas Beth and Yvo Desmedt. Identification tokens - or: Solving the chess grandmaster problem. In Alfred Menezes and Scott A. Vanstone, editors, *CRYPTO*, volume 537 of *Lecture Notes in Computer Science*, pages 169–177. Springer, 1990.

[BDJR97]   Mihir Bellare, Anand Desai, E. Jokipii, and Phillip Rogaway. A concrete security treatment of symmetric encryption. In *Proceedings of 38th Annual Symposium on Foundations of Computer Science (FOCS 97)*, pages 394–403, 1997.

[BDL97]   Dan Boneh, Richard A. DeMillo, and Richard J. Lipton. On the importance of checking cryptographic protocols for faults (extended abstract). In W. Fumy, editor, *Advances in Cryptology - EUROCRYPT '97*, volume 1233, pages 37–51. Springer-Verlag, 1997.

[BDPR98]   Mihir Bellare, Anand Desai, David Pointcheval, and Phillip Rogaway. Relations among notions of security for public-key encryption schemes. In H. Krawczyk, editor, *Advances in Cryptology – Crypto 98 Proceedings*, volume 1462 of *Lecture Notes in Computer Science*, pages 26–46, Berlin – Heidelberg, 1998. Springer Verlag.

[BDPR01]   Mihir Bellare, Anand Desai, David Pointcheval, and Phillip Rogaway. Relations among notions of security for public-key encryption schemes. Full paper, Juni 2001.

[BDSS03]   Carlo Blundo, Paolo D'Arco, Alfredo De Santis, and Douglas R. Stinson. Contrast optimal threshold visual cryptography schemes. *SIAM J. Discrete Math.*, 16(2):224–261, 2003.

[BDU08]   Michael Backes, Markus Dürmuth, and Dominique Unruh. Compromising reflections-or-how to read LCD monitors around the corner. In *IEEE Symposium on Security and Privacy*, pages 158–169. IEEE Computer Society, 2008.

[BDZ03]   Feng Bao, Robert H. Deng, and Huafei Zhu. Variations of Diffie-Hellman problem. In Sihan Qing, Dieter Gollmann, and Jianying Zhou, editors, *ICICS*, volume 2836 of *Lecture Notes in Computer Science*, pages 301–312. Springer, 2003.

[Ben38]   Frank Benford. The law of anomalous numbers. In *Proceedings of the American Philosophical Society*, volume 78, pages 551–572, March 1938.

[BFM88]   Manuel Blum, Paul Feldman, and Silvio Micali. Non-interactive zero-knowledge and its applications. In *STOC '88: Proceedings of the twentieth annual ACM symposium on Theory of computing*, pages 103–112, New York, NY, USA, 1988. ACM.

[BGdMM05] Lucas Ballard, Matthew Green, Breno de Medeiros, and Fabian Monrose. Correlation-resistant storage via keyword-searchable encryption. Cryptology ePrint Archive, Report 2005/417, 2005. http://eprint.iacr.org/.

[Bio06]   BioAPI specification version 2.0 (ISO/IEC 19784-1:2006), 2006.

[BJR⁺06]   John Brainard, Ari Juels, Ronald Rivest, Michael Szydlo, and Moti Yung. Fourth factor authentication: Somebody you know. In *CCS '06: Proceedings of the 13th ACM conference on Computer and communications security*, pages 168–178, New York, NY, USA, 2006. ACM.

[BL96]   Dan Boneh and Richard J. Lipton. Algorithms for black-box fields and their application to cryptography (extended abstract). In Koblitz [Kob96], pages 283–297.

[BL12]   Foteini Baldimtsi and Anna Lysyanskaya. Anonymous credentials light. Cryptology ePrint Archive, Report 2012/298, 2012. http://eprint.iacr. org/.

[Bla79]   George Robert Blakley. Safeguarding cryptographic keys. In *Proceedings of the National Computer Conference*, volume 48, pages 313–317, 1979.

[Bla80]   George Robert Blakley. One time pads are key safeguarding schemes, not cryptosystems fast key safeguarding schemes (threshold schemes) exist. In *IEEE Symposium on Security and Privacy*, pages 108–113, 1980.

[Ble98]   Gerrit Bleumer. Biometric yet privacy protecting person authentication. *Lecture Notes in Computer Science*, 1525:99–110, 1998.

[Bon98]   Dan Boneh. The decision Diffie-Hellman problem. In Joe Buhler, editor, *ANTS*, volume 1423 of *Lecture Notes in Computer Science*, pages 48–63. Springer, 1998.

[Bon99]   Dan Boneh. Twenty years of attacks on the RSA cryptosystem. *Notices of the AMS*, 46(2):203–213, 1999.

[Bor07]   Bernd Borchert. Segment-based visual cryptography. Technical Report WSI-2007-04, Wilhelm-Schickard-Institut für Informatik, Tübingen, 2007.

[Bou54]   Nicolas Bourbaki. *Théorie des ensembles. Livre I, Chapitres 1-2*. Collection: Les structures fondamentales de l'analyse; I Elèments de mathématique: première partie; fasc. XVII Actualits scientifiques et industrielles. Hermann, Paris, 1954.

[Boy04]   Xavier Boyen. Reusable cryptographic fuzzy extractors. In *CCS '04: Proceedings of the 11th ACM conference on Computer and communications security*, pages 82–91, New York, NY, USA, 2004. ACM.

[BP81]   Richard P. Brent and John M. Pollard. Factorization of the eighth Fermat number. *Mathematics of Computation*, 36:627–630, 1981.

[BP97]   Niko Baric and Birgit Pfitzmann. Collision-free accumulators and failstop signature schemes without trees. In *EUROCRYPT 97*, volume 1233 of *Advances in Cryptology*, pages 480–494, 1997.

[BPS00]   Olivier Baudron, David Pointcheval, and Jacques Stern. Extended notions of security for multicast public key cryptosystems. In U. Montanari, J. D. P.

Rolim, and E. Welzl, editors, *Proceedings of the 27th International Colloquium on Automata, Languages and Programming 2000*, volume 1853 of *Lecture Notes in Computer Science*, pages 499–511, Berlin – Heidelberg, Februar 2000. Springer Verlag.

[BR94]   Mihir Bellare and Phillip Rogaway. Optimal asymmetric encryption – how to encrypt with RSA. In A. de Santis, editor, *Advances in Cryptology – Eurocrypt 94 Proceedings*, volume 950 of *Lecture Notes in Computer Science*. Springer Verlag, 1994.

[BR95a]   Mihir Bellare and Phillip Rogaway. Optimal asymmetric encryption – how to encrypt with RSA. Technical report, University of California, 1995.

[BR95b]   Mihir Bellare and Phillip Rogaway. Random oracles are practical: A paradigm for designing efficient protocols. In *First ACM Conference on Computer an Communications Security*. ACM, Februar 1995.

[BR96]   Mihir Bellare and Phillip Rogaway. The exact security of digital signatures - how to sign with RSA and Rabin. In *EUROCRYPT*, pages 399–416, 1996.

[BR08]   Bernd Borchert and Klaus Reinhardt. Anti-tapping and manipulation encoding for online accounts. Patent Publication Number WO/2008/128528, International Application Number PCT/DE2008/000688, International Patent Classification G09C 5/00 (2006.01), October 2008.

[Bra94]   Braille Authority of North America. *English Braille American Edition*. Number 7-35931-00. American Printing House for the Blind, revised 2002 edition, 1994.

[Bra99]   Stefan Brands. A technical overview of digital credentials, 1999.

[Bra07]   Stefan Brands. The identity corner. http://idcorner.org, June 2007. site extinct, accessible via http://web.archive.org.

[Bra13]   Stefan Brands. Credentica homepage. http://www.credentica.com/, May 2013. last accessed 13/05/30.

[Bre80]   Richard P. Brent. An improved Monte Carlo factorization algorithm. *BIT*, 20:176–184, 1980.

[Bre00]   Richard P. Brent. Recent progress and prospects for integer factorisation algorithms. In Ding-Zhu Du, Peter Eades, Vladimir Estivill-Castro, Xuemin Lin, and Arun Sharma, editors, *Computing and Combinatorics*, volume 1858 of *Lecture Notes in Computer Science*, pages 3–22. Springer Berlin Heidelberg, 2000.

[BS99]   Mihir Bellare and Amit Sahai. Non-malleable encryption: Equivalence between two notions, and an indistinguishability-based characterization. In Michael J. Wiener, editor, *Advances in Cryptology – Crypto 99 Proceedings*, volume 1666 of *Lecture Notes in Computer Science*, pages 519–536, Berlin – Heidelberg, Februar 1999. Springer Verlag.

[BS02]   Dan Boneh and Alice Silverberg. Applications of multilinear forms to cryptography. *Contemporary Mathematics*, 324:71–90, 2002.

[BS03]   Johannes Blömer and Jean-Pierre Seifert. Fault based cryptanalysis of the advanced encryption standard (AES). In *Financial Cryptography'03*, pages 162–181. Springer-Verlag, 2003.

[BSB05]   Daniel J. Barrett, Richard E. Silverman, and Robert G. Byrnes. *SSH: The Secure Shell: The Definitive Guide*. O'Reilly, 2nd edition, 2005. ISBN 0-596-00895-3.

[BSKS10]   Heike Busch, Miroslava Sotkov, Stefan Katzenbeisser, and Radu Sion. The puf promise. In Alessandro Acquisti, SeanW. Smith, and Ahmad-Reza Sadeghi, editors, *Trust and Trustworthy Computing*, volume 6101 of *Lecture Notes in Computer Science*, pages 290–297. Springer Berlin Heidelberg, 2010.

[BSN00]   Carlo Blundo, Alfredo De Santis, and Moni Naor. Visual cryptography for grey level images. *Inf. Process. Lett.*, 75(6):255–259, 2000.

[BSS99]   Carlo Blundo, Alfredo De Santis, and Douglas R. Stinson. On the contrast in visual cryptography schemes. *J. Cryptology*, 12(4):261–289, 1999.

[BSSB06]   Abhilasha Bhargav-Spantzel, Anna Squicciarini, and Elisa Bertino. Privacy preserving multi-factor authentication with biometrics. In *DIM '06: Proceedings of the second ACM workshop on Digital identity management*, pages 63–72, New York, NY, USA, 2006. ACM.

[BT09]   Claude Barral and Assia Tria. Fake fingers in fingerprint recognition: Glycerin supersedes gelatin. In Véronique Cortier, Claude Kirchner, Mitsuhiro Okada, and Hideki Sakurada, editors, *Formal to Practical Security*, volume 5458 of *Lecture Notes in Computer Science*, pages 57–69. Springer Berlin Heidelberg, 2009.

[Buc99]   Johannes Buchmann. *Einführung in die Kryptographie*. Springer Lehrbuch. Springer Verlag, Berlin – Heidelberg – New York, 1999.

[BV98]   Dan Boneh and Ramarathnam Venkatesan. Breaking RSA may not be equivalent to factoring. In *EUROCRYPT*, pages 59–71, 1998.

[BVO11]   David Barrera and Paul Van Oorschot. Secure software installation on smartphones. *Security Privacy, IEEE*, 9(3):42–48, 2011.

[Cam08]   Kim Cameron. Fingerprint charade. Kim Cameron's Identity Weblog, `http://www.identityblog.com/?p=981`, May 2008. last access 2013/05/21.

[Cam13]   Kim Cameron. Kim Cameron's identity weblog; identityblog – digital identity, privacy, and the internet's missing identity layer. `http://www.identityblog.com`, 2013. last access 2013/05/21.

[Can05]   Ran Canetti. Decisional Diffie-Hellman assumption. In Henk C. A. van Tilborg, editor, *Encyclopedia of Cryptography and Security*. Springer, 2005.

[CB09]   Rajat Subhra Chakraborty and Swarup Bhunia. Security against hardware trojan through a novel application of design obfuscation. In *ICCAD '09: Proceedings of the 2009 International Conference on Computer-Aided Design*, pages 113–116, New York, NY, USA, 2009. ACM.

[CC02]   Chin-Chen Chang and Jun-Chou Chuang. An image intellectual property protection scheme for gray-level images using visual secret sharing strategy. *Pattern Recognition Letters*, 23(8):931–94, 2002.

[CCI90]   Elliot J. Chikofsky and James H. Cross II. Reverse engineering and design recovery: a taxonomy reverse engineering and design recovery: a taxonomy. *Software, IEEE*, 7(1):13–17, 1990.

[CE87]   David Chaum and Jan-Hendrik Evertse. A secure and privacy-protecting protocol for transmitting personal information between organizations. In *Proceedings on Advances in cryptology – CRYPTO '86*, pages 118–167, London, UK, 1987. Springer Verlag.

[CFN88]   David Chaum, Amos Fiat, and Moni Naor. Untraceable electronic cash. In Shafi Goldwasser, editor, *CRYPTO*, volume 403 of *Lecture Notes in Computer Science*, pages 319–327. Springer, 1988.

[CGG86]   Benny Chor, Oded Goldreich, and Shafi Goldwasser. The bit security of modular squaring given partial factorization of the modulos. In *Lecture notes in computer sciences; 218 on Advances in cryptology—CRYPTO 85*, pages 448–457, New York, NY, USA, 1986. Springer-Verlag New York, Inc.

[CGH98]   Ran Canetti, Oded Goldreich, and Shai Halevi. The random oracle methodology, revisited. Cryptology ePrint Archive, Report 1998/011, 1998. http://eprint.iacr.org/.

[CGM05]   Michel Crouhy, Dan Galai, and Robert Mark. *The Essentials of Risk Management*. McGraw-Hill, 1 edition, December 14 2005.

[Cha79]   David Chaum. Computer systems established, maintained, and trusted by mutually suspicious groups. Technical Report UCBIERL M79/10, University of California,Berkeley, CA, February 1979.

[Cha83a]   David Chaum. Blind signature system. In David Chaum, editor, *Advances in Cryptology – CRYPTO '83*, page 153, New York, 1983. Plenum Press.

[Cha83b]   David Chaum. Blind signatures for untraceable payments. In D. Chaum, R.L. Rivest, and A.T. Sherman, editors, *Advances in Cryptology Proceedings of Crypto 82*, pages 199–203, 1983.

[Cha84]   David Chaum. How to keep a secret alive: Extensible partial key, key safeguarding, and threshold systems. In *CRYPTO*, pages 481–485, 1984.

[Cha85]   David Chaum. Security without identification: transaction systems to make big brother obsolete. *Communications of the ACM*, 28(10):1030–1044, 1985.

[Cha89]   David Chaum. Privacy protected payments: Unconditional payer and/or payee untraceability. In David Chaum and Ingrid Schaumueller-Bichl, editors, *Smart Card 2000: The Future of IC Cards*, pages 69–93, North-Holland, 1989.

[Cha02]   David Chaum. Secret-ballot receipts and transparent integrity. In *Palo Alto Workshop on Information Dynamics in the Networked Economy*, 2002.

[Cha06]   Rafik Chaabouni. Break wep faster with statistical analysis. Technical report, EPFL, LASEC, June 2006.

[CHK$^+$06a] Jan Camenisch, Susan Hohenberger, Markulf Kohlweiss, Anna Lysyanskaya, and Mira Meyerovich. How to win the clonewars: efficient periodic n-times anonymous authentication. In *CCS '06: Proceedings of the 13th ACM conference on Computer and communications security*, pages 201–210, New York, NY, USA, 2006. ACM Press.

[CHK$^+$06b] Jan Camenisch, Susan Hohenberger, Markulf Kohlweiss, Anna Lysyanskaya, and Mira Meyerovich. How to win the clonewars: efficient periodic n-times anonymous authentication. Full version of an extended abstract published in Proceedings of ACM CCS 2006, ACM Press, 2006. 2006/454, IACR Cryptology ePrint Archive, 2006.

[Cia81]   Steve Ciarcia. *Build your own Z80 computer: design guidelines and application notes*. Byte Books. Circuit Cellar, October 1981.

[CKL03]   T. Charles Clancy, Negar Kiyavash, and Dennis J. Lin. Secure smartcard-based fingerprint authentication. In *Proceedings of the 2003 ACM SIGMM workshop on Biometrics methods and applications*, WBMA '03, pages 45–52, New York, NY, USA, 2003. ACM.

[CL01]   Jan Camenisch and Anna Lysyanskaya. An efficient system for non-transferable anonymous credentials with optional anonymity revocation. In *EUROCRYPT*, volume 2045 of *Lecture Notes in Computer Science*, pages 93–118, 2001.

[CL13]   Sébastien Canard and Roch Lescuyer. Protecting privacy by sanitizing personal data: a new approach to anonymous credentials. In *Proceedings of the 8th ACM SIGSAC symposium on Information, computer and communications security*, ASIA CCS '13, pages 381–392, New York, NY, USA, 2013. ACM.

[CLLW92]   Liam D. Comerford, Peter G. Ledermann, Lawrence I. Levy, and Steve R. White. Tamper resistant packaging for information protection in electronic circuitry, May 1992.

[CM07]   Jean-Sebastien Coron and Alexander May. Deterministic polynomial-time equivalence of computing the RSA secret key and factoring. *Journal of Cryptology*, 20(1):39–50, 2007.

[CNO08]   Nicolas T. Courtois, Karsten Nohl, and Sean O'Neil. Algebraic attacks on the Crypto-1 stream cipher in MiFare classic and Oyster cards. Technical Report 2008-166, Cryptology ePrint Archive., 2008.

[Cop93]   Don Coppersmith. Modifications to the number field sieve. *Journal of Cryptology*, 6(3):169–180, 1993.

[CP93]   David Chaum and Torben P. Pedersen. Wallet databases with observers. In *CRYPTO '92: Proceedings of the 12th Annual International Cryptology Conference on Advances in Cryptology*, volume 740, pages 89–105, London, UK, 1993. Springer Verlag.

[CPS04]   Stelvio Cimato, Roberto De Prisco, and Alfredo De Santis. Colored visual cryptography without color darkening. In Carlo Blundo and Stelvio Cimato, editors, *SCN*, volume 3352 of *Lecture Notes in Computer Science*, pages 235–248. Springer, 2004.

[CPS05]   Stelvio Cimato, Roberto De Prisco, and Alfredo De Santis. Optimal colored threshold visual cryptography schemes. *Des. Codes Cryptography*, 35(3):311–335, 2005.

[CPS06]   Stelvio Cimato, Roberto De Prisco, and Alfredo De Santis. Probabilistic visual cryptography schemes. *Comput. J.*, 49(1):97–107, 2006.

[CPS07]   Stelvio Cimato, Roberto De Prisco, and Alfredo De Santis. Colored visual cryptography without color darkening. *Theor. Comput. Sci.*, 374(1-3):261–276, 2007.

[CR07]   Ee-Chien Chang and Sujoy Roy. Robust extraction of secret bits from minutiae. In Lee and Li [LL07], pages 750–759.

[CS98]   Ronald Cramer and Victor Shoup. A practical public key cryptosystem provably secure against adaptive chosen ciphertext attack. In Hugo Krawczyk, editor, *CRYPTO*, volume 1462 of *Lecture Notes in Computer Science*, pages 13–25. Springer, 1998.

[CS03]   Jan Camenisch and Victor Shoup. Practical verifiable encryption and decryption of discrete logarithms. In Dan Boneh, editor, *CRYPTO*, volume 2729 of *Lecture Notes in Computer Science*, pages 126–144. Springer, 2003.

[CSFM05]   Stelvio Cimato, Alfredo De Santis, Anna Lisa Ferrara, and Barbara Masucci. Ideal contrast visual cryptography schemes with reversing. *Inf. Process. Lett.*, 93(4):199–206, 2005.

[CTW08]   Tzung-Her Chen, Kai-Hsiang Tsao, and Chang-Sian Wu. Multi-secrets visual secret sharing. In *The 14th Asia-Pacific Conference on Communications*, pages 1–5, Akihabara, Tokyo, Japan, October 14-16 2008.

[CvH91]   David Chaum and Eugène van Heyst. Group signatures. In *Advances in Cryptology – EUROCRYPT '91*, LNCS, pages 257–265, 1991.

[CvO13]   Jeremy Clark and Paul C. van Oorschot. SSL and HTTPS: Revisiting past challenges and evaluating certificate trust model enhancements. In *IEEE Symposium on Security and Privacy*, May 2013.

[CWP$^+$09]   Rajat Subhra Chakraborty, Francis G. Wolff, Somnath Paul, Christos A. Papachristou, and Swarup Bhunia. Mero: A statistical approach for hardware trojan detection. In Christophe Clavier and Kris Gaj, editors, *CHES*, volume 5747 of *Lecture Notes in Computer Science*, pages 396–410. Springer, 2009.

[Dam07a]   Ivan Damgård. A "proof-reading" of some issues in cryptography. http://www.daimi.au.dk/~ivan/positionpaper.pdf, 2007. Updated version of [Dam07b].

[Dam07b]   Ivan Damgård. A "proof-reading" of some issues in cryptography. In Lars Arge, Christian Cachin, Tomasz Jurdzinski, and Andrzej Tarlecki, editors, *ICALP*, volume 4596 of *Lecture Notes in Computer Science*, pages 2–11. Springer, 2007.

[Dan63]   George Dantzig. *Linear programming and extensions*. Princeton University Press, 1963.

[Dan03]   George Danezis. Statistical disclosure attacks. In Dimitris Gritzalis, Sabrina De Capitani di Vimercati, Pierangela Samarati, and Sokratis K. Katsikas, editors, *SEC*, volume 250 of *IFIP Conference Proceedings*, pages 421–426. Kluwer, 2003.

[dB90]   Bert den Boer. Diffie-hellman is as strong as discrete log for certain primes. In *CRYPTO '88: Proceedings on Advances in cryptology*, pages 530–539, New York, NY, USA, 1990. Springer-Verlag New York, Inc.

[DDN91]   Danny Dolev, Cynthia Dwork, and Moni Naor. Non-malleable crypotography. In *Proceedings of the 23rd ACM Symposium of Theory of Computing 1991*, pages 542–552. ACM, 1991.

[DDN95]   Danny Dolev, Cynthia Dwork, and Moni Naor. Non-malleable crypotography. Technical Report CS95–27, Weizmann Institute of Science, 1995.

[DDN00]   Danny Dolev, Cynthia Dwork, and Moni Naor. Non-malleable crypotography. *Society for Industrial and Applied Mathematics Journal on Computing*, 30(2):391–437, März 2000.

[DDP06]   Ivan Damgård, Kasper Dupont, and Michael Østergaard Pedersen. Unclonable group identification. In Vaudenay [Vau06], pages 555–572.

[Dei10]   Oliver Deiser. *Einführung in die Mengenlehre: Die Mengenlehre Georg Cantors und ihre Axiomatisierung durch Ernst Zermelo*. Springer Verlag, 3rd edition, 2010.

[DeL84]   John M. DeLaurentis. A further weakness in the common modulus protocol for the RSA cryptoalgorithm. *Cryptologia*, 8:253–259, 1984.

[Den06a]   Alexander W. Dent. The cramer-shoup encryption scheme is plaintext aware in the standard model. In Vaudenay [Vau06], pages 289–307.

[Den06b] Alexander W. Dent. Fundamental problems in provable security and crypto-graphy. *Philosophical Transactions of the Royal Society A: Mathematical, Physical and Engineering Sciences*, 364(1849):3215–3230, December 2006.

[DG98] Ed Dawson and Helen Gustafson. A method for measuring entropy of symmetric cipher key generators. *Computers & Security*, 17(2):177–184, 1998.

[DH76] Whitfield Diffie and Martin Hellman. New directions in cryptography. *IEEE Transactions on Information Theory*, 22(6):644–654, 1976.

[Dil12] Clay Dillow. A fingerprint scanner that can capture prints from 20 feet away. `http://www.popsci.com/technology/article/2012-06/fingerprint-scanner-captures-prints-20-feet-away`, June 2012. last accessed 2013/05/25.

[DKL⁺98] Jean-François Dhem, François Koeune, Philippe-Alexandre Leroux, Patrick Mestré, Jean-Jacques Quisquater, and Jean-Louis Willems. A practical implementation of the timing attack. In Jean-Jacques Quisquater and Bruce Schneier, editors, *CARDIS*, volume 1820 of *Lecture Notes in Computer Science*, pages 167–182. Springer, 1998.

[DKRS06] Yevgeniy Dodis, Jonathan Katz, Leonid Reyzin, and Adam Smith. Robust fuzzy extractors and authenticated key agreement from close secrets. In Cynthia Dwork, editor, *Advances in Cryptology - CRYPTO 2006*, volume 4117 of *Lecture Notes in Computer Science*, pages 232–250. Springer Berlin Heidelberg, 2006.

[DLN97] Cynthia Dwork, Jeff Lotspiech, and Moni Naor. Digital signets: Self-enforcing protection of digital information. In *Proc. 28th Ann. ACM Symp. on Theory of Computing*, 1997.

[DM07] Saar Drimer and Steven J. Murdoch. Keep your enemies close: distance bounding against smartcard relay attacks. In *SS'07: Proceedings of 16th USENIX Security Symposium on USENIX Security Symposium*, pages 1–16, Berkeley, CA, USA, 2007. USENIX Association.

[Dob08] Denise Doberitz. Visual cryptography protocols and their deployment against malware. Master's thesis, Ruhr-Universität Bochum, Germany, 2008.

[Dor07] Dorland. *Dorland's Illustrated Medical Dictionary*. W. B. Saunders company, 31st edition, 2007.

[DORS08] Yevgeniy Dodis, Rafail Ostrovsky, Leonid Reyzin, and Adam Smith. Fuzzy extractors: How to generate strong keys from biometrcis and other noisy data. *SIAM Journal on Computing*, 38(1):97–139, 2008.

[DR00] Joan Daemen and Vincent Rijmen. Rijndael for AES. In *AES Candidate Conference*, pages 343–348, 2000.

[DR08]   Tim Dierks and Eric Rescorla. The transport layer security (TLS) protocol, version 1.2, request for comments: 5246. Technical report, The Internet Engineering Task Force, Network Working Group, August 2008.

[DRS04]   Yevgeniy Dodis, Leonid Reyzin, and Adam Smith. Fuzzy extractors: How to generate string keys from biometrics and other noisy data. In *Proceedings of the International Conference on Advances in Cryptology (EUROCRYPT '04), Lecture Notes in Computer Science*. Springer Verlag, 2004.

[Duf08]   Loïc Duflot. CPU bugs, CPU backdoors and consequences on security. In Jajodia and López [JL08], pages 580–599.

[Duf09]   Loïc Duflot. CPU bugs, CPU backdoors and consequences on security. *Journal in Computer Virology*, 5(2):91–104, 2009.

[DY05]   Yevgeniy Dodis and Aleksandr Yampolskiy. A verifiable random function with short proofs and keys. In *Proceedings of the Workshop on Theory and Practice in Public Key Cryptography*, pages 416–431, 2005.

[EG85]   Taher El Gamal. A public key cryptosystem and a signature scheme based on discrete logarithms. In *Proceedings of CRYPTO 84 on Advances in cryptology*, pages 10–18, New York, NY, USA, 1985. Springer-Verlag New York, Inc.

[Eik12]   Eikon. Meet the Eikon Mini – the smallest, low cost USB fingerprint reader on the market today. http://www.authentec.com/Products/TouchChips/Eikonmini.aspx, 2012. Product Website, lasst access 2013/06/11.

[Eik13]   Ronald Eikenberg. Fatale panne bei zertifikatsherausgeber trktrust. http://heise.de/-1776879, January 2013. last access 2013/06/14.

[EMV08a]   EMV. *Book 1: Application Independent ICC to Terminal Interface Requirements*. Integrated Circuit Card Specifications for Payment Systems. EMVCo, LLC, version 4.2 edition, June 2008.

[EMV08b]   EMV. *Book 2: Security and Key Management*. Integrated Circuit Card Specifications for Payment Systems. EMVCo, LLC, version 4.2 edition, June 2008.

[EMV08c]   EMV. *Book 3: Application Specification*. Integrated Circuit Card Specifications for Payment Systems. EMVCo, LLC, version 4.2 edition, June 2008.

[EMV08d]   EMV. *Book 4: Cardholder, Attendant, and Acquirer Interface*. Integrated Circuit Card Specifications for Payment Systems. EMVCo, LLC, version 4.2 edition, June 2008.

[ER77]   Paul Erdös and P. Revesz. On the length of the longest head-run. *Topics in Information Theory, Colloq. Math. Soc. Janos Bolyai, Budapest*, pages 219–228, 1977.

[ES02]   Philip A. Eisen and Douglas R. Stinson. Threshold visual cryptography schemes with specified whiteness levels of reconstructed pixels. *Des. Codes Cryptography*, 25(1):15–61, 2002.

[Fan07]   Wen Pinn Fang. Visual cryptography in reversible style. In *IIH-MSP '07: Proceedings of the Third International Conference on International Information Hiding and Multimedia Signal Processing (IIH-MSP 2007)*, pages 519–524, Washington, DC, USA, 2007. IEEE Computer Society.

[Fan09]   Wen-Pinn Fang. Non-expansion visual secret sharing in reversible style. *IJCSNS International Journal of Computer Science and Network Security*, 9(2), February 2009.

[FBH+05]   Craig Fancourt, Luca Bogoni, Keith Hanna, Yanlin Guo, Richard Wildes, Naomi Takahashi, and Uday Jain. Iris recognition at a distance. In Takeo Kanade, Anil Jain, and NaliniK. Ratha, editors, *Audio- and Video-Based Biometric Person Authentication*, volume 3546 of *Lecture Notes in Computer Science*, pages 1–13. Springer Berlin Heidelberg, 2005.

[FCH+11]   Adrienne Porter Felt, Erika Chin, Steve Hanna, Dawn Song, and David Wagner. Android permissions demystified. In *Proceedings of the 18th ACM conference on Computer and communications security*, CCS '11, pages 627–638, New York, NY, USA, 2011. ACM.

[FDH03]   Shaohua Fan, Charles R. Dyer, and Larry Hubbard. Quantification and correction of iris color. Technical Report 1495, University of Wisconsin-Madison, December 2003.

[Fel08a]   W. Feller. *An Introduction To Probability: Theory And Its Applications*, volume 1. Wiley India Pvt. Ltd., 3rd edition, 2008.

[Fel08b]   Ed Felten. New $2b dutch transport card is insecure. https://freedom-to-tinker.com/blog/felten/new-2b-dutch-transport-card-insecure/, January 2008.

[Fen03]   Stephen Fenner. A physics-free introduction to the quantum computation model. *Bulletin of the European Association for Theoretical Computer Science*, 79:69–85, Februar 2003.

[FFS87]   Uriel Feige, Amos Fiat, and Adi Shamir. Zero knowledge proofs of identity. In *STOC '87: Proceedings of the nineteenth annual ACM conference on Theory of computing*, pages 210–217, New York, NY, USA, 1987. ACM.

[FFS88]   Uriel Feige, Amos Fiat, and Adi Shamir. Zero-knowledge proofs of identity. *Journal of Cryptology*, 1(2):77–94, 1988.

[FH07]   Dinei A. F. Florêncio and Cormac Herley. A large-scale study of web password habits. In Carey L. Williamson, Mary Ellen Zurko, Peter F. Patel-Schneider, and Prashant J. Shenoy, editors, *WWW*, pages 657–666. ACM, 2007.

[FHE+12]   Adrienne Porter Felt, Elizabeth Ha, Serge Egelman, Ariel Haney, Erika Chin, and David Wagner. Android permissions: user attention, comprehension, and behavior. In *Proceedings of the Eighth Symposium on Usable Privacy and Security*, SOUPS '12, pages 3:1–3:14, New York, NY, USA, 2012. ACM.

[FHL09]   Wen-Pinn Fang, Chiu-Jian Hsu, and Mei-Ling Lin. Maximizing the secret hiding ratio in visual secret sharing with reversible property. *IJCSNS International Journal of Computer Science and Network Security*, 9(7), July 2009.

[Fid08]   Fidelica Microsystems. Homepage of Fidelica Microsystems, Inc., 2008. site extinct, accessible via http://web.archive.org.

[Fin03]   Klaus Finkenzeller. *RFID Handbook: Fundamentals and Applications in Contactless Smart Cards and Identification.* John Wiley and Sons, 2nd edition, 2003.

[FJ09]   Jianjiang Feng and Anil K. Jain. Fm model based fingerprint reconstruction from minutiae template. In Massimo Tistarelli and Mark S. Nixon, editors, *ICB*, volume 5558 of *Lecture Notes in Computer Science*, pages 544–553. Springer, 2009.

[FKK96]   Alan O. Freier, Philip Karlton, and Paul C. Kocher. The SSL protocol version 3.0, internet-draft. Technical report, The Internet Engineering Task Force, Transport Layer Security Working Group, November 1996.

[FMS01]   Scott R. Fluhrer, Itsik Mantin, and Adi Shamir. Weaknesses in the key scheduling algorithm of RC4. In Serge Vaudenay and Amr M. Youssef, editors, *Selected Areas in Cryptography*, volume 2259 of *Lecture Notes in Computer Science*, pages 1–24. Springer Verlag, 2001.

[FNB89]   F. Farzin-Nia and M. S. Beg. Alphanumeric persian characters using standard 16-segment displays. *IEEE Transactions on Consumer Electronics*, 35(4):854–857, November 1989.

[FO97]   Eiichiro Fujisaki and Tatsuaki Okamoto. Statistical zero knowledge protocols to prove modular polynomial relations. In Kaliski Jr. [Kal97], pages 16–30.

[For09]   Lance Fortnow. The status of the P versus NP problem. *Commun. ACM*, 52(9):78–86, 2009.

[Fra04]   Matthew K. Franklin, editor. *Advances in Cryptology - CRYPTO 2004, 24th Annual International CryptologyConference, Santa Barbara, California, USA, August 15-19, 2004, Proceedings*, volume 3152 of *Lecture Notes in Computer Science*. Springer, 2004.

[FSF13]   FSF, The Free Software Foundation. bc, an arbitrary precision numeric processing language. http://www.gnu.org/software/bc/, 2013. currently being maintained by Phil Nelson.

[FWDG10]   Dan Frumkin, Adam Wasserstrom, Ariane Davidson, and Arnon Grafit. Authentication of forensic DNA samples. *Forensic science international. Genetics*, 4(2):95–103, February 2010.

[GA03]   Sudhakar Govindavajhala and Andrew W. Appel. Using memory errors to attack a virtual machine. In *SP '03: Proceedings of the 2003 IEEE Symposium on Security and Privacy*, page 154, Washington, DC, USA, 2003. IEEE Computer Society.

[GAFFOG12]   J. Galbally, F. Alonso-Fernandez, J. Fierrez, and J. Ortega-Garcia. A high performance fingerprint liveness detection method based on quality related features. *Future Generation Computer Systems*, 28:311–321, January 2012.

[Gal01]   Steven D. Galbraith. Supersingular curves in cryptography. In Colin Boyd, editor, *ASIACRYPT*, volume 2248 of *Lecture Notes in Computer Science*, pages 495–513. Springer, 2001.

[Gal12]   Javier Galbally. From the iriscode to the iris: a new vulnerability of iris recognition systems. In *Black Hat USA 2012*, July 2012.

[Gan59]   Robin O. Gandy. Review: N. Bourbaki, theorie des ensembles. 1959.

[GdKGM⁺08]   Flavio D. Garcia, Gerhard de Koning Gans, Ruben Muijrers, Peter van Rossum, Roel Verdult, Ronny Wichers Schreur, and Bart Jacobs. Dismantling MiFare classic. In Jajodia and López [JL08], pages 97–114.

[GGM86]   Oded Goldreich, Shafi Goldwasser, and Silvio Micali. How to construct random functions. *Journal of the ACM (JACM)*, 33(4):792–807, 1986.

[Gil77]   John Gill. Computational complexity of probabilistic turing machines. *SIAM J. Comput.*, 6(4):675–695, 1977.

[GM84]   Shafi Goldwasser and Silvio Micali. Probabilistic encryption. *Journal of Computer and System Sciences*, 28:270–299, 1984.

[GMO01]   Karine Gandolfi, Christophe Mourtel, and Francis Olivier. Electromagnetic analysis: Concrete results. In Çetin Kaya Koç, David Naccache, and Christof Paar, editors, *CHES*, volume 2162 of *Lecture Notes in Computer Science*, pages 251–261. Springer, 2001.

[GMR88]   Shafi Goldwasser, Silvio Micali, and Ronald L. Rivest. A digital signature scheme secure against adaptive chosen-message attacks. *SIAM J. Comput.*, 17(2):281–308, 1988.

[GMR89]   Shafi Goldwasser, Silvio Micali, and Charles Rackoff. The knowledge complexity of interactive proof systems. *SIAM J. Comput.*, 18(1):186–208, 1989.

[GO80]   L.J. Guibas and A.M. Odlyzko. Long repetitive patterns in random sequences. *Zeitschrift für Wahrscheinlichkeitstheorie und verwandte Gebiete*, 53:241–262, 1980.

[Gol01]   Oded Goldreich. *Foundations of Cryptography*, volume 1, Basic Tools. Cambridge University Press, 2001.

[Gol02]   Oded Goldreich. Zero-knowledge twenty years after its invention. Cryptology ePrint Archive, Report 2002/186, 2002. http://eprint.iacr.org/.

[Gol04]   Oded Goldreich. *Foundations of Cryptography*, volume 2, Basic Applications. Cambridge University Press, 2004.

[Gol06]   Oded Goldreich. On post-modern cryptography – an essay by oded goldreich. http://www.wisdom.weizmann.ac.il/~oded/on-pmc.html, November 2006.

[GOLFOG12] J. Galbally, J. Ortiz-Lopez, J. Fierrez, and J. Ortega-Garcia. Iris liveness detection based on quality related features. In *Proc. Intl. Conf. on Biometrics, ICB*, pages 271–276, March 2012.

[Goo11]   Dan Goodin. ZeuS trojan attacks bank's 2-factor authentication. *The Register*, February 2011. http://www.theregister.co.uk/2011/02/22/zeus_2_factor_authentication_attack/, last access 2013/06/12.

[Goo13]   Google Inc. Android homepage. http://www.android.com/, 2013. last access 2013/06/26.

[GPR98]   Oded Goldreich, Birgit Pfitzmann, and Ronald L. Rivest. Self-delegation with controlled propagation — or — what if you lose your laptop. In *Advances in Cryptology - CRYPTO '98*, volume 1462 of *Lecture Notes in Computer Science*, pages 153–168, 1998.

[GR04]   Steven D. Galbraith and Victor Rotger. Easy decision-Diffie-Hellman groups. *LMS Journal of Computation and Mathematics*, 7:2004, 2004.

[Gra06]   Amal Graafstra. *RFID Toys: 11 Cool Projects for Home, Office and Entertainment*. Wiley, February 2006.

[Gre07]   Ulrich Greveler. VTANs - Eine Anwendung visueller Kryptographie in der Online-Sicherheit. In Rainer Koschke, Otthein Herzog, Karl-Heinz Rödiger, and Marc Ronthaler, editors, *GI Jahrestagung (2)*, volume 110 of *LNI*, pages 210–214. GI, 2007.

[GRGB+12]   Javier Galballya, Arun Rossb, Marta Gomez-Barreroa, Julian Fierreza, and Javier Ortega-Garciaa. From the iriscode to the iris: A new vulnerability of iris recognition systems. White paper for Black Hat USA 2012, 2012.

[GSW+08]   P. Grother, W. Salamon, C. Watson, M. Indovina, and P. Flanagan. Minex ii – performance of fingerprint match-on-card algorithms phase ii report. Technical Report 7477, Information Access Division – National Institute of Standards and Technology, Februar 2008.

[GSW+09]   P. Grother, W. Salamon, C. Watson, M. Indovina, and P. Flanagan. Minex ii – performance of fingerprint match-on-card algorithms phase ii / iii report. Technical Report 7477, Information Access Division – National Institute of Standards and Technology, May 2009.

[GSW$^+$11] P. Grother, W. Salamon, C. Watson, M. Indovina, and P. Flanagan. Minex ii – performance of fingerprint match-on-card algorithms phase iv report. Technical Report 7477, Information Access Division – National Institute of Standards and Technology, March 2011.

[GT04] Christophe Giraud and Hugues Thiebeauld. A survey on fault attacks. In Jean-Jacques Quisquater, Pierre Paradinas, Yves Deswarte, and AnasAbou Kalam, editors, *Smart Card Research and Advanced Applications VI*, volume 153 of *IFIP International Federation for Information Processing*, pages 159–176. Springer US, 2004.

[GvRVS09] Flavio D. Garcia, Peter van Rossum, Roel Verdult, and Ronny W. Schreur. Wirelessly pickpocketing a Mifare classic card. In *Security and Privacy, 2009 30th IEEE Symposium on*, pages 3–15, 2009.

[HAD06] Feng Hao, Ross Anderson, and John Daugman. Combining crypto with biometrics effectively. *Computers, IEEE Transactions on*, 55(9):1081–1088, 2006.

[Ham50] Richard W. Hamming. Error detecting and error correcting codes. *Bell System Tech. J.*, 29:147–160, 1950.

[Hay08] Brian Hayes. Cloud computing. *Communications of the ACM*, 51(7):9–11, 2008.

[HCL04] Hwa-Ching Hsu, Tung-Shou Chen, and Yu-Hsuan Lin. The ringed shadow image technology of visual cryptography by applying diverse rotating angles to hide the secret sharing. In *Networking, Sensing and Control, 2004 IEEE International Conference on*, volume 2, pages 996–1001 Vol.2, 2004.

[Hel77] Martin E. Hellman. An extension of the Shannon theory approach to cryptography. *Information Theory, IEEE Transactions on*, 23(3):289–294, May 1977.

[Her09] Cormac Herley. So long, and no thanks for the externalities: the rational rejection of security advice by users. In *Pre-Proceedings of New Security Paradigms Workshop 2009*, Oxford, 2009.

[HG05] Edwin Hou and Arthur Glaser. ECE 394 laboratory manual v4.1. ECE 394 Digital Systems Laboratory, Department of Electrical and Computer Engineering, New Jersey Institute of Technology, 2005.

[HGS99] Chris Hall, Ian Goldberg, and Bruce Schneier. Reaction attacks against several public-key cryptosystems. In *Proceedings of International Conference on Information and Communications Security '99*, Lecture Notes in Computer Science, pages 2–12, Berlin – Heidelberg, 1999. Springer Verlag.

[Hil95] Theodore P. Hill. The significant-digit phenomenon. *The American Mathematical Monthly*, Vol. 102(4):322–327, April 1995.

[Hir10] Christian Hirsch. Wirbel um "geheime" Register bei AMD-Prozessoren. http://heise.de/-1139508, November 2010. last access 2013/06/19.

[HK98]   Shai Halevi and Hugo Krawczyk. Public-key cryptography and password protocols. In *ACM Conference on Computer and Communications Security*, pages 122–131, 1998.

[HK99]   Shai Halevi and Hugo Krawczyk. Public-key cryptography and password protocols. *ACM Transactions on Information and System Security*, 2(3):230–268, 1999.

[HKQ00]   Gael Hachez, Francois Koeune, and Jean-Jacques Quisquater. Biometrics, access control, smart cards: a not so simple combination. In A. Watson J. Domingo-Ferrer, D. Chan, editor, *Fourth Working Conference on Smart Card Research and Advanced Applications (CARDIS 2000)*, volume 180 of *IFIP Conference Proceedings*, pages 273–288. Kluwer Academic Publishers, 9 2000.

[HKS00]   Thomas Hofmeister, Matthias Krause, and Hans U. Simon. Contrast-optimal k out of n secret sharing schemes in visual cryptography. *Theoretical Computer Science*, 240(2):471–485, 2000.

[HL11]   Martin Hilbert and Priscila López. The world's technological capacity to store, communicate, and compute information. *Science*, 332(6025):60–65, April 2011.

[HMC05]   Manzurul Hasan, Samiran Mahmud, and Thomas Chowdhury. Designing a 9 segment display for bangla and english numerals. *Asia J. Inform. Technol.*, 4:689–691, 2005.

[HS65]   Juris Hartmanis and Richard Edwins Stearns. On the computational complexity of algorithms. *Transactions American Mathematical Society*, 5:285–306, 1965.

[HT07]   Chih-Ming Hu and Wen-Guey Tzeng. Cheating prevention in visual cryptography. *Image Processing, IEEE Transactions on*, 16(1):36–45, 2007.

[HTBB08]   Richard Howard, Ralph Thomas, Jeff Burstein, and Roxanna Bradescu. Cyber fraud trends and mitigation. *The International Journal of Forensic Computer Science*, 3(1):9–24, 2008.

[HTH06]   Ching-Sheng Hsu, Shu-Fen Tu, and Young-Chang Hou. An optimization model for visual cryptography schemes with unexpanded shares. In Floriana Esposito, Zbigniew W. Ras, Donato Malerba, and Giovanni Semeraro, editors, *ISMIS*, volume 4203 of *Lecture Notes in Computer Science*, pages 58–67. Springer, 2006.

[Hub09]   Douglas W. Hubbard. *The Failure of Risk Management: Why It's Broken and How to Fix It*. Wiley, 1 edition, 2009.

[HyOY96]   Seong-Min Hong, Sang yeop Oh, and Hyunsoo Yoon. New modular multiplication algorithms for fast modular exponentiation. In *Advances in Cryptology – Proceedings of Eurocrypt '96*, pages 166–177. Springer-Verlag, 1996.

[IEE97]   IEEE Standards Board. IEEE std 802.11-1997 information technology –
            telecommunications and information exchange between systems – local and
            metropolitan area networks-specific requirements, part 11: Wireless lan
            medium access control (MAC) and physical layer (PHY) specifications.,
            1997.

[ILL89]   Russell Impagliazzo, Leonid A. Levin, and Michael Luby. Pseudo-random
            generation from one-way functions. In *STOC '89: Proceedings of the
            twenty-first annual ACM symposium on Theory of computing*, pages 12–24,
            New York, NY, USA, 1989. ACM.

[IM03]   Russell Impagliazzo and Sara Miner More. Anonymous credentials with
            biometrically-enforced non-transferability. In *Proceedings of the 2003 ACM
            Workshop on Privacy in the Electronic Society (WPES '03)*, pages 60–71.
            ACM, 2003.

[Int99]   Intel. Intel architecture software developer's manual, volume 2: Instruc-
            tion set reference manual. http://developer.intel.com/design/
            pentiumii/manuals/243191.htm, 1999.

[INT08]   INTEL. Microprocessor quick reference guide. http://www.intel.
            com/pressroom/kits/quickreffam.htm, December 2008. last access
            2013/06/19.

[Iro13]   Ironkey. Ironkey basic S250 and D250 flash drives. http://www.
            ironkey.com/en-US/secure-portable-storage/250-basic.html,
            2013. Product Website, last access 2013/06/11.

[iso06]   ISO/IEC 7816-3: identification cards – integrated circuit cards – part 3:
            Cards with contacts – electrical interface and transmission protocols. http:
            //www.iso.ch, 2006.

[Jab96]   A. Kh. Al Jabri. The unicity distance: An upper bound on the probability
            of an eavesdropper successfully estimating the secret key. *Information
            Processing Letters*, 60(1):43–47, 1996.

[Jai04]   Anil K. Jain. Biometric recognition: how do i know who you are? In
            *Proceedings of the IEEE 12th Signal Processing and Communications
            Applications Conference*, pages 3–5, April 2004.

[Jak07]   Markus Jakobsson. The human factor in phishing. In *Privacy & Security of
            Consumer Information '07.*, 2007.

[JaSP02]   Anil K. Jain and Ruud M. Bolle abd Sharath Pankanti, editors. *Biometrics:
            Personal Identification in Networked Society*, volume 479 of *The Springer
            International Series in Engineering and Computer Science*. Springer-Verlag,
            formerly Kluwer Academic Publishers, 2002.

[JCW02]   Java card biometric API white paper. Biometric Consortium – Interoperabil-
            ity, Assurance and Performance Working Group, August 2002.

[JJ92]   Robert C. James and Glenn James. *Mathematics Dictionary.* Springer Verlag, 5th edition, 1992.

[JJJM07]   Tom N. Jagatic, Nathaniel A. Johnson, Markus Jakobsson, and Filippo Menczer. Social phishing. *Communications of the ACM*, 50(10):94–100, 2007.

[JL08]   Sushil Jajodia and Javier López, editors. *Computer Security - ESORICS 2008, 13th European Symposium on Research in Computer Security, Málaga, Spain, October 6-8, 2008. Proceedings*, volume 5283 of *Lecture Notes in Computer Science*. Springer, 2008.

[JLjQ99]   Marc Joye, Arjen K. Lenstra, and Jean jacques Quisquater. Chinese remaindering based cryptosystems in the presence of faults. *Journal of Cryptology*, 12(4):241–245, 1999.

[JNN08]   Anil K. Jain, Karthik Nandakumar, and Abhishek Nagar. Biometric template security. *EURASIP Journal on Advances in Signal Processing, Special Issue on Advanced Signal Processing and Pattern Recognition Methods for Biometrics*, 2008, 2008. Article ID 579416, 17 pages.

[JW99]   Ari Juels and Martin Wattenberg. A fuzzy commitment scheme. In *Proceedings of the 6th ACM conference on Computer and communications security*, CCS '99, pages 28–36, New York, NY, USA, 1999. ACM.

[KA98]   Markus G. Kuhn and Ross J. Anderson. Soft tempest: Hidden data transmission using electromagnetic emanations. In David Aucsmith, editor, *Information Hiding*, volume 1525 of *Lecture Notes in Computer Science*, pages 124–142. Springer, 1998.

[Kal97]   Burton S. Kaliski Jr., editor. *Advances in Cryptology - CRYPTO '97, 17th Annual International Cryptology Conference, Santa Barbara, California, USA, August 17-21, 1997, Proceedings*, volume 1294 of *Lecture Notes in Computer Science*. Springer, 1997.

[Kat01]   Stefan Katzenbeisser. *Recent Advances in RSA Cryptography*. Kluwer Academic Publishers, Norwell, MA, USA, 2001.

[Kat10]   Jonathan G. Katz. *Digital Signatures*. Advances in Information Security. Springer Verlag, 2010.

[KcKKP03]   Burton S. Kaliski Jr., Çetin Kaya Koç, and Christof Paar, editors. *Cryptographic Hardware and Embedded Systems - CHES 2002, 4th International Workshop, Redwood Shores, CA, USA, August 13-15, 2002, Revised Papers*, volume 2523 of *Lecture Notes in Computer Science*. Springer, 2003.

[Kea09]   Joshua E. Keating. Dead man gets passport. *Foreign Policy*, page 7, December 2009. http://www.foreignpolicy.com/articles/2009/11/30/the_top_10_stories_you_missed_in_2009?page=0,6, lasst accessed 2013/05/24.

[Kee09]   KeeLog. Keydemon, hardware keylogger user's guide. `http://www.keelog.com/`, accessed 7th November 2009.

[Ken05]   Jonathan Kent. Malaysia car thieve steal finger. BBC News, `http://news.bbc.co.uk/2/hi/asia-pacific/4396831.stm`, March 2005. last accessed 2013/05/25.

[Ker83]   Auguste Kerckhoffs. La cryptographie militaire. *Journal des sciences militaires*, IX:161–191, Februar 1883.

[KGHG08]   Gerhard Koning Gans, Jaap-Henk Hoepman, and FlavioD. Garcia. A practical attack on the MiFare classic. In Gilles Grimaud and Franois-Xavier Standaert, editors, *Smart Card Research and Advanced Applications*, volume 5189 of *Lecture Notes in Computer Science*, pages 267–282. Springer Berlin Heidelberg, 2008.

[Kha79]   Leonid Khachiyan. A polynomial algorithm for linear programming. *Doklady Academiia Nauk USSR*, 244:1093–1096, 1979. Englisch Translation in Soviet Mathematics Doklady 20:191-194, 1979.

[Kin00]   United Kingdom. Regulation of investigatory powers act 2000 (c. 23). `http://www.statutelaw.gov.uk/content.aspx?activeTextDocId=1757378`, July 2000. last access 2013/05/08.

[KJJ99]   Paul C. Kocher, Joshua Jaffe, and Benjamin Jun. Differential power analysis. *Lecture Notes in Computer Science*, 1666:388–397, 1999.

[KK99]   Oliver Kömmerling and Markus G. Kuhn. Design principles for tamper-resistant smartcard processors. In *WOST'99: Proceedings of the USENIX Workshop on Smartcard Technology on USENIX Workshop on Smartcard Technology*, pages 2–2, Berkeley, CA, USA, 1999. USENIX Association.

[KKR⁺12a]   Stefan Katzenbeisser, Ünal Kocabaş, Vladimir Rožić, Ahmad-Reza Sadeghi, Ingrid Verbauwhede, and Christian Wachsmann. Pufs: Myth, fact or busted? a security evaluation of physically unclonable functions (pufs) cast in silicon. In Emmanuel Prouff and Patrick Schaumont, editors, *Cryptographic Hardware and Embedded Systems – CHES 2012*, volume 7428 of *Lecture Notes in Computer Science*, pages 283–301. Springer Berlin Heidelberg, 2012.

[KKR⁺12b]   Stefan Katzenbeisser, Ünal Koçabas, Vladimir Rozic, Ahmad-Reza Sadeghi, Ingrid Verbauwhede, and Christian Wachsmann. Pufs: Myth, fact or busted? a security evaluation of physically unclonable functions (pufs) cast in silicon (extended version). *IACR Cryptology ePrint Archive*, 2012:557, 2012.

[KL08]   Jonathan Katz and Yehuda Lindell. *Introduction to Modern Cryptography: Principles and Protocols*. Cryptography and Network Security Series. Chapman & Hall/CRC, 2 edition, 2008.

[Kle07]   Andreas Klein. *Visuelle Kryptographie*. Springer Verlag, 2007.

[KM]   Neal Koblitz and Alfred Menezes. Another look at provable security ii. Technical report.

[KM72]   Victor Klee and George J. Minty. *Inequalities III*, chapter How good is the Simplex Method, pages 159–175. Academic Press, New York, 1972.

[KM04]   Neal Koblitz and Alfred Menezes. Another look at provable security. Technical Report 2004/152, IACR Cryptology ePrint Archive, 2004.

[KM07]   Neal Koblitz and Alfred J. Menezes. Another look at provable security. *Journal of Cryptology*, 20(1):3–37, 2007.

[Knu97]   Donald E. Knuth. *Art of computer programming*, volume 1 Fundamental Algorithms. Addison-Wesley Longman, Amsterdam, 3rd edition, 1997.

[Kob96]   Neal Koblitz, editor. *Advances in Cryptology - CRYPTO '96, 16th Annual International Cryptology Conference, Santa Barbara, California, USA, August 18-22, 1996, Proceedings*, volume 1109 of *Lecture Notes in Computer Science*. Springer, 1996.

[Kob07]   Neal Koblitz. The uneasy relationship between mathematics and cryptography. *Notices of the AMS*, 54(8):973–979, September 2007.

[Koc96]   Paul C. Kocher. Timing attacks on implementations of Diffie-Hellman, RSA, DSS, and other systems. *Lecture Notes in Computer Science*, 1109:104–113, 1996.

[Koo99]   Bert-Jaap Koops. *The Crypto Controversy. A Key Conflict in the Information Society*. The Hague: Kluwer Law International, 1999. ISBN 90 411 1143 3.

[Koo13]   Bert-Jaap Koops. Crypto law survey. http://www.cryptolaw.org/, February 2013. Version 27.0, last access 2013/05/08.

[KS12]   Stefan Katzenbeisser and André Schaller. Physical unclonable functions. *Datenschutz und Datensicherheit*, 36(12):881–885, 2012.

[KTC⁺08]   Samuel T. King, Joseph Tucek, Anthony Cozzie, Chris Grier, Weihang Jiang, and Yuanyuan Zhou. Designing and implementing malicious hardware. In Fabian Monrose, editor, *LEET*. USENIX Association, 2008.

[Lam79]   L. Lamport. Constructing digital signatures from a one-way function. Technical Report CSL-98, SRI International Computer Science Laboratory, October 1979.

[Lau91]   K.T. Lau. Standard sixteen segmented display for thai numerals. *IEEE Transactions on Consumer Electronics,*, 37(1):96–99, February 1991.

[Lev87]   Leonid A. Levin. One-way functions and pseudorandom generators. *Combinatorica*, 7(4):357–363, 1987.

[LHA⁺13]   Michael Ley, Marc Herbstritt, Marcel R. Ackermann, Oliver Hoffmann, Michael Wagner, Stefanie von Keutz, and Katharina Hostert. The dblp computer science bibliography. http://dblp.uni-trier.de/, 2013. last access 2013/06/23.

[LL07]   Seong-Whan Lee and Stan Z. Li, editors. *Advances in Biometrics, International Conference, ICB 2007, Seoul, Korea, August 27-29, 2007, Proceedings*, volume 4642 of *Lecture Notes in Computer Science*. Springer, 2007.

[LM93]   Frank Thomson Leighton and Silvio Micali. Secret-key agreement without public-key cryptography. In Douglas R. Stinson, editor, *CRYPTO*, volume 773 of *Lecture Notes in Computer Science*, pages 456–479. Springer, 1993.

[LMP95]   Steven Low, Nicholas Maxemchuk, and Sanjoy Paul. Anonymous credit card transactions, May 1995. US patent no. 5420926.

[LPM94]   Steven H. Low, Sanjoy Paul, and Nicholas F. Maxemchuk. Anonymous credit cards. In Dorothy E. Denning, Raymond Pyle, Ravi Ganesan, and Ravi S. Sandhu, editors, *ACM Conference on Computer and Communications Security*, pages 108–117. ACM, 1994.

[LRSW00]   Anna Lysyanskaya, Ronald L. Rivest, Amit Sahai, and Stefan Wolf. Pseudonym systems. In Howard M. Heys and Carlisle M. Adams, editors, *Selected Areas in Cryptography, 6th Annual International Workshop, SAC'99*, volume 1758 of *Lecture Notes in Computer Science*. Springer Verlag, 2000.

[LST⁺09]   Stefan Lucks, Andreas Schuler, Erik Tews, Ralf-Philipp Weinmann, and Matthias Wenzel. Attacks on the dect authentication mechanisms. Cryptology ePrint Archive, Report 2009/078, 2009. http://eprint.iacr.org/.

[Lu79]   Shyue Ching Lu. The existence of good cryptosystems for key rates greater than the message redundancy. *IEEE Transactions on Information Theory*, 25(4):475–477, 1979.

[LW92]   Jürgen Lehn and Helmut Wegmann. *Einführung in die Statistik*. Teubner Studienbücher: Mathematik. B. G. Teubner, Stuttgart, 2. überarbeitete edition, 1992.

[LYLL13]   Hsiao-Ching Lin, Ching-Nung Yang, Chi-Sung Laih, and Hui-Tang Lin. Natural language letter based visual cryptography scheme. *Journal of Visual Communication and Image Representation*, 24(3):318 – 331, 2013.

[MAFH02]   Streekanth Malladi, Jim Alves-Foss, and Robert B. Heckendorn. On preventing replay attacks on security protocols. In *In Proc. International Conference on Security and Management*, pages 77–83. CSREA Press, 2002.

[Mah97]   David Paul Maher. Fault induction attacks, tamper resistance, and hostile reverse engineering in perspective. In Rafael Hirschfeld, editor, *Financial Cryptography*, volume 1318 of *Lecture Notes in Computer Science*, pages 109–122. Springer, 1997.

[Mat94]   Mitsuru Matsui. The first experimental cryptanalysis of the data encryption standard. In *CRYPTO '94: Proceedings of the 14th Annual International Cryptology Conference on Advances in Cryptology*, pages 1–11, London, UK, 1994. Springer-Verlag.

[May04]   Alexander May. Computing the RSA secret key is deterministic polynomial time equivalent to factoring. In Franklin [Fra04], pages 213–219.

[MD04]   Nick Mathewson and Roger Dingledine. Practical traffic analysis: Extending and resisting statistical disclosure. In *In Proceedings of Privacy Enhancing Technologies workshop (PET 2004), LNCS*, pages 17–34, 2004.

[MD05]   Steven J. Murdoch and George Danezis. Low-cost traffic analysis of tor. In *IEEE Symposium on Security and Privacy*, pages 183–195. IEEE Computer Society, 2005.

[MDAB10a]   Steven J. Murdoch, Saar Drimer, Ross Anderson, and Mike Bond. Chip and pin is broken. To appear at the 2010 IEEE Symposium on Security and Privacy, January 2010. draft.

[MDAB10b]   Steven J. Murdoch, Saar Drimer, Ross Anderson, and Mike Bond. Emv pin verification "wedge" vulnerability. http://www.cl.cam.ac.uk/research/security/banking/nopin/, 2010. version 2010-02-11 16:45, last access 2013/06/26.

[Men09]   Alexandra Mengele. Security of digital enhanced cordless telecommunication (dect) devices for residential use. Master's thesis, TU Darmstadt, 2009.

[Mer87]   Ralph C. Merkle. A digital signature based on a conventional encryption function. In Pomerance [Pom88], pages 369–378.

[Mer89]   Ralph C. Merkle. A certified digital signature. In Gilles Brassard, editor, *CRYPTO*, volume 435 of *Lecture Notes in Computer Science*, pages 218–238. Springer, 1989.

[Mil75]   Gary L. Miller. Riemann's hypothesis and tests for primality. In *STOC '75: Proceedings of seventh annual ACM symposium on Theory of computing*, pages 234–239, New York, NY, USA, 1975. ACM.

[Mil76]   Gary L. Miller. Riemann's hypothesis and tests for primality. *J. Comput. Syst. Sci.*, 13(3):300–317, 1976.

[MM03a]   Greg Mori and Jitendra Malik. Breaking a visual CAPTCHA. http://www2.cs.sfu.ca/~mori/research/gimpy/, 2003. last access 2013/06/14.

[MM03b]   Greg Mori and Jitendra Malik. Recognizing objects in adversarial clutter: Breaking a visual captcha. In *CVPR (1)*, pages 134–144. IEEE Computer Society, 2003.

[MMC⁺02]   Simon W. Moore, Robert D. Mullins, Paul A. Cunningham, Ross J. Anderson, and George S. Taylor. Improving smart card security using self-timed circuits. In *ASYNC*, pages 211–. IEEE Computer Society, 2002.

[MMJP09]   Davide Maltoni, Dario Maio, Anil K. Jain, and Salil Prabhakar. *Handbook of Fingerprint Recognition*. Originally published in the series: Springer Professional Computing. Springer-Verlag, 2009.

[MMYH02] Tsutomu Matsumoto, Hiroyuki Matsumoto, Koji Yamada, and Satoshi Hoshino. Impact of artificial "gummy" fingers on fingerprint systems. pages 275–289, 2002.

[Mon85] Peter L. Montgomery. Modular multiplication without trial division. *Math. Computation*, 44(170):519–521, 1985.

[MOTW09] H. Gregor Molter, Kei Ogata, Erik Tews, and Ralf-Philipp Weinmann. An efficient fpga implementation for an dect brute-force attacking scenario. *Wireless and Mobile Communications, International Conference on*, 0:82–86, 2009.

[MRS87] Silvio Micali, Charles Rackoff, and Bob Sloan. The notion of security for probabilistic cryptosystems. In *Advances in Cryptology – Crypto 86 Proceedings*, volume 263 of *Lecture Notes in Computer Science*, pages 381–392, Berlin – Heidelberg, 1987. Springer Verlag.

[MS02] Kevin Mitnick and William Simon. *The Art of Deception: Controlling the Human Element of Security*. John Wiley and Sons, Oktober 2002.

[MSK02] Shigeo Mitsunari, Ryuichi Sakai, and Masao Kasahara. A new traitor tracing. *IEICE Trans. Fundamentals*, E85-A(2):481–484, 2002. Electron. Commun. Comput. Sci.

[MSSS11] Dominik Merli, Dieter Schuster, Frederic Stumpf, and Georg Sigl. Side-channel analysis of pufs and fuzzy extractors. In JonathanM. McCune, Boris Balacheff, Adrian Perrig, Ahmad-Reza Sadeghi, Angela Sasse, and Yolanta Beres, editors, *Trust and Trustworthy Computing*, volume 6740 of *Lecture Notes in Computer Science*, pages 33–47. Springer Berlin Heidelberg, 2011.

[Mun10] Randall Munroe. "security" from xkcd – a webcomic of romance, sarcasm, math, and language. http://xkcd.com/538/, February 2010. last access 2013/06/26.

[MV12] Wojciech Mostowski and Pim Vullers. Efficient u-prove implementation for anonymous credentials on smart cards. In Muttukrishnan Rajarajan, Fred Piper, Haining Wang, and George Kesidis, editors, *Security and Privacy in Communication Networks*, volume 96 of *Lecture Notes of the Institute for Computer Sciences, Social Informatics and Telecommunications Engineering*, pages 243–260. Springer Berlin Heidelberg, 2012.

[MvOV97] Alfred Menezes, Paul van Oorschott, and Scott Vanstone. *Handbook of applied cryptography*. Discrete mathematics and its applications. CRC Press, Boca Raton – New York – London – Tokyo, 1997.

[MW96] Ueli M. Maurer and Stefan Wolf. Diffie-hellman oracles. In Koblitz [Kob96], pages 268–282.

[MW99] Ueli M. Maurer and Stefan Wolf. The relationship between breaking the diffie-hellman protocol and computing discrete logarithms. *SIAM J. Comput.*, 28(5):1689–1721, 1999.

[MW00]   Ueli M. Maurer and Stefan Wolf. The diffie-hellman protocol. *Des. Codes Cryptography*, 19(2/3):147–171, 2000.

[Nas82]   L. M. Nashner. Sensory, neuromuscular, and biomechanical contributions to human balance. In *Proceedings from the APTA Forum; Nashville; June 13-15, 1982*, pages 5–12, 1982.

[NBFT$^+$11] Janna Nousbeck, Bettina Burger, Dana Fuchs-Telem, Mor Pavlovsky, Shlomit Fenig, Ofer Sarig, Peter Itin, and Eli Sprecher. A mutation in a skin-specific isoform of SMARCAD1 causes autosomal-dominant adermatoglyphia. *American journal of human genetics*, 89(2):302 – 307, August 2011.

[Nec92]   Vassiliy I. Nechaev. Complexity of a determinate algorithm for the discrete logarithm. *Mathematical Notes*, 55(2):165–172, February 1992. Translated from Matematicheskie Zametki, original article submitted November 1993.

[NESP08a]   Karsten Nohl, David Evans, Starbug, and Henryk Plötz. Reverse-engineering a cryptographic RFID tag. In Paul C. van Oorschot, editor, *USENIX Security Symposium*, pages 185–194. USENIX Association, 2008.

[NESP08b]   Karsten Nohl, David Evans, Starbug, and Henryk Plötz. Reverse-engineering a cryptographic RFID tag. In *Proceedings of 17th USENIX Security '08*, pages 185–193, 2008.

[Net07]   Neil Weinstock Netanel. Temptations of the walled garden: Digital rights management and mobile phone carriers. *J. on Telecomm. & High Tech. L.*, 6:77, 2007.

[New81]   Simon Newcomb. Note on the frequency of use of the different digits in natural numbers. *American Journal of Mathematics*, 4(1):39–40, 1881.

[NH03]   Norman H. Nie and D. Sunshine Hillygus. The impact of internet use on sociability: Time-diary findings. *IT & Society*, 1(1):1–20, 2003.

[nis77]   Data encryption standard (DES). Federal Information Processing Standards Publications 46, January 1977.

[nis09]   Digital signature standard (DSS). Federal Information Processing Standards Publication 186-3, June 2009. third and current revision to the official DSA specification.

[NNR99]   Moni Naor, Yael Naor, and Omer Reingold. Applied kid cryptography or how to convince your children you are not cheating. In *In Proc. of Eurocrypt '94*, pages 1–12, 1999.

[Nor04]   Björn Nordin. Match-on-card technology white paper. Technical report, Precise Biometrics, 2004.

[NP97]   Moni Naor and Benny Pinkas. Visual authentication and identification. In Kaliski Jr. [Kal97], pages 322–336.

[NP02]   Phong Nguyen and David Pointcheval. Analysis and improvement of NTRU encryption paddings. In M. Yung, editor, *Advances in Cryptology – Crypto 02 Proceedings*, volume 2442 of *Lecture Notes in Computer Science*, pages 210–225, Berlin – Heidelberg, 2002. Springer Verlag.

[NP07]   Karsten Nohl and Henryk Plötz. Mifare – little security despite obscurity. Talk at 24th Chaos Communication Congress, December 2007.

[NS94]   Moni Naor and Adi Shamir. Visual cryptography. In Alfredo De Santis, editor, *EUROCRYPT*, volume 950 of *Lecture Notes in Computer Science*, pages 1–12. Springer, 1994.

[NS96]   Moni Naor and Adi Shamir. Visual cryptography ii: Improving the contrast via the cover base. In T. Mark A. Lomas, editor, *Security Protocols Workshop*, volume 1189 of *Lecture Notes in Computer Science*, pages 197–202. Springer, 1996.

[NXP07]   NXP. MIFARE standard 4KByte card IC functional specification. on NXP Semiconductors Website, February 2007.

[NXP13]   NXP. NXP identification product lines. http://www.nxp.com/documents/line_card/75017280.pdf, 2013. last access 2013/06/10.

[NY90]   Moni Naor and Moti Yung. Public-key cryptosystems provably secure against chosen ciphertext attacks. In *Proceedings of the 22nd ACM Symposium of Theory of Computing 1990*, pages 427–437. ACM, 1990.

[NY95]   Moni Naor and Moti Yung. Public-key cryptosystems provably secure against chosen ciphertext attacks. Technical report, Weizmann Institute of Science, Juli 1995. Revision, preliminary version of this paper appeared in Proceedings of the 22nd ACM Symposium of Theory of Computing 1990.

[oEiCI12a] European Network of Excellence in Cryptology II. Discrete logarithms: Hard problems related to the discrete logarithm problem in cyclic groups. Hard Problems in Cryptography wiki, http://www.ecrypt.eu.org/wiki/index.php?title=Discrete_Logarithms&oldid=2536, February 2012. last access 2013/05/13.

[oEiCI12b] European Network of Excellence in Cryptology II. Factoring: Hard problems related to factoring. Hard Problems in Cryptography wiki, http://www.ecrypt.eu.org/wiki/index.php?title=Factoring&oldid=459108, December 2012. last access 2013/05/13.

[OR01]   John J. O'Connor and Edmund F. Roberson. The number e. The MacTutor History of Mathematics archive, September 2001. University of St Andrews Scotland.

[Ora11]   Oracle. Specifications for the Java card 3 platform – version 3.0.4, classic edition. http://download.oracle.com/otn-pub/java/java_card_kit/3.0.4/java_card_kit-classic-3_0_4-rr-spec-pfd-b28-06_sep_2011.zip, September 2011.

[Pap01]   Ravikanth Pappu. *Physical One-Way Functions*. PhD thesis, MIT, 2001.

[Pap08a]   Sebastian Pape. Embedding biometric information into anonymous creden-
            tials. In Karsten Loesing, editor, *Extended Abstracts of the Second Privacy
            Enhancing Technologies Convention (PET-CON 2008.1)*, number 68 in
            Bamberger Beiträge zur Wirtschaftsinformatik und angewandten Informatik,
            February 2008.

[Pap08b]   Sebastian Pape. A survey on untransferable anonymous credentials (ex-
            tended abstract). Technical report, Pre-Proceedings of the IFIP/FIDIS
            Summer School on "The Future of Identity in the Information Society",
            Brno, September 2008.

[Pap08c]   Sebastian Pape. Templateless biometric-enforced non-transferability
            of anonymous credentials (extended abstract). In Michael Gorski
            Ewan Fleischmann, editor, *Book of Abstracts of the 2nd Weekend of Crypto-
            graphy*, Weimar, July 2008.

[Pap09a]   Sebastian Pape. Some observations on reusing one-time pads within dice
            codings (abstract). In *Tagungsband zum 10. Kryptotag, Workshop der
            Fachgruppe Angewandte Kryptologie in der Gesellschaft für Informatik*.
            Arbeitsgruppe Algebra und Zahlentheorie, Technische Universität Berlin,
            Fakultät II, Institut für Mathematik, March 2009. Berlin.

[Pap09b]   Sebastian Pape. A survey on non-transferable anonymous credentials. In
            Vashek Matyáš, Simone Fischer-Hübner, Daniel Cvrček, and Petr Švenda,
            editors, *The Future of Identity in the Information Society*, volume 298
            of *IFIP Advances in Information and Communication Technology*, pages
            107–118. Springer Boston, Brno, Czech Republic, July 2009.

[Pel05]   Thomas R. Peltier. *Information Security Risk Analysis*. Auerbach Publica-
            tions, 2nd edition, April 2005.

[Pfi08]   Andreas Pfitzmann. Biometrics - how to put to use and how not at all? In
            Steven Furnell, Sokratis K. Katsikas, and Antonio Lioy, editors, *TrustBus*,
            volume 5185 of *Lecture Notes in Computer Science*, pages 1–7. Springer,
            2008.

[PGM⁺03]   Sung Bum Pan, Youn Hee Gil, Daesung Moon, Yongwha Chung, and
            Chee Hang Park. A memory-efficient fingerprint verification algorithm
            using a multi-resolution accumulator array. *ETRI Journal*, 25(3):179–186,
            June 2003.

[PH10]   Andreas Pfitzmann and Marit Hansen. Anonymity, unlinkability, undetect-
            ability, unobservability, pseudonymity, and identity management - a con-
            solidated proposal for terminology. http://dud.inf.tu-dresden.de/
            Anon_Terminology.shtml, August 2010. v0.34.

[PK01]   Andreas Pfitzmann and Marit Köhntopp. Anonymity, unobservability, and
            pseudonymity – a proposal for terminology. In Hannes Federrath, editor,

Designing Privacy Enhancing Technologies, volume 2009 of *Lecture Notes in Computer Science*, pages 1–9. Springer Berlin Heidelberg, 2001.

[PMO09]   Alberto Politi, Jonathan C. F. Matthews, and Jeremy L. O'Brien. Shor's quantum factoring algorithm on a photonic chip. *Science*, 325(5945):1221, September 2009.

[Pol75]   John M. Pollard. A Monte Carlo method for factorization. *BIT Numerical Mathematics*, 15(3):331–334, 1975.

[Pom88]   Carl Pomerance, editor. *Advances in Cryptology - CRYPTO '87, A Conference on the Theory and Applications of Cryptographic Techniques, Santa Barbara, California, USA, August 16-20, 1987, Proceedings*, volume 293 of *Lecture Notes in Computer Science*. Springer, 1988.

[Pom96]   Carl Pomerance. A tale of two sieves. *Notices of the AMS*, 43(12):1472–1485, December 1996.

[Pri07a]   Pricewaterhouse Coopers. Economic crime: people,culture and controls – the 4th biennial global economic crime survey. http://www.pwc.com/en_GX/gx/economic-crime-survey/pdf/pwc_2007gecs.pdf, 2007.

[Pri07b]   Pricewaterhouse Coopers. Wirtschaftskriminalität 2007 – Sicherheitslage der deutschen Wirtschaft, 2007.

[Pri09]   Pricewaterhouse Coopers. The 5th biennial global economic crime survey – economic crime in a downturn, November 2009.

[PRTG02]   Ravikanth Pappu, Ben Recht, Jason Taylor, and Neil Gershenfeld. Physical one-way functions. *Science*, 297(5589):2026–2030, 2002.

[PS00a]   Birgit Pfitzmann and Ahmad-Reza Sadeghi. Anonymous fingerprinting with direct non-repudiation. In Tatsuaki Okamoto, editor, *ASIACRYPT*, volume 1976 of *Lecture Notes in Computer Science*, pages 401–414. Springer, 2000.

[PS00b]   David Pointcheval and Jacques Stern. Security arguments for digital signatures and blind signatures. *Journal of Cryptology*, 13(3):361–396, 2000.

[PT67]   Harry E. Petersen and Rein Turn. System implications of information privacy. In *AFIPS '67 (Spring): Proceedings of the April 18-20, 1967, spring joint computer conference*, pages 291–300, New York, NY, USA, 1967. ACM.

[PWP90a]   Birgit Pfitzmann, Michael Waidner, and Andreas Pfitzmann. Rechtssicherheit trotz Anonymität in offenen digitalen Systemen, Kapitel 1 bis 3. *Datenschutz und Datensicherung DuD*, 14(5):243–253, 1990.

[PWP90b]   Birgit Pfitzmann, Michael Waidner, and Andreas Pfitzmann. Rechtssicherheit trotz Anonymität in offenen digitalen Systemen, Kapitel 4 bis 6. *Datenschutz und Datensicherung DuD*, 14(6):305–315, 1990.

[PWP00]   Birgit Pfitzmann, Michael Waidner, and Andreas Pfitzmann. Secure and anonymous electronic commerce: Providing legal certainty in open digital systems without compromising anonymity. IBM Technical Paper RZ3232, 2000.

[PWZ97] Marko Petkovšek, Herbert S. Wilf, and Doron Zeilberger. *A = B*. A K Peters / CRC Press, 1997.

[QGB90] Jean-Jacques Quisquater, Louis C. Guillou, and Thomas A. Berson. How to explain zero-knowledge protocols to your children. In *Advances in Cryptology - CRYPTO '89: Proceedings*, volume 435, pages 628–631, 1990.

[QK02] Jean-Jacques Quisquater and Francois Koeune. Survey of side channel attacks side channel attacks. Cryptographic Algorithm and Related Techniques Evaluation Report 1047, CRYPTREC (Cryptography Research and Evaluation Committees), 2002.

[QS01] Jean-Jacques Quisquater and David Samyde. Electromagnetic analysis (ema): Measures and counter-measures for smart cards. In Isabelle Attali and Thomas P. Jensen, editors, *E-smart*, volume 2140 of *Lecture Notes in Computer Science*, pages 200–210. Springer, 2001.

[QS02] Jean-Jacques Quisquater and David Samyde. Eddy current for magnetic analysis with active sensor. In *Proceedings of Esmart 2002, 3rd edition*, Nice, France, September 2002.

[Rab59] Michael Oser Rabin. Speed of computation of functions and classification of recursive sets. In *Proc. 3rd Conference of Scientific Societies*, pages 1–2, Jerusalem, 1959.

[Rab60] Michael Oser Rabin. Degree of difficulty of computing a function and a partial ordering of recursive sets. Technical report, Hebrew University, Jerusalem, Jerusalem, 1960.

[Rab79] Michael O. Rabin. Digitalized signatures and public-key functions as intractable as factorization. Technical report, MIT Laboratory for Computer Science, Cambridge, MA, USA, January 1979.

[RAG10] Pravin S. Revenkar, Anisa Anjum, and Waman Z. Gandhare. Survey of visual cryptography schemes. *International Journal of Security and Its Applications*, 4(2):49 – 56, 2010.

[RCB01] Nalini K. Ratha, Jonathan H. Connell, and Ruud M. Bolle. Enhancing security and privacy in biometrics-based authentication systems. *IBM Systems Journal*, 40(3):614–634, March 2001.

[RE08] Wolfgang Rankl and Wolfgang Effing. *Handbuch der Chipkarten – Aufbau - Funktionsweise - Einsatz von Smart Cards*. Carl Hanser Verlag München, 5., üeberarbeitete und erweiterte auflage edition, 2008.

[Rel05] FFIEC Press Release. Authentication in an internet banking environment. Technical report, Federal Financial Institutions Examination Council, October 2005.

[Res00]   Eric Rescorla. HTTP over TLS, request for comments: 2818. Technical
            report, The Internet Engineering Task Force, Network Working Group, May
            2000.

[Ric08]   Thomas Ricker. Japan's face-authorizing cigarette machines no match for
            Bruce Willis photo. http://www.engadget.com/2008/07/01/japans-
            face-authorizing-cigarette-machines-no-match-for-bruce-
            w/, July 2008. last access 2013/05/08.

[Rie13]   Frank Rieger. Blackberry 10 macht E-Mail-Passworte für NSA und GCHQ
            zugreifbar. http://frank.geekheim.de/?p=2379, July 2013. english
            summary at the end of the article; last access 2013/07/17.

[RK03]   Ronald Rivest and Burt Kaliski. RSA problem. To appear in Encyclopedia
            of Cryptography and Security (Kluwer)., December 2003.

[RP00]   Eleanor Rieffel and Wolfgang Polak. An introduction to quantum comput-
            ing for non-physicists. *ACM Computing Surveys (CSUR)*, 32(3):300–335,
            September 2000.

[RS92]   Charles Rackoff and Daniel Simon. Non-interactive zero-knowledge proof of
            knowledge and chosen ciphertext attack. In J. Feigenbaum, editor, *Advances
            in Cryptology – Crypto 91 Proceedings*, volume 576 of *Lecture Notes in
            Computer Science*, pages 433–444, Berlin – Heidelberg, 1992. Springer
            Verlag.

[RSA77]   Ronald Rivest, Adi Shamir, and Leonard Adelman. On digital signatures and
            public key cryptosystems. Technical report, MIT Laboratory for Computer
            Science Technical Memorandum 82, April 1977.

[RSA78]   Ronald Rivest, Adi Shamir, and Leonard Adleman. A method for obtaining
            digital signatures and public-key cryptosystems. *Communications of the
            ACM*, 21(2):120–126, 1978.

[RSJ07]   A. Ross, J. Shah, and A.K. Jain. From template to image: Reconstructing fin-
            gerprints from minutiae points. In *IEEE Transactions on PAMI*, volume 29,
            pages 544–560, 2007.

[RU11]   Christian Rathgeb and Andreas Uhl. A survey on biometric cryptosystems
            and cancelable biometrics. *EURASIP Journal on Information Security*,
            2011(1):1–25, 2011.

[SA02]   Sergei P. Skorobogatov and Ross J. Anderson. Optical fault induction
            attacks. In Kaliski Jr. et al. [KcKKP03], pages 2–12.

[SBZ01]   Ron Steinfeld, Laurence Bull, and Yuliang Zheng. Content extraction
            signatures. In Kwangjo Kim, editor, *ICISC*, volume 2288 of *Lecture Notes
            in Computer Science*, pages 285–304. Springer, 2001.

[Sch90]   Mark F. Schilling. The long run of heads. *The College Mathematics Journal*,
            21(3):196–207, May 1990.

[Sch95]   Bruce Schneier. *Applied cryptography (2nd ed.): protocols, algorithms, and source code in C*. John Wiley & Sons, Inc., New York, NY, USA, 1995.

[Sch99a]   Bruce Schneier. Security in the real world: How to evaluate security. *Computer Security Journal*, 15(4):1–14, 1999. The article contains excerpts from a general session presentation delivered at CSI's NetSec Conference in St. Louis, MO, on June 15th, 1999.

[Sch99b]   Bruce Schneier. The uses and abuses of biomoetrics. *Communications of the ACM*, 42(8):136, 1999.

[Sch02]   Bruce Schneier. One-time pads. Crypto-Gram Newsletter, `http://www.schneier.com/crypto-gram-0210.html`, October 2002.

[Sch06]   Bruce Schneier. Security matters – myspace passwords aren't so dumb. wired.com `http://www.wired.com/politics/security/commentary/securitymatters/2006/12/72300?currentPage=all`, December 2006.

[Sch07a]   Bruce Schneier. The psychology of security. *Communications of the ACM*, 50(5):128, 2007.

[Sch07b]   Bruce Schneier. Security matters – secure passwords keep you safer. wired.com `http://www.wired.com/politics/security/commentary/securitymatters/2007/01/72458?currentPage=all`, November 2007.

[Sch08a]   Bruce Schneier. The psychology of security. `http://www.schneier.com/essay-155.html`, January 2008.

[Sch08b]   Bruce Schneier. Rubber-hose cryptanalysis. Schneier on Security – A blog covering security and security technology., October 2008. `http://www.schneier.com/blog/archives/2008/10/rubber_hose_cry.html`.

[Sch09a]   Bruce Schneier. Information leakage from keypads. Schneier on Security – A blog covering security and security technology., Juli 2009. `http://www.schneier.com/blog/archives/2009/07/information_lea_1.html`.

[Sch09b]   Bruce Schneier. People understand risks – but do security staff understand people? *The Guardian, The Sydney Morning Herald, and The Age*, August 2009. available from `http://www.schneier.com/essay-282.html`.

[Sch09c]   Bruce Schneier. Reacting to security vulnerabilities. Schneier on Security – A blog covering security and security technology., December 2009. `http://www.schneier.com/blog/archives/2009/12/reacting_to_sec.html`.

[Sch11]   Bruce Schneier. When it comes to security, we're back to feudalism. `http://www.wired.com/opinion/2012/11/feudal-security/`, December 2011. last access 2013/06/18.

[Sch13a]   Bruce Schneier. Trading privacy for convenience. http://www.schneier.com/blog/archives/2013/06/trading_privacy_1.html, June 2013. last access 2013/06/20.

[Sch13b]   Bruce Schneier. You have no control over security on the feudal internet. *Havard Business Review*, June 2013. http://blogs.hbr.org/cs/2013/06/you_have_no_control_over_s.html.

[Sco02]   Mike Scott. Authenticated id-based key exchange and remote log-in with simple token and pin number. Cryptology ePrint Archive, Report 2002/164, 2002. http://eprint.iacr.org/.

[Sem13]   NXP Semiconductors. MIFARE – contactless smartcard technology, projecthomepage. http://www.mifare.net/, May 2013.

[Seu13]   Karen Seubert. After checking your bank account, remember to log out, close the web browser, and throw your computer into the ocean. the Onion, http://www.theonion.com/articles/after-checking-your-bank-account-remember-to-log-o,32260/, May 2013.

[SF04]   Richard A. Sturm and Tony N. Frudakis. Eye colour: portals into pigmentation genes and ancestry. *Trends in Genetics*, 20(8):327–332, August 2004.

[SFK+10]   Asaf Shabtai, Yuval Fledel, Uri Kanonov, Yuval Elovici, Shlomi Dolev, and Chanan Glezer. Google android: A comprehensive security assessment. *Security Privacy, IEEE*, 8(2):35–44, 2010.

[SG10]   Yannis Soupionis and Dimitris Gritzalis. Audio CAPTCHA: Existing solutions assessment and a new implementation for VoIP telephony. *Computers & Security*, 29(5):603 – 618, 2010. Challenges for Security, Privacy and Trust.

[SGF02]   Gary Stoneburner, Alice Goguen, and Alexis Feringa. Risk management guide for information technology systems. National Institute of Standards and Technology, Technology Administration, U.S. Department of Commerce, Special Publication 800-30, July 2002.

[SH08]   Jörn-Marc Schmidt and Christoph Herbst. A practical fault attack on square and multiply. In *Fault Diagnosis and Tolerance in Cryptography, 2008. FDTC '08. 5th Workshop on*, pages 53–58, Aug. 2008.

[Sha49]   Claude Shannon. Communication theory of secrecy systems. *Bell System Technical Journal*, 28:656–715, Oktober 1949.

[Sha69]   Daniel Shanks. Class number, a theory of factorization, and genera. In *Proc. Sympos. Pure Math.*, volume XX, pages 415–440. Number Theory Institute, State Univ. New York, Stony Brook, N.Y., Amer. Math. Soc., Providence, R.I., 1971., 1969.

[Sha79]   Adi Shamir. How to share a secret. *Communications of the ACM*, 22(11):612–613, 1979.

[Sha93]   Daniel Shanks. *Solved and Unsolved Problems in Number Theory*. Chelsea Pub Co, New York, 4th edition, June 1993.

[She06]   Charles S. Sherrington. *The Integrative Action of the Nervous System*. Charles Scribner's Sons, New York, 1906. Reprinted by Cambridge University Press 1947 and by Yale University Press 1961.

[She08]   James Sherwood.   Photos fool cigarette age-verification software.   http://www.theregister.co.uk/2008/07/01/magazine_age_verification_machine_japan/, July 2008.   last access 2013/05/08.

[Sho94]   Peter W. Shor. Algorithms for quantum computation: Discrete logarithms and factoring. In *FOCS*, pages 124–134. IEEE, 1994.

[Sho97a]   Peter Shor. Polynomial-time algorithms for prime factorization and discrete logarithms on a quantum computer. *SIAM Journal on Computing*, 26(5):1484–1509, 1997.

[Sho97b]   Victor Shoup. Lower bounds for discrete logarithms and related problems. In *EUROCRYPT*, pages 256–266, 1997.

[Sho99a]   Peter W. Shor. Polynomial-time algorithms for prime factorization and discrete logarithms on a quantum computer. *SIAM J.Sci.Statist.Comput.*, 41(2):303–332, 1999. Revised and expanded version of [Sho94].

[Sho99b]   Victor Shoup. On the security of a practical identification scheme. *Journal of Cryptology*, 12(4):247–260, 1999.

[Shy06]   Shyong Jian Shyu. Efficient visual secret sharing scheme for color images. *Pattern Recogn.*, 39(5):866–880, 2006.

[Sig01]   Gesetz über Rahmenbedingungen für elektronische Signaturen, Signaturgesetz vom 16. Mai 2001 (BGBl. i S. 876), das zuletzt durch Artikel 4 des Gesetzes vom 17. Juli 2009 (BGBl. i S. 2091) geändert worden ist.   http://www.gesetze-im-internet.de/sigg_2001/BJNR087610001.html, 2001.

[Sim84]   Gustavus J. Simmons. A system for verifying user identity and authorization at the point-of sale or access. *Cryptologia*, 8(1):1–21, 1984.

[Sim91]   Gustavus J. Simmons. Identification of data, devices, documents and individuals. In *Security Technology, 1991. Proceedings. 25th Annual 1991 IEEE International Carnahan Conference on*, pages 197–218, 1991.

[Sin08]   Ryan Singel. Declassified NSA document reveals the secret history of TEMPEST. http://www.wired.com/threatlevel/2008/04/nsa-releases-se/, April 29th 2008.

[SKK07]   Martin Szydlowski, Christopher Kruegel, and Engin Kirda. Secure input for web applications. In *ACSAC*, pages 375–384. IEEE Computer Society, 2007.

[SNSS08]   Kh. Manglem Singh, Sukumar Nandi, S. Birendra Singh, and L. Shyam Sundar Singh. Stealth steganography in visual cryptography for half tone images. In *Computer and Communication Engineering, 2008. ICCCE 2008. International Conference on*, pages 1217–1221, May 2008.

[Sog08]   Chris Soghoian. Turkish police may have beaten encryption key out of TJ Maxx suspect. CNET News, October 2008. http://news.cnet.com/ 8301-13739_3-10069776-46.html.

[Sol06]   Daniel J. Solove. A taxonomy of privacy. *University of Pennsylvania Law Review*, 154(3):477, January 2006. GWU Law School Public Law Research Paper No. 129. Available at SSRN: http://ssrn.com/abstract=667622.

[Sol07]   Daniel J. Solove. 'I've got nothing to hide' and other misunderstandings of privacy. *San Diego Law Review, GWU Law School Public Law Research Paper*, 44(289), 2007.

[Sol11]   Daniel Solove. *Nothing to Hide – The False Tradeoff Between Privacy and Security*. Yale University Press, May 2011.

[SS08a]   Somitra Kumar Sanadhya and Palash Sarkar. New collision attacks against up to 24-step sha-2. In Dipanwita Roy Chowdhury, Vincent Rijmen, and Abhijit Das, editors, *INDOCRYPT*, volume 5365 of *Lecture Notes in Computer Science*, pages 91–103. Springer, 2008.

[SS08b]   Somitra Kumar Sanadhya and Palash Sarkar. Non-linear reduced round attacks against sha-2 hash family. In Yi Mu, Willy Susilo, and Jennifer Seberry, editors, *ACISP*, volume 5107 of *Lecture Notes in Computer Science*, pages 254–266. Springer, 2008.

[SSA^{+}08]   Alexander Sotirov, Marc Stevens, Jacob Appelbaum, Arjen Lenstra, David Molnar, Dag Arne Osvik, and Benne de Weger. MD5 considered harmful today – creating a rogue CA certificate. http://www.win.tue.nl/ hashclash/rogue-ca/, December 2008. last accessed 2013/06/14.

[ST05]   Andreas Stein and Edlyn Teske. Optimized baby step-giant step methods. *Journal of the Ramanujan Mathematical Society*, 20(1):1–32, 2005.

[ST11]   Adi Shamir and Eran Tromer. Acoustic cryptanalysis – on nosy people and noisy machines – [preliminary proof-of-concept presentation]. http://www. cs.tau.ac.il/~tromer/acoustic/, June 2011. last access 2013/05/08.

[sta04]   starbug. How to fake fingerprints? Chaos Computer Club (CCC), http://dasalte.ccc.de/biometrie/fingerabdruck_kopieren? language=en, October 2004. last access 2013/05/08.

[Sta07]   Richard M. Stallman. Can you trust your computer? In *Selected Essays of Richard M. Stallman, 2nd Edition*. Free Software Free Society, 2007. http://www.gnu.org/philosophy/can-you-trust.html.

[STG09]   Yannis Soupionis, George Tountas, and Dimitris Gritzalis.   Audio
            CAPTCHA for SIP-based VoIP. In Dimitris Gritzalis and Javier López, edit-
            ors, *SEC*, volume 297 of *IFIP Advances in Information and Communication
            Technology*, pages 25–38. Springer, 2009.

[Sul11]   Sean Sullivan. Zeus mitmo strikes again: Polish ING Bank. http://www.f-
            secure.com/weblog/archives/00002104.html, February 2011. last
            access 2013/06/14.

[SW99]   Sean W. Smith and Steve Weingart. Building a high-performance, program-
            mable secure coprocessor. *Computer Networks*, 31(8):831 – 860, 1999.

[SW07]   Robert F. Schmidt and William D. Willis, editors. *Encyclopedia of Pain*.
            Springer Berlin Heidelberg, 2007. ISBN: 978-3-540-43957-8.

[SW09]   Frank Stajano and Paul Wilson. Understanding scam victims: seven prin-
            ciples for systems security. Technical Report UCAM-CL-TR-754, Computer
            Laboratory, University of Cambridge, August 2009.

[SW12]   Sergei Skorobogatov and Christopher Woods. Breakthrough silicon scanning
            discovers backdoor in military chip. In Emmanuel Prouff and Patrick
            Schaumont, editors, *CHES*, volume 7428 of *Lecture Notes in Computer
            Science*, pages 23–40. Springer, 2012.

[Swi04]   Peter P. Swire. A model for when disclosure helps security: What is different
            about computer and network security? *Journal on Telecommunications and
            High Technology Law*, 2, 2004.

[SWT01]   Dawn Xiaodong Song, David Wagner, and Xuqing Tian. Timing analysis of
            keystrokes and timing attacks on ssh. In *SSYM'01: Proceedings of the 10th
            conference on USENIX Security Symposium*, pages 25–25, Berkeley, CA,
            USA, 2001. USENIX Association.

[SWT+10]   Andreas Schuler, Matthias Wenzel, Erik Tews, Ralf-Philipp Weinmann,
            Christian Fromme, H. Gregor Molter, and Harald Welte. dedected.org
            project. www.deDECTed.org, 2010. version 04/04/10 00:29:00, last access
            2013/06/26.

[Syv94]   Paul Syverson. A taxonomy of replay attacks. In *In Proceedings of the 7th
            IEEE Computer Security Foundations Workshop*, pages 187–191. Society
            Press, 1994.

[Tan08]   Andrew S. Tanenbaum. Dutch public transit card broken – RFID replay at-
            tack allows free travel in the Netherlands. http://www.cs.vu.nl/~ast/
            ov-chip-card/, 2008.

[The10]   The Unicode Consortium. Unicode chart U+2800, version 6.0, braille
            patterns. http://www.unicode.org/charts/PDF/U2800.pdf, 2010.

[The11]   The Unicode Consortium. *The Unicode Standard, Version 6.0.0*. Mountain
            View, CA: The Unicode Consortium, 2011. ISBN 978-1-936213-01-6.

[Tra56]   Boris Avraamovich Trakhtenbrot. Signalizing functions and table operators (in russian). *Research Notices of the Pensa Pedagogical Institute*, 4:75–87, 1956.

[Tra67]   Boris Avraamovich Trakhtenbrot. Complexity of algorithms and computations (in russian). Technical report, NGU, Novosibirsk, 1967.

[TS08]   Mohsen Toorani and Ali Asghar Beheshti Shirazi. Lpki - a lightweight public key infrastructure for the mobile environments. In *Proceedings of the 11th IEEE International Conference on Communication Systems (IEEE ICCS '08)*, pages 162–166. IEEE, November 2008.

[Twa71]   Mark Twain. Memoranda. the danger of lying in bed. *The Galaxy*, February 1871.

[TWP07]   Erik Tews, Ralf-Philipp Weinmann, and Andrei Pyshkin. Breaking 104 bit wep in less than 60 seconds. In Sehun Kim, Moti Yung, and Hyung-Woo Lee, editors, *WISA*, volume 4867 of *Lecture Notes in Computer Science*, pages 188–202. Springer, 2007.

[UJ04]   Umut Uludag and Anil K. Jain. Attacks on biometric systems: a case study in fingerprints. In *Proc. SPIE-EI 2004, Security, Seganography and Watermarking of Multimedia Contents VI*, pages 622–633, 2004.

[Uni48]   United Nations. The universal declaration of human rights. http://www.un.org/en/documents/udhr/, December 1948. last access 2013/06/20.

[Unu13]   Roman Unucheck.   The   most   sophisticated   Android   trojan. https://www.securelist.com/en/blog/8106/The_most_sophisticated_Android_Trojan, June 2013. last access 2013/06/10.

[UPPJ04a] Umut Uludag, Sharath Pankanti, Salil Prabhakar, and Anil K. Jain. Biometric cryptosystems: Issues and challenges. In *Proc. of the IEEE, Special Issue on Multimedia Security for Digital Rights Management*, volume 92, pages 948–960, 2004.

[UPPJ04b] Umut Uludag, Sharath Pankanti, Salil Prabhakar, and Anil K. Jain. Biometric cryptosystems: Issues and challenges. *Proceedings of the IEEE*, 92(6):948–960, 2004.

[U.S99]   U.S. Department of Justice. Kevin Mitnick sentenced to nearly four years in prison; computer hacker ordered to pay restitution to victim companies whose systems were compromised. Press release from http://www.justice.gov/criminal/cybercrime/mitnick.htm, August 9th 1999.

[vABHL03] Luis von Ahn, Manuel Blum, Nicholas J. Hopper, and John Langford. Captcha: Using hard ai problems for security. In Eli Biham, editor, *EURO-CRYPT*, volume 2656 of *Lecture Notes in Computer Science*, pages 294–311. Springer, 2003.

[Vau06]   Serge Vaudenay, editor. *Advances in Cryptology - EUROCRYPT 2006, 25th Annual International Conference on the Theory and Applications of*

Cryptographic Techniques, St. Petersburg, Russia, May 28 - June 1, 2006, Proceedings, volume 4004 of *Lecture Notes in Computer Science*. Springer, 2006.

[vdBKV97]   Mark van den Brand, Paul Klint, and Chris Verhoef. Reverse engineering and system renovation—an annotated bibliography. *SIGSOFT Softw. Eng. Notes*, 22(1):57–68, 1997.

[vE85]   Wim van Eck. Electromagnetic radiation from video display units: an eavesdropping risk? *Computers & Security*, 4(4):269–286, 1985.

[Vos08]   David Vose. *Risk Analysis: A Quantitative Guide*. Wiley, 3rd edition, May 2008.

[VP09]   Martin Vuagnoux and Sylvain Pasini. Compromising electromagnetic emanations of wired and wireless keyboards. In *Proceedings of 18th USENIX Security Symposium 2009*, Montreal, 2009.

[VSB⁺01]   Lieven Vandersypen, Matthias Steffen, Gregory Breyta, COnstantino Yannoni, Mark Sherwood, and Isaac Chuang. Experimental realization of shor's quantum factoring algorithm using nuclear magnetic resonance. *Nature*, 414:883–887, Dezember 2001.

[VvT97]   Eric R. Verheul and Henk C. A. van Tilborg. Constructions and properties of k out of n visual secret sharing schemes. *Des. Codes Cryptography*, 11(2):179–196, 1997.

[War05]   Brian Warner. Petmail design. http://petmail.lothar.com/design. html\#auto35, July 2005. last access 2013/06/14.

[War07]   Mark Ward. Campaigners hit by decryption law. http://news.bbc.co. uk/2/hi/technology/7102180.stm, November 2007. Last Updated: Tuesday, 20 November 2007, 09:43 GMT, last access 2013/05/08.

[Way01]   James L. Wayman. Fundamentals of biometric authentication technologies. *Int. J. Image Graphics*, 1(1):93–113, 2001.

[WC98]   C.C. Wu and L.H. Chen. A study on visual cryptography. Master's thesis, Institute of Computer and Information Science, National Chiao Tung University, Taiwan, R.O.C., 1998.

[WC05]   Hsien-Chu Wu and Chin-Chen Chang. Sharing visual multi-secrets using circle shares. *Comput. Stand. Interfaces*, 28(1):123–135, July 2005.

[Wer02]   Annette Werner. *Elliptische Kurven in der Kryptographie*. Springer Lehrbuch. Springer Verlag, 2002.

[Wes10]   Emrys Westacott. Does surveillance make us morally better? *Philosophy Now*, 79, Jun/Jul 2010, Law, Tolerance and Society, 2010.

[WFLY04]   Xiaoyun Wang, Dengguo Feng, Xuejia Lai, and Hongbo Yu. Collisions for hash functions MD4, MD5, HAVAL-128 and RIPEMD. Cryptology ePrint Archive, Report 2004/199, 2004. http://eprint.iacr.org/.

[WgMWC12] Ding Wang, Chun guang Ma, Ping Wang, and Zhong Chen. Robust smart card based password authentication scheme against smart card security breach. Cryptology ePrint Archive, Report 2012/439, 2012. `http://eprint.iacr.org/`.

[Wik13a] Wikimedia Foundation. Wikipedia, the free encyclopedia. `http://www.wikipedia.org`, 2013.

[Wik13b] Wikipedia, the free encyclopedia. Braille. `https://en.wikipedia.org/wiki/Braille`, July 2013. version from 15:08, 6 July 2013.

[Wik13c] Wikipedia, the free encyclopedia. Morse code. `https://en.wikipedia.org/wiki/Morse_code`, July 2013. version from 14:43, 10 July 2013.

[Wik13d] Wikipedia, the free encyclopedia. Thermoception. `https://en.wikipedia.org/wiki/Thermoception`, June 2013. version from 19:47, 2 June 2013.

[Wik13e] Wikipedia, the free encyclopedia. Unary numeral system. `https://en.wikipedia.org/wiki/Unary_numeral_system`, July 2013. version from 16:30, 11 July 2013.

[Wik13f] Wikipedia, the free encyclopedia. Unicity distance. `https://en.wikipedia.org/wiki/Unicity_distance`, June 2013. version from 09:01, 13 June 2013.

[WJMM05] James Wayman, Anil Jain, Davide Maltoni, and Dario Maio, editors. *Biometric Systems – Technology, Design and Performance Evaluation*. Springer Verlag, London, 2005.

[WM13] DJ Walker-Morgan. Android and its password problems open doors for spies. heise security; `http://h-online.com/-1918596`, July 2013. last access 2013/07/17.

[Woo08] Frank W. Wood. Illuminated announcement and display signal. U.S. Patent 974,943, June 1908. issued: Nov 8, 1910.

[WPBC08] Francis G. Wolff, Christos A. Papachristou, Swarup Bhunia, and Rajat Subhra Chakraborty. Towards Trojan-free trusted ICs: Problem analysis and detection scheme. In *DATE*, pages 1362–1365. IEEE, 2008.

[WS96] David Wagner and Bruce Schneier. Analysis of the SSL 3.0 protocol. In *The Second USENIX Workshop on Electronic Commerce Proceedings*. USENIX Press, November 1996.

[WS10] Adam Waksman and Simha Sethumadhavan. Tamper evident microprocessors. In *In Proceedings of the IEEE Symposium on Security and Privacy*, Oakland, California, 2010.

[WY05] Xiaoyun Wang and Hongbo Yu. How to break MD5 and other hash functions. In Ronald Cramer, editor, *EUROCRYPT*, volume 3494 of *Lecture Notes in Computer Science*, pages 19–35. Springer, 2005.

[WY09]   Jonathan Weir and WeiQi Yan. Sharing multiple secrets using visual crypto-
             graphy. In *IEEE International Symposium on Circuits and Systems, ISCAS
             2009*, pages 509–512, Taipei, 2009.

[WYL07]   Daoshun Wang, Feng Yi, and Xiaobo Li. Probabilistic visual secret sharing
             schemes for gray-scale images and color images. *Computing Research
             Repository (CoRR)*, abs/0712.4183, 2007.

[WYL11]   Daoshun Wang, Feng Yi, and Xiaobo Li. Probabilistic visual secret sharing
             schemes for grey-scale images and color images. *Inf. Sci.*, 181(11):2189–
             2208, 2011.

[WYY05]   Xiaoyun Wang, Yiqun Lisa Yin, and Hongbo Yu. Finding collisions in the
             full SHA-1. In Victor Shoup, editor, *CRYPTO*, volume 3621 of *Lecture
             Notes in Computer Science*, pages 17–36. Springer, 2005.

[XB05]   Haidong Xia and José Carlos Brustoloni. Hardening web browsers against
             man-in-the-middle and eavesdropping attacks. In *WWW '05: Proceedings
             of the 14th international conference on World Wide Web*, pages 489–498,
             New York, NY, USA, 2005. ACM.

[YA04]   Susan Young and Dave Aitel. *The Hacker's Handbook – The strategy behind
             breaking into and defending networks*. Auerbach Publications, CRC Press
             LLC, 2004.

[Yan04]   Ching-Nung Yang. New visual secret sharing schemes using probabilistic
             method. *Pattern Recognition Letters*, 25(4):481 – 494, 2004.

[Yao82]   Andrew Yao. Theory and applications of trapdoor functions. In *In Proceed-
             ings of the 23rd Symposium on the Foundation of Computer Science*, pages
             80–91, 1982.

[YL00]   Ching-Nung Yang and Chi-Sung Laih. New colored visual secret sharing
             schemes. *Des. Codes Cryptography*, 20(3):325–336, 2000.

[YWC08]   Ching-Nung Yang, Chung-Chun Wang, and Tse-Shih Chen. Visual crypto-
             graphy schemes with reversing. *Comput. J.*, 51(6):710–722, 2008.

[YWLD07]   Feng Yi, Daoshun Wang, Xiaobo Li, and Yiqi Dai. Colored probabilistic
             visual cryptography scheme with reversing. In Selim Aissi and Hamid R.
             Arabnia, editors, *Security and Management*, pages 138–141. CSREA Press,
             2007.

[YY09]   Dexin Yang and Bo Yang. A new password authentication scheme using
             fuzzy extractor with smart card. In *Computational Intelligence and Security,
             2009. CIS '09. International Conference on*, volume 2, pages 278–282,
             2009.

[Zad80]   Norman Zadeh. What is the worst case behavior of the simplex algorithm?
             Technical Report 27, Department of Operation Research, Stanford Univer-
             sity, May 1980.

[ZH04]   Eberhard Zeidler and Bruce Hunt. *Oxford Users' Guide to Mathematics*. Oxford University Press, 2004.

[ZSNS04]   Fangguo Zhang, Reihaneh Safavi-Naini, and Willy Susilo. An efficient signature scheme from bilinear pairings and its applications. In Feng Bao, Robert H. Deng, and Jianying Zhou, editors, *Public Key Cryptography*, volume 2947 of *Lecture Notes in Computer Science*, pages 277–290. Springer, 2004.

[ZWBK09]   Xuebing Zhou, Stephen D. Wolthusen, Christoph Busch, and Arjan Kuijper. A security analysis of biometric template protection schemes. In Mohamed S. Kamel and Aurélio C. Campilho, editors, *ICIAR*, volume 5627 of *Lecture Notes in Computer Science*, pages 429–438. Springer, 2009.

[ZZT05]   Li Zhuang, Feng Zhou, and J. D. Tygar. Keyboard acoustic emanations revisited. In Vijay Atluri, Catherine Meadows, and Ari Juels, editors, *ACM Conference on Computer and Communications Security*, pages 373–382. ACM, 2005.

List of Symbols and Abbreviations

The following list of symbols is meant for clarity and as aide memoire and not meant to be a replacement for the exhaustive definitions. The duplication of symbols could not be avoided on all occasions, but the intended meaning arises from the particular context.

1^n	string of 1's with length n
a, a_i	integer
$\mathcal{A}$	algorithm
Alice	sender of a cryptographic message
b, b_i	integer
B	bilinear map
Blind	message blinding algorithm
Bob	receiver of a cryptographic message
c, C	ciphertext
$\mathcal{C}$	ciphertext space
$\mathcal{C}_{K,M}$	set of possible encryptions
$c_{\mathcal{M}_i}$	cardinality of encryptions of $\mathcal{M}_i$
CCA	chosen-ciphertext attack
CDH	computational Diffie-Hellman
CPA	chosen-plaintext attack
COA	ciphertext-only attack
d	private exponent (RSA)
D	plaintext redundancy
$\mathcal{D}, \mathcal{D}_I$	domain
Dec, HDec	decryption algorithm
Decode	decoding algorithm
DDH	decisional Diffie-Hellman
DH	Diffie-Hellman
DL	discrete logarithm
DLP	discrete logarithm problem
DNA	desoxyribonucleic acid

e	public exponent (RSA)
e_i	boolean exponent(FFS identification scheme)
e	admissible bilinear map
Enc, HEnc	encryption algorithm
Encode	encoding algorithm
Eve	eavesdropper
F, F_k	efficient, deterministic function
$f(x), f(x)_I$	a function
G	efficient, deterministic algorithm
$\mathbb{G}_1, \mathbb{G}_2, \mathbb{G}_T$	cyclic group
$|\mathbb{G}|$	group order of $\mathbb{G}$
g_1, g_2	group elements of $\mathbb{G}_1$ and $\mathbb{G}_2$, respectively
$\langle g \rangle$	subgroup generated by g
$\gcd(a, b)$	greatest common divisor of a and b
$g(x)$	a function
Gen	parameter-generation algorithm
GenKey, HGen	key-generation algorithm
Γ	alphabet of ciphertext symbols
$h(n, i, j; k)$	hypergeometric distribution
$H(\cdot)$	entropy
$H(\cdot|\cdot)$	conditional entropy
$H^k(s)$	hash of string s with key k
Hash	hash algorithm
I	parameter
$\mathcal{J}, \mathcal{J}_I$	"trapdoor evaluation" algorithm
iff	if and only if
IND	indistinguishability
IOI	item of interest
Ivan	issuer
k, K	key
$\mathcal{K}$	keyspace
$\mathcal{K}_C$	set of possible keys
$\ell(\cdot), \ell'(\cdot)$	polynomial, expansion factor of G
L	language
LOR	left-or-right indistinguishability
Λ	alphabet of key symbols
$\mathcal{M}$	message (plaintext) space
m, M	message (plaintext)
Mallory	malicious adversary
n	modulus, product of two or more large primes (RSA)

n	encoding parameter
n, ν	security parameter
$\mathbb{N}$	natural numbers
NM	non-malleability
$\mathcal{O}, \mathcal{O}_i$	oracle
$\mathcal{O}(f(x))$	Big O notation of $f(x)$
Ω	alphabet of (plaintext) characters
P, p_i	plaintext (Message)
P, P_k	efficient, deterministic permutation
$P(\cdot), p$	probability
$P(\cdot|\cdot)$	conditional probability
P^{-1}, P_k^{-1}	inverse of an efficient, deterministic permutation
Π	family of permutations
p, p_1, p_2	integer, often prime
pk	public key
PA	parallel attack
PIN	personal identification number
PKI	public key infrastructure
$\Pr[event]$	probability of $event$
PRF	cryptographically secure pseudorandom function
PRG	cryptographically secure pseudorandom generator
PRP, PRP_k	cryptographically secure pseudorandom permutation
Peggy	prover
PUF	physically unclonable function
$\phi(n)$	order of the multiplicative group $\mathbb{Z}_n^*$
q	integer, often prime
R	rate (of language L)
R_0	absolute rate (of language L)
$\mathcal{R}$	ressource (of an attacker)
$\mathcal{R}, \mathcal{R}_I$	range
$\mathbb{R}$	real numbers
ROR	real-or-random indistinguishability
s	sign, 1 or -1
s, s'	string
s	random seed
s'	pseudorandom string
s_k	number of spurious key decipherments
s_m	number of spurious message decipherments
s, S	coding
$\mathcal{S}$	coding space

$\mathcal{S}_M$	set of possible encodings
$\mathcal{s}_{\mathcal{M}_i}$	cardinality of encodings of $\mathcal{M}_i$
Samp	sampling algorithm
sk	private key
sk	signing key
Sign	signing algorithm
SDDH	strong decisional Diffie-Hellman
SDDHI	strong decisional Diffie-Hellman inversion
SOR − CO	sample-or-random indistinguishability under ciphertext only
SRSA	strong RSA assumption
SXDH	symmetric external Diffie-Hellman
Σ	alphabet of coding symbols
td, td_I	trapdoor
Unblind	signature unblinding algorithm
vk	verification key
Vrfy	verification algorithm
Victor	verifier
XDH	external Diffie-Hellman
$y = f(x)$	deterministic function or algorithm
$y := f(x)$	deterministic function or algorithm
$y \in_R Y_{f(x)}$	probabilistic function or algorithm
$y \leftarrow f(x)$	probabilistic function or algorithm
y-DDHI	y-decisional Diffie-Hellman inversion
y-DHI	y-Diffie-Hellman inversion
y-SDH	y-strong Diffie-Hellman
$\mathbb{Z}$	integers
$\mathbb{Z}_N$, $\mathbb{Z}/n\mathbb{Z}$	set of congruence classes modulo N
$\mathbb{Z}_N^*$	set of multiplicative invertible elements modulo N
$\perp$	falsum, failure
$\bullet$	invisible dot
$\circ$	visible dot

Index of Keywords

Index of Names